AUTHORITY, IDENTITY AND THE
SOCIAL HISTORY OF THE GREAT WAR

AUTHORITY, IDENTITY AND THE SOCIAL HISTORY OF THE GREAT WAR

Edited by
Frans Coetzee and **Marilyn Shevin-Coetzee**

Berghahn Books
Providence • Oxford

First published in 1995 by
Berghahn Books
Editorial offices:
165 Taber Avenue, Providence, RI 02906, USA
Bush House, Merewood Avenue, Oxford, OX3 8EF, UK

© Frans Coetzee and Marilyn Shevin-Coetzee 1995
All rights reserved.
Reprinted in 2006
No part of this publication may be reproduced
in any form or by any means without the written permission
of Berghahn Books.

Library of Congress Cataloging-in-Publication Data
Authority, identity, and the social history of the Great War / edited
  by Frans Coetzee, Marilyn Shevin-Coetzee.
    p. cm.
  Includes bibliographical references.
  ISBN 1-57181-067-6 (pbk.). -- ISBN 1-57181-017-X
  1. World War, 1914-1918. I. Coetzee, Frans, 1955- .
II. Coetzee, Marilyn Shevin, 1955- .
D521.A98 1995   94-45334
940.3—dc20   CIP

British Library Cataloguing in Publication Data
A catalogue record for this book is available from
the British Library.

Printed in the United States on acid-free paper.

Contents

INTRODUCTION
 Frans Coetzee & Marilyn Shevin-Coetzee   vii

I   THE CONSTRUCTION OF AUTHORITY

1   A "LATECOMER" IN WAR: The Case of Italy
 Giovanna Procacci   3
2   THE POLITICAL POLICE, WAR, AND SOCIETY IN RUSSIA, 1914–1917
 Fredric Zuckerman   29
3   ALL QUIET ON THE HOME FRONT: Popular Entertainments, Censorship and Civilian Morale in Germany, 1914–1918
 Gary Stark   57
4   RESTORING MORAL ORDER ON THE HOME FRONT: Compulsory Savings Plans for Young Workers in Germany, 1916–1919
 Eve Rosenhaft   81

II   SHAPING IDENTITIES: RELIGION, NATIONALITY AND GENDER

5   FRENCH CATHOLICS: *Rumeurs infames* and the *Union Sacree*, 1914–1918
 James F. McMillan   113
6   NATIONALISM IN WARTIME: Critiquing the Conventional Wisdom
 L.L. Farrar, Jr.   133

7 LOVE AND DEATH: War and Gender in Britain,
   1914–1918
   Susan Kingsley Kent 153

8 ITALIAN WIDOWS OF THE FIRST WORLD WAR
   Francesca Lagorio 175

9 FOR FATHERLAND AND JEWISH PEOPLE: Jewish Women
   in Austria during World War I
   Marsha L. Rozenblit 199

III REPRESENTATIONS: IMAGES OF THE SOLDIER

10 SOLDIERS, CIVILIANS AND THE WARFARE OF ATTRITION:
   Representations of Combat in France, 1914–1918
   John Horne 223

11 MASCULINITY, MEMORY, AND THE FRENCH
   WORLD WAR I NOVEL: Henri Barbusse and
   Roland Dorgeles
   Leonard V. Smith 251

12 RUSSIAN GENERAL STAFF TRAINING AND THE
   APPROACH OF WAR
   John W. Steinberg 275

13 KNIGHTS OF THE SKY: The Rise of Military Aviation
   John H. Morrow, Jr. 305

14 COMMUNITIES IN MOURNING
   J.M. Winter 325

NOTES ON CONTRIBUTORS 357
INDEX 360

INTRODUCTION

Frans Coetzee & Marilyn Shevin-Coetzee

Eighty years ago, amidst the oppressive August heat, Europe was plunged into the abyss of war. In their search for a quick but permanent solution to long-standing domestic and international crises, European statesmen resembled the weary desert traveler who in a desperate effort to find relief from the relentless sun found only a mirage rather than the anticipated oasis. Military assurances about the efficacy of the offensive—the quantitative preponderance of their armies and the qualitative advantage of their weaponry—fostered an erroneous, even giddy, assumption about the brevity of a future war and reinforced governmental reluctance to undertake systematic planning and preparation for a prolonged conflict or to address what measures might be necessary to assure domestic tranquility as well as military efficiency. Perhaps the domestic discord so characteristic of the years before 1914, reflected in the militancy of industrial workers and suffragettes, might somehow be supplanted by a call to arms; this hope served in some circles to reinforce the expectation that war would likely bring beneficial consequences.[1]

Rather than being submerged by the call to arms, however, such issues only emerged with renewed force. For 1914, not 1900, marks the beginning of the twentieth century in European history. In a very real sense, the shape of the modern Europe with which we are familiar was forged between 1914 and 1918 in the crucible of the First World War. Empires crumbled, monarchies collapsed, cherished assumptions faded, all victims of this intensive conflict. The very

---

Notes for the Introduction begin on page xx.

map of Europe itself was redrawn to take into account the grave consequences of defeat in that titanic struggle. The emergence of Lenin, Stalin, and the Bolsheviks in Russia, and of Hitler and the Nazis in Germany are inexplicable without reference to the war, as is the growing financial and cultural involvement of the United States in European affairs. Ultimately too, the recurrence of war between 1939 and 1945, and the subsequent bipolarism of the Cold War are themselves part of the legacy of 1914–1918.[2]

Yet to focus exclusively on international relations, however dramatic, is to miss much of what gave the "Great War" (as awe-struck contemporaries were to dub it) its special character and enduring fascination. In August 1914 the various combatant nations, convinced that the conflict upon which they were embarking would be both brief and glorious, were ill-prepared to deal with the realities of modern industrialized warfare. The expected war of movement rapidly degenerated into a stalemate, one which placed the massive and unanticipated demands of a "total war" upon all the participants. Because ultimate victory depended as much upon the productive capacity and moral support of the home front as upon the effectiveness of the troops at the battle front, grasping the war's full dimensions entails analyzing the experiences of, and consequences for, European societies in mobilizing for a war of unprecedented scope and destructiveness.

Of course, all wars impose particular stresses and strains upon their participants, and the impact of the Thirty Years War or the Napoleonic Wars was not lightly forgotten. But the First World War was seared into the popular consciousness in a different sense, reflecting the quantitative and qualitative aspects which distinguished the 1914–1918 conflict from its predecessors. The sheer numbers of soldiers mobilized dwarfed those of previous wars, especially as the global reach of the war justified its lasting designation as a world war. The involvement of so many countries, coupled with the prevalence of universal conscription, though, cannot entirely account for its lasting impact. Given the pull of patriotism, convention, or compulsion, the soldiers who marched off to war in such numbers were arguably a more representative cross-section of their respective populations than their forebears in uniform; certainly they were—in the wake of extended primary education—more literate, more apt to record their experiences and recollections.[3]

If these social and pedagogical factors contributed to what now seems to have been such a literary war, there were other characteristics which set the Great War on a different qualitative footing. Its duration (four years) was not unusual, but its intensity was. Perhaps that intensity made the war seem more prolonged, a feeling reinforced by the all-too-apparent absence of prospects for immediate victory. By late 1914 the war had degenerated into a stalemate in which the technological superiority of the defensive ensured that the earnest efforts to secure a breakthrough simply resulted in squandering the lives of hundreds of thousands of men.

A stalemate would, under any circumstances, have provided ample material for sensitive observers, fodder for their pens no less than for the cannons. Yet the horrors of 1914–1918 were so profoundly shocking because they were so unanticipated. Europeans who pondered the nature of modern war could look to either the Franco-Prussian War or the Russo-Japanese war as likely models, ones in which a decisive outcome was achieved relatively quickly. If history was any guide—and in this case it was not—there was every reason to expect a similarly abrupt decision. Moreover, a process had been underway which one might describe as the "militarization of society," a partial one to be sure, but one which marked the growing acceptance of the inevitability of conflict, the logical place of struggle in the natural order, and the necessary cultivation of properly masculine codes of aggressive behavior.[4]

The failure to achieve an early and decisive victory undercut these assumptions in two ways. First, and most obviously, masculine attributes and a martial spirit were in themselves demonstrably insufficient to manage the burden with which the soldiers had been entrusted by general staffs, newspaper editors, and professed guardians of national culture. This also helps to explain why the Great War was a particularly literary war, given the discrepancy between the expectations of the battlefield as a proper arena for the successful, significant display of masculine ardor and the seeming insignificance of men in uniform once they tested their mettle at the front. The irrelevance of culturally conditioned expectations of masculinity and the inapplicability of traditional military preparation prompted a second unsettling reflection, namely that the emerging war of attrition would shift the dependence of ultimate victory or defeat onto civilian shoulders on the home front.

Whatever their political complexion, the various governments had given insufficient consideration to the requisite measures and probable consequences of mobilizing the home front. Indeed, one reason why it was widely assumed that any war would be short was the expectation that both domestic economies and the network of international commerce and finance could not withstand more than a few months of disruption.[5] Yet the inevitable dislocation and hurried improvisation of the initial months was only one source of strain on the home front. Another was the intractable problem of providing for the huge numbers of men required by armies at the front while simultaneously maintaining (or, in key industries, raising) production levels in the domestic economy. The persistent stalemate, the repetitious slaughter, the incessant need for more military material, only intensified the pressure to find a solution. Accordingly, the responsible authorities, whether government ministers, employers or union leaders, found themselves forced, often with considerable reluctance, to accept substitute labor. In practice this procedure entailed reconfiguring job tasks to accomodate semi- or unskilled workers as well as introducing women into wage labor in greater numbers.

No longer, then, could one imagine that the civilian population could be insulated from the war's disruptive effects.[6] In the First World War, the unanticipated need to mobilize society's resources for a war of attrition, the unforeseen blurring of gender divisions, and the unrelenting lists of casualties all impelled a significant extension of state authority. From the control of information to the organization of production, to the very definition of entitlement and citizenship, governments intruded upon once nearly sacrosanct aspects of civil society. In the process, these imperatives severely strained older, more limited conceptions of the role of the state. Although in retrospect one can discern significant extensions in governmental responsibility in the decades before 1914, the experience during wartime (especially in Britain) eroded the liberal elevation of freedom of conscience and of the rational, responsible individual.

How did the various combatant nations respond to, comprehend, and seek to master the strains and tensions of waging total war? That question is the central theme of this volume which itself is predicated on the argument that a satisfying answer can only be sustained upon a comparative basis. A particular effort has been made to incorporate not just the more familiar experiences of Britain, France, and Germany (though here too there is much to be revealed), but also those of Austria-Hungary, Italy, and Russia. Yet geographic breadth needs to be allied with analytic focus, and so the principal concern of these essays is with the fundamental issues of the wartime construction of authority and identity.

At first glance, such questions of authority and identity might seem unproblematic. Surely in wartime most citizens were willing to tolerate firm governmental action, had little sympathy with dissent, and readily identified with their nation in a spirit of effusive patriotism. But enough has already been said to cast doubt on such complacent formulations; in fact, given the scope and intensity of the conflict, questions of authority and identity go right to the heart of the war experience. How different social and political actors defined what they were fighting or laboring to protect, what initiatives they were willing to accept as being compatible with that definition, and the circumstances under which their conceptions and loyalties might be revised, all were of critical importance in the conduct of the war itself and the subsequent efforts to come to terms with its legacy. Moreover, these central issues overrode the distinctions between the battle front and the home front, and illuminated their essential interdependence.

Surely the most recognizable cutting edge of the constitution of authority was that of the state. Its greater intrusiveness was remarked upon by numerous observers. As one British civilian recalled, "we became increasingly accustomed to restrictions of every sort. When the fourth anniversary came, Government control was so much part of our lives that we found it difficult to jump back in our minds to the prewar world in which we lived in July 1914."[7] Liberals such as J.A. Hobson feared that the wartime extension of state control amounted to an unwarranted and counterproductive restriction of the very individual liberties the war ostensibly was being fought to protect.[8] Yet the phenomenon was not unique to Britain; indeed, the process of state expansion undergone there in some ways narrowed that nation's differences with the continent.

The essays in the first section below illuminate the broader European trend toward greater state control and the ways in which its implementation differed from country to country. In Italy, for example, the absence even of initial consensus on the desirability of entering the war, the nation's fragmented political system and lack of a strong, centralized executive, and its less fully developed industrial base, meant that Italy had simultaneously to undergo rapid economic expansion and find some institutional means of assuring effective direction of the war effort.[9] Giovanna Procacci shows that the eventual result was chaos, in which the militarization of labor discipline and the inability of the government to protect standards of living spawned explosive levels of tension.

Such a scenario is partly reminiscent of Imperial Russia, where the pressures of incompetent leadership and rapid economic modernization proved too great to contain. Here too there were efforts to innovate, to experiment with administrative machinery to deal with problems thrown up by the war (as in the All Russian Union of Zemstvos and the Central War Industries Committee).[10] But there was already a longheld and deeply entrenched bureaucratic tradition, and Frederic Zuckerman's essay helps to explain why government institutions in place proved ineffective. Focusing on the much-feared political police, who envisioned themselves as the state's principal bulwark against dissent or social unrest, Zuckerman demonstrates how patterns of clientage and patronage militated against bureaucratic continuity or efficiency, and how habits of mind shaped by the upheaval of 1905 delayed recognition of the even more explosive situation in 1917.

In unfamiliar situations there is a tendency to insist upon the repetition of more familiar, recognizable patterns of behavior, as with the Russian police's comforting delusion that dissent could be defused simply by depriving it of intellectual leadership. In Germany, this tendency took the form of official insistence that its citizens comported themselves with the serious dutifulness appropriate to the gravity of the situation. Indeed, two points emerge forcefully from the articles by Eve Rosenhaft and Gary Stark: the instrusive concern of the authorities in regard to public morals and morale (and to regard the two as inseparably linked) and the degree to which "authority" in this case was exercised, sometimes at cross purposes, by a variety of military as well as civilian officials.[11] The erosion and eventual collapse of civilian government, and its supersession by a military dictatorship, unable or unwilling to harness special interests, is now a prominent theme in the still modestly developed historiography of the German homefront.[12] Both Stark and Rosenhaft demonstrate how the obsessive concern for the probable disintegration of the social order under the pressure of mobilization proved to be counterproductive, narrowing the acceptable bounds of leisure activity. By denying its citizens opportunities for letting off steam, the state's intrusiveness in Germany accentuated its vulnerability to withstand a deep-seated challenge to its authority.

The exercise and extension of authority involved much more than the frequent recourse to the coercive powers of the state. As we have seen, the authorities in this regard comprised a varied group of officials, but authority itself was negotiated in a variety of contexts. The second section of this book deals more explicitly with the ways in which three concepts integral to the definition of identity within the social order—religion, nationality, and gender—were employed and themselves reshaped during the conflict.

When the war broke out, belligerent clergymen in the various countries assured their respective flocks that in fighting the enemy they were doing the Lord's work, and that with His assistance victory could not be far off. The general idea of suffering, and of Christian sacrifice in particular, provided a readily accessible means of encouraging recruitment, promoting steadfastness, and, eventually, reconciling the grieving survivors in the lines and behind them to the ceaseless carnage.[13] Yet for all their alleged narcotic effects, religious issues had been among the most contentious and divisive of the nineteenth century and in this respect the First World War did nothing to alter the situation. Indeed, prescriptions of unity, couched in religious terms, soon foundered on the rocks of prevailing confessional conflicts.

One can see this particularly clearly in France, where the notion of the nation almost miraculously united against the Germans was explicitly registered as a sacred union. As James McMillan's chapter demonstrates, this comforting construct was soon revealed to be illusory as old conflicts resurfaced. It is striking the degree to which the wartime debate in France between anti-clerical Republicans and Catholic Conservatives interpreted wartime behavior within a framework derived from decades of mutual suspicion. Prejudices fostered during the Franco-Prussian War of clerical assistance to the Germans were resurrected, as were the apprehensions on both sides that the war would be used as an excuse to further entrench or eradicate altogether the influence of the Catholic Church within France.[14] Accordingly, those participants who hoped that the conflict would, like Dr Johnson's prospect of execution, concentrate energies on what bound the nation together rather than upon what divided it, were to be bitterly disappointed. The interwar decades would see no diminution of partisan strife.

Such cleavage suggests that the integrative power of nationalism itself has been overrated, or perhaps more accurately, that as an "imagined community" it often yielded precedence to a variety of ostensibly secondary yet competing forms of identity.[15] Along these lines L.L. Farrar argues that whether one looks to popular attitudes or cabinet-level calculations, less lofty and more practical considerations came into play. In his view the rabid nationalist sentiment characteristic of the period figures more as a legend or a desideratum of anxious politicians hoping to promote a durable spirit of common endeavor they could superimpose upon the fractures observed in their polities. As a convenient umbrella for giving expression to the aspirations of ethnic and cultural minorities it had undoubted force, but in settled countries, once the euphoria (and even this must be qualified) of the early days had diminished, nationalism proved most effective when working with the grain of other allegiances.

Of those other definitions, none was more basic than gender. While scholars have devoted considerable attention to the relations between nations before and during the war, they now recognize the fundamental importance of relations between the sexes to a comprehensive understanding of that conflict.[16] In an obvious sense the outbreak of the First World War re-elevated a conception of gender roles—the martial, protective male and the domestic, vulnerable female—whose legitimacy had come under increasing challenge before 1914. Telling images which drew upon such assumptions evoked the plight of tiny Belgium and the assistance rendered by the powerful Allied guarantors of its neutrality. The sexual connotations, as in the "rape of Belgium" were rarely far from the surface and often were explicit. On the other hand, in an equally obvious way, the importance of the home front and the contribution made by female labor in so many capacities to meet the demands of the war illuminated the limitations and inconsistencies of the first view of a gendered social order. Given such stark alternatives it is no wonder that some civilians felt themselves to be embroiled no less in a war of the sexes than one of armies.

The war produced significant changes in ideas about gender and sexual identity. So contends Susan Kent in her survey of British feminism during the war, but not necessarily in the directions one might have expected. Feminists who before 1914 had repudiated the idea of sexual difference, and the allied notion of separate spheres, were horrified by the bloodthirsty, primitive male passions unleashed by the war, and they therefore embraced the idea of the sexes being both distinguishable and complementary. Interwar feminism, as a result, would not exhibit the same complexion as its prewar predecessor. One of Kent's most important points is that however linked the front and home front may have been, the impact of each upon women contrasted in significant ways. Females who served at the front, she argues, and witnessed firsthand the pervasive vulnerability of soldiers in the face of deadly technology, felt a greater sense of comradeship with men in uniform. Although there is evidence that such attitudes were reciprocated, politicians at home preserved the distinction between the sexes even while conceding what was supposedly the clearest symbol of equality, the franchise in 1918.[17]

The reluctance of the state to set aside gender distinctions was no less prevalent in Italy, as Francesca Lagorio demonstrates. In particular, she focuses upon a group—widows—whose position in society was always problematic, whether as a threat to the sexual order if young, incapable of self-support if old. The war made that problem more pressing, both by dramatically increasing the number of younger widows and by accentuating their right to benefits from the state in compensation for the lost earning power of husbands who would never return home. What ensued was a struggle over entitlements, in the first instance at least, but then more generally over the exercise of legitimate authority in recognition of women's proper place in the social order. The results seemed contradictory, for although widows adopted modern organizational tactics to apply political pressure, they articulated a more traditional conception of womanhood steeped in religious imagery and supplication for paternal assistance (albeit often invoked as a right rather than as charitable aid).[18] Eventually, Lagorio suggests, that more conservative orientation contributed to the susceptibility of the widows' organizations to Italian fascism, and thereby to the failure of efforts to secure a more visible public role.

If much attention has focused on the potential prospects and practical limitations of female emancipation through their wartime assumption of unfamiliar economic roles, it is worth highlighting the degree to which women might nonetheless innovate within traditional forms or adapt existing languages of social relations to their purposes. Moreover, the construction of identity was not a singular process, but involved a more complex sifting through over-lapping distinctions. In no region was this complexity more apparent than the Austro-Hungarian empire, and the degree to which gender, religion, and nationality were interwoven is one theme of Marsha Rozenblit's contribution on Austrian Jewish women. Faced with the challenge of maintaining several different identities simultaneously, Jewish women found an acceptable outlet in voluntary effort in aid of refugees. She suggests that through the medium of social work Austrian-Jewish women enhanced their public image within the Jewish and broader Austrian community.[19] In establishing and successfully managing a network of social-oriented associations, these women evoked the ideal of "spiritual motherhood" (or that of the "nurturant mother," as Rozenblit refers to it) to create a new, dynamic public role for themselves as women in a male-dominated society. On a spiritual plane, their work with the less fortunate fulfilled the Jewish traditions of doing *mitzvot* (good deeds) and of providing *zdakah* (charity or assistance) for those in need. Thus, Austrian-Jewish women, in maintaining the morale and welfare of Austrians on the home front, sought to strengthen their Austrian national identity while simultaneously preserving (and extending) their own importance within the sphere of Jewish cultural heritage.

Forging a secure identity was a means of preserving or reasserting authority; identity and authority were no less critically linked in the military than in the societies from which armies were drawn. Men in uniform struggled with these issues as much as female munitions workers or bereaved widows. And conceptions of gender, of conduct appropriate to a particular sex, or to a certain social position, were no less central at the front. The basic dilemma emerges in all its harsh clarity in both Leonard Smith's and John Horne's essays: codes of behavior conventionally expected of men in combat were no match for machine guns and barbed wire, and the disjunction between the anticipated "imaginary battlefield" and the actual "technological battlefield" repudiated what most recruits had thought it meant to be a soldier, even a man.[20]

Both articles focus upon France, implying that these tensions, so widely felt among soldiers of different armies, carried particular force in French units. Perhaps this should not surprise one, for over the course of the nineteenth century French demographic growth had been especially sluggish, engendering fears of depopulation and insufficient male virility.[21] In any event, from this common point of departure Smith and Horne proceed in different directions to illustrate the responses of French fighting men to the emasculating impact of industrialized warfare. Smith highlights two of that nation's most significant war authors, Henri Barbusse and Roland Dorgelès, whose work reflected the struggle to reimpose a sense of purposeful action. Barbusse believed that the key to reinvigorated masculinity lay in moral certainty, specifically in the conviction of the socialist just warrior, while Dorgelès stressed redemption through the reassuring, guiding intrusion of an omniscient narrator in his text. These approaches represented two ways of invoking authority, provided the reader accepted the inherent justification of French participation or read Dorgelès' text in the prescribed manner.

A linguistic turn is featured in Horne's analysis as well. His concern is with the systems of representation which bound soldiers to their loved ones at home (and even to each other) and within which the unanticipated carnage and stalemate was to be interpreted. In the war's first phase, the public emphasis was upon superior French moral fiber, a certain insouciant courage which the stolid Teuton could neither comprehend nor hope to emulate. Privately, however, doubts crept in among the troops themselves; laughter in the face of danger did not markedly shift the lines of trenches. During the second phase, service at the front was rationalized by the language of sacrifice, a heroic ideal readily retrieved from religion which put a more acceptable public face on casualty lists and denoted the ideal of unity by drawing upon both the Catholic and Protestant faiths. Once again, many soldiers privately felt less enamored of the sacrificial ideal, or more accurately, saw no reason to give their lives to no purpose, for that amounted to suicide, not sacrifice. That distinction helps us to understand the wave of mutinies which wracked the French army in the spring of 1917 in which, despite the troops' refusal to undertake fruitless offensive action, they remained committed to defending French soil and the graves of their comrades. Taken together, the two articles point up the resilience of the French army and the resourcefulness of its men in preserving links to the home front without imperilling domestic morale in the way that a more candid and cynical appraisal of the slaughter might have done.[22]

Refashioning a definition of masculinity and military service that would restore a sense of human agency was only one aspect of the reconstruction of identity in the face of technological warfare. The next pair of essays confront this issue from the perspective of self-legitimation through an ethos of professionalism. That objective is explicit in John Steinberg's analysis of the Russian army's officer corps on the eve of the conflict. In a service, not to mention a social order, in which the prerogatives of birth still held sway, those aspirants lacking privilege faced an uphill struggle, both in attaining high rank on the basis of merit and in exercising command as they saw fit according to professional criteria. Preparations for war, as rehearsed in maneuvers, brought these issues to the fore, especially as they involved the imperial family, the very emblem of privilege itself.[23] Nonetheless, Steinberg argues, men of humbler origins who were imbued with talent and dedication did find their way into positions of authority. The subsequent performance of the Russian army, therefore, was less inept than many initial critics claimed, and the eventual disintegration of the Russian war effort was more a general collapse at many levels.

Struggles over professional expertise as a contested source of authority had been a marked feature of new branches of the military for some time—one need only recall the experience of the young Napoleon Bonaparte in the French artillery. In the First World War, aerial warfare, even if in its nascent stages of development, witnessed just such an effort by aviators (abetted by publicists) to define their military identity. Capitalizing on the prewar fascination with the novelty of powered flight, crack pilots, or "aces" as they would be known, gained enormous popularity for their exploits in the skies. Their identity—and with it their cultural authority—was defined, however, not so much by the modernity and technological complexity of their endeavors as by an aura consciously evoking the supposed glamor and romance of combat in a bygone age.[24] Hailed as knights of the sky, their appellation not only glossed over the mundane realities of many airmen's tasks, such as reconnaisance, but ended up revealing more about the frustrations of so many participants with the course of the war on the ground. Pilots could soar above the stalemate, seek out an identifiable enemy, and feel that they had contributed personally to the war effort. For all their glamor, though, the fighter pilots did not change the direction of the war, and, ironically, the glare of publicity surrounding them partially obscured the development of aerial bombing which would prove significant in the next war.

But whether the emphasis of professionalism stressed the meritocracy of a reformed officer corps or the idiosyncracy of a renewed chivalry among the clouds, it could not disguise the fact that the First World War entailed personal loss and grief on an unprecedented scale. No study of the conflict would be complete, then, without some account of how families, friends, and lovers dealt with the pervasiveness of death. Jay Winter's essay deals with the process of discovery and consolation through which the bereaved passed on the way to commemoration. He illustrates the state's all-too-frequent inability to provide prompt, accurate information concerning a soldier's death (a situation in which its authority did not prove commensurate with its widely accepted responsibilities), but his central point concerns identity, namely the frequent recourse by mourners to "fictive kinship" as a means of reaching out in a broad way for assistance and comfort to others in a similar situation. Once again it is the resourcefulness of ordinary people, seeking the truth rather than lofty platitudes, which is so striking.

In the interwar period, however, a more sanitized version of the war infused the efforts to commemorate it. The neatly arrayed crosses in cemeteries conveyed a certain military precision but their peaceful, orderly alignment belied the brutality and dislocation of the conflict.[25] The sylvan groves in which the fallen warriors were laid to rest exemplified the eternal harmony of nature, yet the landscape soldiers had experienced resembled, in the wake of the incessant shelling, something more like lunar terrain. Even the customary statuary, often modeled on Greek aesthetics, disguised many of the harsh realities of service at the front.

In the process, the cemeteries simultaneously prompted an imagined veneer of continuity upon the war experience, concealing many of its more disruptive aspects. With time the scars upon the earth would heal; commemorative sites would accelerate that process, psychologically as well as environmentally. Historians have embraced this theme, for the thrust of much recent work on the social history of the conflict has been to accentuate the continuity of the war itself with social developments preceding it.[26] Nevertheless, whatever the influence of antecedents, the nearly overwhelmingly urge to return to something approximating "normality" bore witness to the very difficulty of doing so. And in the same vein, the need to commemorate testified to the qualitatively different character of what had been the Great War. It was not merely the horrifying scale of the conflict, the sheer number of casualties which required public tribute; it was the awesome scope, the breadth of participation, which mandated that commemoration be both indistinguishable for public purposes (reflecting the universality of sacrifice) and distinguishable (identifying the individual fallen soldier) for private needs. Public authority and private identity intersected. On whatever level, then, its contemporaries, as well as succeeding generations, might argue about the war's legacy, but it was one they could neither forget nor ignore.

NOTES TO INTRODUCTION

1. Like the suggested readings following each contribution, the citations below are intended to be selective rather than comprehensive; moreover, wherever possible they are weighted toward works readily accessible in English. On the "mood of 1914" and the assumptions of that period's policy-makers, the surest guide is James Joll's *The Origins of the First World War* (London, 1984; 2nd ed., 1992). One might also consult the essays in R.J.W. Evans and H. Pogge von Strandmann, eds., *The Coming of the First World War* (Oxford, 1988) and the series of books approaching the war's origins from the perspective of individual countries. Titles include Zara Steiner, *Britain and the Origins of the First World War* (New York, 1977); J.F.V. Keiger, *France and the Origins of the First World War* (New York, 1983); Volker Berghahn, *Germany and the Approach of War in 1914* (2nd ed., New York, 1993); D.C.B. Lieven, *Russia and the Origins of the First World War* (New York, 1983); Samuel Williamson, *Austria-Hungary and the Origins of the First World War* (New York, 1991). One of the most ambitious efforts to link domestic developments and the outbreak of the conflict has been Arno Mayer's interpretation stressing the counter-revolutionary purposefulness of conservative elites. See his "Domestic Causes of the First World War" in Leonard Krieger and Fritz Stern, eds., *The Responsibility of Power* (New York, 1967), 286–300, and *The Persistence of the Old Regime* (New York, 1981).
2. General accounts include Marc Ferro, *The Great War, 1914-1918* (London, 1973); J.M. Winter, *The Experience of World War I* (Oxford, 1989); Keith Robbins, *The First World War* (Oxford, 1985); Gerd Hardach, *The First World War, 1914–1918* (Berkeley, 1977), an economic study; Modris Eksteins, *Rites of Spring* (Boston, 1989), a cultural study; Bernadotte Schmitt and Harold Vedeler, *The World in the Crucible* (New York, 1984).
3. In addition to Eksteins, see Paul Fussell's classic *The Great War and Modern Memory* (Oxford, 1975); Samuel Hynes, *A War Imagined* (London, 1990); Holger Klein, ed., *The First World War in Fiction* (London, 1976); Phillipp Witkop, *German Students' War Letters* (New York, 1929); L. Housman, ed., *War Letters of Fallen Englishmen* (London, 1930); Eric Leed, *No Man's Land: Combat and Identity in World War I* (New York, 1979); Klaus Vondung, ed., *Kriegserlebnis* (Göttingen, 1980).
4. Sir Michael Howard, "Men Against Fire: Expectations of War in 1914" in Steven E. Miller, Sean Lynn-Jones, and Stephen Van Evera, eds., *Military Strategy and the Origins of the First World War* (Princeton, 1991), 3–19; Anne Summers, "Militarism in Britain before the Great War," *History Workshop* 2 (1976): 104–23; Paul Kennedy and Anthony Nicholls, eds., *Nationalist and Racialist Movements in Britain and Germany before 1914* (London, 1981); Frans Coetzee, *For Party or Country: Nationalism and the Dilemmas of Popular Conservatism in Edwardian England* (New York, 1990); Gerd Krummeich, *Armaments and Politics in France on the eve of the First World War* (Leamington Spa, 1984); Friedrich von Bernhardi, *Germany and the Next War* (London, 1914); Marilyn Shevin Coetzee, *The German Army League: Popular Nationalism in Wilhelmine Germany* (New York, 1990).
5. The classic instance was Norman Angell's *The Great Illusion* (London, 1911). From a modern perspective, see David French, *British Economic and Strategic Planning 1905–1915* (London, 1982).
6. Richard Wall and J.M. Winter, eds., *The Upheaval of War: Family, Work and Welfare in Europe, 1914–1918* (Cambridge, 1988); L. Haimson and G. Sapelli, eds., *Strikes, Social Conflict and the First World War* (Milan, 1992); L. Haimson and C.

Tilly, eds., *Strikes, Wars and Revolutions in International Perspective* (Cambridge, 1989); J.-J. Becker and S. Audoin-Rouzeau, eds., *Les societes europeennes et la Guerre de 1914–1918* (Nanterre, 1990).
7. Arthur Marwick, *The Deluge* (2nd ed., London, 1991), 295.
8. See Hobson's series of articles in *The Nation*, especially his "Liberty as a True War Economy," 29 July 1916. Recent work on the issue includes Kathleen Burk, ed., *War and the State* (London, 1982); James E. Cronin, *The Politics of State Expansion* (London, 1991); Gerry Rubin, *War, Law and Labour* (Oxford, 1987).
9. Giovanna Procacci, "Popular Protest and Labour Conflict in Italy,1915–1918," *Social History* 14 (1989): 31–58; Luigi Tomassini, "Industrial Mobilization and the Labour Market in Italy during the First World War," *Social History* 16 (1991): 59–87.
10. Thomas Fallows, "Politics and the War Effort in Russia: the Union of Zemstvos and the Organization of the Food Supply 1914–1916," *Slavic Review* 37 (1978): 70–90; Lewis Siegelbaum, *The Politics of Industrial Mobilization in Russia, 1914–1917* (New York, 1983); Norman Stone, *The Eastern Front, 1914–1917* (London, 1975); Diane Koenker and William Rosenberg, *Strikes and Revolution in Russia, 1917* (Princeton, 1989).
11. These concerns, of course, preceded the war and persisted after its conclusion, as is evident from Derek Linton, *Who has the Youth has the Future* (Cambridge, 1991); Elizabeth Harvey, *Youth and the Welfare State in Weimar Germany* (Oxford, 1993).
12. The seminal work remains, three decades after its publication, Gerald Feldman's *Army, Industry and Labor in Germany, 1914–1918* (Princeton, 1966). Other significant contributions include Jürgen Kocka, *Facing Total War* (Leamington Spa, 1984); Martin Kitchen, *The Silent Dictatorship* (London, 1976); Ute Daniel, *Arbeiterfrauen in der Kriegsgesellschaft* (Göttingen, 1989); Elizabeth Tobin, "War and the Working Class: the Case of Düsseldorf, 1914–1918," *Central European History* 28 (1985): 257–98; Robert G. Moeller, "Dimensions of Social Conflict in the Great War: the View from the German Countryside," *Central European History* 14 (1981): 142–68; Avner Offer, *The First World War: An Agrarian Interpretation* (Oxford, 1989), 23–78; Richard Bessel, *Germany after the First World War* (Oxford, 1993), 1–90.
13. Good work on this topic remains sparse. Arlie Hoover, *God, Germany and Britain in the Great War: A Study in Clerical Nationalism* (New York, 1989) is inadequate; more rewarding are Alan Wilkinson, *The Church of England and the First World War* (London, 1978) and *Dissent or Conform? War, Peace and the English Churches 1900–1945* (London, 1986), as well as clergyman Andrew Clark's wartime diary, *Echoes of the Great War* (Oxford, 1985). Of course, religious conviction could sustain conscientious objection to military service. On that score, see Martin Ceadel, *Pacifism in Britain 1914–1945* (Oxford, 1980); John Rae, *Conscience and Politics* (London, 1970).
14. German soldiers feared that French priests or soldiers disguised in clerical garb might spearhead the resistance to their advance and occupation. John Horne and Alan Kramer, "German 'Atrocities' and Franco-German Opinion, 1914: The Evidence of German Soldiers' Diaries," *Journal of Modern History* 66 (1994): 1–33.
15. Benedict Anderson, *Imagined Communities* (London, 1991); Eric Hobsbawm, *Nations and Nationalism since 1780* (Cambridge, 1990).
16. Margaret Higonnet et al., eds., *Behind the Lines: Gender and the Two World Wars* (New Haven, 1987); Miriam Cooke and Angela Woollacott, eds., *Gendering War Talk* (Princeton, 1993); Helen Cooper et al., eds., *Arms and the Woman* (Chapel Hill, 1989); Ruth Harris, "The Child of the Barbarian: Rape, Race and

Nationalism in France during the First World War," *Past & Present* 141 (1993): 170–206; Phiippa Levine, "Walking the Streets in a Way No Decent Woman Should: Women Police in World War One," *Journal of Modern History* 66 (1994): 34–78; Susan K. Kent, *Making Peace* (Princeton, 1993); Angela Woollacott, *Upon Her Their Lives Depend* (Berkeley, 1994); Ute Frevert, *Women in German History* (Oxford, 1988); James F. McMillan, *Housewife or Harlot: the Place of Women in French Society, 1870–1940* (Brighton, 1981); Mary-Louise Roberts, *Civilization Without Sexes: Reconstructing Gender in Postwar France 1917–1927* (Chicago, 1994); Wall and Winter, *The Upheaval of War*.

17. Martin Pugh, *Electoral Reform in War and Peace, 1906–1918* (London, 1978); Sandra Stanley Holton, *Feminism and Democracy: Women's Suffrage and Reform Politics in Britain, 1900–1918* (Cambridge, 1986).

18. On the degree to which arguments over entitlement were gendered, see Susan Pedersen, "Gender, Welfare, and Citizenship in Britain during the Great War," *American Historical Review* 95 (1990): 983–1006; idem., *Family, Dependence and the Origins of the Welfare State: Britain and France, 1914–1945* (New York, 1993).

19. Anti-Semitism, either in Austria-Hungary or Germany, did not diminish during the war. See Werner Angress, "The German Army's 'Judenzählung' of 1916," *Leo Baeck Institute Yearbook* 23 (1978): 117–37; Istvan Deak, *Beyond Nationalism* (New York, 1990). Its impact in Britain is recorded by Panikos Panayi, *The Enemy in Our Midst* (Providence, 1991).

20. The tactical implications of industrialized combat are outlined in Tim Travers, *The Killing Ground* (Boston, 1987); Shelford Bidwell and Dominic Graham, *Firepower* (Boston, 1982). Tony Ashworth's *Trench Warfare* (London, 1980) describes one intriguing response, the so-called "live-and-let-live system." See also Allan R. Millett and Williamson Murray, eds., *Military Effectiveness: the First World War* (Boston, 1988).

21. A persistent theme illustrated by Karen Offen, "Depopulation, Nationalism, and feminism in Fin-de-Siecle France," *American Historical Review* 89 (1984): 648–76; Marie-Monique Huss, "Pronatalism and the Popular Ideology of the Child in Wartime France," in Wall and Winter, *The Upheaval of War*, 329–67.

22. Aspects of the French war effort are well covered in J.-J. Becker, *The Great War and the French People* (New York, 1985); Patrick Fridenson, ed., *The French Home Front, 1914–1918* (Providence, 1992); Stéphane Audoin- Rouzeau, *Men at War, 1914–1918* (Providence, 1992); Leonard V. Smith, *Between Mutiny and Obedience* (Princeton, 1994); P.J. Flood, *France 1914– 1918: Public Opinion and the War Effort* (Basingstoke, 1990).

23. For how deeply it was entrenched, see Andrew Verner, *The Crisis of Russian Autocracy* (Princeton, 1990); D.C.B. Lieven, *Russia's Rulers in the Old Regime* (New Haven, 1989).

24. Lee Kennett, *The First Air War* (New York, 1991); John Morrow, *The Great War in the Air* (Washington, 1993); Robert Wohl, *A Passion for Wings: Aviation and the Western Imagination, 1908–1918* (New Haven, 1994).

25. George L. Mosse, *Fallen Soldiers: Reshaping the Memory of the World Wars* (New York, 1990); Sir Frederick Kenyon, *War Graves* (London, 1918); John R. Gillis, ed., *Commemorations* (Princeton, 1994), 150–211.

26. See the editorial comments in Wall and Winter, *The Upheaval of War*; J.M. Winter, *The Great War and the British People* (London, 1986).

I

THE CONSTRUCTION OF AUTHORITY

CHAPTER 1

A "Latecomer" in War
The Case of Italy

Giovanna Procacci

Two factors of a general nature that greatly affected events in Italy must be kept in mind when attempting an analysis of the changes brought about by the war on the socio-economic and political-cultural structures of the country. First, Italy was a "latecomer"—a country which had arrived late at industrial development (this had begun only during the last years of the 19th century). Second, this development had come about in a very limited fashion (more than 55 percent of the population was still actively involved in agriculture on the eve of the war), was unevenly distributed throughout the country, and—according to many observers—had often sacrificed rationality in favor of socio-political compromises.

The fact that Italy belonged to the rank of "second-latecomers" makes its case much more similar to the situation in the Central Empires and Russia rather than to the Western democracies, namely Great Britain and France. This was despite the fact that the young democracy, inaugurated at the beginning of the century (precisely when industrial take-off was beginning) by Giovanni Giolitti, the liberal leader who had governed almost without a break in the fifteen years preceding the war, had tried to draw inspiration from the political and institutional models of these latter countries. In fact, some of the typical traits of the "second-latecomers" had become evident in

---

Notes for this chapter begin on page 26.

that period, such as the state's support for the new industrial concentrations, their conditioning of government policy, and parliament's limited control over the executive power. Moreover, the army had maintained a strong sphere of influence; in addition to the tasks regarding matters of war, the Giolittian regime had assigned a great measure of responsibility for the defense of domestic public order to the army and to its parallel force the Carabinieri.

The characteristics of a country with the structure of a "latecomer" were combined with those traits deriving from the limits of extension of economic, and consequently, social development. The imbalance between north and south had not been resolved at all; on the contrary, it had become even more accentuated since industrial development was almost exclusively confined to the Turin-Milan-Genoa triangle—regions to which productive investments had been directed (and encouraged by the state)—whereas the southern areas had remained untouched by processes of industrial and agricultural modernization. Therefore, agricultural production had continued to fall below national requirements and Italy had continued to depend on foreign countries for some essential products, such as wheat.

From a social point of view, delay, sectorial divisions, and the restricted nature of the development had prevented an improvement in the wretched conditions of most of the rural population. At the same time, the excess of labor had kept the wage levels of the majority of the workers low, with increases confined to small groups of skilled individuals (income per capita on the eve of the war was around half that of Germany and food consumption was more than a fifth below the British average). There had been very few social reforms, and therefore, among all the industrialized countries, Italy took up the rear in terms of working hours, welfare, insurance, and industrial accidents.[1]

The harshness of living conditions, exacerbated by a heavy taxing policy which hit the poorest classes, had meant that even in the Giolittian period, as in the preceding decades, the south of Italy was rocked by violent popular revolts which were bloodily repressed. At the same time, the new democratic policy effected by Giolitti, which guaranteed the freedom to strike, had sparked off a succession of disturbances in the countryside of the Po Valley (where some agricultural modernization had taken place, and where day laborers were used) and in the industrial cities of the north. These had become particularly intense in the years immediately preceding the war, because of the international economic crisis following 1913 and the adoption by entrepreneurs of a progressively more rigid and aggressive attitude.

The nature of these prewar protests was peculiar: in fact, peasants and workers combined their natural hostility towards the "bosses" with increasingly heated resentment towards the state which had allowed the costs of national unity to fall on the poorest classes, and which continued to place the burden of modernization fundamentally on them. But discontent was not unique to the working classes: the middle classes too, comprising the bourgeoisie of white-collar workers and those in professional occupations, education, and business—who had even identified with the battles of the Risorgimento for unity and independence—appeared largely dissatisfied and hostile towards the state, because they felt they had not been assigned a more important socio-political role, while rapid industrialization had brought about the increasing protagonism of the manufacturing, entrepreneurial, and working classes. Therefore, Italy had undergone industrial change without a simultaneous and parallel process of social integration, comparable to that which had taken place in similar phases in the other main industrialized countries. The social fragmentation inevitably had repercussions in the political-cultural sphere: the plan for political mediation attempted by Giolitti was in actual fact too limited to survive the economic crisis and the renewal of acute social conflicts.

Neutrality and Intervention: "The Syndrome of Crimea"

Discontent within the various classes had developed into the radicalization of the political positions hostile to Giolitti, and had brought about his fall in March 1914, with the return to government of an exponent of the conservative agrarian wing. This was Antonio Salandra, an adversary of the line of democratic co-operation and dialogue with the forces of the opposition proposed by his predecessor, and a strong advocate of a return to an authoritarian policy along the lines already implemented in the decades following unity.

It was Salandra's government which denounced the Triple Alliance which Italy had previously signed with the Central Powers, and which declared, upon the outbreak of the world war, that the country would remain neutral.

As is known, the period of neutrality was marked by animated and often dramatic controversy between those who supported Italy's total abstention from the conflict and those who were in favor of the country's entry into war. The majority of the political forces were against the latter proposition. In fact, the enormous Giolittian liberal lineup was in favor of neutrality, being well aware of Italy's lack of preparation, as was the strong Socialist Party, faithful to the old internationalist principles, and a large part of the Catholics. They were joined by a certain number of economic interests, more inclined to exploit the advantages deriving from the possibility of exporting supplies to other belligerent countries than to risk the adventure of a full-scale war economy.

But above all, the people were against the war; in a moment in which the various nations could count on the support—whether enthusiastic or sorrowful—of the masses regarding the decision to intervene, Italy paid for the divide between country and state which had marked its post-unity history. The workers in the big factories were hostile, animated by the pacifism to which the Italian Socialist Party (PSI)—the only one among the big parties of the International—had remained faithful; the great majority of the peasants, to whom any identification with concepts of "nation" and "country" was foreign, were against the war; and a large part of the middle classes was skeptical about the wisdom of the country entering the war, particularly after the military episodes of the first months of the conflict had clearly illustrated the danger that participation in the dreadful conflict would mean for a country with a fragile framework such as Italy.

Therefore, when Italy's intervention was declared in May 1915, there were no signs of enthusiasm which could compare to those previously demonstrated by the populations of the other belligerent countries. Salandra decided to revoke Italy's neutrality, over-riding parliamentary opposition and using the public demonstrations of a few groups of interventionists (among which were Mussolini's followers, renegades from the Socialist ranks).

Thus Italy entered the war without the support of parliament or the majority of public opinion; but also without a suitable productive and financial organization, without autonomy in questions of raw materials for industry and food consumption and, finally, without adequate military preparation. How is it possible therefore to explain the folly of the decision to intervene, taken, moreover, when the reality of the technological war had already become evident on the fronts where the first campaigns, carnage, and experiences of trench warfare had begun?

Despite many doubts and uncertainties, Salandra had persuaded himself of the wisdom of intervention in the conflict on the basis of one conviction: that Italy's participation alongside the powerful British and French allies (whose pressure on Italy must not be underestimated) would be brief. Brief but also profitable; according to Salandra, the certain, rapid victory of the Entente forces, as foreseen by the Italian government, would allow Italy not only to rise finally to become a front-ranking European power, and therefore take part in the division of the spoils, thus resolving the economic stalemate caused by the 1913 crisis and the war itself, but also to realize an enforced consensus within the country, with the submission of the entire population to the war regime and the coercive abolition of conflicts.

Certain victory was clearly considered an inherent part of this plan—the means by which the enforced consensus would be transformed into spontaneous approval and the definitive triumph of a new power coalition over that of Giolitti confirmed. Salandra, who was an exponent of the agrarian right and had always been hostile to Giolitti, also found support for his plan to restore authoritarianism in the areas of new state capitalism from the iron and steel industrialists who during the last years of Giolitti's rule maintained that they had not received adequate government support for their requests for authoritarian social control of the workforce.

Strengthened by such support from the economic powerhouses and driven towards intervention by the Crown and the higher echelons of the army, Salandra had already signed the secret treaty of London in April which committed him alongside the Entente. Perhaps his hope, and that of the forces who supported his plan, was to emulate Count Cavour, the great strategist of the Italian Risorgimento, who by cleverly engineering the participation of his own state, the former kingdom of Sardinia, in the Crimean War alongside the great powers, had thereby achieved its international recognition and benefited from the fruits of a victory obtained with little effort and in a short space of time. This was what I have called "the Syndrome of Crimea," which roused the Italian rulers and military chiefs into action, driving them towards the First (and later the Second) World War, to what would prove to be a lethal undertaking both for them and for the entire country.

The Country at War

What was meant to be a brief military episode, crowned by a rapid and easy victory, soon turned out to be a venture disproportionate with the forces which the state was able to put into the field, both from a military viewpoint and from that of civil organization.

The Italian situation was distinguished from that of the Western Allies (and to a large extent from that of the enemy countries) by two problems. The first was the aforementioned lack of consent to the war by the majority of the population and the liberal lineup which had governed the country for nearly fifteen years; the second concerned industrial and food production which was insufficient to face a long and difficult war.

At the front—mainly the terrible, rocky promontories of the Carso—the soldiers who were mustered there in the autumn and winter of 1915 lacked training and arms; Italy did not possess sufficient heavy and field artillery, machine guns and ammunition, and furthermore, the troops' military preparation and the training of their superiors were wholly inadequate to the situation. Some of these shortcomings were remedied during the war, but they persisted in part until the end of the conflict and even worsened in the period following Caporetto.

But the situation soon assumed dramatic proportions within the country as well. The strong boost given by the state orders to the iron and steel industries, and to all the sectors involved in the war industry, brought about an enormous transformation in the economic structure of the country—which only then changed from being eminently agricultural to eminently industrial.[2] But the privileges granted to industry in terms of finance and the organization of production heightened the divide between this sector and that of agriculture, which had already been seriously hit by the absence of workers summoned to the front. As a consequence, national agricultural production was completely insufficient, making foreign imports even more vital than before the war, although goods were not always available. This resulted in a shortage of supplies in basic foodstuffs, especially wheat, to the extent that the situation in Italy became rather similar—in terms of the problem of hunger—to that of the Central Empires, despite the fact that, unlike them, the country was not subjected to a naval blockade.

The scarcity of essential foodstuffs—linked, as we shall see, to the disorganization of the state in matters of distribution—was accompanied by a sharp rise in prices. In fact, the growing cost of basic foods (and industrial materials) imported from abroad contributed to the increase in prices of essential products and foodstuffs. But, above all, the increase was caused by the inflationary policy decided upon by the government in order to face the costs of the war—costs which were only partially covered by the immense loans from Britain, and later, America. In fact, Italy decided to finance the war not by means of an increase in taxation—as other countries, such as Britain, had done—but through an increase in monetary circulation (the inflation rate was among the highest of the belligerent nations[3]): the cost-of-living index, at 100 in 1913, reached 264 in 1918, wholesale prices more than quadrupled, while retail prices increased even further. Thus, the entire population was burdened with the costs incurred by the war and the poorest classes were those worst hit.

The material hardships, besides the moral sufferings which stemmed from the conflict, increased the hostility of the population towards the war. A widespread, progressive malaise developed throughout the country, ready to explode in 1917, the year of greatest sacrifices and bereavements. As for the majority of the countries at war, this was Italy's *annus horribilis,* ending with the rout at Caporetto. Paradoxically, this saved the Italian state from a fate similar to that of the other "second" or "latecomer" countries, namely, defeat and revolution. In fact, it was only after the military defeat, thanks to greater cooperation with the Allies and a series of measures aimed at coordinating political and military action and reinforcing internal cohesion, that the situation both at the front and within the country itself tended to change. Nevertheless, the serious problems at the root of Italian politics were unresolved—ready to reappear at the end of the conflict.

How then did the Italian ruling class face the tasks which a war of unexpected dimensions and characteristics placed before it? How did it manage to make up for the economic shortages and maintain leadership of a country which from the outset of the conflict had demonstrated its opposition?

The Action of the State. Economic Protection, Repression, and Militarization of Civil Life

In Italy, the action undertaken by the State during wartime was marked by various factors linked to its configuration as a "latecomer."

In fact, along with the Central European powers and Russia, Italy shared strong state intervention, the ever-increasing impact of interest groups on public opinion, the authoritarian and military accentuation of state organization and a growing social dissent.

But compared to the other "latecomers", some of these common traits were even more accentuated in Italy. The country stood out because the state had less control on the private sector, greater power was entrusted to the armed forces, and finally, if we exclude Russia, there was more animated and widespread popular and worker opposition to the war.

In fact, economic backwardness compelled the government to protect excessively (and without the controls which even in Germany public influence had managed to impose) the development of the industrial sectors for arms' manufacturing. Because any form of inquiry regarding the organization of the businesses, their accounts, and the actual costs of the manufactured articles was excluded, the state procured raw materials for industry at subsidized prices, and paid for the products without making any check on the prices demanded. At the same time, it diminished the burden of wage increases by an enormous inflationary maneuver, and, as we have already pointed out, did not take any steps to create a new form of direct taxation, while increasing the indirect taxes. These economic policy choices, allowing the industrialists to reap huge profits, favored a rise in productivity but also provoked an uncoordinated expansion in production and an exorbitant rise in prices, while wages and salaries were continually cut back by inflation and taxation. This situation demonstrates the extent of the power of economic groups and their influence in controlling government policy.

As in Germany and Austria, the war government favored industry by effecting the militarization of the working class (which we will examine later), thus realizing the requests for greater coercion which the entrepreneurs had failed to obtain under the Giolittian regime. Generally speaking, in Italy the social control of the country was realized much more by repressive means than by any search for approval.

The firm belief that the war would be short-lived had in fact led to the consideration that propaganda in favor of the conflict was a secondary issue; something that was in any case not easy in a country which was pulled apart by the controversy between neutralist and interventionist options and which had gone to war on the basis of an executive *coup de main*. During the period of neutrality, the recurring themes of propaganda—the struggle to free the "unredeemed" lands still under Austrian rule, and the "democratic" war against the continental autocracies—had scarcely aroused the interest of the majority of the population. Besides, the motivation of a battle for democracy was in clear contrast with the regime of strict authoritarianism begun by Salandra's government. Even in the years which followed, up until 1918, any action of persuasion carried out by the state was extremely limited (and aimed essentially at the Giolittian sentiments of the middle classes, to persuade them to support the government in the war). In concrete terms, most of the propaganda was conducted by private patriotic associations. It was only after Caporetto that the government concerned itself to a certain extent with popular approval and tried to obtain it with a campaign of persuasion, mainly developed at the front, and through some improvements in the conditions of the troops. But the attention paid to the civilian population by the central public power, in terms of both propaganda and welfare, was still negligible.

In fact, welfare was transferred to local bodies, the communes, which in turn relied on private charitable organizations and patriotic associations. This volunteer work was sporadic in big cities and nonexistent in smaller towns, the countryside, and poorer areas. Consequently, it was wholly inadequate in comparison to the needs. The only actions accomplished by the government in the social sphere were first, as we shall see, a few interventions in favor of workers in the factories and countryside—linked to the requirements of food and industrial production and the consequent necessity of putting an end to strikes and protests—and second, the granting of subsidies to the poorer families of men called up, whose level, already among the lowest of all the countries at war, nevertheless remained unchanged for the first two years of the conflict, and was rapidly eroded by inflation.

The knowledge that the country was overwhelmingly against Italy's entering the war was an element which immediately favored authoritarian decisions and encouraged an increasingly frequent recourse to them—above all, from the moment in which the war became one of attrition and the country's capacity to resist became central to the military outcome. This factor strengthened the determination to use repression, thereby, as we know, corresponding to the practice of "latecomers," and consolidating Salandra's conservative-authoritarian outlook. It was necessary to silence public opinion with every preventive and repressive means available. To this end, a series of decrees was issued at the moment of intervention, limiting—practically to the point of abolition—the freedom to meet and associate and freedom of speech. Although not publicly declared, even freedom of thought was placed under heavy restrictions. In fact, the measures concerning censorship allowed the military authorities to open letters coming from and going to the front and the war zones, and permitted the prefects to do likewise in the rest of the country. If the correspondence contained expressions held to be dangerous for the maintenance of social peace, the senders were reported to the authorities. Most of the proceedings for crimes of opinion were assigned to the military tribunals. The senior authorities ordered that the regulations of the military penal code be severely applied in order to act as a deterrent in respect to public opinion.

During the war, this exceptional legislation was constantly harshened in response to the growing dissent which the country expressed against the conflict. In particular, the repression in the last year of the war became more marked, when, following the defeat of Caporetto—which was, as is known, attributed falsely to the soldiers' abandoning of the front, and not to the recognized faults of the military high command—the government favored an aggressive campaign against "defeatism." Many of the most animated socialist groups were broken up (youth branches, workers' associations) and many of the opposition activists were imprisoned or condemned to house arrest in distant places in the islands and south of Italy. But above all, ordinary dissent was hit—a phenomenon without equal in the other countries—and many citizens were tried and imprisoned for trivial reasons, often on the basis of simple suspicions. Arturo Labriola, a member of parliament who had actually supported intervention, declared to the House on 17 October 1917, "No European government was ever armed with so many and such strict laws against its own citizens as that of Italy".[4]

At the same time as this attempt to silence public opinion was going on, the war regime also resulted in parliament being deprived of its duties. All the legislation regarding the key sectors such as defense, public order, and the economy, was placed in the hands of the government. In fact, the legislative assembly was only convened when it was impossible to do otherwise, for example, to approve the budget, or whenever a government crisis had been declared.

The importance given to a policy of repression forced the government to seek the determining support of the armed forces, to whom complete freedom of action at the front was entrusted, while most of the management of public life was also assigned to them. Huge areas, considered to be strategic from the war viewpoint or particularly exposed to the danger of workers' protests, were placed under exclusive military jurisdiction (all northern Italy after Caporetto), and the manufacturing of arms was largely run by the military authority. The power of the armed forces in the factories was still superior to that of their German counterparts, since in Italy they were also present *within* the factories, where they controlled production and discipline. Numerous offenses were removed from the competence of civil courts and assigned to the military tribunals. Moreover, the defense of public order, both preventive, by means of censorship, and repressive, was placed almost completely in the hands of the military authorities.

In this situation little space remained for the political currents which had opposed intervention to make themselves heard. Nevertheless, even if the Socialist opposition was more of a principle than a fact, having condemned the war, it appeared in the eyes of public opinion as the main instigator of any movements for peace. For the interventionists—who made the Socialists the prototypes of the "internal enemy" and accused them of being responsible for all the demonstrations of hostility throughout the country—the PSI was to blame for "defeatism," whereas the opposing side saw it as the symbol of the struggle against injustice and oppression. Thus, the PSI constituted a magnet which attracted not only the pacifist opposition but, after the February revolution, also the first cores of revolutionary intransigence.

As the war continued and the prospect of an easy victory slowly disappeared to the point of becoming an unattainable dream in 1917 (and especially after Caporetto), for its part, the interventionist movement—a jumble of positions which went from the Salandrian conservative right and the nationalists to the "interventionist revolutionary" factions of Mussolini's followers and the "democratic interventionist" social reformers—continually moved towards increasingly controversial antisocialist positions and made itself an advocate, alongside Cadorna, of an iron fist policy towards any form whatsoever of dissent. The plan for a *coup d'état* in order to establish a government of public safety headed by a soldier—perhaps Cadorna—which appeared briefly in the summer of 1917 was also part of this perspective, although it failed because of the estrangement of the more moderate interventionists, including the Salandrian conservative group.

Industrial Mobilization

It was in this period—perhaps also in relation to the thwarted putsch attempt—that the organization of Industrial Mobilization (MI) was partially modified. This was a body created at the beginning of the war to control worker conflicts, and which provided that internal factory discipline be placed under the direct management of the military command. In July 1917, disciplinary supervision in the factories was removed from the control of the Supreme Command and permanently assigned to those military forces which depended directly on the MI. The latter, having first been responsible to the Ministry of War (and therefore to the Supreme Command) now became autonomous, part of the new Ministry of Arms and Munitions, headed by General Alfredo Dallolio. Compared to the approach of the Supreme Command, that of General Dallolio was certainly less strict, both as regards the disciplinary standard within the factories, and the concessions (above all in terms of wages) to be granted to the working class. It was not a coincidence that only in this period were the trade union representatives allowed into the MI Central Committee, the body which made the final decisions regarding controversies about work.

Borrowed from the German and Austrian experiences, the MI had been created with the precise aim of placing labor relations under state—and, in particular, military—control, and of preventing conflicts, by means of the militarization of the workers. The distinguishing feature of this body—which at war's end counted 1,976 businesses with 903,000 workers, spread throughout all the industrial sectors, but mainly iron, steel, and mechanics—was that of having abolished the right to strike in the factories under it and having introduced forced labor. In fact, the workers were unable to leave their place of work for any reason (moving to another job, health, or family reasons, etc.). Abandoning the workplace was made the equivalent of desertion.

Labor disputes had to be resolved through a system of arbitration. Conciliation was in the hands of MI regional committees, in which specific commissions, composed of army officers, industrialists, and workers' representatives (usually picked by the industrialists) had the job of dealing with disputes which had arisen in the factories under their control. Conflicts resolved by local bodies swelled from 122 in 1915–16 to 1,284 in 1917–18. Appeals could be made to the Central Committee.

Workers, including women and children, were subject to the military penal code and to military courts. Discipline was determined directly by army officers, who decided on punishments and, in the more serious cases, on whether a worker should be sent to the military court or directly to the front. The coercive level was higher in Italy than in the Central Powers. In Germany, for example, the trade-unionists managed to mitigate many regulations, such as that binding workers to their workplace, and in Austria women were not subject to militarization.

The disciplinary questions, and in general all those regarding the organization of work within the factory, were not subject to arbitration. In these areas, the industrialists enjoyed complete freedom and only had to come to an agreement with the local military headquarters, on which, until July 1917, as we have seen, the officers assigned to discipline depended. But in 1917, General Dallolio decided to interfere within the labor organization too, in an attempt to rationalize the entire industrial production and render it more efficient. The MI concerned itself with safety and hygiene conditions in the factories—in most of them work was carried out in overcrowded conditions, given the rapid rate of development of production and the consequent need to increase labor—and promoted an accident insurance system which Italy, unlike the other industrialized countries, did not possess. Moreover, as had already happened in the other warring nations, an industrial relations modernization policy was set up by the bodies of the MI. In 1917, the arbitration process came into operation and, with the entry of the trade unions into the MI Central Committee, three-sided contacts began among the sides in conflict—entrepreneurs and workers' representatives—and the state. These were the main experiences of modernization brought to Italian industrial relations by the war, some of which (such as the three-sided consultations) were destined to disappear with the end of the conflict.

The MI intervention within labor organization was met with hostility from the entrepreneurs. They had agreed to wage increases so long as their power within the factories was not affected. From mid-1917 onwards—regarding the new MI policy—the industrialists began to criticize Dallolio, actually managing to bring about his fall in May 1918, and have him replaced by the Secretary of State for War, Zupelli, a loyal executor of the Supreme Command's dictates.

Living Standards

Despite the MI's attempts at regulation, work in the Italian factories was subject to conditions rarely experienced in the other main warring nations. Given the level of industrial backwardness, during the conflict there were situations typical of exploitation during the first phase of industrialization, justified to public opinion by the needs of war. Common features were long hours, compulsory overtime (reaching even 16- 18 hours a day, with consecutive shifts of 36 hours), and low wages of unskilled workers, usually based on piece work, and—despite increases—always below the level of the rise in the cost of living. Conditions were sometimes so bad that in certain cases soldiers sent to work in the factories requested to be transferred to the front.

The difficulties of life within the factory were combined with those outside, mainly involving the shortage of essential foodstuffs. Inadequate wheat production and the consequent need for foreign imports, as was the case for other essential items, produced a growing food shortage, especially from the end of 1916 onwards. On several occasions in the course of 1917 no bread was to be had in the main cities.

Besides the difficulty of receiving supplies from abroad, the scarcity of essential foodstuffs was also linked to poor distributional organization by the state. A law prevented foodstuffs from being transferred from one province to another, so that it was not unusual for one area to be short of necessary provisions while in another supplies requisitioned in the countryside went unused and spoiled. Conflicting orders from the civil and military authorities concerning rationing and requisitions, bureaucratic chaos, and the incompetence of individuals all contributed to bring about an emergency situation in all the main cities and in many lesser towns.

It must also be remembered that in the big Italian cities—owing to the rapid and immense industrial change of the war years—the hardships created by the conflict were added to those linked to the industrialization process itself, which transferred thousands of rural families to the main northern urban centers. These families crowded the poor districts, living in makeshift accommodations, six or seven to a room. There was practically no assistance to speak of in these areas of the cities and less food was available. Indeed, the presence of these new city dwellers weighed negatively on the supplies to the whole city, as these were distributed—especially flour for bread-making—on the basis of the number of inhabitants registered in the previous census of 1911, and therefore the new workers and their families were not taken into consideration in the calculations. Consequently, a lack of sufficient supplies for the needs of the swollen population was common in the industrial cities and it is not surprising that some of the main urban protests—in particular, the one in Milan in the spring of 1917 and the Turin uprising in August of the same year—began precisely because of the lack of bread in the shops.

Consumption levels fell dramatically in the cities, especially from 1916 onwards. According to studies carried out on workers' families in Milan, their calorie intake was so low that it was unthinkable that it could decrease further without provoking pathological forms of malnutrition. Between 1917 and 1918, when essential foodstuff rationing began, bread rations were even reduced to less than 200 grams a day in some cities. Considering the level of prices and the fact that many products were exclusively to be found on the black market, only families with more than one working member were saved from a pitiful standard of living. But many combatant soldiers' families could only count on the meager government subsidy, which in many cases was not granted. Among other reasons, it was denied to those whose inability to work was not recognized, those in possession of properties (regardless of size), widowed mothers of soldiers whose wives received subsidies, and boys over twelve years of age. Welfare action was therefore completely insufficient. The rise in infant mortality during the war—one of the highest in Europe—growth in lung disease, and a serious decline in the birthrate, are all indications of the degree of extreme material hardship which hit the poorest classes.

In the country and small urban centers living standards were less dramatic compared to the cities, as subsistence was usually guaranteed by means of vegetable plots or rearing animals. But life was certainly not easy, especially for some categories, such as laborers, whose families often lived on the state subsidy alone. Jobs, for those who could count on them, meant greatly increased physical effort. In Italy—unlike other European countries, with the partial exception of France—it was mainly the women who had to compensate for the absence of the male members of the family. Sometimes they went to carry out seasonal work as laborers (in particular as rice-weeders in the rice-growing areas of the north), performing extremely heavy tasks, such as plowing, hoeing, and loading hay. Their wages fluctuated between a third and a fifth of that received by their male counterparts for the same job. Some were used to agricultural work, for others, such as the women from the south, it was a completely new experience, because in those areas agricultural work was an all-male domain because of tradition and productive structure. Nevertheless, they were also forced to work—since many were deprived of subsidies, as these were not granted to the families of draft dodgers, most of whom were southern peasants who had emigrated to America— and endured conditions of exploitation often superior to the women of other areas in Italy.

The intervention by the state to meet the needs of the rural population was limited, as far as production was concerned, to the granting, on a very restricted basis, of exemptions and licenses. For labor relations this entailed the extension of contracts until the postwar period, rent restrictions, and a decree concerning farming-related accidents, while for family welfare it meant the donation of subsidies. But the effects of the legislative regulations on labor relations varied from area to area, and were only marginally controlled by the state.

Generally speaking, on the one hand inflation produced a rise in agricultural prices and a consequent advantage for the producers. On the other, requisitions, price fixing, enforcement of non-remunerative prices, bans on the transfer of certain products from one province to another, and reduced production owing to the lack of labor, combined to worsen the conditions of economic hardship which the Italian countryside had always known.

The "Moral Revolt"

It has already been noted that the hostility of the population towards the war from the very beginning of the conflict was a situation peculiar to Italy. And we have also seen that it was this knowledge which forced the government to issue severe exceptional legislation. By virtue of this, dissent was concealed for the first one and a half years of the war. Until the autumn of 1916, social protest was limited— apart from some demonstrations at the departure of troops and various strikes in the non-militarized factories outside the areas controlled by the armed forces (where striking was obviously forbidden).

Besides, the arrival in the factories of a large number of unskilled workers, who knew that their jobs were temporary, created some confusion and slowed down the protests. The skilled working class of the auxiliary plants or those within the war zones had been rendered powerless by the exceptional legislation and by militarization.

In evaluating the absence of open forms of protest against the war—anonymous ones, such as graffiti, leaflets, shouts and catcalls against the patriotic speakers and police forces continued to be frequent—it must also be remembered that in the first months of the conflict the country was unaware of the actual situation at the front. The sufferings of the recruits, their terror before a hitherto unknown condition of death—the technological death produced by the new instruments of a mass war—and the impact with the cruel disciplinary laws, were all unknown to the families, who were informed by the press (or by the patriotic authorities of the country) about a situation which was hugely different from reality, imbued with bombastic rhetoric and therefore incomprehensible to the majority. Censorship, for its part, prevented any dramatic news contained in correspondence from reaching relatives; and the severe punishments which were inflicted when the authorities identified the senders discouraged the soldiers themselves from informing their families of their actual conditions. It was only with the first permits for leave—very belatedly granted by the Supreme Command, knowing the effect that the soldiers' tales could have on the state of mind of the population—that the country came to learn of the real conditions of the infantrymen. This was the reason which, even more than hunger, often compelled the people to demonstrate against the war.

With the winter of 1916 approaching—Italy's second winter at war—the whole of the country was involved in a series of popular protests. They began in the countryside and were led by women; each one stemmed from immediate causes—the delay in the delivery of the monthly subsidies, the lack of bread in the village bakeries—but soon developed into a protest against the war, demanding the return of their relatives at the front. During 1917, the peasant revolts became increasingly frequent, often taking on the characteristics of a real popular uprising. It was always the women who began as most of the men were at the front and, besides, the risk they ran was evidently less.

These rebellions resembled the former peasant revolts, through which, especially in the south, the people had demonstrated their anger toward the forms of oppression which first the previous rulers and later the new unitary state had imposed upon them. But during the war the rebellion against the state took on new dimensions: it was no longer a protest in defense of violated collective rights and, therefore, in favor of the reinstatement of regulations which had been infringed.[5] The war and the February revolution in Russia had lent a new meaning to the anti-authoritarian protests, because they were also naïvely attributed to the power to produce a change in the decision to continue the conflict, and an overturning of the political and social hierarchies. "Peace or revolution," "bread or revolution" were the slogans uttered by the crowds of demonstrators, written on the walls of the cities, or included in the numerous anonymous letters which private citizens sent to the "powerful."

Women were the main protagonists of the peasant revolts, and of those in the factories and cities. In the countryside, the principal episodes of conflict involving mainly the north and center of the country were caused by them, left to work the fields. In Lazio and the south—where there was a growing phenomenon of occupied lands in those years—the protests were carried out by the women. In the cities, they were the ones who mostly had to endure the burden of the war, looking after the children alone, standing in endless queues to buy food, and observing the constant and often prohibitive rise in prices. And once more it was the women who, entering the factories en masse from the end of 1916 onwards, experienced, often for the first time, work in the plants, enduring the harshness of the pace imposed and the rigors of the disciplinary regime, being paid wages which were not only greatly inferior to those of their unskilled male peers but sometimes of even the boys.

The first spate of factory protests, begun in the second half of 1916, therefore mainly consisted in young female workers (who did not risk, like the men, being sent to the front as a punishment) abandoning their jobs. The reasons usually stemmed from the belief that they had been victims of an abuse of power: the dismissal of a colleague, a fine for unintentional lateness, punishment for an unfinished job or an action considered to be disobedient, etc. The protest would begin with a request for the reinstatement of the previous conditions—abolition of the fines, or the punishments—but it sometimes passed to a more general request for improvements in the working conditions, and—above all in 1917—to pacifist demonstrations.

Therefore, an identical mechanism to that of the countryside operated for the women in the factories too. The protests characteristic of "moral economy" turned into struggles against the factory system and the policy of war.

From the beginning of 1917 onwards, the women's protests were increasingly supported by those of the male workers. Despite strikes being forbidden and the arbitration process set up, even in the militarized factories there were many cases of strikes involving a large number of workers, including the men. Usually a protest arose precisely because the arbitration system worked badly—long periods passed between the workers' requests and the decisions of the MI regional committees—or because it did not satisfy the workers. But often strikes were declared for solidarity—such as dismissal or unfair punishments meted out to colleagues—and therefore took on characteristics which went beyond the economic elements or the organization of labor to become—as in the case of the main workers' protests in the Ligurian and Neapolitan steelworks—a form of collective protest against the system of coercion and militarization in the factories. In these cases, the strikes acquired a "moral" value, such as the reacquisition of professional freedom and dignity, both injured by authoritarianism.

On other occasions, as in the main protest episode of the war in Turin in August 1917—where barricades were erected in the workers' districts and the rebels confronted the army for three days—it was an explicit protest by all the workers and poor of the city against the war regime: arising from a collective reaction to the lack of bread, it soon transformed into a real revolutionary uprising along Russian lines.

Therefore, what was shared by all the rural and urban protests during the war, within and without the factories, was a "moral revolt" against the injustice perpetrated towards individuals, a community, or the entire nation; a form of injustice which was constantly brought to the fore by the authoritarian system and the incapacity of the state and which was made most obvious by the war itself. "Do like in Russia" became the slogan which summarized this desire—still more moral than political—to install a "new order," a hierarchy of values and methods which opposed those imposed and endured during the war.

As the conflict continued, the differences between the conditions of the poor and the well-off grew more obvious. These not only involved living standards but life itself. In fact, public opinion very soon realized that while the poor—peasants and workers—had to go and fight in the front line, the sons of the ruling classes managed to be exempted or sent to the rear, to the Red Cross and the offices of the Supreme Command in Rome, or to the factories as surveillance officers.

The resentment of the phenomenon of shirkers combined with that produced by the knowledge that a part of the population—the "sharks," traders, and speculators—was benefiting from the conflict. As the war continued, the certainty that only the poor went to die at the front and that they were the only ones to suffer from hunger strengthened in the minds of the people. They were equally convinced that the country's rulers were incompetent and corrupt and that they favored the industrialists and speculators. Thus, they came to the conclusion that the war had been desired to promote the interests of the "rich" against those of the "poor."

After Caporetto

Caporetto marked a change in the running of the state and in the mentality of the population. Regarding the former, the fear of defeat—both military and political—forced those of the ruling class who had wanted the war to demand a policy from the government which was more decidedly oriented to the right. From the eve of Caporetto, the government had been led by a liberal moderate, Vittorio Emanuele Orlando. He had previously been Home Secretary in the Boselli government which had been formed in June 1916, after the fall of the Salandra government, and open to all the interventionist groups, and as such had demonstrated his inclination towards a policy of mediation. But the fear that military defeat could be a prelude to an internal insurrection—it must be remembered that Caporetto took place a few days before the October Revolution—convinced even the most moderate to agree to an authoritarian stance. After Caporetto, any demonstration of dissent whatsoever was hit by a more widespread and merciless form of repression than before. The country lived in a climate of witch-hunts, consisting of anonymous denunciations and convictions. As already mentioned, this penalized the exponents of the Socialist opposition and ordinary citizens, guilty only of not falling within the criteria of a patriotism which was as fanatical as it was intolerant.

Furthermore, after Caporetto, living standards worsened: consumption was further cut back, ration cards were adopted for the main foodstuffs (which, however, did not prevent privileged situations continuing), and youths not yet twenty years old were called up, the so-called "boys of '99" (but avoidance of military service was not eliminated). Rural requisitions became more widespread, provoking a state of malaise which was not compensated by the granting of more leave for the soldiers in order to carry out work in the fields. Although the insurrectional-type protests of the previous year almost stopped—made impossible by legislation—the persistent and increasingly sullen and brooding discontent towards the government was communicated with apprehension by the various prefects, as they noted the sentiment throughout the country of favor towards the enemy. The people hoped that Caporetto had marked Italy's defeat, and that therefore the country would soon be occupied by the Austrians.

Despite the fact that the MI body of legislation forbade striking, dissent remained unchanged in the factories too. In 1918, although the number of strikes was reduced in favor of controversies resolved by arbitration—because almost all the industrial areas had been declared war zones and the trade unions had acquired more power—there was greater unity in the demands of the skilled and unskilled working classes and many militarized workers took part in the strikes.

In the countryside, spontaneous revolts decreased whereas demonstrations aimed at fulfilling specific aims became more numerous. These were the symptoms of greater cohesion among the workers and a renewed relationship with the trade-union organizations, but, above all, they were indicative of a change in the spirit of protest, now less violent (dare we say less "moral" in the sense used above), more organized and aimed at obtaining concrete results.

But the growing sense of class identity and the attainment of certain objectives in the struggles (thanks also to trade-union mediation) did not bring about a change in the relationship with the state as regards the creation of unitary national consciousness and consequent patriotic solidarity (as in Britain, for example). On the contrary, the knowledge of the role they had played within industry and at the front—and the contractual victories themselves—reinforced the belief of the workers and peasants that a new social order had to arise from the war, within which new rights and economic and political powers would be recognized.

At the same time, however, other sectors too demanded compensation from the state for the hardships and burdens endured. These were, for example, the middle classes who had suffered reductions in their fixed incomes because of inflation, and had shared the food shortages with the poorer classes and seen their sons called to the front. Some of these, belonging to the higher levels of society, had also supported all the welfare and propaganda action, with practically no help from the state. Therefore, they considered themselves entitled to economic, social, and political recognition for this work carried out in support of the country at war. On the other hand, the industrialists put forward no less serious demands for protection, in the knowledge that many advantages obtained from the war would no longer be forthcoming with the end of the conflict. The landowners also demanded measures in their favor, having experienced more costs than advantages in the war.

The experience of war had, therefore, produced a kind of corporative social subdivision of opposing groups, all equally convinced that they ought to receive recognition and compensation.

This was exactly the opposite of the reaction hoped for by those who had forced the country into the war. Conceived of as a means of blocking the process of internal democratization and opening to the masses, it had instead reinforced their tendency to emerge. Moreover, it had not created a unitary national consciousness, nor brought about a social reorganization around the existing ruling class. On the contrary, it had strengthened remarkably all the prewar elements of disintegration, heightening the hostility of the majority towards the state, promoting the internal unity of the opposing classes of entrepreneurs and workers, and creating new centers of irreconcilable political-cultural conflict between the champions of the war (who had turned out to be the most unscrupulous supporters of the violation of democratic rules) and those who had declared themselves contrary to the war and had tried to defend legality and right from the attacks of the former (finding themselves however outmaneuvered on their left by the ideology which preached the overcoming of democratic mediations, and which had found its concrete realization in Russia).

The unresolved internal tensions, and the subdivision of the requests and objectives of the various social groups succeeded only in underlining the absence of a leadership capable of creating a new plan to integrate the masses into the state. In a fragile socio-political structure such as Italy's, the trauma of the war had produced changes which could not be absorbed.

The Paradox of the Latecomers

I would like to conclude with some remarks on the role of the state regarding "second (or late) comers," especially in Italy.

In all these countries in which the war caused a crisis of regime the action of the State showed itself to be inferior to the task, and far less efficient when compared to that realized by Britain and France.

This may appear paradoxical: in fact, where state interventionism had proven experience behind it—as in the "second" or "latecomer" countries—it was here that it showed its inability to cope with the complex problems which a mass war continually put forward, linked to production, supplies and distribution, monetary and tariff policies, and the relation between means of repression and consent.

What were the reasons for this? I think one can suppose that this depended greatly on the variety of centers of power from which orders were transmitted—government, military commands, economic interests. Unlike what happened in Britain and France, the powerful interest groups were not subjected (especially in Italy) to government control, and (once more, especially in Italy) military power took over increasingly vast areas of civilian life. Thus, instructions issued by public bodies were often subjected to obstructionism by economic groups, and, in their turn, the military powers challenged orders from civil powers, even issuing contradictory measures. Furthermore, two different lines of action were created within each of these bodies, one more moderate which tried to seek consent, the other more severe, convinced of the need to favor repressive choices (represented in Italy by Dallolio-Cadorna and Orlando-Salandra). The result was that, lacking a single policy, these regulations, which were determined by different interests and policies, tended to be superimposed on each other and were often contradictory.

It must be added that—in the attempt to maintain control of its own management—the state tended to increase the bureaucratic process: bodies sprang up, within both the political and military spheres, whose task was to supervise the application of the regulations, and sometimes even the work carried out by other offices which the various senior departments did not trust. In the face of the inefficient running of the administrative and bureaucratic structures, and consequent inability to control the situation, the state reacted by stepping up the compulsory measures.

The organizational deficiencies—which introduced the country to the specter of hunger—and the priority given to the policies of repression compared to those of consent, deprived the governments of the support and legitimization which in countries without a tradition of state interventionism, such as Britain and France, were obtained instead by a line of policy more attentive to material living conditions and the mood of the population. Although these nations had also faced the problem of inequality in the experience of hardships and losses, a policy which was careful not to lay the sacrifices only on the poorest classes prevented the differences from turning into open class conflict. In Great Britain, as has been shown, the standard of living of some of the poorest classes improved: unlike Italy, the wages of unskilled workers increased considerably, and a policy of progressive taxation made the war almost seem a system of redistribution of the collective burdens. At the same time, a shrewd policy concerning consumption and a high level of agricultural production saved the country from great hardships. In France much the same situation pertained.

These political choices allowed the state to appeal to the consensus of the population when facing the war of attrition. The obtaining of cohesion within the country by means of persuasion and civil mobilization, with a marginal use of repressive means, favored the consolidation of a strong sense of national identity—which the war tended to increase rather than diminish—and strengthened the power of the ruling classes in office. On the contrary, in the "second" or "latecomer" countries, the emphasis was transferred to coercive methods. As we have seen, these were favored particularly in Italy, where the state responded to the growing hostility towards the war by increasing the repressive forms of social control, and conceding extremely limited space to welfare measures and the regaining of consent.

In the postwar period in Italy, the political leadership did not succeed in bridging the gap which separated it from the country, and creating the bases for a democratic revival. The war had emphasized the handicaps of the outset—economic backwardness and lack of consent of the majority of the country—and had made the fragile socio-political framework even more vulnerable to traumas. In the face of the worsening economic situation, the violent expression of popular dissent, and the pressures on the state practised by groups of entrepreneurs and factions of the political-military right, the solution which the Italian state adopted was that already tested in the war years: the authoritarian and repressive crushing of dissent.

Notes for Chapter 1

1. Between 1901 and 1913 per capita industrial production rose by 2/3 and industrial production by 87%; the average increase in Europe was 56%. The active population employed in industry rose from 22.5% in 1901 to 25.5% in 1911 (in agriculture it fell from 59.4% to 55.4%, and in services it went from 18.1% to 19.1%). But the distance between Italy and other industrialized countries remained considerable; the ratio between per capita income in the United King-

dom and in Italy decreased from 2.3 to 2 between 1881 and 1913. In 1911 the companies which employed more than 250 people and used machines of over 250 cv were only 0.3 to 0.4% of the total. The number of people forced to emigrate was extremely high; in 1913 alone, when the active population of Italy was around 16 million, 872,600 people were forced to emigrate.
2. The industrial sector went from 25% of the total private GNP in 1914 to 31.5% in 1917, and to 30.6% at the end of the war. The capital of all industrial limited companies increased between 1913 and 1918 by 56% (that of engineering companies by 252%). Private consumption rose from 79,500 million lire in 1913 (1938 prices) to 84,600 million lire in 1918. There was an enormous increase in employment in many of the big industries: workers at Fiat, for example, increased from 4,000 to 40,000 in 1918.
3. The wholesale price index—100 in 1914—was 425 in Italy in 1918, 329 in France, 227 in the United Kingdom, 205 in Germany.
4. Some examples of trials—among many. A priest who tried to console a dying man by saying that his son, missing in action, had probably been taken prisoner was convicted and the sentence was confirmed on appeal; the police began a search for the parents—in order to try them—of a little girl who on Christmas Eve had prayed to a venerated statue of the Christ child that peace should come soon; a street trader was charged for selling chocolate figures representing the various crowned heads of Europe, among which was Franz Josef.
5. The reference is to the work on the "moral economy" by E.P. Thompson, *The Moral Economy of the English Crowd in the XVIIIth Century,* in "Past and Present," 38, 1967 and 50, 1971.

Select Bibliography

L. Tomassini, "Industrial Mobilization and the Labour Market in Italy during the First World War," *Social History,* (1991), as well as his "Industrial Mobilization and State Intervention in Italy in the First World War: Effects on Labor Unrest," in Haimson and Sapelli eds., *Strikes, Social Conflict and the First World War: An International Perspective* "Annali della Fondazione G. G. Feltrinelli", 1992. Offers insight into the Italian state's intervention into the war economy.

S. Musso, "Political Tension and Labor Union Struggles: Working Class Conflicts in Turin during and after the First World War," in L.Haimson and G. Sapelli eds., *Strikes, Social Conflict and the First World War,* cit. Discusses protest in the countryside and in the factories.

Giovanna Procacci, *Soldati e prigionieri italiani nella Grande guerra* (Rome: Editori Riuniti, 1993). Focuses on the military situation, the penal military regime, and the condition of the soldiers and the prisoners.

_____, ed., *Stato e classe operaia in Italia durante la prima guerra mondiale* (Milan: Angeli, 1983). A collection of essays on Italy during the Great War.

_____, "Popular Protest and Labour Conflict in Italy, 1915—1918," in *Social History* (1989), 1.

_____, "State Coercion and Worker Solidarity in Italy (1915-1917): The Moral and Political Content of Social Unrest," in Haimson and Sapelli eds., *Strikes, Social Conflict and the First World War,* cit.

CHAPTER 2

THE POLITICAL POLICE, WAR, AND SOCIETY IN RUSSIA, 1914–1917

Fredric S. Zuckerman

The First World War placed the political police system of Russia on alert. The forces of order, like so many others in Russia, believed that the outbreak of war had merely granted Russia a reprieve from revolution. Thus on 2 September 1914, while other nations marched more-or-less joyously off to war under the unifying atavistic banner of rabid nationalism, the Department of Police (nicknamed Fontanka after the St. Petersburg Quai upon which its headquarters resided) pleaded for a different sort of united front, against the internal enemy, against revolution.[1] In response to this fear Tsardom reinforced the essential role already played by the political police in the defense of the monarchy, granting it vast resources to protect Russia's ruling (the court and aristocracy) and governing (senior officialdom) elites from the people.[2] No other combatant nation during the First World War imposed such a heavy weight of responsibility for the internal security of the state upon its political police forces. Yet neither the Tsarist government nor its forces of order considered this to be an exceptional duty given the unstable political environment that permeated Russian life in August 1914 (as we shall soon see) and the historically based role of the political police system as a bulwark against the subversion which the forces of order believed perpetually threatened the Tsarist regime.[3]

Notes for this chapter begin on page 52.

Nevertheless, despite the dedication of its officers to fulfilling this assignment and the vast resources the government placed at their disposal for this purpose, Russia's political police proved remarkably ineffective in sustaining its traditional role as the first line of defense against revolution. Why was this so?

In order to understand the role and the behavior of the Tsarist political police during the First World War and thereby be able to respond to this question, we must first review the integral role the political police played in the evolution of Russian society—the protection and even sustenance of the "two Russias" culture[4]—in the generation or so before August 1914.

The Political Police and Russian Society, 1881–1914

Tsardom's striking lack of trust in the population at large during what should have been a period of national unification and reconciliation after August 1914 and the central role of the political police system in preventing any such convergence between state and society was the product of the political cultural phenomenon known as the "two Russias." The "two Russias" societal pattern rigidly maintained the political and socio-economic *status quo*. It isolated the ruling and governing elites from the remaining segments of society—the "other" Russia of peasants, intelligentsia, professionals, merchants, workers whose aspirations the ruling and governing elites had desperately struggled to contain. This struggle allowed the political police to increasingly extend its tentacles throughout Russian society between 1881 and 1914.

We can begin to understand the complexion of the "two Russias" political culture by recognizing that all Russians high and low lived without the protection of personal inviolability. The weakness of such laws on personal inviolability that did exist in the face of overpowering legislation enabling the political police to prevent crime and preserve the tranquillity of the state led to the unwarranted intrusion into the lives of Russia's population by over zealous police and law and order officials. This state of affairs was best exemplified by the promulgation of the Exceptional Measures on 14 August 1881. These "temporary" regulations remained in force until the end of the regime within as many as two-thirds of Russia's fifty provinces.

The Exceptional Measures capped a long series of repressive decrees, and served as a declaration of Tsardom's lack of confidence in its people. Instead it relied upon the bureaucracy's administrative authority to judge, convict, and sentence not only those persons who committed crimes against the state, but those whom it charged with merely contemplating the commission of such crimes or, worse, those accused by local officials of just behaving suspiciously! The penalties most commonly evoked under the rubrics of this process were exile and a procedure called open police surveillance (*glasnyi politseiskii nadzor*). There were two types of exile: *vyssylka* and *ssylka*. *Vyssylka*, the milder and more common form of punishment, prohibited the "criminal" from living within certain proscribed areas of the empire. Its victims were usually persons suspected of being "politically unreliable," a phrase often used to condemn individuals not for something they had done but for something they might do in the future. *Ssylka* or deportation to a definite location was a much more severe penalty, as it condemned the accused to a particular residence, usually in Siberia, for a period of up to five years or sometimes ten years for hardened political criminals. A person could be sentenced to *ssylka* merely for having made some offhand remarks that the chief of the local political police bureau construed as dangerous to society.[5]

Exile of either sort went hand in hand with open surveillance, a form of harassment designed to remind the victim that the slightest deviation from normal behavior patterns would come to the attention of the authorities. This barbarous form of persecution reduced its victims to despair and poverty, destroying their health and driving some to suicide.[6]

The brutality and capriciousness of the political police's tactics struck fear into Russian society,[7] but did not eliminate dissent. To eradicate dissent the forces of order led by the political police undertook to silence those who disseminated unwelcome ideas and the makers of public opinion.[8] Yet Russia's professional people, its intellectuals, and its students, all tainted to one degree or another by foreign ideas which challenged Russia's traditional political culture, were steadily increasing in number. Paradoxically, despite their alien views, these members of unofficial Russia were essential for Tsardom's survival in the competitive arena of international development, and the demands of this competition forced Russia's educational institutions to produce more graduates. Within this environment (at the beginning of the twentieth century) Tsardom's refusal to permit popular discussion of the critical issues confronting it, let alone its refusal to allow any public involvement in the government's policy-making created an intense hostility between the "two Russias" that made the gap between the "two Russias" appear insurmountable. Tsardom, therefore, strove to protect itself through the rapid, substantial expansion of the political police.[9] Needless to say, increased repression in the face of an increasingly literate, politically aware population only served to increase the volatility of the relationship between the new elements of Russian society and the traditional elites.

The Security Divisions served as the principle political police weapon against society. The Ministry of Internal Affairs established these bureaus throughout Russia wherever subversion existed. Only three Security Divisions—Petersburg, Moscow, and Warsaw—were established by statute, all the others were created by edicts issued over the signature of the Minister of Internal Affairs.

The heart of each Security Division was its agents: the detectives (*filery*) and secret agents (*sekretnye sotrudniki*). Security Division detectives maintained surveillance over suspicious individuals and groups, over their residences and the venues of their meetings. Russia's secret agents infiltrated both subversive groups and parties and to a lesser degree the organizations of the legal opposition (including the press of all of these groups) in order to inform on their members and/or disrupt their activities.

Tsardom's first line of defense against its people was its detectives. The absence of personal inviolability in Russia is clearly exemplified by the "watching brief" assigned to Russia's detectives. People in all walks of life, but especially the intelligentsia, regularly fell under secret (*neglasnyi politseiskii nadzor*)—as opposed to open—surveillance. This large group of victims included known revolutionaries, persons who had completed their sentences as state criminals (such as the victims of the Exceptional Measures), high school and university students and their teachers, persons occupied in various aspects of publishing, the employees of libraries and reading rooms, and members of the military—officers and ordinary soldiers. Places as well as people were kept under secret surveillance: shops, restaurants, inns, and public houses; indeed any place where suspects met and where agitators dispensed their propaganda. The political police usually maintained surveillance over a suspect for two years. If at the end of two years the Special Section (the guiding administrative and intelligence processing directorate of the political police system) had convinced itself that the object of surveillance did not present a threat to state security, observation of the suspect was discontinued.[10]

It is a measure of the detectives' success that the revolutionaries believed that most large Security Divisions—such as those located in St. Petersburg, Moscow, Warsaw, and Kiev—maintained thousands of surveillance personnel. In reality, there were probably no more than a thousand professional political police detectives throughout Russia. Yet the average revolutionary on the run in St. Petersburg, for example, could seldom dodge the political police for more than three months.[11] Despite abuse by their superiors, chronic low pay, and long hours, these detectives were among the most loyal of Tsardom's servants.[12]

The secret agents were a completely different kettle of fish. Political police detectives supplied only relatively obvious—though extensive—intelligence to the Special Section. The detectives did not have access to the core of Russia's numerous revolutionary and opposition groups. Nonetheless, the political police desperately wished to unravel the programs, tactics, and internecine politics of these circles in order to develop effective counter-surveillance. Some of this intelligence could be gleaned from the multitude of revolutionary and oppositionist publications available to Fontanka, though the aspects of these groups that most interested the political police rarely appeared in print. This information could only be gleaned by special teams of secret agents who masqueraded as revolutionaries (sometimes as constitutionalists), infiltrating the decision-making center of the targeted group and making themselves indispensable members of the organization. The Security Divisions protected agent identities so assiduously that the exact number of secret agents employed by the political police probably will never be known. However, the impact upon the *mentalité* of Russian educated society of this insidious intrusion into their lives can be gauged from the claim in 1918 by one of the first historians of the Tsarist political police:

> [There] was not a single party, nor a single mill, factory, nor a single organization, nor society, union, club committee, university, institute, there was not even a single newspaper editorial staff in which among its members and collaborators there would not have been several secret agents.[13]

Is it no wonder that respect for the law rapidly diminished amongst the masses to the point where the assassination of the despised Minister of Internal Affairs, V.K. Plehve, on 22 July 1904, sparked universal rejoicing.[14] The gap between the people and the elites had never been so wide.

The assassination of Minister of Internal Affairs Plehve served as a catalyst, releasing the tensions of Russian society. Plehve's replacement Prince P.D. Sviatopolk-Mirskii, a moderate reformer, briefly contained popular hostility to the regime by promising political reform. His efforts, however, were thwarted by a recalcitrant government in December 1904.

Within a month the "two Russias" were at war. The ferocity of the 1905 Revolution and the extent of anti-government solidarity startled the government. A broad spectrum of political opinion from the extreme left (the socialist parties) to the moderate right (Russia's industrialists and *haute* bourgeoisie) demanded fundamental alterations to the Tsarist political structure. While these political groups entertained different goals (running the gamut from moderate constitutional monarchy to socialism), they shared one immediate aim: that Russia must adopt some form of parliamentary government in which the Tsar would play a constitutional rather than an autocratic role.

The Revolution established the Duma or Legislature, which along with an upper house, the State Council (the elites' house brandishing a veto over legislation and large sections of the budget) formed the legislative institutions of the post 1905 government. The radical composition of the first two Dumas made cooperation with the government impossible. Finally, by using a successful political police provocation as an excuse, the government prorogued the Second Duma and illegally revised the electoral law so that the newly limited franchise would guarantee the election of a conservative legislature. This incident, known as the *Coup d'Etat* of 3 June 1907 is considered the finale of the 1905 Revolution.

The victory of the forces of order over the Revolution, though it preserved the "two Russias" political culture, came at a terrible price. Although the exact number of political police killed during the 1905 Revolution is unknown,[15] enough perished so as to create panic among them.[16]

Both the brutality of the political police and the extent of popular violence combined to make an indelible impression on the collective *mentalité* of the Tsar's police. In the aftermath of the 1905 Revolution, Russia's political police uniformly perceived the Russian people as united in their intent to destroy the monarchy and with it them. This perception led the police to vilify all forms of opposition to the monarchy, and, most important, not to distinguish adequately between the intensity and types of dissent abroad in Russia during the First World War.

The political police suffered the humiliation of having failed to carry out its brief. The Security Divisions failed to forewarn the government of potential trouble, while the repression they employed against dissent merely exacerbated public hostility toward the regime. Indeed, the political police, obsessed with the dynamics of the 1905 Revolution, used that uprising as the model for any future revolutions. As we shall see, looking backwards became an integral part of its wartime activity. Between 1908 and 1912, however, the exhausted and defeated dissident movements allowed the political police to bask in the illusion that any further disturbances of this magnitude were a long way off into the future. Fontanka's complacency masked the subtle transformation of Russian politics of the previous decades and the recent Revolution (especially with regard to a more sophisticated public opinion).

The new Fourth Duma, elected in 1912, became the beacon of Russian public opinion and, along with its moderate and liberal deputies, the *bete noir* of political police concerns. The Fourth Duma became the protagonist of two of the most powerful weapons deployed against Tsardom: legality and public opinion. The public opinion stimulated by its newspaper-reported debates drove the political police to distraction. General K.I. Globachev, chief of the political police in the capital, clearly remembered his frustration with the Duma. As we will shortly observe, he focused much of his attention on the moderate and liberal Duma Deputies and in the end he blamed them and the Duma (which served as their rostrum) for the collapse of Tsardom.[17]

The labor movement too continued its evolution between 1907 and 1914, even though for quite some time after the dissolution of the Second Duma in 1907 the magnitude of the defeat of the working class at the hands of the counter-revolution obscured exactly how much the cauldron of revolution had tempered it. The political dynamics of the 1905 Revolution taught the laboring masses about themselves, the elites who ruled over them, and the society of which they were now a part.[18]

This is not to say that the years between 1907 and 1912 were notable for a booming labor movement, for clearly they were not. However, the form of self-improvement adopted by Russia's workers in their trade unionism and enlightenment circles boded well for their future. Indeed, despite the interminable police harassment they endured, the legal and semi-legal trade unions became the single most important outlet for worker expression and mechanism for learning about practical labor politics.[19] Between 1907 and 1912 the police closed 214 unions and many others ceased to exist as result of political and economic circumstances. Nonetheless, the number of unions never dropped below 200 and, significantly, by the end of 1912 their number began to increase, reaching 234 in 1913.[20]

Yet political police analysts underestimated the potential for political unrest in Russia in 1912, assuming it would be a relatively quiet year.[21] The violent reaction to the Lena goldfield massacre of April 1912, in which troops shot at a peaceful crowd of miners and their families, killing or wounding more than a hundred of them, quickly swept this assumption aside. The magnitude of the strikes in response to this incident stunned the Department of Police.[22]

By the end of 1913 the political police's confidence in its ability to contain the strike movement began to erode. Labor unrest continued to mount. The Special Section, convinced that systematic revolutionary agitation (particularly by the social democrats) was to blame for the unrest, ordered its Security Divisions to embark upon mass arrests "that would paralyze them [the revolutionary organizations], preventing these groups from carrying out their criminal activities."[23] However, these arrests did not prevent a massive wave of strikes (with its epicenter located in St. Petersburg) from spreading throughout Russia in early July 1914 . Using the threat of impending war as an excuse for sweeping legality aside, the Minister of Internal Affairs employed stern measures against the strikers, their unions, and the radical intelligentsia whom the police considered to be their leaders. All unions were closed, policemen wrecked *Pravda's* editorial offices, closed down the Menshevik paper *Luch* (*The Light*), while the Petersburg Security Division made a large number of arrests.[24] The July strikes petered out, dissipating as the workers' energy diminished in the face of police counter measures.[25] The forces of order still expected the worst.[26] For them the international crisis and the collapse of the strike movement were a case of simple cause and effect—that the July strikes signaled the beginning of a new revolution, something only interrupted by the onset of the First World War.[27]

The Tsarist Political Police and the First World War, 1914–1917

From the autumn of 1914 the political police sought to rely more than ever before upon the investigative and interpretive skills of its intelligence gathering and processing specialists. These individuals served as Tsardom's early warning system, seeking to ensure that neither the Department of Police nor its masters would be caught off guard again as had happened in January 1905.

This responsibility fell most heavily upon the shoulders of General K.I. Globachev and Colonel A.P. Martynov, the political police chiefs of the Petrograd (the wartime name of St. Petersburg) and Moscow Security Divisions respectively. The political police chiefs who occupied the Moscow and St. Petersburg posts (those of the two capitals) carried exceptional status in the eyes of their superiors. Thus, their analyses of events and the advice they offered normally carried special value for the Ministry of Internal Affairs. For this reason we will concentrate mainly—though not exclusively—upon Globachev's and Martynov's capacity to evaluate the socio-economic and political crises of the First World War.

Why did the police, despite the dedication of Globachev, Martynov and their colleagues, fail in its role as the traditional bulwark of the Romanov dynasty? The explanation is to be found both in the Byzantine politics that increasingly dominated the of Ministry Internal Affairs and the court during the First World War and in the "habits of mind" to which the political police succumbed that caused it to misinterpret events and to respond improperly to them.

The influence of court politics on police affairs preceded the outbreak of war. During the conflict, however, Fontanka's leadership completely immersed itself in the phantasmagoric obscurantism of the court. In its desire to preserve the political *status quo*, however, the police leadership interfered with increasing irresponsibility into the processes of government management. Ministers of Internal Affairs, Assistant Ministers and some of Fontanka's Directors became alienated from their Security Division chiefs as the chain-of-command became riddled with mistrust and at times open hostility between field and administrative personnel. For example, the infamous and long-standing performance known as "ministerial leapfrog" made policy formulation an impossibility particularly during times of crisis. Because Tsarist ministers owed their positions solely to the whim of the Tsar, tenure was insecure at the best of times. However, to make matters worse, each new Minister was the head of a lengthy patron-clientele network which required servicing. Therefore, they often took advantage of the privilege of choosing their own Assistant Ministers and directors of the various ministerial departments within their jurisdictions, who subsequently often selected a new group of subordinates as well. This form of musical chairs took place irrespective of the quality of the incumbents replaced. "Ministerial leapfrog" and the internecine politics that accompanied it played havoc with political police administration and severely undermined its capacity to maintain order.

Between 1915 and 1917 the Ministry of Internal Affairs endured six Ministers, who in turn were served by five directors of the Department of Police. These five men ruled over a Special Section led by two non-entities—the first a journeyman bureaucrat and the second an alcoholic. Constant reshuffling meant that the perpetually new officials had little if any time to learn their jobs, were indecisive and, therefore, could not develop any policies. Prince V.M. Volkonskii, who served five of the Ministers, recalled that the Ministry sank into chaos.[28] Under such conditions none of these Ministers could win the respect of their political police.[29] Loss of confidence led to indecision, confusion and eventually inertia at the highest level of the Ministry of Internal Affairs.

In particular, the tenures of three of Tsardom's wartime Ministers of Internal Affairs—A.N. Khvostov, B. V. Shturmer, and A.D. Protopopov—were notable for their terrible relations with the police. Khvostov, an unsavory man with a well-deserved odorous reputation, was once described by General A.I. Spiridovich, Chief of the Tsar's personal bodyguard and one of Russia's most able political policemen, as "an ignoramus in both politics and police."[30] B.V. Shturmer, like his predecessor, was a self-serving schemer, who regularly quarreled with his colleagues, and used his office for petty matters and personal vendettas. The Minister launched one of his vendettas against E.K. Klimovich, appointed by his predecessor to the directorship of the Department of Police. The public bickering between Shturmer and Klimovich from March to September 1916 demoralized the Department of Police. Klimovich declared that Shturmer failed to offer any leadership to Fontanka, which, as a result, "was completely without a rudder, without a sail, not knowing what to do." Police affairs became so chaotic that the frustrated Klimovich "asked God above to give me some kind of general directives."[31] Finally, the bickering between the two men climaxed with the competent Klimovich's dismissal.[32]

The Shturmer-Globachev relationship was not much better. Shturmer developed a close relationship with a shady sometime official and confidant of Rasputin, I.F. Manasevich-Manuilov, who considered himself an expert on political police affairs. Although ostensibly serving only as Shturmer's private secretary, this extraordinarily impudent man ordered Globachev—a major general and the most powerful political policeman in Russia—"to dance to his tune and if he refused to do so he would see to it that Globachev was sacked within 24 hours." Globachev ignored him and retained his job,[33] but the humiliating episode hardly endeared Russia's most important political police official to his Minister.

By the autumn of 1916, therefore, just as the political police awakened to the depth and the nature of the crisis confronting them, the lack of confidence and degree of animosity between police chiefs and Ministers was undermining what remained of the Ministry of Internal Affair's chain of command. The process of disintegration, however, had begun before the war.[34] In 1916 that lack of communication became endemic as Ministers and Assistant Ministers lost themselves completely in the machinations of the court and their own petty intrigues.

Under A.D. Protopopov, Tsardom's last and most incompetent Minister of Internal Affairs and a man who inspired only ridicule,[35] the crisis of confidence within the Ministry reached its peak. In matters of internal security Protopopov ignored the advice of both his Assistant Minister charged with managing the police as well as the Director of Fontanka. Instead Protopopov deferred to the views of his "best friend and pal,"[36] P.G. Kurlov, a former Assistant Minister of Internal Affairs, managing the police, who, although possessing both ability and considerable experience in police matters was a corrupt and venal man. Kurlov carried the well-deserved reputation of an intriguer *par excellence* and had been previously dismissed in disgrace from government service for negligence. His former colleagues within the Department of Police despised him. Even Tsar Nicholas II, who still valued his service, refused to fulfill Kurlov's deepest desire to be reappointed as Assistant Minister.

The first and most damaging instance of Kurlov's influence came with the appointment of A.T. Vasil'ev as Director of the Department of Police. To be sure, Vasil'ev was awarded the post after a lengthy career within Fontanka, including a stint as chief of the Special Section. Yet in the final crisis of the Romanov dynasty the political police found him wanting. A colleague characterized Vasil'ev as a "drab man ... He was one of Kurlov's boys, simply occupying a place." [37] The combination of a non-entity as director of Fontanka and Protopopov's reliance on Kurlov erased any remaining confidence the political police chiefs such as General Globachev in Petrograd and Colonel A.P. Martynov in Moscow had in their superiors.[38]

* * *

Within the maelstrom of the Ministry of Internal Affairs' internal disintegration the Special Section and its field bureaus struggled to contain a disillusioned and disgruntled society. They glumly confronted a revived and reinvigorated strike movement, and opposition members of the Duma, industrialists, and *zemstva* professionals enraged by what they perceived to be the government's inept prosecution of the war and by the demeanor of the government itself. As a result, they formed organizations designed to integrate educated society into the war effort. The first of these groups was the Progressive Bloc which comprised six Duma caucuses—about 241 of the 407 deputies in the Duma. The Kadets (Constitutional Democrats), Progressists, and the Left Octobrists formed the "liberal" segment of the Bloc, at least on most issues, while the Centrists, Zemstvo Octobrists, and Progressive Nationalists constituted its more conservative wing. Established in August 1915, the Progressive Bloc soon became a rump parliament, substituting for the prorogued Fourth Duma (interrupted in September 1915 by a disgruntled government) as a forum for public opinion. Its legislative program was quite moderate, focusing particularly on civil rights and labor and trade union policy. The police viewed the Progressive Bloc as a serious challenge to the government in that it symbolized the termination of the Duma's unconditional parliamentary support for the government offered at the beginning of the war.[39]

The establishment of the Progressive Bloc coincided with the growing involvement of the so-called "public organizations" in the war effort. The principal public organizations were the All-Russian Union of Zemstvos for the Relief of Sick and Wounded Soldiers and the Union of Towns. At first the two unions limited themselves to the relief of the sick and wounded, establishing hospitals, maintaining hospital trains, canteens and medical stores. In 1915 the two organizations began to participate in the process of military supply. A joint committee for the supply of the army united the two unions in this endeavor. This united organization, known by the acronym *Zemgor*, placed war orders, assisted in the establishment of factories, the shipment of supplies to the front and so on. Though not without major shortcomings, *Zemgor* enjoyed great popularity and commanded the allegiance of thousands of employees.[40] These organizations presented a serious challenge to the government's desire to conduct the war and supply the army on its own. As in the 1880s in the war against subversion and terrorism, Tsardom wanted the support, but not the participation of its people in these endeavors. The privilege of conducting the war belonged to the ruling and governing elites alone.

These circumstances set alarm bells ringing within the Special Section and its Security Divisions, particularly those in Moscow and Petrograd. The political police had to discover exactly what the impact of this new political environment would be upon the *status quo*. But its ability to interpret events suffered from the limitations imposed upon it by both the habits of mind common to all political policemen and the physical limitations forced upon the Special Section and the Security Divisions by the exigencies of war.

The Special Section's and its agencies' ability to divine the signs of oncoming turmoil were critically affected by their reliance on previous actions of their opponents to analyze the present and predict the future. Tsarist political policemen were no different from their colleagues in other countries in searching the Special Section's archives in order to discover what to expect next from the population under surveillance. This meant that even at best the Special Section's analysts were usually a step behind events. It was a foot race they were bound to lose.

Thus, Fontanka's analysis of the mood of Russian society during the First World War was deeply colored by the experiences of the 1905 Revolution. Indeed, the Department of Police tried to prevent its memory of 1905 from degenerating into a hazy useless impression by constructing an etiology of the 1905 Revolution. The Special Section's analysts were sufficiently intelligent to realize that the dynamics of one revolution were unlikely to be exactly duplicated in a subsequent rebellion. "It is not possible to conjecture on the form of new revolutionary struggles," Fontanka told its political police, "but nonetheless we must be ready to meet further revolutionary excesses."[41] During the First World War scarcely a significant intelligence survey did not reflect the conclusions drawn by this etiology.[42]

This etiology enshrined one of the most common beliefs of political policemen—that only an elite could bestir the masses to revolution. In 1905 the police concluded that the Union of Unions—a combination of professional and liberal associations—and the St.

Petersburg Soviet of Workers' Deputies were responsible for unifying and guiding the workers and peasants "with the goal of forcibly attaining a constitution."[43] This is a credible though overly simple explanation for what transpired in 1905.

The leadership syndrome, rather than a belief in spontaneous discontent always appealed to the police mentalité.[44] Indeed, by emphasizing the role of political agitators real or imagined, the forces of order in their own minds made the massive discontent throughout Russia seem manageable. Such a state of mind invariably led the political police to underrate popular protest as an expression of deeply felt grievances and overrate the influence of agitators hard at work, driving the ordinarily placid masses into opposition.

The quality of political police intelligence was further reduced by the impact of the First World War upon the staffing of Fontanka's political police bureaus. During the war the Tsarist police suffered from a serious shortage of undercover agents, trained officers, and chancery staff. The accuracy and quality of intelligence gathered from the field depended in large part on the placement of undercover agents within groups targeted by the Special Section or by its Security Divisions. The number and quality of these people considerably diminished between 1914 and 1917 as the government drafted secret agents into the army. At the same time field bureaus found it increasingly difficult to recruit new undercover agents.[45]

In a foolhardy attempt to compensate for this critical shortage the Special Section demanded the collection of more political intelligence by any means from its Security Divisions. Much of the material collected in this manner, often taken from newspapers, was of dubious value and the sheer volume of it overwhelmed political police chanceries already experiencing critical staff shortages. It became impossible for the large Security Divisions such as the one in Moscow to adequately process intelligence or to retrieve it from their files quickly on demand.[46]

* * *

Burdened with limitations on their intelligence gathering and processing machinery and suspicious as well as disdainful of their superiors within the Ministry of Internal Affairs, Globachev, Martynov, and their fellow Security Division chiefs confronted a society undergoing socio-economic and political transformations the values of which the forces of order either rejected or did not understand. The images of 1905 resurfaced as these police chiefs projected their fear as hatred for the people and institutions the regime considered responsible for the turmoil that shook the monarchy during the war years. The political police especially focused its suspicion and hatred upon the Duma system and the wartime organizations which arose from the new post-1905 political culture that the Duma represented. Globachev, for example, claimed that the Duma drove the government into retreat before the wave of opposition its deputies had aroused against the regime. Like most of his colleagues, Globachev became entranced by the emotional speeches of the moderate and liberal deputies from the Duma's rostrum. One speaker after another would decry the deteriorating state of Russian society, attack the credibility of the government, ridicule the diminishing authority of the monarchy, and even advocate taking "part in a revolution in order to organize a new 'healthy' government, which would finish off the existing system," replacing it with a democratic republic.[47] Mistaking opposition rhetoric for programs of action, a common political police habit of mind,[48] the Special Section did not evaluate the capacity of these loquacious groups to implement their threats—it just assumed that they would. It could hardly have done otherwise seeing as the Special Section possessed only one unreliable secret agent within the liberal movement.[49]

As a result, Globachev and his colleagues, mistakenly applying the precedent of 1905, believed that they were witnessing the rejuvenation of liberal politics and thus the vanguard of revolution. They feared that the Progressive Bloc and *Zemgor* would be able to rectify two of the flaws which had condemned the 1905 Revolution to defeat: the absence of a unified, premeditated plan of action and, once the revolution appeared victorious, the victors' inability to reconcile the differences between their competing political programs.[50] The Department of Police forewarned the government that *Zemgor* under the *aegis* of the Progressive Bloc, itself guided by the liberal intelligentsia "who like in 1904—1905 are the leaders of the revolutionary movement" will "bring about an onslaught [against the government] at the triumphant conclusion of the war" hand-in-hand with the Russian masses.[51]

Globachev despised the liberal intelligentsia, proclaiming that, "history does no know similar examples of treason.... All the subsequent work of socialists and bolsheviks [*sic*!] toward the decomposition of Russia is only the logical consequences of the treason of these traitors [the liberal intelligentsia]." Globachev believed that the State Duma had declared revolutionary war on the nation and by 1916 had formed "a definite revolutionary center" with the silent blessing of M.V. Rodzianko, the President of the Duma. Accordingly, Globachev claimed that this "revolutionary center" was closely associated with the Progressive Bloc, *Zemgor*, and especially with the Central War Industries Committee (CWIC). This committee, composed of prominent merchants, industrialists, and representatives of labor, controlled smaller war industries committees located throughout provincial Russia. The establishment of these committees, whose purpose was the self-mobilization of industry for national defense, arose from the initiative of business circles.[52] The Chief of the Petrograd Security Division reserved his greatest suspicion for the Workers' Group of the CWIC, which he claimed linked the laboring masses to the Duma, giving "the revolutionary center" the ability to lead these people in whatever direction it chose. And Globachev believed that he knew exactly what that direction would be. To the Petrograd political police chief the CWIC was nothing more than "a political organization that served the exclusive aim of laying the ground work for revolution." Other police chiefs shared Globachev's opinion as well.[53]

A.P. Martynov, the Chief of the Moscow Security Division, though a more level-headed and intelligent surveyor of Russian society than his Petrograd colleague, still believed that the legal opposition was only one step, maybe less, away from being revolutionary itself. To Martynov, the legal opposition served as an introduction to the delights of rebellion. He imagined a symbiotic relationship emerging among the opposition parties, the revolutionaries, and the Russian people. The Department of Police elaborated at length on how this relationship would function. It concluded that while the public organizations (*Zemgor* and the CWIC) under the guidance of the liberal intelligentsia strove to direct the home front in wartime, members of the currently atomized and ineffectual (thanks to police arrests) revolutionary parties joined these organizations in order to spread their own propaganda. The Tsarist police claimed that this propaganda crystallized "the amorphous mass" of the population by whipping up the sedition "the constitutionalists had sown." Clearly, the police believed that the next stage on the road to revolution, according to its etiology of the 1905 Revolution (armed demonstrations, terrorism directed against officialdom, partisan crimes, and agrarian and industrial terror) was being prepared. This interpretation led the Special Section's analysts to conclude that the situation in the early summer of 1916 paralleled that of 1904—1905 so closely that "the present moment is extremely dangerous." [54] Extremely dangerous, without doubt, but not as the result of the machinations of the Progressive Bloc or any of the public organizations.

The reality of political life within the Progressive Bloc (Globachev's imagined "revolutionary center") was quite different from the partial truths and hyperbole of the political police. As early as the spring of 1916, the liberals themselves recognized what should have been apparent to the political police—that their efforts to organize the masses under bourgeois leadership through wartime public organizations could not succeed. Progressive Bloc members of every political stripe feared the workers' movement and, therefore, never seriously encouraged it to join the opposition's harassment of the government. After all, the workers, unimpressed with the politicians' passivity, would transform words into action, and the strikes of a politically active labor force would undermine the war effort. No one, including the Workers' Group of the CWIC, wished to encourage that.[55]

A few political police analysts, however, did not succumb to the image of popular discontent formulated by the majority of their brethren from past events and personal prejudice. As early as 1915, worrying unorthodox observations began to creep into Martynov's reports, indicating that he was becoming sensitive to the changing political chemistry of society at large and of the factory floor in particular. Martynov expressed growing discomfort with the outdated Special Section axiom that the masses were little more than a collective *tabula rasa* naturally imbued only with traditional loyalties and burning patriotism[56] and he began to dispute this prejudice of his superiors as best he could.

For example, as the situation deteriorated at the front and home front, the strike movement reconstituted itself with unexpected vigor.[57] The Moscow tram strike of September 1915, in which workers in defense plants joined tramway men in a work stoppage until thirty-two plants were involved, was one of the most significant instances of unrest. Typical of strikes during the war years, no leadership cadre could be found to have instigated or directed this work stoppage, although the network of illegal and legal organizations probably facilitated the communications necessary for its coordination.[58] Yet Fontanka's leadership refused to believe that the strike was leaderless, despite Martynov's reports to his superiors in Petrograd. The Director of the Department of Police rejected Martynov's conclusion, arguing that the demands of the strikers were inspired by the local social democrats and that members of the strike committee were in fact Bolsheviks. Martynov refused to give ground to his chief's opinion. "No," he replied, "I do not have such facts at my disposal."[59]

As the political crisis intensified Martynov became bolder. During the winter of 1916 he warned that "the prestige of the supreme authority [the Tsar] has palled," and that the anti-dynastic movement "is spreading appreciably here," courageously conveying the unadulterated truth—something he would do with increasing frequency over the next several months, by placing the responsibility for this state of affairs squarely on the ineptitude of the government and the scandalous behavior of the court.[60]

The Department of Police ignored Martynov's conclusions. As the strike movement intensified the forces of order relied on time-worn traditions of repression and arrest to contain it. Fontanka had forgotten its own post-1905 dictum: when confronting widespread discontent mass arrests do not resolve anything. The forces of order, motivated by their misguided concern over the essential role of an instigating elite and unable to conquer the Duma system, returned to their pre-1905 opinion that opposition to the government was confined to isolated self-contained groups which could be eliminated by mass arrests.[61] This illusion offered only temporary comfort for the majority of political police officers and none at all for Martynov.

What Martynov honestly reported in the case of the tramway strike reinforced his view that something else was transpiring in Russia's factories and work places: an awakening more or less independent of revolutionary agitation or propaganda.[62] Martynov, however, did not develop a coherent overview of Russian politics and society incorporating his unorthodox insights until October 1916. By that time the demoralizing failure of the Brusilov offensive against the Austrians in June 1916 awakened even the dullest political police officer at least partially from his stupor. An air of helpless desperation crept into the police's phrases. What Martynov had been writing for months now rang true. But it was Martynov's analysis which had differentiated between the societal dynamics that energized the revolutionary mood of 1905 and those that provoked the mood of mid-1916. He courageously passed on his opinion to his superiors in Petrograd.

The following two reports on the state of society prepared in October 1916 by Martynov and Globachev corroborate and exemplify what has just been discussed. In 1915 the Ministry of Internal Affairs ordered its political police bureaus to prepare monthly reports surveying the political and economic situation of Russian society under their supervision and to send these surveys to the director of the Department of Police.[63] The Martynov and Globachev reports[64] were responses to this order. The two reports followed the general guidelines set by the Ministry and thus focused on the same topics and contained similar information. Both authors described the collapse in morale brought about by repeated military defeats, the hyper-inflation of the ruble, and shortages of food and heating fuel resulting from the collapse of the transportation system and the corruption of lower officialdom. The two police chiefs recognized that by the autumn of 1916 the intensity of popular hostility toward the government had become unparalleled. Martynov wrote despairingly, "that it is difficult to say what measures could be undertaken to rekindle the patriotism of the people." Both men sensed an air of defeatism amongst the Moscow and Petrograd populations. Some of Moscow's intelligentsia called for a separate peace during the few victorious days of the Brusilov offensive and felt a growing antipathy toward Great Britain, whose leaders they blamed for the continuation of the war, a war which they decried would destroy not only Germany, but France and Russia as well.

Significantly, despite their common overview of the crisis confronting the monarchy, Martynov's and Globachev's reports exhibited a fundamental difference. In the usual style of such surveys, Globachev filtered his analysis through the political cultural prism of the "two Russias" which prevented him from understanding the new sociopolitical dynamics. For example, like Martynov, he blamed the obdurate behavior of the factory workers on economic misery. Yet Globachev appeared perplexed that despite his strategy of employing systematic mass arrests against the Petrograd social democrats, which disrupted and seriously weakened the underground, strikes continued spontaneously. Announcing that "every kind of strike has blazed up purely by chance," he seemed amazed that the strikes taking place under his jurisdiction initially did not appear to exhibit "any clear political program." Once set in motion they became "unconditionally and clearly political." Unlike his Muscovite counterpart, Globachev refused to accept the logical implications of his own observations. The "two Russias" syndrome which he swore to uphold blinded him, forcing Globachev to fall back on time-worn traditional explanations. He insisted that the bitterness of the masses was directed only against the government's "forgetting" their needs. For this political police chief the onus for the discontent spreading throughout the capital remained with the people. With a lack of sensitivity and a crudity of expression even for a gendarme, Globachev chastised not the government, but the people themselves for their "wearying craving for the rapid satisfaction of their immediate needs ...." Globachev's reporting—self-contradictory, drawing stale, familiar conclusions from observations that described an unfamiliar reality—gave his report a perplexing air that reflected the clash between illusion and reality which characterized the behavior of the government throughout Tsardom's final months.

Despite their common overview, Martynov's survey revealed that he had rejected the analytic structure conventionally employed by the forces of order to evaluate Russia's current political crisis. Unlike Globachev's observations, Martynov's report bridged the political and cultural gap that divided the "two Russias." Martynov constructed his survey from the perspective of the people rather than that of the Ministry of Internal Affairs. "It is difficult," Martynov wrote, "to name a class of society which would stand solidly with the government," not even Tsardom's civil servants, whose lives were being ruined by hyper-inflation.

Martynov, unlike Globachev, transferred the onus for this crisis from the opposition and subversive elements of society to the government itself. He stood the traditional police formula of revolution—a *sine qua non* of Special Section's philosophy—on its head by proclaiming to the Department of Police that a revolutionary elite was not necessary for driving the population to rebellion, though revolutionaries would certainly take advantage of this situation once given the opportunity. Globachev, not nearly so astute as Martynov, came to understand this last critical point only in retrospect.[65]

As a result, Globachev's report—replete with the "treasonous" activities of subversive and opposition groups—told his superiors what was happening, but misled them about this crisis' dangerous complexion. Even so, the fact that the future of the regime was so seriously thrown into doubt appeared to matter less to Globachev's superiors than his traditional explanation for this state of affairs. Perhaps they took comfort in blaming the governing elites' traditional enemies—the press, the Duma, the radical and oppositionist intelligentsia, the people—for the erosion of their authority. Clearly, the elite of Russia had become isolated even from its own political police. No fresh analysis of the dynamics of mass dissent, therefore, could penetrate beyond the outer offices of the Department of Police. As the official who read Martynov's report noted:

> A report composed with excessive caution, apparently the most critical moments are not reflected in it. Order the Chief of the Moscow Otd. po okhr. [Martynov] that especially on these [vital] questions he should not be afraid to get closer to the truth.[66]

How much closer to the truth could Martynov get? This survey, *written from the perspective of the people*, is remarkable for its distinct absence of villains—except for the government itself. Martynov described a mass movement that had surpassed the bounds of the Ministry of Internal Affairs' and the elites' understanding and had entered the realm of culture.[67] It is this factor which disturbed the note-writing official so deeply.

A movement generated by this sociological transformation could not be contained by police measures. As P.G. Kurlov remarked in his memoirs, his acquaintance with the affairs of the Department of Police in October 1916 forced him to conclude that Tsardom confronted a form of threat against which it "was extremely difficult to contemplate undertaking [any sort of] police measures which would possibly restore order."[68] But if this was his contemporary opinion, not even he, Minister of Internal Affairs Protopopov's "pal," could convince the Minister or his director of the Department of Police of this fact. At one time the leadership of the forces of order listened closely to the innovative ideas of their political police chiefs.[69] Now, this relationship had been dissolved owing to ministerial "leap frog" and court politics which installed men, solely concerned with their own position *vis-à-vis* the court, in positions of power.

Both Martynov and Globachev, from different perspectives and at different levels of sophistication, had fulfilled the brief assigned to them by the government in September 1914. Yet they found themselves to be whistling into the wind. Isolated from both a changing society it no longer could contain and from an officialdom which refused to listen to its message, the Tsarist political police had become an island within the flow of volatile socio-economic and political movements.

* * *

Nothing exemplifies the breakdown in the relationship between the political police and its superiors within the Ministry of Internal Affairs more clearly than Globachev's experiences during the four months prior to the February Revolution. As the late autumn passed, Globachev reported his concern "that an unavoidable rapidly approaching catastrophe was clear,"[70] to every Petrograd official responsible for law and order within the capital.[71] However, he found no one who would act upon his warning. Director of the Department of Police Vasil'ev, despite the reports he received daily from Globachev was convinced that all would be well as long as the rural majority remained calm, "even satisfied ... and almost indifferent to all that is so worrisome to the urban population." Despite the evidence supplied to him, Vasil'ev persisted in the view that the inability of the opposition to join with the revolutionaries for decisive action against the government, combined with their failure to organize the peasantry into a revolutionary juggernaut, meant that "a revolutionary action in the near future is not practicable."[72]

Vasil'ev was not alone in ignoring the signs of impending revolutions. How much did Protopopov know about the perilous state of Tsardom? P.P. Zavarzin, chief of the Warsaw Security Division, claimed that the Minister of Internal Affairs understood the desperate political situation, but chose to ignore it, keeping Nicholas II and Alexandra in the dark.[73] According to Globachev, however, Protopopov "saw nothing and understood nothing and confused everything."[74] One thing is certain, Protopopov refused to acknowledge the slightest possibility of revolution.[75]

Globachev, Martynov, and their colleagues frightened and leaderless, did not possess the luxury of simple, passive self-delusion. The warnings of oncoming catastrophe arising from the intelligence their bureaus gathered were unmistakable. Russia's political police chiefs found themselves in an untenable position. On the one hand they could not convince government officials of the seriousness of the situation, and on the other hand, they were impotent *vis-à-vis* the deepening political crisis. They could not face the fact that the police system could no longer serve as the traditional bulwark of the regime. As a consequence, Russia's political policemen, despite evidence of their growing impotence, stubbornly fulfilled the requirements of their ethos—to reaffirm the monarchical principal when it weakened and defend it when it was attacked—by traditional means of repression (arrest and exile). Such behavior only exacerbated the crisis.

Globachev, in particular, became a victim of what Karl Mannheim labeled "utopian thinking," which condemns its sufferers to be "not at all concerned with what really exists, rather in their thinking they seek to change the situation that exists."[76] Globachev's "utopian thinking" not only led him to strike out against those whom he perceived to be the opponents of the regime, but paradoxically convinced him that the employment of traditional methods of harassment and arrest against specific groups would actually save the regime. But even in this last desperate endeavor he was stymied by the disintegration of the entire government which had been overcome by apathy, inertia, and confusion.[77] Globachev remained convinced that the crisis could still be defused if only Protopopov would dissolve the Duma, thereby "liquidating the 'revolutionary center'" and with it the influence of its ringleaders located in the CWIC, the public organizations, and the Progressive Bloc. When Protopopov asked the exasperated Globachev for advice, the Petrograd Security Division chief presumptuously offered his Minister two choices: dissolve the Duma or retire![78]

Globachev made his arrests. By mid-February, however, the entire apparatus of the Department of Police, the Corps of Gendarmes, and the Petrograd *Gradonachalnik* (Mayor) girded themselves for revolution.[79] Nevertheless self-delusion persisted in the Ministry of Internal Affairs. Vasil'ev informed the Tsaritsa, "that revolution as such was quite impossible." Finally, in the face of increasing unrest such illusions crumbled. On the morning of 23 February 1917, Vasil'ev warned a surprised Protopopov that the workers' movement displayed a massive character in which neither discipline nor leadership could be discerned, but the director of the Department of Police expressed his hope that the strikers would return dutifully to work in the morning. When that did not happen Vasil'ev informed Protopopov that, "the situation was more confused than it had [previously] seemed." He then turned to Globachev, ordering him to collect fresh intelligence in order to sort things out.[80]

Fresh intelligence poured in from Globachev's bureau and other sources as well depicting a mass movement taking on nightmarish proportions. The Petrograd Security Division worried especially about the news that the police were arresting people who had never been arrested before.[81] Helpless and perplexed, Globachev explained to his chief: "The uprising has risen into a blaze without any party preparation and without preliminary discussions or plans of action." Globachev continued:

Now everything depends on the line of conduct of the military, if at last, it does not come down on the side of the proletariat then the movement will quickly wane, but if the military rejects the government then nothing will save the country any longer from revolutionary turmoil. Only decisive and immediate action can weaken and halt the rising movement.[82]

The revolution had driven the political police system—a symbol of the entire state order—into a *cul-de-sac* from which both Globachev and Martynov conceded they were powerless to retrieve the situation.[83] The political police had neither the physical resources to subdue large scale popular unrest nor the capacity to restore the regime's corroded authority. Still, the slowness with which the police moved from illusion to reality—burdened as it was by habits of mind and traditional prejudices, and by the exigencies of war—minimized the value of the political police to the faltering regime.

Notes to Chapter 2

1. M.V.D., Department of Police, Circular no. 175641, 2 September 1914, FAAR [Archive of the Paris Office of the Tsarist political police, Hoover Institution], [Box] 194 [Index no.] XVI(b) (6), (c), [Folder] 2.
2. A.A. Miroliubov, "Dokumenty po istorii Departamenta politsii perioda pervoi mirovoi voiny," *Sovetskie Arkhivy* 3 (1988): 81.
3. Ministerstva Vnutrennikh Del. Departament Politsii. Po 2 Deloproizvodstva, *O preobrazovanii politsii v Imperii*, 1 Sentiabria 1913 g. no. 20.083, 1–2.
4. In my view the concept of the "two Russias" is most clearly espoused by Dominic Lieven in his book, *Russia's Rulers under the Old Regime* (New Haven: Yale University Press, 1989).
5. Marc Szeftel, "Personal Inviolability in the Legislation of the Russian Absolute Monarchy," *American Slavic and East European Review* 17 (February 1958): 23–24.
6. V.M. Gessen, *Iskliuchitel'noe polozhenie* (St. Petersburg: 1908), 14–5.
7. A.V. Bogdanovich, *Tri poslednikh samoderzhtsa: Dnevnik A.V. Bogdanovich[a]* (Moscow: 1924), 33.
8. IU. Delevskii, *Protokoly sionskikh mudretsov: Istoriia odnogo podlega* (Berlin: 1923), 124–125.
9. Ellis Tenant, "The Department of Police 1911–1913: From the Recollections of Nikolai Vladimirovich Veselago," MS Hoover Institution, 17; Maurice LaPorte, *Histoire de l'Okhrana la police secrete des tsars* (Paris: Payot, 1935), 29; A.P. Martynov, *Moia sluzhba v Otdel'nom korpuse zhandarmov: Vospominaniia* (Stanford: Hoover Institution Press, 1972), 324 n. 10; V.N. Russiian, "Rabota okhrannykh v otdelenii v Rossii," MS Moravsky Collection, Hoover Institution, n.p.
10. "Rossiia pod nadzorom politsii," *Osvobozhdenie*, 1903, no. 11 (35),185,187; V.M. Gessen, *Iskliuchetel'noe polozhenie*, 12.
11. M.E. Bakai, "Iz vospominanii M.E. Bakaia: Provokatory i provokatsiia," *Byloe*, Paris, 1908, no. 8: 108–9; V. Zhilinskii, "Organizatsiia i zhizn' okhrannago otdeleniia vo vremena tsarskoi vlasti," *Golos Minuvshago*, 1917, nos. 9/10: 258; Z.I. Peregudova, "Istochnik izucheniia demokraticheskoogo dvizheniia v Rossii

(materialy fonda departamenta politsii), *Voprosy Istorii*, 1988, no. 9: 97: Michael Futrell, *The Northern Underground: Episodes of Russian Revolutionary Transport and Communications Through Scandinavia and Finland, 1863–1917* (London: Faber & Faber, 1963), 112.
12. A good example of this loyalty is the statistic revealing that the large majority of detectives served for more than twenty years. Zhilinskii, "Organizatsiia zhizn'," 42.
13. A. Volkov, *Petrogradskoe okhrannoe otdelenie* (Petrograd: 1917), 14.
14. E.J. Dillon, *The Eclipse of Russia*, (New York: George M. Doran, 1918), 133; "Samoderzhavie nakanune revoliutsii: Vnutripoliticheskii kurs V.K. Pleve," in B.V. Anan'ch, R. Sh. Ganelin, B.B. Dubentsov, et. al., *Krizis Samoderzhavie v Rossii, 1895–1917* (Leningrad: 1984), 153.
15. A.I. Spiridovich, *Revoliutsionnoe dvizhenie v Rossii: Partiia Sotsialistov-Revoliutsionerov i eia predshestvenniki*, pt. 2 (Petrograd: 1916), 158–59, 272; *Boevyia predpriiatiia sotsialistov-revoliutsionerov v osveshchenii okhranki* (Moscow:1918), 102–7; P.P. Zavarzin, *Rabota tainoi politsii* (Paris: 1924), 73, 126, 130; A.I. Spiridovich, "Pri Tsarskom rezhime," *Arkhiv Russkoi Revoliutsii* 15 (1924): 201, 203–4: M.E. Bakai, "Iz zapisok M.E. Bakaia," *Byloe*, Paris, 1909, nos. 9/10: 199.
16. M.A. Osorgin, "Dekabr'skoe vozstanie 1905g. v Moskve v opisanii zhandarma," *Golos Minuvshago*, 1917, nos. 7/8: 359–60; A.V. Gerasimov, *Na lezvii s terroristami* (Paris: YMCA Press, 1985), 143, 145–46.
17. K.I. Globachev, "Pravda O Russkoi Revoliutsii: Vospominaniia byvshago Nachal'nika Petrogradskago Okhrannago Otdeleniia," MS Bakhmeteff Archive, Columbia University, 14.
18. For example see: Victoria E. Bonnell, *Roots of Rebellion: Workers' Politics and Organizations in St. Petersburg and Moscow, 1900–1914* (Berkeley and Los Angeles: University of California Press, 1983), 321–22.
19. R.C. Elwood, *Russian Social Democracy in the Underground: A Study of the R.S.D.R.P. in the Ukraine 1907–1914*, Publications on Social History, issued by the International Institute of Social History, no. 8 (Assen: Van Gorcam and Comp., 1974), 193.
20. B.I. Grekov, K.F. Shatsillo, V.K. Shelokhaev, "Evoliutsiia politicheskoi struktury Rossii v kontse XIX-nachale XX veka (1895–1913)," *Istoriia SSSR*, 1988, no. 5: 44–45.
21. For example, the expected mass demonstrations and strikes to commemorate Bloody Sunday, despite fears to the contrary, did not eventuate. F.L. Aleksandrov and L.M. Shalagnova, "Den' 9 Ianvaria v Rossii v 1908–1917 (Obzor dokumentov TsGIAM)," *Istoricheskii Arkhiv* 1 (1958): 215.
22. G.A. Arutiunov, *Rabochee dvizhenie v Rossii v period novogo revoliutsionnogo pod"ema 1910–1914 gg.* (Moscow: 1975), 153, 179; M.V.D., From the Office of the Vice Director of the Department of Police, 30 September 1912, Circular no. 106452, FAAr, 34, IVe, 2.
23. M.V.D., Department of Police, Circular no. 172874, issued by the Ninth Secretariat, 14 June, FAAr, 158, XIIId(1), 11.
24. Arutiunov, *Rabochie dvizhenie v Rossii*, 368.
25. For a recent interpretation of the role of the wartime strike movement upon the stability of the regime, see Diane P. Koenker and William Rosenberg, *Strikes and Revolution in Russia , 1917* (Princeton: Princeton University Press, 1989).
26. Martynov, *Moia sluzhba*, 153–54.
27. M.V.D., Department of Police Circular no. 175641, 2 September 1914, FAAr, 194, XVIb (6), (c), 2.
28. "Pokazaniia kn.Volkonskogo," *Padenie Tsarskoe Rezhima: Stenograficheskie otchety doprosov i pokazanii dannykh v 1917 g. v Chrezvychainoi Sledstvennoi Komissii*

Vremennogo Pravitel'stva, [hereafter *P.Ts.R.*] vol. 6 (Moscow-Leningrad, 1924–1927), 138.
29. Globachev, "Pravda O Russkoi Revoliutsii," 51, 63.
30. A. IA. Avrekh, *Tsarizm nakanune sverzheniia* (Moscow: 1989), 110.
31. "Dopros gen. E.K. Klimovicha," *P.Ts.R.*, 1:72.
32. "Pokazaniia S.P. Beletskogo," *P.Ts.R.*, 4: 514–15; "Dopros B.V. Shturmer," *P.Ts.R.*, 1: 268–72.
33. "Dopros kn. M.M. Andronnikova," *P.Ts.R.*, 1: 388.
34. Fredric S. Zuckerman. "Political Police and Revolution: The Impact of the 1905 Revolution on the Tsarist Secret Police," *Journal of Contemporary History* 27 (1992), 279–300.
35. V.S. Diakin, "The Leadership Crisis in Russia on the Eve of the February Revolution," trans. Michael Melancon, *Soviet Studies in History* 23 (Summer 1984): 18.
36. Globachev, "Pravda O Russkoi Revoliutsii," 68, 71.
37. "Dopros M.S. Komissarova," *P.Ts.R.*, 3: 73.
38. Globachev, "Pravda O Russkoi Revoliutsii," 69; "Dopros kn. M.M. Andronnikova," *P.Ts.R.*, 1: 400; "Pis'mennyi obiasneniia A.T. Vasil'eva," *P.Ts.R.*, 1: 423.
39. Michael F. Hamm, "Liberal Politics in Wartime Russia: An Analysis of the Progressive Bloc," *Slavic Review* 33 (September 1974): 453; Michael T. Florinsky, *The End of the Russian Empire* (New York: Collier Books, 1961), 102–3.
40. Michael T. Florinsky, *Russia: A History and An Interpretation* (New York: MacMillan, 1953), 2: 1366–67.
41. M.V.D., Department of Police Circular no. 175641, 2 September 1914, FAAR, 194, XVIb (6), (c), 2.
42. For example, B.B. Grave, ed., *Burzhuaziia nakanune Fevral'skoi Revoliutsii* (Moscow: 1927), 45; "Politicheskoe polozhenie Rossii nakanune Fevral'skoi Revoliutsii v zhandarmskom osveshchenii," *Krasnyi Arkhiv* 17 (1926): 6; "V nachale 1916 goda (Iz dokumentov)," *Krasnaia Letopis'*, 1923, no. 7: 208.
43. "Uchet departament politsii opyta 1905 goda," *Krasnyi Arkhiv* 18 (1926): 224.
44. For the classic discussion of political police reporting see Richard Cobb, *The Police and the People: French Popular Protest 1789–1820* (Oxford: Oxford University Press, 1970), 3–81.
45. S.B. Chlenov, *Moskovskaia okhranka i ee sekretnye sotrudniki: Po dannym komissi po obespecheniiu novogo stroia* (Moscow: 1919), 19; Fredric S. Zuckerman. "Vladimir Burtsev and the Tsarist Political Police in Conflict, 1907–14," *Journal of Contemporary History* 12 (January 1977): 193–219.
46. P.G. Kurlov, *Gibel' imperatorskoi Rossii* (Berlin: 1923), 30; Chlenov, *Moskovskaia okhranka*, 10; "Moskovskaia okhranka v 1915g.," *Golos Minuvshago*, 1918, nos. 1–3: 283.
47. Globachev, "Pravda O Revoliutsii," 11–12, 49.
48. Lucien W. Pye, "The Roots of Insurgency and the Commencement of Rebellions," in *Internal Wars: Problems and Approaches*, ed. Harry Eckstein (London: Free Press, 1964), 150.
49. A. IA. Avrekh, "Dokumenty Departamenta politsii kak ustochnik po izucheniiu liberl'no-oppozitsionnogo dvizheniia v gody pervoi mirovoi voiny," *Istoriia SSSR*, 1987, no. 6: 37–40, 47–48; Grave *Burzhuaziia*, vi.
50. M.V.D., Department of Police, Dispatch no, 2, 1916 FAAR, 189, XVIa, 2.
51. Grave, *Burzhuaziia*, 333–38; "Obshchee polozhenie k iiuliiu 1916 g.: Zapiska departamenta politsii," *Byloe*, n.s., 1918, no. 3 (31): 26–27.
52. Florinsky, *A History of Russia*, 2:1370.
53. Globachev, "Pravda O Russkoi Revoliutsii," 23–25; P.P. Zavarzin, *Zhandarmy i Revoliutsionery: Vospominaniia* (Paris: 1930), 201–3.

54. M.V.D., Department of Police Circular no. 175641, 2 September 1914, FAAr, 194, XVb (6), (c), 2; Grave, *Burzhuaziia*, 33–8.
55. Hamm, "Liberal Politics," 465–66, 468.
56. Globachev, "Pravda O Russkoi Revoliutsii," 49.
57. M.V.D., Department of Police no. 412, "Obzor deiatel'nosti Rossiiskoi sotsial-demokraticheskoi ..., FAAr, 194, XVIa, 2.
58. Diane Koenker, *Moscow Workers and the 1917 Revolution* (Princeton: Princeton University Press, 1981), 89.
59. Martynov, *Moia sluzhba*, 279–80.
60. Grave, *Burzhuaziia*, 65, 75–81.
61. *Ibid.*, 75–81.
62. *Ibid.*, 33–38; B. Grave, *K istorii klassovoi bor'by v Rossii v gody imperialisticheskoi voiny: Iiul' 1914-Fevral' 1917g.* (Moscow: 1926), 129.
63. "Tsarskaia okhranka o politicheskom polozhenie v strane v kontse 1916 g." *Istoricheskii arkhiv* no.1 (1960): 203
64. Martynov's report is to be found in *Ibid.*, 204–9; Globachev's report is in "Politicheskoe polozhenie Rossii nakanune Fevral'skoe revoliutsii v zhandarmskom osveshchenii" *Krasnyi Arkhiv*, no. 4 (17) (1926): 4–35.
65. Globachev, "Pravda O Revoliutsii," 14–16
66. "Tsarskaia okhranka," 204.
67. For example, Diane Koenker describes the evolution of an urban working class culture which although shared by "a relative minority of Moscow workers, had assumed a distinct form, characterized by self-improvement, sobriety, collegiality and pride in class identity." This is the phenomenon Martynov had identified, but could not define. Koenker, *Moscow Workers*, 93.
68. Kurlov, *Gibel'*, 211.
69. Fredric S. Zuckerman, "In the Name of the Tsar: The Tsarist Secret Police and Russian Society, 1880–1917," chapters 7, 10, 12.
70. Globachev, "Pravda O Russkoi Revoliutsii," 14, 17.
71. *Ibid.*, 13–14.
72. Grave, *Burzhuaziia*, 136–39; "Politicheskoe polozhenie Rossii," 20.
73. Zavarzin, *Zhandarmy*, 208.
74. Globachev, "Pravda O Russkoi Revoliutsii," 71–72.
75. Diakin, "The Leadership Crisis," 12.
76. Karl Mannheim, *Ideology and Utopia: An Introduction to the Sociology of Knowledge* (London: Routledge and Kegan Paul, 1960), 36.
77. D.S. Diakin, *Russkaia Burzhuaziia i tsarizm v gody pervoi voiny, 1914–1917* (Leningrad: 1967), 274–75; Tsuyoshi Hasagawa, *The February Revolution: Petrograd, 1917* (Seattle: University of Washington Press, 1981),152–53.
78. Globachev, "Pravda O Russkoi Revoliutsii," 25, 27, 70.
79. "Pokazaniia A.D. Protopopova," *P.Ts.R.*, 4: 86–87, 89; "Pis'mennye obiasneniia A.T. Vasil'eva," *P.Ts.R.*, 1: 424–25; L.P. Leiberov, *Na shturm samoderzhaviia: Petrogradskii proletariat v gody pervoi mirovoi voiny i fevral'skoi revoliutsii (iiul' 1914-mart 1917g.)* (Moscow: 1979), 132–33.
80. "Pokazaniia A.D. Protopopova," *P.Ts.R.*, 4: 95, 98; Zavarzin, *Zhandarmy*, 236.
81. "Fevral'skaia revoliutitsii," 161–62.
82. *Ibid.*, 173–74.
83. *Ibid.*, 169; Leiberov, *Na shturm samoderzhaviia*, 229–30; Martynov, *Moia sluzhba*, 297.

Select Bibliography

Burdzhalov, E.N., *Russia's Second Revolution: The February 1917 Uprising in Petrograd* (Bloomington: Indiana University Press, 1987). An important work, translated from Russian, offering a refreshing analysis of the socio-political dynamics of the February Revolution.

Lincoln, W. Bruce, *Passage through Armageddon: The Russians in War and Revolution 1914–1918* (New York: Simon and Shuster, 1986). A general history, although not entirely satisfactory.

Koenker, Diane and William G. Rosenberg, *Strikes and Revolution in Russia, 1917* (Princeton: Princeton University Press, 1989). An important contribution to the social history of the period, albeit with some methodological imperfections.

Melancon, Michael S., *The Socialist Revolutionaries and the Russian Anti-War Movement 1914–1917* (Columbus: Ohio State University Press, 1990).

Siegelbaum, Lewis H., *The Politics of Industrial Mobilization in Russia, 1914–1917* (New York: St. Martin's Press, 1983).

Stone, Norman, *The Eastern Front, 1914–1917* (London: Hodder & Stoughton, 1975). Idiosyncratic but stimulating study.

CHAPTER 3

ALL QUIET ON THE HOME FRONT
Popular Entertainments, Censorship, and Civilian
Morale in Germany, 1914–1918

Gary D. Stark

In the initial months of the First World War, one of the district military commanders who had assumed authority over domestic administration in Germany issued directives for the local press. He reminded journalists and the military censors who monitored them that, during the war, most domestic issues are also of military importance because such issues might touch upon the economic war effort, hearten Germany's enemies or dishearten Germans, undermine faith in the government, or internally divide the nation and destroy its wartime solidarity. Consequently, the commander declared, the press and the military must be equally vigilant against anything that "unnecessarily irritates the national temper and cripples its powers of resistance. Nowadays we need the psychological powers [*seelische Kräfte*] of every individual just as much as their physical and material powers," and mass media such as the press had a duty to help strengthen the civilian population's wartime morale.[1]

As this commander recognized, it was no longer possible to draw sharp distinctions between frontline and home front, military and civilian, or foreign and domestic. In the dawning age of "total war," governing authorities in the belligerent nations realized that victory demanded not only that the nation's military and economic resources

---

Notes for this chapter begin on page 77.

be fully mobilized, but that the collective energies of the masses be mobilized as well. To generate public support for the war effort and sustain civilian morale, leaders everywhere sought to organize, cultivate, and direct popular enthusiasm and nationalist passions; to do this, they quickly realized, required organizing, cultivating, and directing the media of mass communications and, increasingly, of mass entertainment.[2] German wartime censors, seeking "to avert the disclosure of anything that would, either directly or indirectly, jeopardize or make more difficult attaining our war aims,"[3] carefully monitored not only the activities of the daily popular press, but also those of many popular entertainment media: the "legitimate" theater and opera, the "popular" stage (cabarets, variety theaters, music halls, revues, cafés chantants), the cinema, humor magazines and humorous postcards, and escapist popular fiction.

II

Prewar Europe witnessed an unprecedented growth in popular amusements and entertainments—especially cheap, undemanding, and largely passive ones requiring a minimum of education or interpretation for their enjoyment. By the end of the nineteenth century, urbanization and a mature industrial economy had produced a mass urban population that enjoyed an increasing amount of leisure time and disposable income. With more vacant time to fill, these masses sought amusement and diversion, and entire new industries arose, such as the popular press and the commercial cinema, to supply these mass consumers with the inexpensive entertainments and regalements they craved.[4]

On the eve of the First World War, for example, German–speaking Europe sustained nearly 600 public or privately owned theaters, and the German Reich supported about 2,000 daily newspapers (some with circulations of as high as 200,000); an even larger number of cinemas—approximately 2,400—drew an estimated 1.5 million filmgoers per day. Berlin alone supported nearly 40 public theaters and opera houses, between 200 and 350 cinemas, six circuses, and about 150 cabarets, music halls, and vaudeville or variety stages; over 100 daily newspapers and over 1,200 weekly or monthly periodicals were also published in the capital. Cheap, escapist popular literature ("pulp fiction") was also enormously popular. Although sensationalistic crime and detective stories, hair-raising wild-west or war adventures, sentimental romance novels, and titillating accounts of illicit love and crimes of passion were broadly condemned by contemporaries as *Schundliteratur* ("trashy literature"), there was a massive demand for them. An estimated 20 million German customers spent 50 million marks annually on serialized stories peddled door-to-door by 30,000 to 40,000 itinerant colporteurs, while the more established booktrade sold millions of copies of brief but thrilling "dime novels."[5]

Because of their potential for influencing public opinion—and because of a growing prewar concern about the increasing moral degeneracy of modern society, which many observers blamed primarily on "immoral" art, reading matter, films, stage performances, and other mass entertainments—in prewar Germany, as elsewhere, the government subjected the popular press, the colportage booktrade, the public stage, and other public amusement and entertainment media to various forms of censorship and control. Although the Imperial Press Law of 1874 abolished government licensing of the press and all pre-publication censorship of printed material, it retained the state's right to be fully and immediately informed about the contents of all periodical publications that were not purely technical or scholarly in nature: under the Press Law, a copy of every such publication had to be submitted to local police at the place of publication once distribution of the work had begun. Beginning in the 1880s, the German government also began policing lowgrade, sensationalistic pulp fiction: local authorities could ban from the colportage trade any printed or pictorial material they considered morally or religiously offensive, and after 1900 it became a criminal offense for colporteurs to distribute to minors anything which, although not legally obscene, might seriously offend the public.

Public theaters, cabarets, music halls, and various other public amusements in prewar Germany were subject to even stricter legal restraints, including state licensing and, in most locales, stringent prior censorship. Throughout much of the Reich, local ordinances stipulated that no drama, skit, song, or recitation could be performed on a public stage unless it had first been expressly approved by the police, who could ban (or require substantial alterations in) any performance they believed might endanger public peace, order, or security or that might threaten the existing moral or political order. Beginning around 1906, most German cities and towns also brought the popular new medium of the cinema under state control: youths under the age of sixteen were allowed to attend only specially supervised children's matinees, and most films that were to be shown publicly now also had first to be submitted to the police for their approval.

As in all belligerent nations, in Germany state control of printed material, public amusements, and other forms of public discourse and entertainment expanded enormously during the First World War. On 31 July 1914, Emperor Wilhelm II declared a state of war to exist in the Reich, and formally imposed a legal state of siege (*Belagerungszustand*). During this state of siege (which remained in force until November 1918), the German military enjoyed extraordinary power over civil life: executive authority was now placed in the hands of the military commanders in each of the Reich's 26 Army Corps districts. Although civilian administrators and communal officials continued performing their normal functions, they were now obligated to follow the orders and special ordinances of the commanders, who in turn were answerable only to the Emperor. Virtually autonomous and enjoying broad powers to protect a loosely defined "public order," the commanders had the right to monitor all political activity, regulate or even close down commercial enterprises (including public entertainments), and censor the press, the mails, telegram traffic, and all public meetings and announcements.[6]

The relative freedom of the press that existed in prewar Germany ended under the state of siege, for all non-scholarly publications were now subject to prior military censorship. Each district military commander established a press censorship office (*Zensurstelle*) for his area to ensure that no information harmful to the war effort would be published. Because early censorship policies and decisions varied widely among military districts, however, in October 1914 the Chief of the General Staff established a special Central Censorship Office (*Oberzensurstelle*) to coordinate the activities of the various district censorship offices. Although the Central Censorship Office attempted to set general guidelines and issued detailed instructions about what could and could not be published concerning the war effort, in fact its directives were advisory only, and (at least until mid-1917), each district military censorship office continued to set and enforce its own censorship policies, which frequently gave rise to confusion and contradictory decisions.

While requirements varied somewhat among districts, any information touching upon military matters had to be approved by the local military censors prior to publication in all districts; by 1917, most books or journals that were to be distributed abroad likewise had to obtain the censors' prior approval. Immediately upon publication, one copy of all other printed matter (excluding purely scholarly or scientific publications) had to be submitted to local civil authorities who checked it carefully for deviations from the elaborate guidelines about wartime information. Punishments ranging from warnings to a permanent cessation of publication were meted out to journalists and/or publications that violated these guidelines.

Public speeches, performances, and amusements were also placed under tighter controls. In the Berlin and most other military districts, a written text of any public lecture or presentation in which military affairs were to be discussed or mentioned had to be submitted for police approval at least 48 hours in advance. Prewar Germany's elaborate system of prior censorship of theaters, cinemas, and other public entertainments was now also extended and made more rigorous. The military, for example, considered it a "regrettable inconvenience" that the prior censorship of public amusements was so uneven throughout the nation, and that in some communities there was no censorship at all. To facilitate "a more uniform execution of censorship," therefore, several district commanders used their wartime emergency powers to introduce formal prior censorship of public entertainments in communities where this had not existed prior to 1914. The police officials charged with censoring theatrical, cinema, and other performances were to first obtain the approval of the district commander for all except the most routine, harmless works, and any bans issued under his authority could be appealed only to the Minister of War. Whereas before the war any play, skit, or film that had already been approved once by the local censor did not need to be resubmitted again if others wanted to perform it later, the authorities now declared that any works approved before the outbreak of war had to resubmitted for new approval.[7]

III

With the outbreak of hostilities, prewar concerns about the immoral content and demoralizing influence of many popular amusements were immediately compounded by a new prudish suspicion that the fatuous, inane nature of much mass entertainment was not only shamefully ill-suited to the grave crisis the nation now faced, but that foolish, frivolous, and immoral amusements were actually detrimental to the war effort because they diverted people's energies, wasted scarce national resources, and undermined traditional morality. Increasingly, German authorities saw civilian wartime morale and public morals as closely linked, and because the popular entertainment media were assumed to exert a powerful influence upon both, those media were subjected to ever more stringent oversight and control.

On 4 August 1914, immediately after Germany's declaration of war against France, public theaters, popular cafés chantants, music halls and cabarets, and many other amusements in Berlin and most other German cities were ordered closed; a few days later the Bavarian government ordered the upcoming *Oktoberfest* canceled because of the "present political situation." When most theaters and other amusements were allowed to reopen a week or two later, their operations were strictly curtailed: cafés chantants, music halls, and cabarets, for example, were severely limited in the hours they could operate and in their serving of alcohol, while the legitimate stage now had to conclude its performances by 11 p.m.

Because German authorities considered frivolous, escapist mass entertainments during a time of national crisis and popular sacrifice to be undignified, even sacrilegious, they also demanded that popular amusements exhibit a new moral gravity appropriate to the solemn national challenges ahead. Less than a fortnight after the outbreak of the war, for example, civil authorities in Berlin decreed that henceforth "in music halls and cinemas, only performances will be permitted that correspond to the seriousness (*Ernst*) of the times." The Prussian War Minister was especially concerned that, given the gravity of the times, far too many shallow, downright silly films, mostly of foreign origin, were being shown and that these were "poisoning [the people's] healthy national sentiment." Rather than offering all that imported "trash," the minister suggested cinemas show more serious films that would strengthen the nation's patriotic will and promote good morals.[8] In the regular theaters, too, censors were no longer willing to approve works that lacked a sufficiently serious tone. From the earliest days of the war on, local authorities across Germany banned numerous operettas, musical comedies, farces, vaudeville acts, and other types of public performances (including ragtime music!) that had routinely been permitted before the war because these were now considered too "burlesque," "frivolous," "bawdy," or simply because they were "not serious enough." Similarly, local military commanders ordered that all low-grade adventure films, comedies, and other "trashy movies" (*Schundfilms*) be completely banned from their districts on the grounds that such films were, by their very nature, unsuitable for the "gravity of the times."[9]

These early ascetic measures were instituted when most Germans expected the war to be over in a few weeks; when the illusion of a short war was shattered and it became clear the war might drag on for years, authorities imposed additional austerities. In 1916, for example, after the Emperor himself denounced the "shameless misconduct" of Berlin's youth and the capital city's unseemly nightlife—which he said was increasingly offensive to his soldiers "in these trying times"—the Berlin police conceded that cabarets and music halls in the city

> have enjoyed a significantly more lively business [during the war] than before and, under the special circumstances of the war, exert a morally destructive impact on broad segments of the populace.

They assured the Emperor and Interior Minister, however, that in Berlin they were instituting

> significantly more stringent guidelines both in the prior censorship of scripts as well as in the monitoring and punishment of violations. Any expressions of a morally lax lifestyle here are rigorously suppressed.

Since the outbreak of the war, Berlin's police had carried out over 1,700 on-site checks, and discovered over 900 violations; several comedians had been punished for reciting smutty jokes, some cafes and cabarets had been closed down for a month because of "indecent and burlesque incidents," and others had been threatened with closure. Nevertheless, to further limit the immoral impact of theaters and music halls, in late 1916 the mandated closing time was moved up from 11 to 10 p.m.; in addition, officials in Berlin and most other localities refused all applications for new theater licenses after 1914 on the grounds that opening such undertakings was "not in keeping with the seriousness of the present times."[10]

German cinemas, too, faced a number of new restrictions during the latter half of the war, especially after local officials, religious leaders, the regional press, and others complained about the moral dangers of the many "insipid and disgraceful" popular films still being shown and about the attention-getting flyers, banners, posters, and placards that the highly competitive cinema industry commonly used to advertise new films. (Many conservative Germans found these garish, eye-arresting cinema posters with their screaming, suggestive slogans to be both highly offensive and completely contrary to the austere wartime mood.) First, the government instructed civil authorities across Germany to be even more vigilant in preventing morally questionable films from being shown "in these serious times" and reminded them they were not obliged to permit a film in their more conservative locales simply because it had been passed by the more liberal film censors in Berlin. Second, the concern that, as more fathers were called to the front and more mothers went to work, children would spend more of their time and money at the cinema, led military commanders to raise the minimum age for cinema admission. Third, the commanders took decisive action against the plague of crass cinema posters: the size of posters was strictly regulated; they could be displayed only in movie theaters and could not be visible from the street; they could announce only the titles of coming attractions, without any embellishment or commentary; they could contain only printed words, no illustrations; and in some localities, posters, like films, first had to be approved by the police before they could be displayed.[11]

Fourth, because many observers were convinced that immoral, sensationalistic films, crass advertising posters, and other excesses of the commercial cinema ultimately stemmed from the excessive proliferation of cinemas in recent years and the ruthless, unscrupulous competition between cinema owners that resulted, there were also new efforts to address this problem. Although prewar attempts to license cinema owners and control the number of new movie houses had come to naught, the solemn wartime mood and the suspension of normal administrative procedures created a new opportunity for the state to halt the inordinate spread of cinemas. Thus, in 1916 the commander for the Berlin district decreed that no new cinemas could be opened there for the duration of the war unless specifically approved by local authorities; other commanders soon followed suit. Soon thereafter, a broad-based movement of private moral reformers and conservative political parties launched a campaign to pass new legislation that imposed licensing on the entire German cinema industry. Hoping to make permanent the *ad hoc* licensing measures instituted by various military commanders, in early 1918 the imperial cabinet drafted a bill that would license all cinema operators and empower the authorities to close down extant cinemas if they violated any provisions of the commercial code. Political collapse and revolution in late 1918 prevented the imperial Reichstag from considering the bill, but in May 1920 the Weimar republic enacted a national Film Law that, although it did not provide for licensing of cinemas, did incorporate some of the wartime controls, including a more centralized, nation-wide system of prior censorship.[12]

After 1915 the government also deployed new, more effective weapons against cheap pulp fiction. Producers of such reading matter had quickly capitalized on the war, changing the settings of many of their stories to the battlefield; indeed, a whole new genre of *Kriegsschundliteratur* ("trashy war literature") appeared that dealt with combat heroes, foreign spies, flying aces, romances between soldiers and nurses, and other wartime themes. In November 1915 the Prussian Interior Ministry banned from the colportage trade a long list of such works, and urged local authorities to use both their legal powers and moral persuasion to prevent their distribution.[13] In contrast to civil authorities, who under existing law were powerless to prevent established bookstores from selling a wide range of *Schundliteratur*, Germany's district military commanders enjoyed much wider latitude. As the commander of the Kassel district pointed out, the new legal situation created by the state of siege created for him and his colleagues "the possibility of achieving a goal previously raised in peacetime and one made even more pressing now: the suppression of all *Schundliteratur* aimed at youth."[14] Acting largely independently, during the winter of 1915–16 several commanders drew up their own lists of popular fiction that was to be banned not merely from the colportage trade, but also from display in established bookstores and from sale to anyone under 17 years old. At the urging of the War Minister and other high civil authorities, commanders in most other areas soon issued similar orders designed "to uphold the security of the Reich by preventing the poisoning of the next generation of youth by *Schundliteratur*"; in the interests of uniformity, most of these commanders also agreed to accept a common, centrally-compiled list of banned titles drawn up by the Prussian Interior Ministry.[15]

These measures against pulp fiction met with enthusiastic support from some frustrated civil officials, who praised "this completely new and ... exemplary way of suppressing the excesses of inferior popular literature." Conservative political parties such as the Catholic Center also applauded the commanders' efforts "to protect the spiritual and moral development of young people [from the] war's heightened dangers" and demanded that, as part of the imperial government's military preparation of German youth, all military commanders adopt identical measures designed to protect the nation's young people from "trashy" novels and films. In July 1917, the few commanders who had not yet joined the campaign to combat undesirable *Schundliteratur* were in fact required to do so by the Supreme Commander, who acknowledged that these uniform measures "create a more legally secure basis, which in peacetime can be further built on."[16]

In mid-1918 the Prussian Interior Ministry, hoping to codify and make permanent the extraordinary wartime measures the various military commanders had taken against offensive pulp fiction, began drafting a comprehensive law governing the sale and distribution of *Schundliteratur*. Like the proposed film law, this legislation was temporarily delayed during the revolution of 1918–19, but was eventually resurrected after the war: the Harmful Publications Act of 1926 made permanent the military commanders' *ad hoc* measures of 1915-17 by establishing government censorship boards that compiled lists of reading material that could not be sold or distributed to anyone under 18 years of age.[17]

IV

Wartime control of popular entertainments in Germany extended well beyond their general operations and availability: authorities scrupulously censored the specific content of the entertainments as well.

Although Germany's central and district military censors often diverged on the day-to-day implementation of wartime press censorship, they agreed on its general, guiding principles:

   a) Nothing can be published that could give the enemy valuable military, political, or economic information;
   b) Anything that could shake the unity of the populace's determination for victory (*die Einheitlichkeit des auf den Sieg gerichteten Volkswillens erschüttern*) should be avoided;
   c) Public confidence in the government and in the Supreme Command must be preserved.[18]

In recognition of the importance of popular entertainments within modern society, the military applied these same broad guidelines to public amusements as well. (As First General Quartermaster Erich Ludendorff declared in 1917, "If we forbid anything to be published in the press and so forth that can unfavorably affect the public's attitude toward the war, then it shouldn't be permitted to spread such ideas to the populace through the far more impressionable form of a theatrical performance.")[19] Civilian and military censors in wartime Germany vigilantly monitored theater, cabaret, and vaudeville performances, the cinema, and other popular amusements to ensure that nothing in the entertainment media undermined public trust in the government or the military, disrupted the nation's unified commitment to the war, or divulged valuable military, political, or economic information.

To preserve public confidence in the Hohenzollern dynasty, for example, one patriotic historical drama, "Frederick the Great," was banned by Berlin police in 1917 because some in the Emperor's entourage feared its portrayal of a harshly militaristic ruler (the protagonist's father, Frederick William I), of war-mongering Prussian generals, and of Frederick the Great's unleashing of an aggressive war to satisfy his ego and lust for conquest would all cause political and morale problems on the home front. Moreover, they worried that Frederick's preemptive attack on Saxony in 1756 might remind contemporaries of Germany's attack on Belgium in 1914![20] Censors were particularly watchful for anything that might diminish the public's image of the German military in general, and of the officer corps in particular. Thus O.E. Hartleben's popular drama "Monday Before Lent: An Officer's Tragedy," the story of a young officer driven to suicide because his colleagues did not consider the girl he loved socially acceptable for an officer, which had enjoyed a huge success in Germany before the war, was banned in Breslau in 1917 because it implied that the despicable behavior of a few officers was representative of many. "This piece," the censor said,

> seeks nothing less than to tendentiously pillory what our enemies (both domestic and foreign) denounce as 'militarism.' Permitting this work at the present time—just when the officer corps is so heroically bleeding and proving itself, and when we must avoid anything that might arouse ill-will against the army—is out of the question.[21]

Likewise, military authorities in several Prussian and Bavarian cities ordered the drama "Blue and Red" banned because it allegedly caricatured the German officer corps and "might occasion an unfavorable view of the life and activities within military circles." The light farce "Night Maneuvers," a play about the amorous adventures of officers, was banned in Berlin in 1916 for the same reason.[22]

Popular films that might undermine confidence in the military were suppressed with equal vigor. The spy film "Guilt's Penitent," for example, was banned in late 1914 because the authorities believed it was not only likely to inspire similar imitative acts of espionage, but also because the film's characters, who "are in prominent, highly responsible military positions, ... are portrayed as flagrantly and unscrupulously violating their service duties," something that could "destroy [public] trust in the fealty and integrity of the officer corps."[23] Later in the war (1917), the Prussian War Ministry requested that the patriotic film "Sword and Hearth," which advocated that soldiers wounded in the war be resettled on parceled-out aristocratic estates, be banned because it depicted the class of aristocratic estate owners—the traditional source of the Prussian officer corps—in a false and unfavorable light and was likely for that reason "to cause harm."[24]

Wartime censors also kept watch over public entertainments for anything that, by violating the so-called *Burgfrieden* ("civil truce within the fortress"), might undermine the solidarity of the German people and their united commitment to victory. During this increasingly tenuous internal truce, the government and the nation's various political parties, religious confessions, and other domestic factions were to renounce conflict with each other and unite in defense against the common foreign enemy. Because the Supreme Command considered this new domestic party unity and near-unanimous support for the war absolutely crucial for a successful war effort, it quickly instructed all district military commanders to use their censorship powers to "immediately and energetically suppress even the slightest attempt to disturb the unity of the German people."[25] In the interests of the civil peace and national cohesion, military censors refused to allow in the press or in the entertainment media anything that cast doubt on the nationalist sentiment or determination of any German or group,

> any insults to others ... , especially any terms of abuse, derogatory comparisons, or degrading insinuations, ... any attempts to impute to others selfish or base motives in the pursuit of political goals, any needless rekindling of old quarrels, and any insults between social classes, occupational groups, or religious confessions.[26]

(With astonishing naiveté, the military even urged the civilian government to avoid in its domestic polices "anything that would appear likely to call attention to party-political or confessional conflict, not to mention sharpening it.")[27]

Thus, references in public entertainment to Germany's often bitter prewar confessional rivalries between Catholics and Protestants were frequently suppressed. German theater censors, for example, banned such dramas as Lion Feuchtwanger's "Jew Süß" and Hermann Essig's "Pastor Rindfleisch" because it was feared the former's portrayal of 18th-Century religious rivalries in Württemberg and the latter's depiction of a Protestant clergyman as petty, greedy, and duplicitous would cause offense, generate Catholic-Protestant antagonism, and endanger the confessional peace.[28]

Authorities were especially concerned about popular stage plays, films, or pulp fiction that exacerbated Germany's class tensions by portraying the upper classes in inaccurate, stereotyped ways that would generate envy and resentment among the lower classes. One Reichstag delegate, for instance, complained that in many adventure films, popular romances, melodramas, and comedies, barons and industrial magnates were always portrayed as being "filthy rich" and as leading

> a kind of life that simply does not exist in reality. [In the films] they always drive big automobiles, carry bulging pocketbooks but never pay for anything, are constantly drinking champagne, and generally lead a life of total pleasure and sensuality. ... By portraying in such a matter-of-fact way things that, in real life, are rare individual cases, and by raising these almost to a norm, many popular films not only falsify and distort people's view of the world but also distort the social behavior of certain types of people.[29]

Similarly, a Prussian school inspector charged in 1915 that popular films invariably depicted the upper classes as an elite that never worked, lived in opulent luxury, led decadent lives, and tended either to scorn or to mistreat those lower down on the social ladder. "What false perceptions and distorted images are perpetuated in the minds of countless moviegoers concerning the lives of the better-situated social classes," he complained,

> especially when most moviegoers come from the lower classes. Hardworking, honest industrialists who feel deeply responsible for the millions of marks and thousands of workers in their charge; the anxious, often frantic existence of our great merchants; the responsible work being done by our higher civil servants and officers; the unceasing exertions of the productive middle classes—of these, one never catches even a glimpse in the cinema. The masses, in short, are getting only a social caricature [of the upper classes].

Similar sentiments were expressed by a county director in wartime Baden, who warned of the "false images and misperceptions" that the great box office hits were creating about the values and lifestyles of the propertied classes.[30]

Accordingly, numerous popular films were banned for allegedly heightening class tensions, as were two more serious works of social criticism by the noted dramatist Carl Sternheim. His "The Snob" and "1913," both part of his cycle "From the Heroic Life of the Bourgeoisie," dealt with a social-climbing parvenu who becomes a ruthless, cynical industrial tycoon and marries into the nobility. Upon the wishes of the military commander for the Berlin district, both plays were banned there in 1915/16 (and subsequently in many other German cities) because their depictions of the upper bourgeoisie and nobility were "inclined to disturb the inner peace." In the opinion of the censors, Sternheim's dramas presented

> an untrue, distorted mirror of the leading circles of the German people. ... [In these plays] the conflicts between the various strata of the population, instead of being reconciled, are sharpened .... The presentation of such a picture of our populace and social life seems in itself questionable. But at the present time, in a work that purports to depict Germany on the eve of the war, it must certainly be inadmissible to portray certain sectors of the society—which have certainly done their duty regarding the war—as decadent, unscrupulous, or egotistical, and thus as inimical to the national interest. This constitutes an attack upon members of our national community, something that must be absolutely avoided during the civil truce.[31]

Still another internal division the authorities sought to ban from popular entertainments was the general problem of Germany's national minorities, and the French population of Alsace-Lorraine in particular, where French revanchism and the problem of divided nationalist loyalties posed a serious problem now that Germany and France were at war. Soon after the outbreak of the war, the Provincial Governor of Alsace-Lorraine secretly asked the help of all local police throughout the Empire in suppressing any public discussion about the physical impact of the war upon Alsace-Lorraine or about the general stance of the local population toward the war.[32] This latter issue was precisely what interested the young Alsacian writer René Schickele, however, whose 1914 drama "Hans of Schnackenloch" explored, in a balanced and sensitive way, some of the dilemmas the war presented to French families in Alsace, where one son might fight on the German side and another on the French. After the Berlin police in late 1916 allowed the performance of an extensively-edited version of the play, from which all politically sensitive passages had been removed, it became a box office success in the capital and several other major cities. In the Spring of 1917, however, First General

Quartermaster Ludendorff complained that this drama "glorified anti-German Alsacianism" and created in those who saw it "an inner estrangement [*innerlichen Abkehr*] from the war"; because the Supreme Command considered any treatment about the German-French conflict in Alsace-Lorraine to be inappropriate, he demanded that when the theater season ended in two weeks, "Hans of Schnackenloch" must no longer be performed.[33]

Friction between Germany and its wartime ally Austria-Hungary was still another kind of division the military censors refused to allow to be portrayed in popular entertainments. In November 1914, for example, the military commander for the Berlin district protested to the police there about an actor's anti-Austrian remark during a theatrical performance. Police investigated and found that the actor had momentarily forgotten his lines; he improvised a bit in order to pick up the thread of the dialogue again but unfortunately chose some remarks that made light of Austrians. The police solemnly warned the theater that this was a most serious matter and must not happen again or the play would be closed down.[34] Later in the war (January 1916), Frank Wedekind's drama "Bismarck," which touched upon the Austro-Prussian war, was banned by the Berlin police because it might prove offensive to Austria. And in 1918 the Prussian Interior Minister forbade the performance of Ernst von Wildenbruch's patriotic work "The Field Commander," which was set during the Thirty Years War; it had as its protagonist a member of the Hohenzollern family who is executed by the Habsburg emperor and contained some dialogue that disparaged the house of Habsburg. Now, more than ever, the Minister argued, this anti-Austrian work threatened the German-Austrian alliance; furthermore, he said, "it is not advisable to remind the public, under present circumstances, of the beginnings of the Thirty Years War, which after all is somewhat comparable to the present."[35]

Finally, censors sought, as they did in the press, to suppress from the stage, the cinema, and from other entertainment forums any potentially valuable military, political, or economic information. The German General Staff took over from civilian censors the censorship of all films that in any way touched upon military affairs or war industries. To guard against false rumors and misinformation as well as to prevent the unauthorized disclosure of important military information, Berlin authorities in December 1914 further ordered that, when (silent) films about the war were shown in cinemas, there could be no accompanying live narration or commentary, and that no public announcements about war developments (victories, defeats, etc.) could be made in theaters, music halls, or cinemas unless the reports had first been confirmed by the Wolff Telegraph Bureau (an officially sanctioned source for all war information that stood under military press censorship.)[36]

More important, the authorities were keen to keep out of popular amusements any potentially valuable—or domestically disturbing—information relating to Germany's serious economic difficulties. In 1915, as rising prices, shortages of food and other commodities, and deteriorating living conditions dampened war enthusiasm and led to a rising level of public complaints and the first signs of war weariness, the military authorities became concerned about the effects of this on civilian morale. Too much public discussion of declining material conditions on the home front, the military censors concluded, could seriously damage the war effort. "Frivolous, one-sided, or exaggerated reports of distress are doubly harmful in that they arouse greed and avarice on the one hand and alarm and panic-buying on the other and thereby cause additional price increases." Producers and distributors of scarce materials were essential to the war effort and to the common good and thus had to be protected against sweeping, unjust, stereotypical attacks that might question their right to an adequate profit and thereby curtail their future expansion. While the government could be criticized for its handling (or mishandling) of Germany's economic situation, it must be protected from "constant, generally contemptuous *(abfällig)* judgments" that could undermine the public's trust in it and thereby create new public resistance to the implementation of additional economic measures.[37] Military authorities were concerned, too, that any increase in German press coverage of poor economic conditions at home could be used by the enemy to bolster their population's morale and determination to persevere until Germany's defeat. In the latter half of 1916, therefore, the censors attempted to crack down on the German public's "increasing excitation about the supposed inadequacies of our economic institutions" and sought to prohibit even joking references to the shortages of food and other commodities.[38] Thus, military press censors were instructed that "the shortage of food should not become a topic of jokes in *Witzblätter*" (cheap, mass circulation newspapers or magazines specializing in jokes, comics, and humorous caricatures).[39] When war postcards began circulating in Frankfurt that poked fun at rationing and shortages with innocuous humorous jingles, the military commander of the region declared that, because of the "public discord" such postcards arouse and because of the growing paper shortage, in the future permission to print them would no longer be granted.⁴⁰ Likewise, after the popular Munich cabaret entertainer Karl Valentin delivered a short humorous monologue in 1917 about deteriorating living conditions for soldiers and civilians while Bavaria's king continued to lead a comfortable, ostentatious lifestyle, police there forbade him from performing on-stage again for six weeks.⁴¹ Later that year, a play entitled "Hamster," about a wealthy Berliner's attempts to purchase and hoard rationed foodstuffs, was banned by authorities in Magdeburg because they feared it would fuel urban-rural antagonisms and contribute to popular resentment of the rich.⁴²

In their broad efforts to mobilize and manipulate public opinion on the home front and stoke the nationalist passions of the civilian population, German censors also paid close attention to the general patriotic tone of the communications and entertainment media. Civilian film censors during the early days of the war urged cinema operators to show only films that corresponded to the patriotic mood of the nation.⁴³ Any material considered pacifist or insufficiently pro-war was of course banned. In 1917, for example, when war weariness and the desire for peace was rising, Berlin authorities banned an adaptation of Aristophanes' "Peace" and the city of Flensburg suppressed a historical play about the fall of Vineta because the censor found it a pacifist, anti-military work that failed to sufficiently recognize the interests of the national community.⁴⁴

For the authorities, monitoring nationalist sentiment usually meant suppressing material that (in their opinion) might somehow cause Germans to doubt not merely the righteousness and superiority of Germany's war aims, but also the goodness and supremacy of Germany's national history and culture. For example, when a critical biography of Bismarck by the popular novelist Gustav Frenssen appeared early in the war, several citizens protested that it distorted the historical facts, was a derogatory insult to the great national leader, and defamed not only Bismarck's memory, but the piety and devotion of the German nation as well. Although he acknowledged he lacked the legal power to ban this book, the military commander for the Altona district (where Frenssen lived) confidentially urged all civilian authorities under his jurisdiction to use whatever means they considered appropriate to prevent or discourage book dealers from stocking and selling it.⁴⁵

At times, military authorities launched xenophobic campaigns to insulate German civilians from certain non-German, foreign cultural influences during the war. Shortly after the outbreak of the war, for example, the German government banned the importation of all new foreign-made films. Popular films produced in the "enemy" nations of France, England, or Italy, it was feared, however innocent they might appear, could surreptitiously be spreading false, anti-German ideas among the nation's cinema audiences. Censors thus were instructed in 1915 not to approve any films that had been produced in foreign nations since the outbreak of the war, regardless of the actual content of the film. (The reasons for this action were as much economic as ideological: the ban on imported films, which comprised the overwhelming majority of films shown in Germany, also helped Germany's beleaguered and critical balance of trade by providing a boon to the native German film industry, which, protected now from foreign competition, expanded enormously after 1914.)[46]

While it proved relatively easy to ban imported, foreign-made cultural commodities like popular films, it proved more difficult to ban non-German literary products. Some authorities attempted to routinely ban from German theaters any dramas or operas either written by a foreign—and particularly by an "enemy" (i.e., French, British, or Russian)—author, or works that had a "foreign" content. Thus in the early weeks of the war Berlin police banned a play (by a German author) about the French Foreign Legion and later a burlesque operetta which had an "Anglo-American" content; the Dresden police banned one operetta because it was set in Paris and London and another because it included characters portraying the diplomats of enemy nations; the authorities in Hannover banned the play "Lady Hamilton" because of its English theme and content; and the Breslau police once attempted to ban one of Tschaikovsky's operas because it was written by a Russian (although protests about the absurdity of the decision persuaded them to rescind the ban). The general policy finally adopted by the Berlin authorities, and adopted also by most other areas, was to ban works written by living authors of "enemy" nations, but to allow works written by authors who had died before 1914, so that the classic works of "enemy" artists such as Shakespeare, Moliere, Tolstoy, or Tchaikovsky could be performed. In exceptional cases, however, the censors permitted the performance of works by living authors from belligerent nations who, in their opinion, had retained their "objectivity" toward Germany—for example, George Bernard Shaw's anti-English, pro-Irish drama "Johns Bull's Other Island."[47]

On the other hand, maintaining the proper nationalist fervor of the civilian population at times required the wartime censors to dampen, rather than fuel, war enthusiasm and zealous German chauvinism, especially in the war's early, most heady weeks. As the Prussian War Ministry pointed out in one of its earliest directives to the German press, "The language used against the enemy may be harsh. But an insulting, abusive tone, or one that underrates the opponent is no sign of strength. The purity and greatness of the movement that has seized our nation requires dignified language."[48] Thus, in the first days of the war civilian film censors sought to ensure that no films were shown that might arouse overzealous patriots to commit acts of violence against foreign nationals residing in Germany.[49] Soon thereafter, the military commander for the Berlin district, concerned about an extemporaneous remark by an actor during a theater performance, instructed police there to be especially vigilant about any dramatic dialogue that contains "a boastful anticipation of our final victory, [or speaks of] our invincibility, or disparages the enemy's courage, and so forth." (When the Berlin Police President passed on this directive to his subordinates, he promised that in the future, this policy would be "carried out especially severely [*besonders scharf durchgeführt*]".)[50] Soon thereafter Berlin police banned the play "Two Against Twenty" because it ridiculed and excessively denigrated the enemy. That same month police in Bremen forbade the sale of a series of popular patriotic postcards there that depicted a huge German soldier pounding a puny enemy soldier and effortlessly sweeping him aside. According to the police, such overeager expressions of enthusiasm were undesirable because they portrayed the difficult struggle ahead too lightly and treated the enemy with derisive scorn. Victory over the enemy, the police lectured, will be no easy matter or trivial amusement, and moreover, defeating a small, weak enemy demeans, rather than honors our nation's soldiers. Because the population must recognize that this war is a serious matter and Germany's enemies are strong and formidable, postcards such as these could not be allowed.[51]

V

Like the disciplined and austere ancient Spartans, to whom they were often compared, Germany's military and civilian leaders in the First

World War were convinced that victory depended to a great extent upon the citizenry's endurance and cohesion. To preserve and nurture civilian unity and the capacity and will to fight on—particularly among youth, on whom fell the primary burden of military service— German authorities orchestrated and manipulated public opinion on the home front with censorship, propaganda, and other "munitions of the mind" (Philip Taylor).[52] Popular amusements and entertainments became an important battlefield on which this psychological warfare was waged; moral laxity, flagrant self-indulgence, unseemly frivolity, wasteful dissipation of material and spiritual resources, embarrassing or divisive allusions, and misplaced patriotic zeal were among the many elusive enemies to be combated.

The paternalistic censoriousness of the German ruling elite toward the nation's popular entertainment media sprang from complex fears, many of which predated the war, over the potentially harmful effect of many mass amusements: for example, that they were morally corrupting; that they fostered false, distorted popular perceptions of social realities; or, conversely, that they only too accurately depicted and popularized unpleasant social realities the elites would prefer to keep hidden.

Although the restraints on and censorship of popular amusements that Germany imposed between 1914 and 1918 built on and extended several existing prewar policies, the extraordinary conditions created by the war allowed the authorities to enact more stringent, centralized, and standardized controls than would have been possible before. While some of the more repressive wartime measures were lifted in 1918, others (e.g., a national system of film censorship and the indexing of popular reading materials that could not be distributed to youth) were carried over into the postwar era. Germany's censorship of mass communications and entertainment media in the First World War is thus both a culmination of pre-1914 trends and a foreshadowing of similar, but more systematic and far reaching state efforts to control and manipulate these media in the Second World War.

Notes to Chapter 3

1. Censorship guidelines issued by commander of the VII. Army Corps [hereafter: A.C.], June 1915, reprinted in *Militär und Innenpolitik im Weltkrieg 1914—1918*, ed. Wilhelm Deist, 2 vols. (Düsseldorf, 1970), 95—98. These are elaborations of guidelines issued by his predecessor on 27 Aug. and 20 Nov. 1914.
2. Jack Roth, ed., *World War I: A Turning Point in Modern History* (N.Y., 1967), 109.
3. Transcript of meeting of leaders of the military censorship agencies, 28–29 Feb. 1916, in Deist, *Militär*, 110–16 (here p. 113).
4. See my "Cinema, Society, and the State: Policing the Film Industry in Imperial Germany," in *Essays on Culture and Society in Modern Germany*, ed. Gary D. Stark and Bede K. Lackner (College Station, Tx., 1982), 163; also Edward Tannenbaum, *1900. The Generation Before the Great War* (Garden City, N.Y., 1976), 191–237.
5. Charlotte Engel Reimers, *Die deutschen Bühnen und ihre Angehörigen. Eine Untersuchung über ihre wirtschaftliche Lage* (Leipzig, 1911), 26–31; Modris Eksteins, *The Limits of Reason. The German Democratic Press and the Collapse of Weimar Democracy* (Oxford, 1975) 13, 73; Kurt Koszyk, *Deutsche Presse 1914–1945* (Berlin, 1972), 23; James Retallack, "From Pariah to Professional? The Journalist in German Society and Politics, from the Late Enlightenment to the Rise of Hitler," *German Studies Review*, XVI, nr. 2 (May 1993): 179; Stark, "Cinema," 158, n. 100; Brandenburgisches Landeshauptarchiv, Potsdam, Rep. 30 Berlin C, Tit. 74 [hereafter: BrLHA/74], Th 135; Karl Baedeker, *Berlin and its Environs. Handbook for Travellers*, 5th ed. (Leipzig, 1912); Georg Jäger, "Der Kampf gegen Schmutz und Schund. Die Reaktion der Gebildeten auf die Unterhaltungsindustrie," *Archiv für Geschichte des Buchwesens*, 31 (1988): 163–91.
6. Hans Fenske, "Die Verwaltung im Ersten Weltkrieg," pp. 866–908, in: *Deutsche Verwaltungsgeschichte, Band 3: Das Deutsche Reich bis zum Ende der Monarchie*, ed. Kurt G. A. Jeserich, et. al (Stuttgart, 1984); and Diest, *Militär*, XXXI-XLVII, 1–59.
7. Order of the III. A.C. commander, 1 Oct. 1914, III. A.C. commander to Prussian War Minister [hereafter: WM], 29 Dec. 1914 and Prussian Interior Minister [hereafter: IM] to Police Presidents [hereafter: PP], 7 May 1917, BrLHA/74, Th 134; Wolfgang Schulze-Olden, "Die Theaterzensur in der Rheinprovinz (1819–1918)" Inaug. diss. (Cologne, 1965),99–100.
8. Berlin police decree 11 Aug. 1914, BrLHA/74, Th 134; Stark, "Cinema," 155–56.
9. John Williams. *The Other Battleground. The Home Fronts. Britain, France and Germany 1914–18* (Chicago, 1972), 31. For some specific titles of plays and films banned in Prussian, Saxon, and Bavarian cities early in the war, see BrLHA/74, Th 36 and Th 37; Schulze-Olden, "Theaterzensur," 100–1; Hessisches Hauptstaatsarchiv, Wiesbaden, Abt. 407 [hereafter: HHStA/407], Nr. 409; and Stark, "Cinema," 157–58.
10. Wilhelm II to Berlin PP, 16 July 1916, Berlin police report by Brunner, May 1916, and by Carnapp, 22 July 1916, BrLHA/74, Th 134; Glasenapp to Berlin PP, 25 July 1916, and Berlin police order of 31 Dec. 1916, BrLHA/74, Th 1. See also Williams, *Other Battleground*, 31; Robert E. Sackett, *Popular Entertainment, Class, and Politics in Munich, 1900–1923* (Cambridge, Mass., 1982); 75, 78; and Schulze-Olden, "Theaterzensur," 126.
11. Stark, "Cinema," 156–59; Guben police to District President, Frankfurt/Oder, 27 Feb. 1915, 19 Dec. 1915, and 31 Jan. 1916, BrLHA, Rep 3B, Abt. I, Bd. 1431; Baden IM memo of 11 Dec. 1915 to local County Administrators, Generallandesarchiv Karlsruhe, Abt. 357 [hereafter: GLA/357] Nr. 13077; and Württemberg State Police to Württemberg IM, 9 Oct. 1917, Hauptstaatsarchiv [hereafter: HStA] Stuttgart, E151cII, Nr. 287.

12. Stark, "Cinema," 159–60, and Paul Monaco, *Cinema & Society. France and Germany During the Twenties* (N.Y., 1976), 52–61.
13. Prussian IM to District Presidents, 1 Nov. and 15 Nov. 1915, BrLHA/74, Tit. 121, Bd. 16985.
14. Quoted in Jäger, "Kampf," 180.
15. Ibid.; copies of decrees of several military commanders found in HStA Stuttgart, M77/1, Bü 60, in GLA/356/1969/10, Nr. 1180, and in Staatsarchiv [hereafter: StA] Darmstadt, G15 Freidberg, XX; order of the commander of the III. A.C., 22 Mar. 1916, Prussian WM and IM memos of 23 May 1916, decree of commander of XIX. A.C., 29 May 1916 and Saxony IM memo of 20 June 1916, and report of Karl Brunner to Prussian IM, 29 July and 17 Sept. 1916, in BrLHA, Rep 121, Bd. 16985.
16. Wolfgang Hütt, *Hintergrund: Mit den Unzüchtigkeits und Gotteslästerungsparagraphen des Strafgesetzbuches gegen Kunst und Künstler 1900-1933* (Berlin, 1990), 32, 139–40; order of Supreme Military Commander, 20 July 1917, in Geheimes Staatsarchiv Preußischer Kulturbesitz, Abt. Merseburg, Rep. 77 [hereafter: GStAM/77], Tit. 380, Bd. 11, Bl. 353ff.
17. Hütt, *Hintergrund,* 33–34, 137–46; Jäger, "Kampf," and Klaus Petersen, "The Harmful Publications (Young Persons) Act of 1926. Literary Censorship and the Politics of Morality in the Weimar Republic," *German Studies Review*, 15, nr. 3 (Oct. 1992): 505–23.
18. Acting General Staff memo, early September 1915, in Deist, *Militär,* 104–07 (here 105).
19. Ludendorff to Berlin police, 19 May 1917, as quoted in Heinrich Houben, *Verbotene Literatur. Von der klassischen Zeit bis zur Gegenwart. Ein kritisch-historisches Lexikon über verbotene Bücher, Zeitschriften und Theaterstücke, Schriftsteller und Verleger* (2 vols.; Berlin, 1924), II: 514–15.
20. Berlin police memo to Prussian IM, 15 Sept. 1917, BrLHA/74, Th 36.
21. Houben, *Verbotene Literatur,* II: 268. On the earlier cuts, see Dr. Müller's comments in *Stenographische Berichte über die Verhandlungen des Reichstages,* 10. Leg. Per., 2. Sess, 37. Sitzung vom 30 June 1901, Bd. 180, p. 1023.
22. BrLHA/74; Roswitha Flatz, *Krieg im Frieden. Das aktuelle Militärstück auf dem Theater des deutschen Kaiserreichs* (Frankfurt, 1976), 324, 338.
23. Prussian Supreme Administrative Court decision of 16 Nov. 1914.
24. Prussian WM memo of 19 Apr. 1917, Württemberg WM to Württemberg IM, 26 Apr., Stuttgart Police to commander of the XIII. A.C., 5 May 1917, in HStA Stuttgart, E151cII, Nr. 287.
25. Chief of General Staff to all federal War Ministries and General Commanders, 13 Aug. 1914, in Deist, *Militär,* I:193–94.
26. Prussian IM to local police, 9 Feb. 1915, as quoted in Kurt Koszyck, "Entwicklung der Kommunikationskontrolle zwischen 1914 und 1918," in: *Pressekonzentration und Zensurpraxis im Ersten Weltkrieg. Text und Quellen,* ed. Heinz-Dietrich Fischer (Berlin, 1973), 164; and Oberzensurstelle to all Zensurstellen, 25 Nov. 1916, reprinted in Deist, *Militär,* I:456; also commander of the VIII. A.C. to civilian and military officials, 28 Nov. 1914, ibid., 83–84.
27. Bavarian WM to Kultusminister, Oct. 1914, quoted in Michael Körner, *Staat und Kirche in Bayern 1886–1918* (Mainz, 1977), 184.
28. William Small, "In Buddha's Footsteps. Feuchtwanger's Jud Süß, Walther Rathenau, and the Path to the Soul," *German Studies Review,* 12, nr. 3 (Oct. 1989): 470; Houben, *Verbotene Literatur,* II:72–76.
29. Quoted in Friedrich Zglinicki, *Der Weg des Films* (Frankfurt, 1976), 367.
30. Guben county school inspector to District President, Frankfurt/Oder, 27 Sept.

1915, BrLHA, Rep 3B, Abt. I, Bd. 1431; County office of Schwetizngen to Baden IM, 2 May 1917, GLA/362, Nr. 174.
31. Berlin police to commander of III. A.C., early 1915, and 13 Dec. 1915; commander of III. A.C. directive of 1 Feb. 1915 and 17 Dec. 1915, BrLHA/74, Th 134 and 319, and partially quoted in Karl Deiritz, *Geschichtsbewußtsein. Satire. Zensur. Eine Studie zur Carl Sternheim* (Königstein, 1979), 171–72.
32. Confidential memo of Prussian IM to local police directors, 4 Nov. 1914, BrLHA/74, Th 134. Soon thereafter, some military commanders issued decrees forbidding any press discussion of Alsace-Lorraine's future legal/international status. Censorship guidelines issued by commander of the VII. A.C., June 1915, Deist, *Militär*, 95–98.
33. The account that follows is taken from Houben, *Verbotene Literatur*, II: 508–18, who reprints in full most of the documents without, however, indicating his source.
34. Report of PP of Berlin-Schöneberg, 2 Nov. 1914, BrLHA/74, Th 134.
35. Artur Kutscher, *Frank Wedekind. Sein Leben und sein Werke* (3 vols.; Munich, 1922-23) 209; GStAM/77, Tit. 1000, Nr. 5, Fasc. 2, Bl. 165–72.
36. War Press Office to Württemberg WM, 1 Dec. 1917, HStA Stuttgart, E 151c/II, Nr. 286.
37. Oberzensurstelle to all Zensurstellen, 27 Dec. 1915, in Deist, *Militär*, I:279–82.
38. Oberzensurstelle to all Zensurstellen, 29 Nov. 1916, in ibid., 457–58.
39. Ibid., referring to press briefing Nr. 151 of 21 July 1916.
40. HHStA/407, Nr. 530. The verse was:
Für Fleisch, fur Brot und Butter
Für Milch und Hundefutter
Petroleum und Licht
Für seife, Zucker, Eier,
Für Wurst und "Tante Meier" (toilet paper)
. Man *Karten* nur verspricht—
Doch *Ware* kriegst Du nicht!
41. Sackett, *Popular Entertainment*, 92.
42. BrLHA/74, Th 36.
43. Berlin police memo, 11 Aug. 1914, ibid., Th 134.
44. Ibid., Th 36.
45. Commander of IX. A.C. to all civil authorities, 20 Feb. 1915, Staatsarchiv Bremen, 4, 14/1–Kr.A.14.b.
46. Memo of Prussian IM, 7 Feb. 1915, BrLHA, Rep 2, Abt. I, Nr. 3446; order of IX. A.C. commander, 23 Oct. 1915, StA Bremen, 4,20–Nr. 352; memo of Hessian IM, 21 May and 14 Oct. 1915, StA Darmstadt, G15 Friedberg, XIX. Abt., III. Abschnitt, Bd. II. See also Horst Knietzsch, *Film gestern und heute: Gedanken und Daten zu sieben Jahrzehnten Geschichte der Filmkunst*, 3d ed. (Leipzig, 1972), 31; Siegfried Kracauer, *From Caligari to Hitler. A Psychological History of the German Film* (Princeton, 1947), 22, 35; and Peter Dittmar, "Berlin und die Filmindustrie," in *Berlin und die Provinz Brandenburg im 19. und 20. Jahrhundert*, ed. Hans Herzfeld (Berlin, 1968), 850.
47. BrLHA/74; Breslau PP to Berlin PP, 20 Feb. 1918, Glasenapp to Breslau PP, 16 Mar., and Glasenapp to Royal State Court II, 11 May 1918, in BrLHA/74, Th 135. On the wave of anti-foreign popular sentiment in the Munich theaters, see Sackett, *Popular Entertainment*, 74–75.
48. Prussian WM to military commanders, 9 Nov. 1914, in Diest, *Militär*, 81–83.
49. Berlin police memo, 11 Aug. 1914, BrLHA/74, Th 134.
50. Commander of III. A.C. to Berlin police, 20 Oct. 1914, and Berlin PP to suburban police presidents, 22 Oct. 1914, BrLHA/74, Th. 134.

51. Bremen police memo, 15 Oct. 1914, StA Bremen, 4, 14/1–Kr.A.14.d.
52. Philip M. Taylor, book review in *Journal of Modern History*, 58, nr. 4 (Dec. 1986): 923.

Select Bibliography

Modris Eksteins, *Rites of Spring: The Great War and the Birth of the Modern Age* (Boston, 1989). An innovative study of the cultural impact of the war.

Heinz-Dietrich Fischer, ed., *Pressekonzentration und Zensurpraxis im Ersten Weltkrieg. Text und Quellen* (Berlin, 1973). A useful collection of essays and documents about the German press and German press censorship during the war.

Jürgen Kocka, *Facing Total War. German Society, 1914—1918* (Cambridge, MA, 1984). A pathbreaking study of the war's impact on the various German social classes.

John Williams, *The Other Battleground. The Home Fronts. Britain, France and Germany 1914–1918* (Chicago, 1972). A readable, if impressionistic, account of everyday life on the home front.

J. M. Winter, *The Experience of World War I* (New York, 1989). A recent, comprehensive overview of the war and its aftermath.

CHAPTER 4

RESTORING MORAL ORDER ON THE HOME FRONT
Compulsory Savings Plans for Young Workers in Germany, 1916–19

Eve Rosenhaft

During the spring and summer of 1916, German public opinion was aroused by a series of measures through which the authorities in various parts of the country attempted to limit young workers' spending power. These measures took the form of schemes for compulsory savings through deductions from the young workers' wages *(Lohnsparzwang* or *Sparzwang)*. Policies of this kind had been applied by individual employers since the middle of the nineteenth century. Aimed specifically at young workers, compulsory savings was seen as contributing to their moral education, although the fact that in some cases the schemes were applied to workers as old as 25 suggests that maintaining a stable and disciplined workforce by tying workers to the firm and providing them with the means to establish households upon marriage was an important consideration here, as in so much of nineteenth-century employer paternalism. The idea of requiring that *all* workers pay some part of their wages into a savings fund had been discussed in social policy circles before the war; it was recommended variously as a form of insurance against unemployment (the one major risk to workers' livelihoods not covered by Bis-

---

Notes for this chapter begin on page 104.

marckian social insurance) and as a way of financing housing for the working class, which would in turn contribute to the founding of families and the raising of the birth rate. Once the *Sparzwang* had been implemented by the military authorities, there was considerable discussion in the same circles about whether it should be maintained in peacetime.[1] As it happened, the schemes were brought to an end with the demobilization at the end of the war, and their reintroduction was never seriously considered. At the time, however, they exercised public opinion. They drew representatives of the military, national and local government, industry, labor, the legal, teaching, and caring professions and the youth movement into a discussion that exposed anxieties about generational and gender power, consumption, social equity, the wartime emergency and the postwar future. In Berlin, the administration of the schemes produced a new articulation between municipal administration and the global ambitions of voluntary social work agencies; in northwestern Germany, their imposition precipitated one of the earliest mass protests in which young workers, adult trade unionists, and women as consumers acted in concert, the beginning of a wave of strikes and hunger demonstrations that would continue and grow in intensity until the end of the war.

As a practical measure, the *Sparzwang* originated with the military authorities. Under the Law of Siege of 1851, Germany was divided up into 24 army corps districts. When this law was invoked on the outbreak of war in 1914, the Commanding Generals in the respective districts took over extensive powers for the maintenance of "public safety."[2] The first step was taken in March 1916 by the Commanding General in Kassel (11th district), who ordered that minors who were guilty of "gross violation of their duty to their dependents" (that is, those who failed to use their wages to support their families) should have an "appropriate" but unspecified proportion of their wages withheld and kept in a savings account until their twenty-first birthday. Young workers subject to this provision could also be prohibited from leaving their place of residence without official permission. Within ten days of the Kassel order, the Military Commander for Berlin and Brandenburg issued a decree affecting all workers under the age of 18; they were to receive 18 marks from their wages and one-third of the remainder; the rest was to be paid into a savings account by the employer. Payments could be made out of the withheld sum, where a worker had "a legal or moral duty" to support dependents or his or her "considered interests" made it desirable. Local governments were charged with administering applications for refunds. On 22 April 1916, the Commanding General for the 10th district, covering Hannover, Oldenburg, and Braunschweig, introduced a particularly draconian version of the *Sparzwang*. Up to their eighteenth birthday, young workers could receive no more than 16 marks out of their weekly wage; workers between 18 and 21 could receive an additional one-third of the remaining sum. Refunds could be made out of savings with the permission of the municipal authorities. At the same time, all young workers were forbidden to leave the district unless their families moved or they were requisitioned for war work. In May 1916 compulsory savings was introduced by the military authorities in Saxony (4th district), and as late as July 1918 it was introduced in Alsace-Lorraine. In the Bremen-Altona area (9th district) and in Westphalia (7th district), the schemes were considered by the military commanders during 1916 and rejected after consultation with the civilian authorities. Similarly, the Commanding General in Bavaria (1st district) refrained from introducing compulsory savings, although Bavaria did follow the widespread practice of instituting a range of measures to restrict the undesirable activities of young people, including the imposition of curfews and bans on the consumption of alcohol and tobacco.[3]

In some areas, the civilian authorities, too, were active on this front. In September 1916 the Prussian War Ministry wrote to all the Commanding Generals to propose a uniform introduction of the *Sparzwang*, and the Prussian cabinet considered the possibility of introducing a Prussian-wide statute to that effect.[4] Analogous measures were already available in statute law; paragraph 119a of the Reich Industrial Code allowed for local governments to order that the wages of young workers be paid to their parents or guardians. In the earliest discussions of the impact of the war on young people, this was the measure that had been invoked as a possible antidote to indiscipline. In March 1916, the Ministry of the Interior in Württemberg recommended that municipalities use their powers under para. 119a, and in other regions individual localities did so on their own initiative.[5] On the whole, though, advocates of the *Sparzwang* thought the provisions of the Code did not provide sufficient guarantee that money would not fall into the hands of the young workers themselves.

Once promulgated, the *Sparzwang* suffered varying fates in different parts of the country. In Saxony and Northwest Germany (Hannover, Braunschweig, Oldenburg) it was lifted rapidly after public protests, which will be discussed further below. In Kassel, its provisions were so selective as not to have any significant impact, although young people were sufficiently aware of them (it was reported) to see to it that they did their spending away from their own communities to avoid the danger of being publicly identified as spendthrifts.[6] It was in Berlin-Brandenburg that the scheme established itself most effectively, coming to an end only with demobilization at the end of 1918. In January of 1917 it was estimated that 100,000 accounts had been opened in the army district as a whole, with combined deposits of five and a half million marks.[7] By the summer of 1918, the Berlin savings scheme alone had amassed over six million marks in more than 100,000 accounts (see Table). The numbers of workers leaving the scheme upon reaching their eighteenth birthday was more than counterbalanced by the effect of continuously rising nominal wages, and this in spite of the fact that the portion of the wage payable before savings was raised repeatedly, until at the end of the war it had reached 36 marks plus one-third of the remainder. Given that the estimated number of young workers in the city in 1916 was about 90,000, the *Sparzwang* can reasonably be said to have affected the whole of the underage workforce—including those who chose to find ways of evading it. Through these young workers, a sizeable proportion of the working-class population of the city was touched by the *Sparzwang*, since the vast majority of young workers were living at home.[8]

What the *Sparzwang* meant for the households affected was first and foremost a forced reduction in family income. The presumption behind the measure was that young people were earning more than they had earned in peacetime, and more than they needed, but this was a presumption that was widely challenged even at the time. There is no question that the labor force participation of young people increased in wartime, or that the combination of new job opportunities and wage inflation contributed to a rise in their nominal incomes. In 1916, there were just over a million men and over 350,000 women aged 14 to 17 in industrial work in Germany; about 40 per cent of the males and more than half of the females in industrial work were under 16. Young people made up over 25 per cent of the workforce. Even for the young and unskilled, the move into industry, and more particularly the move into war-related industries, meant that nominal wages could rise as much as 2-300 per cent over the course of the war. The chemical industry recorded an increase in the weekly wage of young male workers from 20 marks at the beginning of the war to 39 marks in October 1917 to 49 marks in October 1918.[9] In the footwear industry in the Southern Palatinate, young men of 15 and 16, who would have earned between six and twelve marks per week in 1914, were taking home up to 33 marks at the end of the war, while the Bavarian factory inspectorate noted that there had been complaints and even workplace protests over the fact that young unskilled laborers were earning more than apprentices and even the fathers of families.[10] In the Berlin area, the *Sparzwang* discussion threw up reported cases of young men earning 135 marks a week, and wages of 40-50 marks per week were common by the end of the war.[11] This compared with an average for young unskilled workers of 15 marks at the beginning of the war. By the end of 1916, it was reported, 60 per cent of young workers in Berlin were earning enough to fall under the *Sparzwang*.[12] At the beginning of 1917, however, the number of savings accounts open under the scheme was fewer than half the estimated number of young workers in the city, which suggests that in fact low wages were still common; this was acknowledged to be the case particularly with girls.[13] Nor were the increases in wages that drew public attention universal. Even within the metal trades vital to the war effort, wage rates continued to vary from one region to another, and so did the rate of increase; on a national scale, wages in Berlin were relatively high.[14] When invited to consider the introduction of the *Sparzwang*, the Bremen city fathers stated categorically that high wages were an exception in their area.[15]

The Bremen authorities, like most observers who looked closely at the issue, also made the point that as high as wages were, they were not keeping pace with the rising cost of living. High aggregate wages commonly reflected more than an increase in basic rates; they bespoke a struggle for existence: a combination of long hours worked at punishing piece-rates, topped up by supplements which were intended to adjust income to price-rises but never did. It has been estimated that a working-class family spent 31 marks per head a week on food in 1917, and a contemporary estimate set the minimum weekly income necessary to support a family of four in Berlin in 1917 at between 89 and 95 marks.[16] A wage of 40 marks for a single family member was thus by no means high. Apart from the cost of food, the rocketing price of clothing and footwear was a constant concern; the need to replace worn-out work clothes, or in the case of clerks and shopgirls, to maintain a smart appearance, and the constant call for the purchase of mourning dress provided occasion for the bulk of applications for refunds from the savings schemes.[17] Looking back from the spring of 1918, the municipal officer responsible for administering the *Sparzwang* in Berlin admitted:

> For innumerable families living on the earnings of such young people this meant the complete undermining of their living conditions, made them all at once dependent for their livelihoods on the good will and the social consciousness of a public agency, and all this at a time when the prices for all foodstuffs were rising in an unprecedented way.[18]

The authorities' persistence in enforcing a measure whose main rationale was manifestly hollow suggests that there were other, less pragmatic, motives behind the imposition of the *Sparzwang*. In fact, there are a number of contexts in which the *Sparzwang* may be located, a number of concerns which it addressed and appeared to answer. The foremost of these was a growing anxiety over the moral condition of young people in wartime. The problems of young people had been at the center of public discussion since the 1890s, and even at that time the function of such concern as an expression of wider social and political anxieties was apparent. During the war, their moral development was an object of acute anxiety, and this was expressed most openly in discussions of juvenile delinquency. The question of the character and incidence of juvenile crime during the First World War is an open one. Crime statistics for the war years were not published until the 1920s. By that time a consensus had already developed among criminologists that juvenile crime had increased between 1914 and 1918,[19] although the published figures are suspect for a number of reasons. During the war itself, the idea of a rise in juvenile crime developed from a prediction to a hypothesis, but in the absence of firm evidence it was never uncontested. Significantly, it was in February 1916 that a new phase in the public discussion of the issue was opened, in a speech delivered to Berlin lawyers. The speaker, Franz von Liszt, was a well-known spokesman for the juvenile court movement and a Liberal *Reichstag* deputy. He expressed some skepticism about claims that the incidence of juvenile crime was rising abnormally, but was most decided in his assertion that the danger of such an increase existed. He cited individual examples of youthful criminality, including activities directly related to war like forging passes or stealing food in order to take gifts to relatives at the front and less directly related ones, like extortion, gang robbery, and murder, as symptoms of *Verwahrlosung* (a combination of neglect, degeneracy, and waywardness). The elements of the wartime situation that von Liszt adduced to account for this situation were: inadequate supervision, the overstimulation of youthful fantasies by official and unofficial war reports and propaganda, and, not least, the availability of exorbitant wages and extensive responsibilities to people too young to manage them.[20] Von Liszt was the first to propose publicly that the Industrial Code be used to limit young people's access to their earnings, and his speech, along with the discussion it sparked off in the press, was widely seen as having motivated the *Sparzwang*.

The link between high incomes and crime was, *prima facie*, a tenuous one. The fundamental objection to high wages was that they exposed inexperienced youngsters to new temptations, and particularly those of dangerous or illegitimate consumption. Drinking, smoking, and cinema-going were the most obvious activities of this kind, and young people's access to them was directly blocked by military decrees in many areas. The Commander in Berlin-Brandenburg made particular reference to the way in which young workers were falling prey to prostitutes. But it was also argued that young workers' sudden access to wealth could lead them into crime through a fatal combination of heightened desires and financial mismanagement: In April 1916, Berlin's respectable liberal newspaper the *Vossische Zeitung* reported on a murder: an 18-year-old metalworker earning 55 marks a week bought a coat for 69 marks; soon short of money in spite of his generous salary, he sold it, and killed the new owner while trying to steal it back.[21]

Concern thus focused not only on unhealthy habits and dangerous entertainments, but on conspicuous consumption as such. The head of the Berlin office responsible for processing refund applications remarked in his first report on the *Sparzwang* that the number of applications suddenly being made for large sums to pay for clothing and boots was suspicious, "as though it were a deliberate challenge to official compulsion." In the same report he deplored the fact that

> the generous income of youths ... often tempts them into leading the life of young gentlemen, a life which often enough requires a tailor-made suit for 85 marks (and even a silk waistcoat), even for an unskilled laborer.[22]

Similarly, those who commented on the behavior of young women workers, while generally observing that they tended to be more thrifty than boys, remarked that when they did waste their money it was too often on dressing up.[23] Between 1914 and 1918, though, conspicuous consumption was not simply a matter of private morality. By early 1916, it had become clear that the regulation of consumption was an important instrument for guaranteeing social equity. Public discontent over the unequal distribution of severely limited food supplies was voiced everywhere, leading to open protest demonstrations in some places (including Berlin). Who got how much of what became a central issue of everyday politics in the streets and neighborhoods, while the profits and lifestyles of industrialists notoriously improved.[24] The vision of the young worker in his silk waistcoat picking up prostitutes mirrored the popular image of the war profiteer. The curfews, bans on cinema-going and cinema displays, prohibitions on entering public houses, smoking, and drinking alcohol, and even the closure of ice cream parlors that were imposed in various parts of Germany were lobbied for and justified by the authorities as measures for the protection of youth from moral and physical endangerment.[25] Viewed in the context of a politics of consumption, these new controls can also be seen as measures for policing the street scene. In this context, the *Sparzwang* had the uniquely important function of limiting the consumption of working-class families in advance (a function more effectively fulfilled by reducing young people's wages at the source than by handing them over to adult members of the household).

Last not least, the *Sparzwang* presented itself as a means for redressing a perceived imbalance in authority within the family, a perception which reflected anxieties about the threat to social hierarchy in general and the gender order in particular. It was the conviction of the military authorities who introduced the *Sparzwang* that high spending power went along with an exaggerated sense of independence and lack of respect for authority. In his report on the origins and operation of the scheme, the Commander in Berlin-Brandenburg attributed to local employers the hope that it would have "a positive influence on the arrogance of young people, which on occasions is barely to be tolerated."[26] One observer from industrial circles deplored the "greater self-confidence, more immodest manner, greater unmanageability and higher wage-demands"[27] of young workers in wartime, but such complaints were by no means typical of the public statements of employers. While they would continue to resist any measures that extended rights and powers to the labor movement, industrialists were primarily interested in keeping a free hand in their dealings with their own workers. On the whole, the employers of young workers either displayed an indifference to the principle of the *Sparzwang*, combined with concerns about the costs of administering it and fears that it might reduce the stability and motivation of the workforce (this seems to have been the mood of Berlin employers), or else they positively rejected it as unnecessary and disruptive (as did a meeting of employers convened under the chairmanship of the Mayor of Gelsenkirchen).[28] The head of one Prussian engineering firm went so far as to issue a testimonial to his workforce in the *Berliner Volkszeitung*, concluding:

> In a word, I cannot claim that our youth has run wild under the influence of the war. Of course, I don't regard it as a sign of degeneracy when a sixteen- or seventeen-year-old lad smokes the odd cigarette or goes to the movies.[29]

The idea that young workers stood at the forefront of a general collapse of the structures of authority was a particular preoccupation of the military authorities themselves, for whom moral, social, industrial, and political indiscipline were intimately connected and equally menacing. This view was expressed by Lieutenant Colonel Max Bauer, Head of Operational Department II (heavy artillery) in the Supreme Command, in a memorandum of March 1917, in terms that echo those applied to overspending young people:

> It cannot have escaped the alert observer that ... on the domestic scene the German qualities of loyalty, decency, and sense of duty are taking giant steps downhill. In all occupations and social groups the pursuit of gain, profiteering, hedonism, and extravagance are taking over. Hand in hand with this there goes a remarkable arrogance, presumptuousness, the demand for rights,... and a complete indifference to the soldiers who have to bear the burden of the war.[30]

The threat to traditional authority was thus voiced in terms of an opposition between the fighting front and the home front, across a gap which was marked by gender and generation. Well beyond military circles, the threat to the prewar order was articulated as a challenge to patriarchal authority, a challenge which came into its own with the departure of a large section of the adult male population on military service. Again, the discussion of juvenile delinquency made this explicit: the loss of a firm masculine hand at home was itself an invitation to indiscipline and crime, "for it is almost always the father who maintains discipline and order among the children; the mother has a soft temperament and can't really be strict."[31] In schools, too, the fact that schoolmasters at the front were replaced by women was cited as a feature of the general breakdown of the system contributing to the uncontrollability of the young.[32] Public discussion of changes in workplace relations was also colored by this anxiety. The urgent mobilization of the young for war work led to an erosion of formal structures of vocational training, including apprenticeship. Young people began to abandon apprenticeships for better-paying, lower-status work early in the war; by 1916 the number of apprentices in Berlin had dropped from 25,000 to 7,800. On a larger scale, observers recognized a general collapse of industrial training, officially encouraged by the running-down of vocational schools, by the recommendations of some regional military authorities that "as little time as possible" should be spent on training new workers, and by the provisions of the Auxiliary Service law of December 1916, which automatically nullified the apprenticeship obligations of any youth called up for war work. Trade unionists, conservatives, and moral and industrial reformers alike regarded this development with dismay, for it appeared to jeopardize the postwar prospects of individual young workers and German industry as a whole. At the same time, comments on the breakdown of the apprenticeship system, like disapproving reports of cases where apprentices took over the running of workshops when the master and journeymen were called up, were often tinged with nostalgia for an institution in which the young paid for future security in deferred gratification and personal subordination to an employer-patriarch.[33]

In the context of an anxiety about the decay of patriarchal relations, the *Sparzwang* had a dual force: it was formulated as a measure to protect mothers, but in terms that implicitly and explicitly shifted the blame for collapsing moral order onto them. In the language of the military authorities, the working sons of men at the front faced the accusation that they abused their high incomes not only through profligacy but also by neglecting their duty of support towards their mothers and younger siblings. Worse still, "in many cases, once in possession of their own money, [they] set themselves up at home as tyrants over their mothers."[34] The idea that overpaid young workers tyrannized their mothers coincided with a popular view of working-class women as victims of conditions on the home front, but it also merged into a vision of lone mothers as at best weak and at worst irresponsible. Explanations for juvenile delinquency (again) were sought not only in the absence of paternal discipline, but also in maternal neglect resulting from women's war work.³⁵ The persistent suspicion of woman-dominated households is reflected in a sentence that appeared in an official report of late 1916 on the effect of the *Sparzwang* and was picked up and incorporated in several later accounts: "Only in the case of weak mothers, whose husbands are at the front, do young workers continue to keep back too much [of their wages] for themselves."³⁶

"The fathers," one of the accounts went on to say, "are quite satisfied with the *Sparzwang.*"³⁷ The same message was conveyed in an article published in the journal of the German Schoolmasters' Association (*Deutscher Lehrerverein*), which introduced a favorable account of the *Sparzwang* with a vignette from the front: twenty soldiers, mostly workers from the industrial east of Berlin, in their thirties, chat about the scheme ...

> and amazingly: they all found the decree very sensible,... [This was partly a selfish attitude, the author continues] for they repeatedly expressed dissatisfaction that others, especially men so much younger, could now earn such high sums, while they could not. But when they came to explain their views ..., then they delivered all sorts of judgments about young people's fun-seeking, about the need for tight discipline [*stramme Zucht*], about the lack of thrift, about the value of every penny.³⁸

The invoking of male working-class opinion is particularly interesting in this context, for a later editorial in the same journal reflects the way in which the conditions that produced the *Sparzwang* activated specifically middle-class status anxieties. "As a primary schoolteacher," remarked the author, summarizing a report on young workers' wages, "you can only look up with amazed envy to these lads who just two or three years ago sat before you in short trousers and have now risen to such proud—and for a teacher unattainable—economic heights."³⁹ For male schoolteachers, gender- and class-consciousness were in any case organically linked. Among the Association's wartime activities was a campaign against the replacement of serving schoolmasters with female staff, a campaign in which arguments about juvenile indiscipline were freely deployed.⁴⁰

A consideration of the terms in which people sought to justify the *Sparzwang* thus confirms one observation that several historians have recently made about the effects of First World War on German society: it intensified anxieties about gender identity in ways that were manifested in a range of cultural attitudes and practices both during and after the war.⁴¹ Misogyny, the focusing of social antagonism on women as a group, was not confined to any single class; in the first months of the war soldiers' wives were objects of widespread hostility on account of their privileged access to state benefits, so that "women" (regardless of their actual class) were set against "workers" in the popular mind.[42]

If it seems unlikely that by the spring of 1916 working-class men were generally satisfied with measures that struck at the livelihoods of working-class mothers and their children, the attitude adopted by the adult male leadership of the labor movement to the *Sparzwang* betrays a certain ambivalence. In Berlin, for example, the members of the socialist Free Trade Unions consulted in preparation for the drafting of the decree first voiced their opposition but then went on to suggest significant amendments, which were finally incorporated: they insisted on equal treatment of all categories of young workers; the limitation of the *Sparzwang* to workers under 18; guarantees that employers would have no say in the disposition of the funds saved and that the workers could check that the funds really had been paid into their savings accounts; and a sympathetic machinery for appeal. The unions also made a strategic decision to cooperate in the administration of the *Sparzwang*, with the result that it was believed in some parts of the country that the Berlin workers had instigated the measure.[43] Similarly, the Free Trade Unions and the official Socialist Youth movement, failing in a petition to the Prussian War Ministry that the *Sparzwang* be lifted, sought to soften it by encouraging the Ministry to advise the military commanders to apply the decrees only to those whose "style of life makes compulsory intervention necessary"—a proposal that reflected the persistence of a distinction between rough and respectable workers in Social Democratic thinking.[44] The Social Democratic press often reported uncritically the findings of criminologists who argued that there had been a significant increase in waywardness and delinquency among working-class youth, although Socialists usually drew conclusions that emphasized the destructiveness of war and the need for new social policies in peacetime.[45] When the Majority Social Democrats tabled a resolution in the *Reichstag* calling for the lifting of the *Sparzwang*, it was clear that they were being pushed from below by their own youth and from the left by the caucus of oppositional anti-war Social Democrats, the Social Democratic Collective (*Sozialdemokratische Arbeitsgemeinschaft*), which had already presented a motion for repeal.[46]

The non-socialist trade unions were still more uncertain in their attitudes. Opinion in the mainly Catholic Christian and the liberal

(*Hirsch-Dunker*) and "yellow," or company unions, varied between levels of leadership and regions. The leadership of the Christian unions initially accepted the *Sparzwang* as a necessary measure for the duration of the war, but their representatives in Saxony and the Rhineland opposed it, as did leading members of the Catholic Young Men's Association; by early 1917 their official paper was publishing oppositional statements.[47] The liberal and "yellow" unions accepted the principle of the *Sparzwang* in Württemberg, but, again, rejected it in Saxony and the Rhineland.

In general, both organized and unorganized workers who were directly affected by the *Sparzwang* opposed it. In the Rhineland and the Ruhr, the danger of opposition from an increasingly insubordinate and excitable workforce was sufficient to motivate the civilian authorities to reject the scheme in advance.[48] In Braunschweig, the introduction of the *Sparzwang* on 1 May 1916 was answered by strikes in the major factories which spread to involve nearly all of the city's young workers. Noisy and increasingly violent protests against the decree merged with the actions of women and children demonstrating against food shortages. They received the support of the local trade union secretariat, whose representatives first persuaded the military commander to raise the savings threshold. When this was rejected by a mass meeting of young workers, the city was occupied by troops; the trade unions responded by threatening a general strike and demanding the lifting of the *Sparzwang* as well as the implementation of measures to improve the supply and equitable distribution of foodstuffs. Young workers had also gone on strike in Hannover (in this case, against the express advice and sustained disapproval of trade union leaders), and in response to the workers' actions, both the civilian government of Braunschweig and the local employers had begun to urge that the military decree be lifted or at least modified. As a result, the *Sparzwang* was rescinded a week after it first went into effect, and the general responsible for it resigned a few weeks later.[49]

Similar events occurred in Magdeburg, in the Saxon military district, where spontaneous strikes by young metalworkers were joined by adult women workers. Here, too, the strikes elicited the support of the leadership of all trade union groups, whose formal request for the repeal of the decree was backed up by popular demonstrations. Crowds surged through the main shopping streets throughout the two nights preceding the day when the decree was due to come into effect. The Commanding General refused to repeal the decree, but in the course of events its implementation was suspended indefinitely and the strikers were persuaded to return to work.[50]

In Berlin, there was no such concerted action. Police agents confirmed the general opposition to the *Sparzwang*, and in June the Chief of Police, clearly worried about signs of discontent among both workers and employers, urged the military authorities to reconsider the operation of the scheme. The police anticipated that the Socialist Youth movement would attempt to organize public protests. In fact, socialist youth in Berlin, already divided between a leadership allied with the Social Democratic Party majority and an activist group associated with the left-Social Democrat opposition, was further split by debates over what to do about the *Sparzwang*; the majority leadership thought it was pointless to attempt more than formal submissions to the authorities.[51]

There were some sporadic work stoppages when the first reduced pay packets were handed out, but in the capital and the hinterlands resistance generally took the form of evasion. Employers never ceased to complain that workers were leaving the district to seek work elsewhere. This practice was most common in border areas, particularly those nearest to the Saxon district where the *Sparzwang* had been suspended. Even under the *Sparzwang*, though, the city of Berlin was still a desirable place to live and work. Some young workers evaded the scheme by repeatedly changing jobs, or taking on several low-paid jobs, thus doubly frustrating its stated intention of instilling discipline and respect for authority.[52]

Popular discontent was most commonly expressed through applications for refunds from savings. Large numbers of young workers and their guardians (usually their mothers) resorted to refunds in the first weeks after the decree came into effect, in spite of the fact that it was a time-consuming and sometimes humiliating process. The Berlin Guardianship Bureau (*Vormundschaftsamt*), charged with reviewing applications, opened a special ground floor office near the center of town and appointed 45 new staff members. Their job was to check the eligibility of each applicant in terms of his or her amount and sources of income, contributions to the household, and general behavior ("Thrifty or wasteful?").[53] A reader's letter of February 1917 to the Social Democratic *Vorwärts* describes how the process looked from the worker's point of view:

> If the saver or his parents wants to take out some money to buy clothes, a monstrous bureaucratic machinery is set in motion. First you have to go in and make an application. Eight days later an officer comes to inspect

your circumstances. Another eight days later a parent has to go in, and is subjected to the third degree [*wird bis auf die Nieren ausgefragt*]. And in such tones! You often feel like a real beggar! Another eight days later you finally get the news that 30 marks has been released. So the money just goes up in smoke, for where can you find clothes for 30 marks?[54]

By mid-June 1916 28 per cent of savers had applied for refunds, and 17 per cent of the saved funds had been paid back.[55] This was interpreted at the time as a sign that the *Sparzwang* was producing hardship, as it certainly was. But the insistence on claiming one's rights in this context had a political quality. The applications were couched in terms of (in the words of one official) "boundless embitterment," and offices where applications were received became sites for individual protest. Moreover, the incidence of applications was sensitive to the political context; officials reported that the *Reichstag* debate of 19— 20 May on the Social Democratic motions for repeal of the *Sparzwang* decrees touched off "a veritable popular uprising. A flood of refund applications engulfed the [bureau], and the applicants demonstrated such a degree of excitement that genuinely innocent bureau staff had to suffer the wildest insults and scenes."[56] As late as the spring of 1918 it was reported that while there were fewer applications displaying open hostility to the decree itself, "the population is still extraordinarily excitable and often expresses its agitation in the most violent language and reproaches to the staff."[57]

In the absence of primary documentation of the appeals process, it is not easy to assess the attitudes of those workers who were individually affected by the *Sparzwang*. There are some clues in the published accounts. A general suspicion of the authorities was reflected in speculation that the whole scheme was designed to prop up the savings banks or to divert workers' money into war loans.[58] The most common objection to the *Sparzwang*, of course, was that it produced hardship, but this appeared in various guises. It was pointed out that official notions about young workers' needs were unrealistic: a young woman wrote to the Social Democratic newspaper in Hannover complaining that her family was threatened with penury because she and her sister would now lose nearly one-fifth from their take-home pay; the *Sparzwang* took no account of their need, as clerical workers, to keep themselves in decent clothing.[59] If young workers were seen eating sweets and confectionery, apparently luxury items, this could be because these were unrationed—the only kind of high-calorie food they could get for cash.[60] Arguments regarding hardship insisted that wages were not too high, and often turned the claims of the authorities on their heads: women and children were victims not of irresponsible youth but of the *Sparzwang*; morality was endangered not by high earnings but by reductions in the wages of young women that forced them onto the street. And the extent to which the decrees had disrupted domestic relations that they were meant to be restoring is reflected in the comment of a mother: "It used to be that children supported their parents; now the parents have to support their children."[61]

There are very few comments from the public at large that reflect on the character of the *Sparzwang* as an intervention in industrial relations. Complaints focused on employers' failure to keep workers informed about the state of their savings accounts, on the decision of some employers to dismiss young workers rather than take on the administrative burden of the *Sparzwang*, or on the way in which the *Sparzwang* reinforced the existing imbalance of power: why should a worker who could never know the extent of his employer's war profits have his own wages subject to scrutiny and control?[62] The press of the official Socialist Youth movement insistently emphasized the hypocrisy of the authorities who would intervene to control young people's morals but declined to enforce the health and safety regulations that would guarantee their physical well-being.[63] A longer view was taken in the socialist trade union press, where the *Sparzwang* was identified as having a tendency to depress wages generally. It was also noted that once the measure had been imposed on young workers, it could be imposed on all workers. Hermann Mattutat, a leading Württemberg trade unionist, argued that the employers were behind proposals for an extension of the *Sparzwang* to the whole country, their object being to increase the dependency of workers and rob them of their freedom of movement.[64]

Among themselves, trade union leaders of all persuasions expressed their suspicion of any measure that would add to the power of employers, who were already exploiting the wartime emergency by evading regulations and victimizing workers.[65] In Mattutat's article, though, as in most public statements, the emphasis was on the workers' rights as citizens rather than as workers. The limitation on freedom of movement, both actual and implied, constituted one of the chief grounds of principle on which trade unionists and radical socialist politicians attacked the *Sparzwang*. It was characterized as "exceptional legislation more backward than the codes governing the treatment of domestic servants [*Gesindeordnungen*],"⁶⁶ a violation of civil rights outside the legal competence of the military even under a declared state of siege. Indeed, the fact that the country was at war ought to place all thoughts of discrimination beyond the pale. The historic image of socialist workers as "men without a country" was subliminally invoked and parried with the reminder of their contribution to the war effort:

> It cannot be allowed that the young workers of the 10th army corps district, who in a few months will have to serve the German *Reich* with their blood, or have already done so, should enjoy fewer rights than other Germans.⁶⁷

Thus the resolution of the trade unions in Braunschweig, where the issue of freedom of movement was reportedly the most explosive one for the young workers themselves. But what the labor movement complained about equally vociferously was the interference of the military in the lives of working-class families, the "intrusion in the most fundamental rights of parents." This was an affront to the civil rights of parents ("the few rights that *are* guaranteed"), but it went beyond that. Not only the young people but their parents were *bevormundet*, reduced to the status of minors, by these measures. The *Sparzwang* was also described as *ehrverletzend*—an affront to parental honor.⁶⁸ In a similar vein, a representative of the Protestant Worker's Association, speaking at a meeting of trade unionists in Düsseldorf, characterized the *Sparzwang* as not only unjust but shaming. His colleague from the Catholic Trade Unions spoke of a crude interference in family relationships; there was a danger, he said, that the organic ties of family might be broken by measures that put too great an emphasis on cash transactions, turning parents and children into mere landlords and lodgers.⁶⁹

In the polemics of the trade unions, both the language of shame and honor and the emphasis on the integrity of the family invoked prewar discourses. Honor (*Ehre*) was one of the key terms in the construction of social identity before 1914. Originating as an affect of nobility enshrined in the conventions of the duel, in the nineteenth century honor was appropriated as part of the self-image of bourgeois masculinity.⁷⁰ Turn-of-the-century feminists in their turn argued that the police harassment of suspected prostitutes was an offense against "female honor," while striving to replace the predominant sexualized definition of honor in women with one based on "valuing the human personality" regardless of sex or class.⁷¹ In this light, the claim to honor on the part of working-class parents (or in their name) represents a claim to moral equality with other sections of society, analogous with the claim to civic equality embodied in the parallel discourse of civil rights. Both of these claims were potentiated by the reference to workers' participation in the common war effort.

Emphasis on the integrity of the family does not seem out of place among confessional trade unionists; it was one of the preoccupations of the Catholic Center Party.[72] It seems less self-evidently appropriate to the politics of the Socialist trade unions. In fact, the language of labor-movement opposition to the *Sparzwang* has clear echoes of prewar debates on youth policy. In 1901, laws were promulgated in Prussia and several other states that granted new powers to the state to remove endangered young minors from their homes into a program of corrective "welfare education" (*Fürsorgeerziehung*). The public and parliamentary debates over this policy expressed the conflict between the principle of caring intervention that motivated many "progressive" social reformers and the liberal-patriarchal insistence on the sanctity of the family, recently reasserted by the Civil Code of 1900. In these debates, both Socialists and Catholics deployed the argument of parents' rights in the hope of protecting families which might have been targeted for intervention on account of their political non-conformity.[73]

The labor movement, then, addressed the *Sparzwang* primarily as a matter of social and family policy. This represents an accurate reading of the intentions of its proponents, for while the *Sparzwang* responded to a range of social and political imperatives, it executed all its functions through working-class families, and represented a practical denial of their competence. It was a radical extension of prewar initiatives in youth policy which rested on the conviction that working-class families in general could not be relied on to socialize their children. Significantly, the perception of the *Sparzwang* as an intrusion on the rights of parents was shared by social policy professionals. Their concern, though, was to justify the intrusion, on the understanding that it was controversial, and to see that it was exercised in such a way as to make it acceptable to all involved. This had been a central object of the expanding voluntary social-work establishment before the war, when bourgeois social reformers and in particular representatives of the women's movement had pioneered the professionalization of social work as a combination of sympathetic care, or "organized motherliness," and social prophylaxis (or social hygiene). The First World War led to a proliferation in the functions of voluntary social work and to an increasing articulation between the state and voluntary sectors, as local government took responsibility for caring for the families of serving soldiers and working mothers. These developments prompted the first moves towards rationalizing the welfare functions of the municipalities in statutory institutions, including youth and welfare bureaus, that would be features of the welfare state in the Weimar Republic.[74] Writing on the present and future role of welfare bureaus in early 1918, Marie Baum celebrated the achievements of wartime, which had made the figure of the social worker into a familiar one; but she warned: "This intrusion into personal freedom is tolerable only when it is carried out by sensitive hands."[75]

In Berlin, the *Sparzwang* had a particular role to play in this development. Voluntary welfare associations, the German Central Bureau for Private Welfare (*Deutsche Zentrale für private Fürsorge*) and the German Central Bureau for Youth Welfare (*Deutsche Zentrale für Jugendfürsorge*) were invited to assist the Guardianship Bureau in processing applications for refunds. As the staff of the Bureau grew to meet the administrative burden, the specific task of the voluntary social workers changed; the Bureau now passed on to them only problem cases, "cases in which apart from the savings refund the whole family situation seems to demand intervention."[76] In effect, the refund mechanism developed into a system for screening the young working population. It was the view of the *Sparzwang* administrator in Berlin's neighboring city, Charlottenburg (which operated the same system) that the appeals system was the most important feature of the scheme, whose object was to bring the young into contact with the caring agencies.[77] Many social workers and youth workers remained agnostic on the question of whether the war had ruined young people, but welcomed the *Sparzwang* as an opportunity to extend the net of their caring activities. The Central Bureau for Private Welfare reported that of the 785 young people on whom files had been opened in the course of the appeals administration in 1916 and 1917, only 40 had previously been known to the Bureau.[78] The social workers involved in the appeals system, nearly all of them women, tended to emphasize the helping and educative aspect of the *Sparzwang* against its disciplinary and punitive features—to the point sometimes of producing guidelines that contradicted the intentions of the authorities.[79] At the same time, it is difficult to disentangle professional altruism from the element of empire-building in their response to the scheme.

When the role of the voluntary agencies was first publicized, the editors of the official Socialist Youth journal expressed their doubts about this "'care,' which notoriously has a nasty sound to it."[80] Called to respond to the *Sparzwang*, the labor movement was drawn into a debate about the character of the working-class family. This was a discussion that had been going on with increasing intensity for a generation, but the war added a new angle and gave it a new urgency. The wartime emergency which gave the socially conservative military establishment a free hand in policy-making foregrounded the gender issue as a question of conflict and variation *within* the working-class household; as Ute Daniel has pointed out, the model of family life that informed the *Sparzwang* was an authoritarian-patriarchal one, in which woman-headed households were defined in advance as being inadequate and requiring intervention.[81] The *Sparzwang* and the circumstances that produced it also gave young workers a distinct status and identity as social actors in their own right, and the result was that even on the workers' side, different kinds of arguments were being made about how working-class families functioned, and different kinds of realities were being acted out. Trade union leaders and socialist politicians talked about the rights of families and parents, implicitly challenging the military's vision with one of harmony and cooperation. Young workers emphasized their role and rights as individuals within the family, and in practice this went along with taking action to defend their interests independent of their "fathers" in the movement and even against their advice. But they also presented their own vision of family solidarity, and it was one in which mothers figured significantly both as fellow sufferers and as collaborators in the struggle for survival:

> Last week my mother could have bought some cabbage for pickling if I'd been able to give her all my wages. But now [i.e., since the *Sparzwang*] I can't. My mother doesn't want to withdraw the money, because she says, as hard as it is for her, it's my money. But it's hard for me too, to have to watch while we run out of everything at home.[82]

This statement from a young Catholic worker, like references in the Socialist Youth press to "worried mothers" and "mothers' sympathy with their hard-working children,"[83] proposes a positive alternative to the visions of military and trade union leadership alike. This, too, was realized in action when mothers accompanied their sons (and daughters) to apply for refunds or when women, children, and young workers demonstrated together against *Sparzwang* and food shortages.[84]

The *Sparzwang* thus opened up a space in which new experiences of gender and generation could be articulated. The language used by the principal protagonists in the *Sparzwang* discussion, however, was still largely that of prewar policy debates. From this point of view, the *Sparzwang* discussion is a good reflection of the general crisis of 1915/16, a crisis of the adaptation of prewar institutions to the demands of general mobilization. It exposed the contradictions of official policy, which attempted to forestall the breakdown of social order by intervening in the family while it connived at the undermining of "normal" relations in home and workplace through an opportunist approach to questions of industrial regulation and manpower. The *Sparzwang* debate also caught the Social Democratic labor movement at a significant moment of transition from its early enthusiasm for the war effort to a more critical stance. By the end of 1916, some of these ambivalences were on the way to resolution. The state had taken effective control of food supply, and machinery for manpower deployment had been set up which incorporated the trade unions in ways that prefigured the corporatism of the Weimar Republic. Production and reproduction were fused in a single realm of public competence. This did not prevent a spiraling growth of popular opposition, in which youth and women played a leading role. But the stability of the republic ushered in by revolutionary action in 1918 depended on a process of orderly military and industrial demobilization. This meant the removal of women and young people from industrial work to make way for breadwinners returning from the front.[85] Utopias of subversive unity disappeared behind new frontiers of class compromise. After 1919, the Social Democratic labor movement would become an active proponent of interventionist social policies and a pillar of the voluntary social work establishment, abandoning the language of honor for that of social hygiene.[86]

In the context of the *Sparzwang*, the change in tone of public policy from the war years to the new sobriety of Weimar is neatly illustrated by two public appeals to youth. The first was issued by the military commander in the Bremen-Altona area, after the decision had been made not to institute a *Sparzwang* there:

To the youth of the 9th Army Corps District
Perform your own war service! Be pious to God! Be obedient and respectful towards your rulers, you fathers and mothers, teachers and masters!

Follow the voice of your conscience and discipline yourselves! Stay away from low pursuits, bad books, unclean living! Always use your time well! Be good humored, but respectful! You belong to your fatherland with body and soul! Toughen your body, dear youth, and increase the fighting strength of our people! Help your mothers and younger brothers and sisters in every way you can! Be thrifty with your earnings. Save for times of want! Be strong, true and pure, German youth![87]

The second is the notice included in all savings books returned by the Charlottenburg authorities in 1918:

To young savers!
The *Sparzwang* is over! The savings books are in your hands! The money is at your disposal! What counts now is making good use of the savings that you made in the days of high wages. The times that lie before us are difficult and uncertain. Take the money to support yourself only in an emergency! Don't buy expensive clothes needlessly! Think of your future! Use the money to acquire skills, the basis for getting on better in life! Take up apprenticeships, complete interrupted apprenticeships! Educate yourselves! The *skilled* worker will always be able to earn! For those of you who don't need to touch your savings [now], let it form the basis for a future and a household of your own![88]

Compulsory Savings Accounts, City of Berlin

Date of reporting	Number of savers	Deposits (M)	Withdrawals (M)		Total in accounts		Applications for refund	Applications for refund		Long-term refunds granted	Accounts closed
			Amount (M)	As % of deposits	Amount (M)	As % deposits		Number	As % of savers		
1 May 1916	19,316	381,622	26,095	6.8	355,527	93.2	4,241	3,476	18.0		
1 July 1916	25,622	939,210	192,777	20.5	746,433	79.5	11,710	7,233	28.2	257	
1 Oct. 1916	35,838	1,837,233	588,215	32.0	1,249,018	68.0	25,131	12,668	35.4	629	2,620
1 Jan. 1917	50,766	2,988,819	1,133,746	38.0	1,855,073	62.0	40,586	17,906	35.3	879	6,690
1 April 1917	62,932	4,126,209	1,619,465	39.2	2,506,744	60.8	50,375	21,401	34.0	1,033	10,725
1 July 1917	71,489	4,959,196	2,200,173	44.4	2,759,023	55.6	58,368	24,398	34.1	1,095	14,792
1 Oct. 1917	83,524	5,958,644	2,695,716	45.2	3,262,928	54.8	65,515	27,058	32.4	1,180	17,861
1 April 1918	103,979	8,786,473	3,722,320	42.4	5,064,153	57.6	81,180	33,477	32.2	1,335	23,217
1 Sept. 1918[1]	90,730				6,161,255						
30 April 1919[1]	55,046				2,111,331						

Source: Dr. Schoenberner, "Der Sparzwang für Jugendliche in Berlin (2)," *Blätter für Kriegswohlfahrts- Armen- und Waisenpflege*, vol. 8, no. 1 (1918), p. 13; [1] *Die Sparkasse*, 1919, Nr 899, p. 223.

Notes to Chapter 4

1. R., "Über Lohnzahlung an Minderjährige," *Concordia*, vol. 23 (1916), pp. 146–48; Dr. Wygodzinski, "Der Sparzwang für Jugendliche," *Daheim* vol. 53, no. 2 (1917), pp. 18f. Cf. G. Schulz, "Fabriksparkassen für Arbeiter—Konzeption und Inanspruchnahme einer betrieblichen Institution," *Zeitschrift für Unternehmensgeschichte*, vol. 25 (1980), pp. 145–78; J. Reulecke, "Bürgerliche Sozialreformer und Arbeiterjugend im Kaiserreich," *Archiv für Sozialgeschichte*, vol. 22 (1982), pp. 309ff.
2. G.D. Feldman, *Army, Industry and Labor in Germany, 1914–1918* (Princeton University Press, Princeton, 1966), p. 31. Cf. Dr. Feisenberger, "Zur Rechtsgültigkeit der Verordnungen der Militärbefehlshaber betr. Bekämpfung der Verwahrlosung der Jugendlichen," *Zentralblatt für Vormundschaftswesen, Jugendgerichte und Fürsorgeerziehung* [*ZfVJF*], vol. 8, no. 2 (1916), pp. 13f
3. Announcements of the various measures in: *Soziale Praxis und Archiv für Volkswohlfahrt* [*SP*], vol. 25, no 22 (1916), p. 528; *SP*, vol. 25, no. 41 (1916), p. 914; *SP*, vol. 27, no. 50 (1919), p. 780; *ZfVJF*, vol. 8, no. 1 (1916), p. 12; cf. the Statement of the Bavarian government on youth policy in wartime of 17 January 1917, published in full in *ZfVJF*, vol. 9, no. 1 (1917), pp. 10f.
4. Memorandum of War Ministry to Commanding Generals, 15 September 1916, Staatsarchiv Bremen [StABr] 3-M.2.h.2.Nr 79 (Senats-Registratur), vol. 4, no. 6; *Verhandlungen des Reichstags*, vol. 307, p. 1135; cf.U. Daniel, *Arbeiterfrauen in der Kriegsgesellschaft* (Vandenhoeck & Ruprecht, Göttingen, 1989), pp. 165f.
5. "Schärfere Erziehungsmaßnahmen für die Jugendlichen in Württemberg," *SP*, vol. 25, no. 12 (1915/16), pp. 284f.; *Jahresberichte der Gewerbeaufsichtsbeamten und Bergbehörden für die Jahre 1914–1918* (Berlin, Statistisches Reichsamt, 1920), Section 5 (Baden), pp. 48f, Section 7 (Mecklenburg-Schwerin), p. 17.
6. Commanding General 11th Army Corps District to Commanding General 9th Army Corps District, StABr 3-M.2.h.2.Nr 79, vol. 4, No. 9.
7. H. Reusch, "Die Entwicklung der Jugend-Zwangssparkasse Berlin und der Provinz Brandenburg," *Die Sparkasse*, 1917, no. 842 (1.4.17), p. 98.
8. C. Lewy, "Jugendfürsorge und Sparzwang," *Jugendfürsorge*, vol. 12, no. 819 (1917), pp. 6f; H. Götz, "Für den Sparzwang der Jugendlichen," *Die Lehrerin*, vol. 33 (1916/17), pp. 202f.
9. D.S. Linton, *"Who Has the Youth Has the Future." The Campaign to Save Young Workers in Imperial Germany* (Cambridge University Press, Cambridge, 1991), pp. 198–201.
10. *Jahresberichte der Gewerbeaufsichtsbeamten*, Section 2 (Bayern), pp. xxx, 23, 126.
11. Götz, "Für den Sparzwang," p. 203; "Geschäftsbericht ... über die Tätigkeit des Magistrats bei Ausführung der Bekanntmachung ... im Gemeindebezirk der Königlichen Residenzstadt Charlottenburg ... 1. April 1917 bis 31. März 1918," Landesarchiv Berlin [LABln] Rep. 142/StB/3828. For presentations of the situation in the popular press, see: F.N., "Mit 17 Jahren 105 M. Wochenlohn," *Vossische Zeitung*, 3 May 1916 (morning edition); "Die Durchführung des Sparzwangs," *Vossische Zeitung* 26 April 1916 (morning edition).
12. "Berliner Arbeitslöhne im Kriege," *SP*, vol. 26, no. 8 (1916), p. 156.
13. Wygodzinski, "Sparzwang;" Lewy, "Jugendfürsorge."
14. Cf. "Eine lohnstatistische Erhebung über die Rüstungsarbeiterverdienste," *SP*, vol. 27, no. 46 (1918), pp. 713–15.
15. StABr 3-M.2.h.2.Nr 79, vol 4, nos. 13–16; cf.*Jahresberichte der Gewerbeaufsichtsbeamten*, Section 23 (Bremen), p. 54.
16. Daniel, *Arbeiterfrauen*, p. 210; A. Triebel, "Variations in patterns of consumption

in Germany in the period of the First World War" in R. Wall and J. Winter (eds.) *The Upheaval of War* (Cambridge University Press, Cambridge, 1988), p. 162.
17. "Geschäftsbericht ... Charlottenburg"; cf.Linton, *Who Has the Youth*, p. 202.
18. Dr. Schoenberner, "Der Sparzwang für Jugendliche in Berlin (1)," *Blätter für Kriegswohlfahrts-, Armen und Waisenpflege*, vol. 8, no. 1 (1918), p. 4.
19. Cf. M. Liepmann, *Krieg und Kriminalität in Deutschland* (Carnegie Foundation, Stuttgart/Berlin/Leipzig, 1930); W. Flitner, "Der Krieg und die Jugend" in O. Baumgarten *et al.*, *Geistige und sittliche Wirkungen des Krieges in Deutschland* (Carnegie Foundation, Stuttgart/Berlin/Leipzig, 1927).
20. [F.] von Liszt, "Der Krieg und die Kriminalität der Jugendlichen," *Zentralblatt für die gesamten Strafrechtswissenschaften*, vol. 37 (1916), pp. 496–516.
21. "Der Überfall in der Ackerstraße," *Vossische Zeitung*, 14 April 1916 (evening edition).
22. Dr. Schoenberner, "Der Sparzwang für Jugendliche in Berlin," *ZfVJF*, vol. 8, no. 5/6 (1916), pp. 52f.
23. Gewerberat Schmidt, "Der Sparzwang für Jugendliche und seine Wirkungen auf dem Arbeitsmarkt," *Der Arbeitsnachweis in Deutschland*, vol. 3 (1915/16), p. 219; Gewerbelehrer Orf, "Vorschläge zur Förderung des Jugendsparwesens," *Die Westfälische Fortbildungsschule*, vol. 12 (1916), pp. 197–200. Cf. A. Salomon, "Weibliche Jugend im Kriege," *Die Frauenfrage*, vol. 17 (1915), p. 122.
24. See A. Offer, *The First World War: An Agrarian Interpretation* (Oxford University Press, London, 1989); B. Davis, *Home Fires Burning: Politics, Identity and Food in World War I Berlin* (Doctoral Dissertation, University of Michigan, 1992, forthcoming Oxford University Press).
25. For examples of lobbying, and the case of ice cream parlors, see StABr 3-M.2.h.2.Nr 79, vol. 1 (Rauchverbot für Jugendliche); vol. 3, nos. 12 and 17; vol. 4, no.3; cf. Linton, *Who Has the Youth*, pp. 204–6.
26. "Denkschrift zur Bekanntmachung des Oberkommandos in den Marken vom 18. März 1916," StABr 3-M.2.h.2.Nr 79, vol. 4, no. 8, p. 6.
27. Schmidt, "Der Sparzwang für Jugendliche," p. 219.
28. Dr. Rocke, "Der Sparzwang für Jugendliche," *Der Arbeitgeber. Zeitschrift der Vereinigung der Deutschen Arbeitgeberverbände*, 1916, no. 18, pp. 103f; Dr. H., "Sparzwang für jugendliche Arbeiter," *ibid.*, no. 8, pp. 30f.
29. Cited in "Zum Sparzwang für jugendliche Arbeiter," *SP*, vol. 25, no. 32 (1916), p. 736.
30. W. Deist (ed.), *Militär und Innenpolitik im Weltkrieg 1914–1918* (Droste, Düsseldorf, 1970), p. 574; on Bauer, cf. E. Domansky, "Der Erste Weltkrieg" in L. Niethammer *et al.*, *Bürgerliche Gesellschaft in Deutschland* (Fischer, Frankfurt a.M., 1990), p. 317.
31. Center Party Deputy Belzer, *Verhandlungen des Reichstags*, vol. 312, p. 5117.
32. Flitner, "Der Krieg und die Jugend," p. 257; Liepmann, *Krieg und Kriminalität*, p. 86; and below, n. 40.
33. Liepmann, *Krieg und Kriminalität*, pp. 83–85; *Rechenschaftsbericht der Generalkommission der Gewerkschaften Deutschlands vom 1. Juni 1914 bis 31. Mai 1919* (Generalkommission der Gewerkschaften Deutschlands, Berlin, 1919), p. 40; L. Schultz, "Der Krieg und das gewerbliche Lehrverhältnis," *SP*, vol. 25, no. 8 (1915), pp. 171f; H. Burghart, "Die Not im Lehrlingswesen," *SP*, vol. 28, no. 14 (1918), pp. 204f. For a discussion of differences of attitude between trade unions and employers to the whole apprenticeship system, which predated the war and persisted into the Weimar Republic, see E. Harvey, *Youth and the Welfare State in Weimar Germany* (Clarendon Press, Oxford, 1993), pp. 62–70.
34. "Denkschrift zur Bekanntmachung des Oberkommandos in den Marken," p. 6.
35. Liepmann, *Krieg und Kriminalität*, p. 94; K. Gaebel, "Die Beeinträchtigung der

Kindererziehung durch die mütterliche Erwerbstätigkeit," *Zeitschrift für Armenwesen*, vol. 16 (1915), pp. 103–10.
36. "Wirkungen des Sparzwangs," *Arbeiter-Jugend* [*AJ*],1916, no. 23, p. 183; "Über die Wirkungen des Sparzwanges auf die Jugendlichen," *Die Sparkasse*, 1916, no. 824, p. 219.
37. Rocke, "Der Sparzwang."
38. G. Wolff, "Pädagogische Anmerkungen zum Sparzwang für Jugendliche," *Pädagogische Zeitung* [*PZ*], vol. 46 (1917), p. 217.
39. "Die Wirkungen des Sparzwanges," *PZ*, vol. 46 (1917), p. 460.
40. "Verwahrlosung der Jugend?," *PZ*, vol. 46 (1917), p. 32; "Die Durchsetzung der Volksschullehrerschaft mit Lehrerinnen," *PZ*, vol. 46 (1917), pp. 90f. Cf. *Verhandlungen des Reichstags*, vol. 313, pp. 5791f.
41. E.g. Domansky, "Der Erste Weltkrieg"; K. Theweleit, *Male Fantasies* (Cambridge, Polity Press, 1987–89); K. Hausen, "Mothers, sons and the market in symbols and commodities," in H. Medick and D. Sabean (eds.), *Interest and Emotion: Essays on the Study of Family and Kinship* (Cambridge University Press, Cambridge).
42. Davis, *Home Fires Burning*, pp. 70–92
43. *27. Jahres- und Kassenbericht der Gewerkschaftskommission Berlins und Umgegend* (Gewerkschaftskommission, Berlin, 1917), pp. 12–15; cf. "Denkschrift zur Bekanntmachung des Oberkommandos in den Marken," pp. 6f.
44. "Eine Einschränkung des Sparzwangs bevorstehend?," *AJ*,1917, no. 2; "Wo bleibt die Einschränkung des Sparzwangs?," *Vorwärts* 11 February 1917.
45. E.g., "Krieg und Kriminalität der Jugendlichen," *Vorwärts* 29 January 1917; "Der Krieg als Jugendverderber," *AJ*, 1917, no. 4, pp. 31f.
46. *Verhandlungen des Reichstags*, vol. 318, pp. 485, 492.
47. "Der Sparzwang der Jugendlichen," *Zentralblatt der christlichen Gewerkschaften Deutschlands*, vol. 16, no. 7 (1916), pp. 51–53; C. Noppel, "Der Sparzwang für Jugendliche in Berlin," *Jugendführung*, vol. 4 (1917), pp. 13–21; "Gegen den Sparzwang!," *AJ*, 1917, no. 3.
48. Daniel, *Arbeiterfrauen*, pp. 164f.
49. Linton, *Who Has the Youth*, pp. 210f; F. Boll, *Massenbewegungen in Niedersachsen 1906–1920* (Neue Gesellschaft, Bonn, 1981), pp. 223–32.
50. "Aufhebung eines Sparzwangerlasses," *AJ*, 1916, no. 14.
51. I. Materna and H.J. Schreckenbach (eds.), *Dokumente aus geheimen Archiven, Band 4: Berichte des Berliner Polizeipräsidenten zur Stimmng und Lage der Bevölkerung in Berlin 1914–1918* (Böhlau, Weimar, 1987), pp. 131, 160f.
52. Schoenberner, "Der Sparzwang" (n. 22); Noppel, "Der Sparzwang," p. 18.
53. E. Friedeberg and S. Wronsky, *Handbuch der Kriegsfürsorge im Deutschen Reich* (Vahlen, Berlin, 1917), p. 254.
54. "Wo bleibt die Einschränkung des Sparzwangs?".
55. "Der Sparzwang für Jugendliche und seine Wirkungen auf dem Arbeitsmarkt," *Der Arbeitsnachweis in Deutschland*, vol. 3 (1915–16), p. 221.
56. Schoenberner, "Der Sparzwang (1)" (n. 18), p. 4; cf *Verhandlungen des Reichstags*, vol. 307, pp. 1115–251.
57. Dr. Schoenberner, "Der Sparzwang für Jugendliche in Berlin (2)," *Blätter für Kriegswohlfahrts-, Armen und Waisenpflege*, vol. 8, no. 2 (1918), p. 10.
58. Noppel, "Der Sparzwang," p. 20.
59. Quoted in "Die Sparzwangerlasse," *AJ*, 1916, no. 11, p. 87.
60. "Ihr sprecht von hohen Löhnen stets…," *AJ*, 1917, no. 6, p. 48.
61. Noppel, "Der Sparzwang," p. 17.
62. Schoenberner, "Der Sparzwang" (n. 22); letter to Hannover *Arbeiterwillen*, reprinted in "Die Sparzwangerlasse"; cf *Verhandlungen des Reichstags*, vol. 307, pp. 1130–35.

63. E.g., "Gegen den Raubbau an der Jugend," *AJ*, 1917, no. 14, p. 111.
64. H. Mattutat, "Die allgemeine Einführung des Sparzwanges für Jugendliche in Deutschland," *Correspondenzblatt der Generalkomission der Gewerkschaften Deutschlands*, vol. 26 (1916), pp. 537–39.
65. See for example "Protokoll der Verhandlunger [sic] von Arbeiterführern über den Sparzwang der Jugendlichen am Freitag, den 10. Oktober 1916," Hauptstaatsarchiv Düsseldorf, Bestand Regierung Düsseldorf Nr. 33555.
66. "Ungeeignete Maßnahmen gegen Minderjährige," *Correspondenzblatt der Generalkommission der Gewerkschaften Deutschlands*, vol. 26, p. 117; *27. Jahres- und Kassenbericht*, p. 15; *28. Jahres- und Kassenbericht der Gewerkschaftskommission Berlins und Umgegend* (Gewerkschaftskommission Berlins und Umgegend, Berlin, 1918), p. 20; *Verhandlungen des Reichstags*, vol. 307, pp. 1159–64.
67. "Der Sparzwang für die jugendlichen Arbeiter und die Lebensmittelfrage vor den Gewerkschaften," *Volksfreund* (Braunschweig), 5 May 1916. [Men were subject to call-up for military service from their eighteenth birthday, but the Sparzwang in the 10th District was intended to apply to workers up to 21.]
68. Resolution of trade union leaders, Braunschweig, 4 May 1916, *ibid.*; "Der Lohn der Jugendlichen," *Volksfreund*, 27 April 1916; "Zum Sparzwang der Arbeiterjugend," *Volksfreund*, 2 May 1916.
69. "Protokoll der Verhandlunger [sic] von Arbeiterführern," pp. 2f, 9.
70. U. Frevert, "Bourgeois honour: Middle-class duellists in Germany from the late 18th to the early 20th century" in D. Blackbourn and R.J. Evans (eds.), *The German Bourgeoisie* (Routledge, London, 1991), pp. 255–92.
71. M. Raschke, "Die weibliche Ehre" (1897), cited in E. Meyer-Renschhausen, "Zur Geschichte der Gefühle. Das Reden von Scham und Ehre innerhalb der Frauenbewegung um die Jahrhundertwende" in C. Eifert and S. Rouette (eds.), *Unter allen Umständen. Frauengeschichte(n) in Berlin* (Rotation, Berlin, 1986), p. 102.
72. See the comments of the Center spokesman in the *Reichstag* debate on the *Sparzwang, Verhandlungen des Reichstags*, vol. 307, p. 1169.
73. Linton, *Who has the Youth*, pp. 63f; D. Peukert, *Grenzen der Sozialdisziplinierung. Aufstieg und Krise der deutschen Jugendfürsorge 1878 bis 1932* (Bund, Cologne, 1986), pp. 117–29; R. Ahlheim *et al.*, *Gefesselte Jugend. Fürsorgeerziehung im Kapitalismus* (Suhrkampt, Frankfurt a.M., 1976), pp. 260–64; K. Liebknecht, *Ausgewählte Reden und Schriften I* (Europäische Verlagsanstalt, Frankfurt a.M., 1969), pp. 285f.
74. Cf. C. Sachße, *Mütterlichkeit als Beruf* (Suhrkamp, Frankfurt a.M., 1986); Y.-S. Hong, "The contradictions of modernization in the German welfare state: gender and the politics of welfare reform in First World War Germany," *Social History*, vol. 17 (1992), pp. 251–70.
75. Marie Baum, "Aufgabe, Einrichtungen und Organe von Wohlfahrtsämtern in Stadt- und Landkreisen," *SP*, vol. 27 (1918), p. 307.
76. *Tätigkeitsbericht der Zentrale für private Fürsorge e.V. für die Kriegsjahre 1916–1918* (Stalling, Oldenburg, [1918]), p. 19.
77. "Geschäftsbericht ... Charlottenburg."
78. *Tätigkeitsbericht der Zentrale für private Fürsorge*, p. 19.
79. Friedeberg/Wronsky, *Handbuch*, p. 255; [E.] Friedeberg, "Der Sparzwang der Jugendlichen in der Mark Brandenburg," *Jugendfürsorge*, vol. 11, no. 4/5 (1916), pp. 9f. Cf. Report on the activities of the Central Office for Public Welfare (*Zentralstelle für Volkswohlfahrt*), *Concordia*, vol. 28 (1918), pp. 24f; reports on the Congress of Juvenile Court Officers, April 1917, in *Deutsche Strafrechts-Zeitung*,

vol. 4 (1917), pp. 228; *SP*, vol. 9, no. 3/4 (1917), pp. 35–39; *Jugendführung*, vol. 4 (1917), pp. 182–85.
80. "Wirkungen des Sparzwangs," *AJ* 1916, no. 23, p. 183.
81. Daniel, *Arbeiterfrauen*, pp. 166f.
82. Cited in Noppel, "Der Sparzwang," p. 17.
83. "Where can you get food without stealing ration cards? That's the big question for young workers and their worried mothers.... Gnawing hunger and the mothers' sympathy with their hard-working children lead to extraordinary expenditure on food.": "Ihr sprecht von hohen Löhnen stets...," p. 48.
84. Ute Daniel refers to this as a "subversive unity of action": *Arbeiterfrauen*, p. 167. Cf. R. Sieder, "Behind the lines: working-class family life in wartime Vienna" in R. Wall and J. Winter (eds.) *The Upheaval of War* (Cambridge University Press, Cambridge, 1988), pp. 109–38.
85. Daniel, *Arbeiterfrauen*, pp. 118–24; R. Bessel, "'Eine nicht allzu große Beunruhigung des Arbeitsmarktes'. Frauenarbeit und Demobilmachung in Deutschland nach dem Ersten Weltkrieg," *Geschichte und Gesellschaft*, vol. 9 (1983), pp. 211–29; R. Bessel, *Germany after the First World War* (Clarendon Press, Oxford, 1993).
86. See most recently C. Eifert, *Frauenpolitik und Wohlfahrtspflege. Zur Geschichte der "Arbeiterwohlfahrt"* (Campus, Frankfurt a.M./ New York, 1993); D. Crew, "German Socialism, the state and family policy, 1918–33," *Continuity and Change*, vol. 1 (1986), pp. 235–63.
87. StABr 3-M.2.h.2.Nr. 79, vol. 6, no. 1.
88. Dr. Schoenberner, "Die Aufhebung des Sparzwangs für Jugendliche," *ZfVJF*, vol. 10, no. 19/20 (1919), p. 202.

Select Bibliography

Bessel, Richard. *Germany after the First World War* (Oxford: Clarendon Press, 1993). The first general survey of the immediate aftermath of the war, demobilization, and its consequences.

Boll, Friedhelm. *Massenbewegungen in Niedersachsen 1906–1920* (Bonn: Neue Gesellschaft, 1981). A regional study of popular protest with general implications.

Daniel, Ute. *Arbeiterfrauen in der Kriegsgesellschaft* (Göttingen: Vandenhoeck & Ruprecht, 1989). A highly detailed and well-argued account of the experience of working-class women.

Feldman, Gerald D. *Army, Industry and Labor in Germany, 1914–1918* (Princeton: Princeton University Press, 1966). Still the only, and authoritative, monographic study in English of military-industrial relations and questions of manpower mobilization.

Harvey, Elizabeth R. *Youth and the Welfare State in Weimar Germany* (Oxford: Clarendon Press, 1993). A study of postwar youth policy which draws out continuities with pre-1914 and wartime policy.

Kocka, Jürgen. *Facing Total War. German Society 1914–1918* (Oxford: Berg, 1984). A revised version of a 1973 original, with strong emphasis on the general interpretation of wartime developments in terms of changes in class relations.

Linton, Derek S. *"Who Has the Youth Has the Future." The Campaign to Save Young Workers in Imperial Germany* (Cambridge: Cambridge University Press, 1991). Includes a chapter on youth and youth policy in wartime.

Mai, Gunther. *Kriegswirtschaft und Arbeiterbewegung in Württemberg 1914–1918*

(Stuttgart: Klett-Cotta, 1983). A rare regional case-study of military policy and the labor movement.

Offer, Avner. *The First World War: An Agrarian Interpretation* (London: Oxford University Press, 1989). A study of the war in terms of the food-supply problems of the respective combatant powers, with extensive discussion of Germany.

Whalen, Robert W. *Bitter Wounds. German Victims of the Great War, 1914–39* (Ithaca: Cornell University Press, 1984). A study of the experience of and attitudes to returning veterans, including the impact of the war on intra-familial relationships.

II

SHAPING IDENTITIES:
RELIGION, NATIONALITY AND GENDER

CHAPTER 5

FRENCH CATHOLICS
Rumeurs Infâmes and the *Union Sacrée*, 1914–1918

James F. McMillan

In his illuminating study of French morale and public opinion during the Great War, Jean-Jacques Becker posed the question of what it was that enabled the French people to hold out over four long years of suffering and privation until final victory was achieved. He concluded that the crucial factor may well have been the notion of a "sacred union", the agreement to bury long-standing political and ideological animosities in response to President Poincaré's appeal to put national unity first. The *union sacrée*, Becker suggests, acted as a kind of "magic potion" which bound people together. Moreover, it was a sign of an even deeper reality—the consciousness, developed over centuries, in the minds of French men and women that they were a historic nation, with a powerful sense of their identity as an "imagined community."[1] The purpose of the present chapter is not to challenge the Becker thesis, but rather to suggest ways in which it might be nuanced. From the time of the French Revolution, the idea of the nation had come to mean different things to different sections of the French population,[2] and over four years of warfare the *union sacrée*—essentially a political truce—was subjected to considerable strain. As is well known, it had broken down on the Left by 1917.[3] Less well studied is the extent to which the "sacred union" was

---

Notes for this chapter begin on page 129.

jeopardized by the survival in wartime of the bitter antagonism between republican anticlericals and the Catholic Church.

A profound anticlericalism was an integral part of French republican political culture.[4] For political leaders of the Third Republic such as Léon Gambetta, Jules Ferry, and Emile Combes, the creation of an *état laïc*, a completely secular state and society, was the very *raison d'être* of the regime: hence the enactment of anticlerical legislation (the *lois laïques*) in the 1880s and the renewed anticlerical attack on the Church at the turn of the century, which culminated in the passing of the Law of 1905 separating church and state. The list of republican objections to the Church was long, but prominent among them was the allegation of anti-patriotism and loyalty to a foreign head, the Pope. Because it was an international body, anticlericals argued that the Church could not but be a threat to the nation, all the more so in that by educating Catholic youth in its own schools rather than in state schools, it reared generations in ideals contrary to the national interest. Clericalism, declared Gambetta, was the enemy and "Jesuitism" was always a threat to the *patrie*, all the more insidious because it tended to rise up precisely when the *patrie* was down.

The tradition which identified the Church as the enemy of the nation can be traced back to the first French Revolution, and it is worth emphasizing that it flourished not only among politicians and intellectuals but was deeply rooted in popular mentalities. By inventing the doctrine of popular sovereignty, the Revolution made the nation rather than the monarch the mainspring of authority and legitimacy in the state. To be an enemy of the revolutionary state was therefore also to be an enemy of the nation. Under the First French Republic, perhaps the most zealous champions of this doctrine were the soldiers of the *armées révolutionnaires*, the militants charged with exporting the Revolution to the French provinces. As their historian, Richard Cobb, has shown, in the eyes of the *armées* a Catholic, by definition, could never be considered a patriot, but was rather a fanatic, an enemy of the Republic and an accomplice of the Ancien Régime. Catholicism, in a word, represented the counter-revolution, epitomized by the rising in the Vendée which saw credulous peasants manipulated against the Republic by an alliance of unscrupulous priests and aristocrats. Echoes of these charges resurfaced during subsequent wars in the nineteenth century. During the Crimean War, there were rumors at Carmaux that the clergy was contributing financial support to Russia in the hope of facilitating a Bourbon restoration under Henri V.[6] During the Italian War of 1859, some people in Savoy accused Bishop Dupanloup of trying to raise money for the Austrians.[7] The disastrous Franco-Prussian War of 1870/71 gave rise to still more widespread accusations. For instance, in the Tarn, the local Republican press denounced the alliance of the *château* and the sacristy and accused the clergy of not only failing to support the Provisional Government but of playing the game of the Prussians. According to *Le Patriote Albigeois* (13 November 1870):

> The *curés* thwart the measures demanded by public safety: they form secret divisions: masters of the minds of women through the confessional, they make use of this dangerous power to sow the seeds of discouragement and to enervate those who would like to take up arms. They should remember that before they are priests, they are Frenchmen![8]

Likewise in Brittany there were denunciations of priests who preached that the evils of the war were a kind of divine retribution, and rumors went around that some clerics were handing over their collections to the Prussians and acting as spies on their behalf.[9] Similar charges were made elsewhere, along with the accusation that collusion with the Prussians was intended to bring about a monarchical restoration and the reimposition of the tithe. A priest at Le Mans complained:

> People turned against the priests and the *châteaux* with blind stupidity. The most impossible calumnies were produced and soon believed ... the poor village *curé* who can hardly live on his modest salary was supposed to be sending millions (to the Prussians).[10]

It was during the First World War, however, that such scurrilous stories, indignantly repudiated by churchmen as "'infamous rumors" or *rumeurs infâmes*, were to gain even greater currency, thus highlighting the extreme fragility of national unity achieved under the *union sacrée*. In the pages of well-known anticlerical newspapers (for example *Le Bonnet Rouge, La Dépêche de Toulouse, L'Humanité*) but also in the files of the *Police générale* series at the Archives Nationales, there is ample evidence that the First World War, far from liberating France from outmoded religious quarrels, as is often assumed, served rather to provoke fresh outbreaks of animosity against the Church. Before examining particular "infamous rumors" in detail, however, it will be helpful to look first at the attitude of French Catholics towards the *union sacrée* and at the position adopted by the Papacy with regard to the war.

Anticlerical allegations of lack of patriotic fervor were deeply resented by the French Church and by the French Catholic community. While it is true, certainly, that Catholics refused to identify with the idea of the nation as developed in the Republican and Jacobin tradition and as symbolized by the figure of the peasant girl Marianne, they vehemently insisted that they had their own alternative, and more exalted, patriotic ideal. Like the integral nationalists of the *Action Française*, they drew a distinction between the *pays légal* and the *pays réel*, that is between the official republican regime on the one hand, and "real," "eternal," France on the other—a France best embodied by the Army and by the Catholic Church. Catholic nationalism, however, though overlapping with that of *Action Française* in many regards (not least in the belief that the country was ruled by a nefarious coalition of Jews, Protestants, and Freemasons), was a distinctive entity in its own right. It was a kind of "clerical" nationalism, or perhaps better, a "national Catholicism," strongly linked to French conservatism as expressed in organs such as the daily newspaper the *Echo de Paris*. Catholic nationalists stressed the idea of France as the "eldest daughter of the Church," and liked to recall the close links which had existed historically between church and state. France, according to them, could only be France if it continued to be a country of Catholic Christianity. Religion, contrary to the affirmations of the masters of the Third Republic, was not simply a matter for individual consciences, but a vital social force, upon which the moral and spiritual welfare of the nation depended. Against the corroding effects of secularization, Catholics urged the need for rechristianization, in order to rebuild a Christian society and to make France once again a genuinely Catholic country. Joan of Arc, not Marianne, was their inspiration: hence the vigorous campaign in the Belle Epoque to reclaim the Maid from the godless republicans and have her canonized as a saint of the Church. For Catholics, Joan was the perfect symbol of the indissoluble bond between religion and patriotism and the promotion of her cult was in itself a refutation of the anticlerical assertion that it was impossible to be both Catholic and patriotic.[11] As the Archbishop of Toulouse, Mgr Despez put it, Joan was "the virgin divinely sent to France to prevent her from ruin, and to conserve for the defense of the faith the nation so justly called the eldest daughter of the Church".[12] Having been among the most ardent supporters of the "National Revival" which characterized the years immediately preceding 1914, Catholics greeted the outbreak of hostilities as an opportunity to demonstrate the full depths of their patriotism. There were to be no stronger defenders of the *union sacrée*.[13]

When Germany declared war on France on 3 August 1914, the throne of Peter was still occupied by Pius X, under whom relations between France and Rome had reached their nadir in modern times. Formal diplomatic relations between France and the Holy See had already been severed on 30 July 1904, even before the Separation Law of 1905 widened the breach between Rome and the Republic. The death of Pius on 20 August 1914, followed by the election of his successor Giacomo della Chiesa, who took the title of Benedict XV, initially raised hopes that the new Pope might be more sympathetic to France, as he was a career diplomat in the tradition of Leo XIII and his Secretary of State Cardinal Rampolla, who in the *Ralliement* of the 1890s had called on French Catholics to abandon their attachment to the monarchist cause and accept the Republic as the legitimate form of government. Benedict's choice of Cardinal Ferrata as Secretary of State was interpreted as an encouraging sign, since he had been papal nuncio in Paris at the time of the *Ralliement*. And though Ferrata died after only a month in office he was replaced by another known Francophile, Cardinal Gasparri, who had taught for twenty years as a professor at the Institut Catholique in Paris. Other signs of *rapprochement* were the handwritten letter given by the new Pope to Cardinal Amette, the Archbishop of Paris, to be passed on to President Poincaré to inform him of the outcome of the papal election, and the invitation extended in turn by Amette to Poincaré to be represented at the funeral Mass for the deceased pontiff at Notre Dame cathedral in Paris.[14]

Despite these early gestures of sympathy towards France, however, from the very beginning of his pontificate Benedict XV revealed his determination to maintain his predecessor's strict neutrality in the European conflict.[15] His desire for a return to peace was proclaimed two days after his enthronement, when he announced that he hoped to be able to serve as an intermediary in the conflict, and reiterated in his first message to the world, on 8 September 1914, in which he denounced war as a "scourge." In his first encyclical, *Ad Beatissimi*, issued on 1 November 1914, he blamed the war on a deep malaise within modern society, manifested in various disturbing developments such as racial hatred, class antagonisms, lack of respect for authority, the decline of family values and the spread of immorality, especially among youth. But Benedict's commitment to peace went beyond the uttering of pious platitudes. He launched countless initiatives on behalf of prisoners, refugees, the wounded and the sick, often in collaboration with the Red Cross. By way of spiritual action for peace, he ordered public prayers to be said from January 1915 and composed a prayer for peace of his own which he urged Catholics throughout the world to recite. Most controversial of all, the Pope embarked on a series of diplomatic maneuvers aimed at securing a negotiated—compromise— peace.

His first attempt was made in 1916, when he tried without success to persuade President Wilson of the United States to act as a mediator. The second and more ambitious effort was undertaken in 1917 at a moment when both sides appeared to be flagging from war weariness and when the prospect of a military solution seemed more remote than ever. In a Peace Note published on 16 August 1917, Benedict called for a suspension of hostilities and simultaneous disarmament on the part of the belligerent powers, to be followed by international arbitration, the results of which were to be binding and backed by sanctions. Another clause stipulated freedom of movement on the seas and freedom of movement for peoples. There were to be no war indemnities, each side being responsible for the payment of its own expenses contracted under the war. Occupied territories were to be returned to their previous owners: France would be evacuated, the Germans would regain their overseas colonies, and Belgian independence was to be guaranteed. Disputed territories (such as Alsace-Lorraine and the Trentino) were to be settled by negotiation and in conformity with the wishes of the local populations. The belligerent powers, however, gave short shrift to Benedict's peace formula. Germany, which initially had seemed amenable (the ground having been prepared by Pacelli, papal nuncio in Munich and the future Pius XII), was no longer interested after the removal from office of the German Chancellor Bethmann Hollweg and the effective assumption of power by the military. In Austria-Hungary, both the Emperor Karl and his Foreign minister Czernin, along with the main press organs, were all opposed to a negotiated peace. The Allied Powers simply failed to respond and, disillusioned, the Pope gave up his efforts to end the conflict by negotiation.[16]

French reactions to Benedict's wartime diplomacy were particularly unfavorable. Overall French public opinion (including Catholic opinion) saw neutrality as an unacceptable position: it was widely felt that there were rights and wrongs in the conflict, and that the Pope should be on the side of right (i.e., France). Neutrality was interpreted as in effect opting for the Central Powers: hence the cool reception given to Benedict's first encyclical, which according to a police report of 25 November 1914 created "complete disillusionment" among French Catholics.[17] Indeed, in some quarters the reaction was much stronger. The Catholic novelist and polemicist Léon Bloy described the encyclical as being of "an astonishing mediocrity" and as representing a missed opportunity. In his view, the Pope should have taken up an emphatically anti-Austrian position and placed the Empire under Interdict, and then broken off diplomatic relations with "heretical and brigand Germany."[18] *Le Temps* (known to be close to French government thinking) likewise articulated its regret at the Pope's refusal to take sides. Neutrality, it argued, was an understandable and acceptable stance on the part of secular governments. The papacy, however, was not a temporal but a spiritual power, and its neutrality was not political but moral. It was therefore incomprehensible, given German aggression and war crimes, that Benedict should refuse to side with the cause of justice.[19]

In 1916 the sensational publication of an interview with the Pope conducted by the journalist Latapie exacerbated anti-papal feeling for it appeared to confirm the pontiff's equivocal position regarding the violation of Belgian neutrality in particular and German war crimes generally (which allegedly included the destruction of churches and the execution of priests). Additionally, Latapie implied that Benedict had intrigued to try to prevent the entry of Italy into the war on the Allied side. Such was the furor stirred up in France by the article that Cardinal Amette, on behalf of the French episcopate, was obliged to write to the Pope to inform him of the profound distress caused by his remarks. In his reply, Benedict claimed that he had been misrepresented, and that Latapie had published his piece without authorization, despite a promise to submit it for approval to the Vatican. Gasparri called the journalist "a vulgar liar" and tried to limit the damage by stating explicitly in a letter of 11 July 1915 that the violation of Belgian neutrality by Germany was indeed one of the "injustices" to which the Pope had alluded in an allocution of 22 January 1915 (a statement which, to the satisfaction of the French, gave rise to protests from Germany). Gasparri also confirmed that the Pope was most indignant about the treatment of Cardinal Mercier, Archbishop of Mâlines, and of other Belgian bishops and priests, and that he was outraged at the destruction of religious buildings. The creation of three new French cardinals in 1916 was a gesture further designed to reassure the Church in France that the Pope was not anti-French.[20]

Yet doubts continued to linger as to where the pontiff's real sympathies lay. The French government considered prayers for peace as likely to spread defeatism, and would not permit them to be said. Catholic newspapers which defied the ban and attempted to publish Benedict's own prayer for peace were seized by order of the censor. Not all Catholics objected to such measures. Léon Bloy declared that Benedict should change his name to "Pilate XV."[21] But it was above all the Pope's diplomatic maneuvers which aroused the most suspicion and hostility. The veteran priest-eater, Georges Clemenceau, told his readers in *L'Homme Enchaîné* that there could be no question of impartiality between right and barbarism, or victim and criminal.[22] Catholic reactions were by no means dissimilar. Already by 1916 some French Catholics were disconcerted by the way the war was being reported in the official Vatican organ, the *Osservatore Romano*,[23] which they thought could be better renamed the *Osservatore Tedesco*. The Pope's peace proposals of 1917 were roundly condemned by "Pertinax" in the *Echo de Paris* (which had a large Catholic readership) as seriously lacking in justice,[24] while the *Action Française*, the organ of French integral nationalism and neo-royalism, also read by many Catholics who appreciated its defense of the Church, flatly refused to go along with the peace plan. Hitherto the paper had tried to show understanding for the difficulties and delicacy of the Pope's position, but in 1917 it affirmed that there could be no peace before a final victory for French arms.[25]

Even the French bishops were at best ambiguous in their response to the papal peace initiative, and the well-known Dominican, Father Sertillanges, spoke for a great many of his co-religionists when, at a religious and patriotic ceremony to launch a third national loan subscription held at the Church of the Madeleine, he gave a resounding *non possumus* to the Pope's peace proposals. He declared:

> Most Holy Father, we cannot for the moment answer your calls for peace ... .\Our enemies remain powerful, the invasion has not affected them ... .\We are sons who sometimes say, like the apparent rebel in the Gospel: No! No![26]

Sertillanges was to be the object of ecclesiastical sanctions for this declaration of filial disobedience and patriotic faith, but it should be stressed that his text had been cleared in advance both by the superiors of his Order and by Cardinal Amette, who presided over the ceremony, which was also attended by Mme Poincaré. His text was reproduced in the *Echo de Paris*, which made no secret of its approval, and, more discreetly, in Catholic journals such as *La Croix* and the *Revue du clergé français*.[27] In the face of such intransigence on the part of French Catholics, it is hardly surprising that Benedict was obliged to desist from further attempts to secure a negotiated peace after the rejection of his initiative in 1917.

Thus far, it could be argued that the similar attitudes of both Catholics and republicans to the peace proposals of Benedict XV confirm the Becker thesis that the sense of national unity remained strong in France throughout the duration of the war and underlay the country's firm resolve to fight on to an ultimate victory achieved by force of Allied arms. The Church never wavered in its commitment to the *union sacrée*. Yet there was another set of responses to papal policy which suggest that, however great the identification on all sides with the defense of the *patrie*, there remained deep rifts in French national life which not even the notion of "sacred union" could bridge. Anticlericals seized on the attitude of the Holy See to question the genuineness of the French Church's commitment to victory and to resurrect the old anticlerical war cry of *Le cléricalisme! Voilà l'ennemi!* Scarcely had hostilities begun when rumors began to be bruited with the familiar insinuation that Catholicism and patriotism were incompatible, and, as never before, the Church found itself obliged to try to give the lie to a whole series of *rumeurs infâmes*.

The first to emerge was that the war had actually been started by the clergy. As early as September 1914 *Le Correspondant* had to defend Catholics against the accusation that the war had been initiated by "nobles and priests".[28] In December 1915, the Bishop of Montauban, Mgr Marty, wrote an open letter to the government complaining that "just about everywhere" he encountered "this monstrous accusation" that "the priests are the cause of the war: the priests are sending money to the Prussians."[29] The echoes of 1870 are unmistakable. In January 1916 it was the turn of *La Croix* to respond to the smear campaign, widespread in the south of France, which branded priests as the originators of the war. Ironically, the reason that the rumor was spreading, according to *La Croix*, was because so many of the journalists who worked on its regional editions were not around to combat them, as they were away doing their patriotic duty at the front, and, regrettably, moderate newspapers were afraid to speak up for the clergy lest they too were attacked as clerical.[30] This particular *rumeur infâme* was kept up right through the war and was still being propagated even after the cessation of hostilities. A police report from Quimper, dated 10 July 1920, commented on a brochure which emanated from the publishing house *L'Idée Libre* with the title of *La France dans les bras du pape*. On its cover it represented a Jesuit in the form of a vulture along with the inscription: "*Voilà l'ennemi!*" Inside, it reproduced the argument that while the country had been at war, it was all the time being subverted by an internal enemy: "this eternal and evil-doing enemy is the Jesuit, the Black Party, Popery." It was they who had provoked the war in the first place, thanks to their secret internal organization, with a view to creating chaos and disorder, from which they could profit. And indeed, with the renewal of diplomatic relations between France and the Vatican in sight, they were close to realizing their objectives—which was all the more shameful when one recalled "what a sickening role Benedict XV had played during the war."[31]

A second *rumeur infâme*, a refinement of and addition to the thesis that the clergy had started the conflict for their own ends, was that they continually sought to exploit the circumstances of the war for their own purposes, most notably by attempting to use the war to encourage a great religious revival, both at the front and the rear. While the claim was by no means totally inaccurate—churchmen *did* hope that the war would encourage a return of lost sheep to the fold—there was no mistaking the sectarian thrust of the anticlerical attacks. The whole notion of a "religious revival," scoffed Clemenceau, was just a device to inveigle poor, crazed, souls into the churches.[32] But the radical and socialist press was not always so sanguine and seized on suggestions from the pulpit that the war might be a punishment sent from God to chastise France for the sins committed by their anticlerical political leaders who had persecuted the Church and carried out the Separation. Thus, in the Isère the socialist newspaper *Le Droit du Peuple* ran a regular column from October 1914 in which clerics were accused of subverting the *union sacrée*. Their zeal did not go unrewarded as the authorities took such denunciations seriously. In November 1915 the curé of Montalieu was prosecuted and sentenced to three months imprisonment, with a two hundred-franc fine, for using words likely to spread panic among the population.[33] Similarly, in November 1915 to the delight of *La Lanterne*, a priest in the Seine-et-Marne who had outraged local people in the village of Coulommiers by preaching that France was now paying for its impiety in the recent past was first denounced by the vigilant editor of the local republican newspaper, *Le Démocrate de Seine-et-Oise*, and then prosecuted for pronouncing "words likely to disturb public order."[34]

Anticlericals also accused the Church of inventing new "miracles" to further its interest, and in particular the "miracle of the Marne". A police report of 1915 noted how the "clerical milieux" were spreading the story told by certain German prisoners captured after the battle who reported that they had seen a great, white, vaporous form in the sky, in the shape of a winged warrior, hovering above the French troops, which had spoken to the Germans and convinced them to give themselves up. The report commented: "These stories transport fervent clericals, especially the right-thinking feminine element."[35] Anticlerical journalists like the socialist Sixte-Quenin who wrote violently anticlerical pieces for *Humanité* and other journals (interestingly, like Combes, he had once been a seminarian) were incensed by such attempts on the part of Catholics to attribute the victory of the Marne to the status of France as the eldest daughter of the Church. If there was any superior moral force behind the success of French arms, he affirmed, it came from the Revolutionary tradition rather than God.[36]

Another way in which the clergy were said to be taking advantage of the circumstances of the war was by building up a formidable network of charities and associations under the guise of patriotism that in reality reinforced clerical power. Here the bad faith of the anticlericals was specially obvious, for it was of course true that the Church at both the national and local level engaged in all kinds of *oeuvres de guerre* to help the war effort. Special collections were taken up at church functions for soldiers, Catholic women were encouraged to knit for the *patrie*, and parishes dispatched clothes, blankets and the like to the front. Yet the fact that the Church organized its own good works independently from the efforts of local municipalities very quickly led to a resumption of clerical-anticlerical antagonisms at the local level. Evidence from the Isère reveals cracks in the *union sacrée* caused by competition between rival charities: those of the *Association Catholique de Secours aux Blessés et d'Assistance par le Travail* and those of the municipalities. Left-wing communes would not support Catholic efforts while conservative municipalities withheld their support from the state ones. Catholic ladies collecting for the *Association* were likely to meet with verbal abuse or be told that the Pope was rich enough already.[37] According to the Anticlerical League in Albi, clerical contributions to the war effort were in reality a plot "to extend their tentacles over all charitable activity, indubitably for political purposes."[38] Similarly base motives were attributed to nuns working as nurses in military hospitals. According to the likes of Sixte-Quenin, they surrounded their patients with religious effigies and made assiduous efforts to convert them while they were at their lowest ebb. Even worse, it was suggested that the wounded were not given proper medical care and attention unless they promised to become practicing Catholics.[39] *Le Bonnet Rouge* claimed that Muslim patients were particularly subject to this kind of harassment in attempts to convert them.[40]

A third, and widespread, *rumeur infâme* was that the clergy were *embusqués*, cowards who shirked their patriotic duty—a claim hard to reconcile with the fact that over 30,000 priests had been mobilized to serve with the French armed forces (prominent among them were many members of religious orders expelled from their country by the Law of 1904 against the congregations but who returned voluntarily to enlist). Sixte-Quenin's article in *L'Humanité* of 14 November 1915 was typical. Why, he demanded of Minister of War Millerand, had some 12,580 *"célibataires"* (i.e., priests) not been sent to the front line? Did they perhaps have hidden influence?[41] A particularly nasty variant on this theme was to be found in newspapers such as the *Dépêche de Toulouse*, which, when listing citations for bravery, deliberately refused to mention that some of the heroes happened to be clergymen. Instead, they preferred to remind their readers of the need for vigilance against the dreaded Jesuit, as in the story printed by *Humanité* concerning a père Boutin S.J, who was said to have been sending postcards from his sector of the front illustrated by photographs which could give away the French plan of battle. In reality, far from being a German agent, the same captain Boutin was in fact laying down his life for his country, and the editor of *Humanité* was obliged to publish an apology.[42] The Briand government itself was obliged to repudiate the allegations of clerical shirking, while *La Dépêche de Toulouse*, having been threatened by a libel action by the novelist and right-wing nationalist Maurice Barrès, likewise began to cite the names of priests and religious among the dead and the decorated. Nevertheless, the rumor was not easily stopped. Renewed anticlerical pressure on the Chamber of Deputies produced the Sixte-Quenin amendment of 3 February 1917, a modification to the conscription laws of 1889 and 1905 which henceforth permitted priests to be mobilized not merely in the auxiliary services but as fighting men.[43]

The most serious of the *rumeurs infâmes*, however, which was not confined to the anticlerical press or local malicious gossip but expressed also in French government circles, was the one which represented the Pope and the French Church as the enemy of France. As has been seen, papal policy during the war was not popular in France, even among Catholics. But the "infamous rumor" about him went well beyond a refusal to accept his peace proposals and, in fact, identified the Vatican as actively plotting against France and favoring the cause of the Central Powers, above all with a view to preserving Austria-Hungary, the leading Catholic power in Europe. That such notions were entertained in government circles is attested by a lengthy memorandum in the French police archives, dated 3 February 1916, which analyzed papal policy in detail. It argued that, at first, the Pope had believed that the most likely outcome of the war would be victory for the Central Powers—an illusion nourished by his largely Germanophile entourage. At this stage, therefore, he had wished to be on good terms with Germany and Austria so that he could have a say in the peace settlement. Once it became clear that France could never be conquered, however, he was left with only two options. On the one hand, he could sit back and allow the war to run its course, in which case he would witness the defeat of Catholic Austria and victory for the Allies, namely republican and officially atheist France, Protestant England, and schismatic Russia. This was not a scenario which the *monde noir* of Rome could view with equanimity, especially since they considered that from the point of view of the clergy in France it would amount to a crushing blow for the Church. Not only would the republican regime be consolidated but the rise of socialism and other revolutionary ideologies would be encouraged, with the consequence that the French Church would never have any redress for its grievances against the French state and therefore might even have to face the renewal of religious persecution.

Alternatively, the Pope could pursue the goal of a compromise peace, in the hope of maintaining the status quo. This was the solution which appealed to Rome, not least because it would keep intact the Pope's own authority and prestige with the Great Powers. It was also desirable for the sake of the clerical party in France, which could only benefit from an inconclusive outcome to the war. After the shedding of so much blood and the experience of so much suffering to no obvious purpose, the French people would be inflamed against their political leaders and be ready to sweep away the republican regime, allowing the *parti de l'ordre* to take over. Betraying its indebtedness to the myth of the Jesuit plot, the report concluded:

Therein lies the secret of pontifical policy, obviously inspired by Berlin, of the intended clerical maneuvers at the front and in the country, and of the enticements held out to Belgium.[44]

The police report claimed to be based on disclosures from a well-placed religious source, one actively involved in the formulation of clerical and royalist policy. The informant had posed the question: "To the general interest of the Roman Church should the Pope prefer the interest of an erring nation whose victory would bring a return of religious battles?' The answer of the Jesuits to such a question had to be: "*Non*".[45]

The same thesis, propounded in even more virulent language was to be found in the anticlerical press. In 1916 *La Lanterne* ran a series of articles entitled *Catholicisme et papauté* written by Paul Massoulier, who claimed to have inside information in the shape of two secret memoirs drawn up by well-connected French ecclesiastical sources in Rome. Massoulier alleged that, whereas the right-wing press had not been slow to denounce the pacifist maneuvers of the international socialist gathering at Kienthal, they had overlooked the fact that there was another international at work—the *international noir*. The documents in Massoulier's possession, however, made it clear that the Pope favored a shabby, compromise peace, rather than the triumph of justice. Because Rome had failed to give a proper lead, it was argued by the authors of the memoirs that it was the responsibility of the French and Belgian bishops to speak out and ease Catholic consciences troubled by the Pope's silence—a silence which *La Lanterne* described as the "coupable mutisme" of "le pape bochophile Benoît XV."[46]

Ecclesiastical appointments were adduced as further evidence of the Pope's treachery. Extremely sinister for the anticlerical press was the election of the Pole Wladimir Ledowchowski to be the new General of the Jesuit Order. Clemenceau waxed indignant in *L'Homme Enchâiné*, citing the event as a victory of the German party over the French party within the Order.[47] A press release which appeared in leading newspapers such as *Le Temps*, *Le Figaro*, and *L'Information*, with obvious approval from the government, observed: "Father Ledowchowski was Provincial in Germany. He is so *germanisant* that several Polish Jesuits have left the Society of Jesus."[48] *Le Journal* did not mince its words: "The new 'black pope' is the man of Berlin."[49] Similarly, the elevation of the nuncios in Berlin and Vienna to the College of Cardinals came in for criticism. A police report commented: "it's the German nuncio, the nuncio of the Kaiser who receives the (cardinal's) hat, alongside the one of Franz Joseph."[50]

If, as we have seen, French Catholics were themselves not a little disconcerted by the general direction of papal policy, they were not slow to appreciate that anticlericals wished to represent it in the worst possible light for their own sectarian purposes. Filial disobedience to a premature call for peace was one thing, acceptance of the *rumeur infâme* about a Vatican-inspired plot against France something else entirely. Rebuttals were soon forthcoming which in the virulence of their language and in their similar recourse to conspiratorial explanations of motive amounted to clerical equivalents of the original accusations. In the Gironde one priest, claiming to speak for an organization called *The Three Ave Marias*, published a brochure which warned the Catholics of France to be on their guard against being duped by the pernicious slanders against the papacy. Benedict XV had raised his voice in support of a just peace, he claimed, and it was only lackeys of the *Boches* who claimed that he wanted a German peace. Many Frenchmen had been the beneficiaries of the Pope's humanitarian efforts, yet no one seemed to wish to publicize them. The charges against the Pope were total calumnies and derived ultimately from Bismarck, who had well understood that in order to confuse the French and diminish their place in the world it was vital to weaken the bonds between France and the Holy See.[51]

The theme of playing Bismarck's game by giving credence to anti-Roman fabrications was picked up by other clerical authors, whose vehement denunciations of the government gave the police cause for concern and generated fears that the distribution of them would result in public disorder. One brochure argued that the only reason that neutral nations were more favorably inclined to Germany than to France was that France was "anticlerical, atheistic and hostile to the Pope, while even Protestant Germany has nothing of this anticlericalism or atheism."[52] Another suggested that the article by Latapie was a prime example of the kind of plot favored by Bismarck to keep the French divided, and condemned it as a "cowardly and criminal outrage against our prisoners and against our war victims." It was thanks to the Pope that considerable improvements had been made in the conditions of French prisoners and wounded soldiers, and the point of the Latapie interview was an attempt to create a scandal which would divert attention away from the very real achievements of the papacy, in conformity with orders emanating ultimately from Bismarck. The article added that it was precisely the same men who were orchestrating the campaign against General Joffre and the General Staff as well as against the Pope, which was proof positive that not all the enemies of France were to be found in Germany.[53]

Not all Catholic responses to the *rumeur infâme* about Benedict XV and other infamous rumors were expressed in quite such violent terms. All, however, are indicative of the deep divisions which continued to beset French society and of fundamental disagreements over the issue of what it meant to be French. *La Croix* tried to reassure its readers that there was nothing sinister about the Pope's silence, as the Holy See was not in a position to make public all its actions. Rather, there was much to be said for giving the Pope a free hand to operate behind the scenes as best he could. In any case, according to the correspondent, the Pope had indeed spoken out, notably at his allocution of 22 January 1915, and he was thus a much less neutral figure than the Heads of State of, say, the USA or Spain.[54] "Franc" wrote in the same newspaper in March 1915 that too many Catholics failed to see the base objectives which the *rumeur infâme* was designed to serve, and ridiculed the audacity of anticlericals attempting to dictate to the Pope on matters such as ecclesiastical appointments.[55]

The right-wing press took a similar line. *La Libre Parole* warned Catholics not to be the dupes of the press campaign against Benedict XV, arguing that the campaign had resulted precisely from the very correctness of Catholic attitudes to the war, which had left anticlericals floundering and increasingly desperate to find any means that would resuscitate their flagging cause. They had trained their fire on the Pope because he, too, had behaved impeccably, and to the dismay of anticlericals had succeeded in raising the prestige of the papacy through his humanitarian endeavors. It was more than a little ironical, the article suggested, to see people who denied the official existence of the Pope wax indignant at his refusal to take sides. What was necessary was the restoration of the French embassy at the Vatican, although even some Catholics now seemed to doubt its utility as a result of the scurrilous press campaign.[56] Likewise, *L'Echo de Paris* put the case for the renewal of diplomatic links with Rome in order to counteract the Germanophile influences at work there, and it identified the persistence of the kind of sectarianism which had produced the separation of church and state as the main obstacle to the resumption of diplomatic relations.[57] *Action Française*, from the first, stigmatized all *rumeurs infâmes* as attempts to create division and confusion among Catholics in France.[58] The resignation of Denys Cochin from the Ribot government in August 1917 was another gesture of protest at the spread of the rumors and a sign that Catholic politicians could no longer give their support to the *Union sacrée*.

Two general conclusions emerge from this brief survey of the controversies surrounding the attitude of the Papacy and the French Church to the First World War. One is the continuing vigor of anticlericalism, too often regarded as a force which was fast becoming extinct by 1914. While it is true that relations between church and state improved dramatically in the immediate aftermath of the war as a result of the electoral swing to the Right in 1919, the return of the Left in 1914 was to be accompanied by another anticlerical outburst which delighted in harking back to the rumors concerning the role of Benedict XV and French Catholics between 1914 and 1918. It is also worth recalling that the main argument invoked by the political establishment of the Third Republic against the enfranchisement of women in the interwar period was the alleged persistence of the "clerical threat".[59] The idea that the First World War prepared the way for a "second Ralliement" is, at the very least, debatable.[60] A second conclusion is quite simply that nationalism divided the French more than it united them, even in the circumstances of their struggle for survival during the Great War. The "'infamous rumors" revealed the durability of old hatreds and the fragility of the "Sacred Union."

I wish to thank the British Academy for a research grant which enabled me to spend time in Paris carrying out the research necessary for the preparation of this chapter. An earlier version of the text was given as a paper at the French History Society conference in London in March 1992 and I am grateful for helpful comments and suggestions made by participants. I am especially indebted to Dr. Ralph Gibson of Lancaster University who subsequently forwarded to me a number of illuminating nineteenth-century references.

Notes to Chapter 5

1. J-J Becker, *The Great War and the French People* (Leamington Spa, 1986). The idea of the nation as an "imagined community" is developed by B. Anderson, *Imagined Communities:Reflections on the Origin and Spread of Nationalism* (3rd ed., London, 1986).
2. R. Tombs, ed., *Nationhood and Nationalism in France: from Boulangism to the Great War 1889-1918* (London, 1991) and B. Jenkins, *Nationalism in France: Class and Nation since 1789* (London, 1990).

3. Cf. A. Rosmer, *Le mouvement ouvrier pendant la première guerre mondiale*, 2 vols.,(Paris, 1936–1959) and A. Kriegel, *Aux origines du communisme français (1914–1920)* (2 vols., Paris, 1964).
4. R. Rémond, *L'anticléricalisme en France de 1815 à nos jours* (Paris, 1976), especially pp. 176–90. Antijesuitism has now been thoroughly explored by G. Cubitt, *The Jesuit Myth: Conspiracy Theory and Politics in Nineteenth-Century France* (Oxford, 1993).
5. R. C. Cobb, *The People's Armies* (London and New Haven, 1987), pp. 442–79.
6. J. Faury, *Cléricalisme et anticléricalisme dans le Tarn (1848-1900)* (Toulouse, 1980), p. 51.
7. Abbé F. Lagrange, *Vie de Monseigneur Dupanloup, évêque d'Orléans* (6th ed, Paris 1886), vol. 2, p. 202.
8. Quoted by Faury, *Cléricalisme et anticléricalisme*, pp. 88-9.
9. G. Cholvy and Y.-M. Hilaire, *Histoire religieuse de la France contemporaine*, (3 vols., Toulouse, 1985–8), vol. 2, p. 189.
10. *Matériaux pour l'Histoire religieuse du peuple français*, ed. F. Boulard, vol. 1, (Paris 1982–86), p. 342.
11. J.F. McMillan, "Reclaiming a Martyr: French Catholics and the Cult of Joan of Arc, 1890–1920," in *Martyrs and Martyrologies. Studies in Church History*, vol. 30, ed. D. Wood, (Oxford, 1993).
12. *L'Univers*, 6 September 1890.
13. The fullest study is J. Fontana, *Les catholiques français pendant la Grande Guerre* (Paris, 1990). See also J.D. Holmes, *The Papacy in the Modern World 1914–1978* (London, 1981) and the article by J.-M. Mayeur, "La vie religieuse en France pendant la Première Guerre Mondiale" in *Histoire vécue du peuple chrétien*, vol. 2 (Toulouse, 1979).
14. R. Poincaré, *Au service de la France*, vol. 5, (Paris, 1928), pp. 304–7.
15. J. Fontana, *Les catholiques*, p. 173ff.: J.D. Holmes, *The Papacy*, ch. 1: S. Marchese, *La Francia ed il problema dei rapporti con la Santa Sede 1914–1924* (Naples, n.d.).
16. D. Stevenson, *The First World War and International Politics* (Oxford, 1988), p. 162ff: J. Leflon, "L'action diplomatico-religieuse de Benoît XV en faveur de la paix durant la première guerre mondiale", in *Benedetto XV, i cattolici e la prima guerra mondiale. Atti del Convegno di Studi tenuto a Spoleto nei giorni 7-8-9 settembre 1962* (Rome, 1973), pp. 33–70.
17. Archives Nationales (AN) F7 12881: report of a correspondent, Paris, 25 November 1914.
18. L. Bloy, *Journal* vol. 4, *Au seuil de l'Apocalypse. La porte des humbles* (Paris, 1963), p. 124.
19. *Le Temps*, 2 August 1915.
20. On the Latapie affair, see Fontana, *Les catholiques*, p.187ff. and *annexe v*, which gives the text of the interview as reported by Latapie.
21. L. Bloy, *Au seuil de l'Apocalypse*, p. 142.
22. *L'Homme Enchaîné*, 22 February 1915.
23. AN F7 12881, report of a correspondent, Paris, 19 February 1916.
24. Cited by Cholvy and Hilaire, *Histoire religieuse*, vol. 2, p. 255.
25. Cf. C. Maurras, *Le pape, la guerre et la paix*, (Paris, 1917).
26. P. Sertillanges, *La Paix française* (Paris, 1917), p. 10.
27. Fontana, *Les catholiques*, pp. 210, f. 221.
28. *Le Correspondant*, 25 September 1914.
29. Cited by Fontana, *Les catholiques*, p. 152.
30. AN F7 12881: report of a correspondent, Paris, 29 January 1916.

31. AN F7 12881: commissaire spécial to Director of Sûreté Nationale, Quimper, 10 July 1920.
32. *L'Homme Enchaîné*, 22 February 1915.
33. P.J. Flood, *France 1914–1918: Public Opinion and the War Effort* (London 1990), p. 104.
34. *La Lanterne*, "La propagande noire," 19 October 1915.
35. AN F7 12881: report of a correspondent, Paris, 30 September 1915.
36. Sixte-Quenin, *L'Humanité*, 10 November 1915. reproduced in *Le cléricalisme et la guerre* (Villeneuve-Saint-Georges, 1917).
37. Flood, *France*, p. 106.
38. Cited by Fontana, *Les catholiques*, p. 129.
39. Sixte-Quenin, *Le cléricalisme et la guerre*, p. 58ff.
40. *Le Bonnet Rouge*, 9 May 1915.
41. Sixte-Quenin, *L'Humanité*, 14 November, 1915.
42. Fontana, *Les catholiques*, p. 147.
43. Ibid., p. 159ff.
44. AN F7 12881 Paris, 3 February 1916.
45. Ibid.
46. *La Lanterne*, 29 August 1916.
47. *L'Homme Enchaîné*, 13 February 1915.
48. Cited by Fontana, *Les catholiques*, p.144.
49. *Le Journal*, 12 February 1915.
50. AN F7 12881: note of 12 November 1915.
51. AN F7 12881: Prefect of the Gironde to Minister of the Interior, 6 December 1915.
52. AN F7 12881 Paris, report of 1916, commenting on brochure *Ah! de grâce qu'on cesse d'obéir à Bismarck* by "Jean Lenoir".
53. Ibid, brochure *Que penser du complot Latapie. Un lâche attentat contre nos prisonniers et contre toutes les victimes de guerre*.
54. *La Croix*, 25 February 1915.
55. *La Croix*, 24 March 1915.
56. *La Libre Parole*, 8 February 1915.
57. *L'Echo de Paris*, 17 February 1915.
58. Cf. *Action Française*, 4 October 1915 and C. Maurras, *Le pape, la guerre et la paix*.
59. See J.F. McMillan, *Housewife or Harlot: The Place of Women in French Society, 1870–1940* (Brighton and New York, 1981).
60. Cf.H.S. Paul, *The Second Ralliement: The Rapprochement between Church and State in France in the Twentieth Century* (Washington, 1967).

Select Bibliography

The major study to date of French Catholics during the period of the First World War is the thesis of J. Fontana, *Les catholiques français pendant la grande guerre* (Paris 1990). There is no comparable study in English, though J.D. Holmes, *The Papacy in the Modern World 1914–1978* (London, 1981) has a chapter on Benedict XV, and the Pope's diplomatic initiatives are surveyed succinctly in D. Stevenson, *The First World War and International Politics* (Oxford, 1988). The strength of the *union sacrée* is fundamental to the argument of J.J. Becker, *The Great War and the French People* (Leamington Spa, 1988), while good introductions to the varieties of nationalism to be found in Modern France can be found in R. Tombs (ed.), *Nationhood and Nationalism in France: From Boulangism to the Great War 1889–1918* (London, 1991) and B. Jenkins, *Nationalism in France: Class and Nation since 1789* (London, 1990). An excellent study of anti-jesuitism is G. Cubitt, *The Jesuit Myth: Conspiracy Theory and Politics in Nineteenth Century France* (Oxford, 1993), which complements the wider treatment of anticlerism by R. Rémond, *L'anticléricalism en France de 1815 à nos jours* (Paris, 1976).

CHAPTER 6

NATIONALISM IN WARTIME
Critiquing the Conventional Wisdom

L.L. Farrar, Jr.

Introduction

The First World War is a major landmark of the twentieth century and indeed of modern history. Likewise, nationalism is generally regarded as a primal force and distinguishing feature of the modern world. Nationalism and the war are in fact bound together like Siamese twins, causes and consequences of one another, a relationship which is fundamental to our explanation of the period. It is useful from time to time to re-examine such operating assumptions so as to confirm their validity or to adjust them in light of new information or interpretations.

According to the prevailing wisdom, the war and nationalism are linked. The war is widely seen as fostering nationalism, leading "to the most far-reaching triumph of nationalism to date."[1] Nationalism is perceived as intensifying and/or lengthening the conflict which is frequently viewed as "a supremely nationalistic war."[2]

The question of wartime nationalism has profound consequences. It implicates our understanding of the war's inner dynamic, i.e., how it was conducted and why it continued. Nationalism's role in the war also significantly affects our interpretation of nationalism in general, its forms and power as a historical force, as well as its definition.

Notes for this chapter begin on page 147.

Finally, an evaluation of nationalism's role in the war influences our system of historical periodization which separates modern history—and especially the twentieth century—from its predecessors by identifying such distinctive elements as nationalism.

Nationalism took a variety of forms corresponding to the war's basic elements, namely, public opinion at home and at the front, propaganda, war aims, wartime diplomatic policy and strategy, and the sub-nationalities. An evaluation of nationalism's wartime role requires a consideration of each of these areas. In doing so, the conventional usage is accepted, i. e., whatever is called nationalism is taken as such. The issue of defining the term will then be raised at the end of the essay.

Home

It is argued by many historians that the masses were motivated by an aggressive nationalism. During the First World War "mass armies were supported by the fanatical nationalism of the civilian populations."[3] Such fanaticism is seen to be a driving force in the war and a constraint on policy-makers in how they conducted the war. This contention must be evaluated in the war's context.

The initial public response to the war was widely viewed as overwhelmingly positive. The so-called August enthusiasm has long been the most accepted fact of wartime public opinion because "militant nationalism ... without exception inflamed all European states."[4] Yet the unanimity, universality, and duration of this enthusiasm has subsequently been questioned; it seems to have been relatively brief and evidenced primarily by the urban middle/upper classes, while most workers and peasants remained passive.[5] For each who cheered, there may have been dozens who worried or grieved.[6] Most, like "the French, did not depart with the enthusiasm of conquerors but the resolution of a duty to be accomplished."[7] In short, defensive patriotism rather than expansive nationalism was characteristic of the early weeks of the war.

The two salient features of public opinion from September 1914 to early 1918 were the simultaneous diminution of initial enthusiasm as well as a relative lack of protest. While there was certainly some chauvinism among intellectuals, businessmen, and the upper and middle classes,[8] the sense of resigned resolution to fight on was much more widespread.[9] Precisely because it operated against a background of deepening war fatigue and pacifism by late 1915, this lack of resistance is both more significant and enigmatic.[10] The strikes of 1916 and then, increasingly, in 1917 and 1918 were essentially protests against working and living conditions (above all, food shortages) but were by implication a protest against the war which created them.[11] During the final weeks of the war, there was a revival of enthusiasm in the victorious countries, though probably due as much to sheer relief as aggressive nationalism.[12] The fact remains that the overwhelming majority of belligerent populations made the war possible by working, paying taxes, and, above all, by not revolting against it. And yet we cannot be sure of their motives for it is difficult, perhaps impossible, to know what most Europeans felt about the war.[13] For not only the impenetrability and paucity of evidence but also the ambivalence of many contemporaries toward the war complicates any analysis of their attitudes.[14]

What conclusions can we draw? There is little evidence for the extreme interpretation that the masses were driven by aggressive nationalism which in turn determined government policy. Likewise, the contention that the masses were pacifist and/or rebellious is difficult to demonstrate. The central fact remains that the masses not only did not revolt but also supported the war effort, and regarding their motives we are, however, left with a question mark: were they convinced or merely obedient? What is clear is that mass aggressive nationalism cannot be demonstrated and thus was more than likely not a significant factor.

Front

Troop morale is an element at once more inherently critical as well as easier to control through military discipline and, for the same reason, even more difficult to fathom than civilian opinion.[15] Traditionally, there have been two largely contradictory interpretations of soldier morale at the front which might be called horror/pacifism and heroism/nationalism. In the first view, encouraged by postwar disenchantment, the war is presented in all its horror with the soldiers cynical about the war and their governments, hating the guns, sometimes empathizing with the enemy, isolated from the home front, and fighting only for their "mates." The second view, certainly fostered by wartime propaganda and postwar nostalgia, emphasizes the pathos, poignancy, and bravery of one's own side and the impersonality of the enemy.[16] A more realistic estimate seems to lie somewhere in between.

Morale at the front evolved during the course of the war. The prewar phobias of governments about resistance to mobilization proved unfounded.[17] At least some soldiers mobilized in the large cities shared the August enthusiasm of some civilian counterparts: part of the war's mythology includes photos of soldiers flower-bedecked by girls and trains inscribed with "A Berlin" or "Nach Paris."[18] Less credulous reports from the cities and from smaller towns and the countryside, however, lacked this bravado and recount much more silent, even sullen obedience.[19] One historian in fact asserts that "'the national fever' of summer 1914 was a myth and that only a minority of conscripted men felt enthusiastic at the start of the war."[20] Whatever enthusiasm there was in early August was dissipated by the reality of war and replaced during the next two years by tenacity marred by notably little failure of discipline even from the multi-national troops of the Habsburg and Romanov armies.[21] In 1917, however, the edifice showed signs of cracking—first the Russian army, then the French mutinies—but the Russian army was cobbled back together for another six months and the French mutinies proved to be a protest against pointless attack but not defense.[22] Although the Russian army collapsed, the Habsburg army persevered until near the end, while the German army maintained discipline in retreat and the navy suffered mutinies only when ordered to undertake a pointless suicide mission.

What is striking about this record is the apparent absence of aggressiveness or enthusiasm as motivators of soldiers the front. "Here again, there is hardly any trace of true nationalism."[23] In fact, whenever they were exposed to nationalist propaganda, the troops seem to have been at best bored, at worst alienated.[24] What kept the troops in the trenches was less aggressive nationalism than dogged defense of homeland, even when occupying foreign territory, as in the case of German soldiers resisting the British attack at the Somme in 1916,[25] as well as a narrower but more compelling loyalty to comrades.[26] Finally, there was also a sense that they had little choice: "It is no longer a question, as in August 1914, of patriotism but of submitting to a destiny inflicted by the order of things."[27]

Propaganda

The acknowledged purpose of propaganda was to fabricate nationalism. Governments "set up machinery to manipulate public opinion towards continued support of the war."²⁸ In its extreme form, the task of propaganda was "to mobilize the animosity of the country against the enemy"²⁹ H.G. Wells observed in 1914 that "the ultimate purpose of this war is propaganda, the destruction of certain beliefs, and the creation of others."³⁰ Thus propaganda became the personification of wartime nationalism.

In fact, propaganda's role was less grandiose but hypothetically more critical. It appeared necessary to mobilize whole populations for total war.³¹ By September 1914 governments decided that the initial enthusiasm had diminished and they all to greater or lesser degrees resorted to establishing propaganda ministries and launching campaigns.³² These official efforts were supplemented by semi-official activities of schools,³³ churches,³⁴ the press,³⁵ military leagues,³⁶ graphic artists,³⁷ and intellectuals.³⁸ These campaigns were intensified as the war lengthened but the critical issue became much more to discourage defeatism than to encourage aggressive nationalism. A committee set up in England in 1917 was a bellwether: its primary purpose was to "counteract pacifist propaganda" and "strengthen the national morale."³⁹ To this end, censorship functioned as a form of negative propaganda, protecting the public from "information likely to cause disaffection."⁴⁰ A French prefect articulated the assumptions and practice of censorship: "It is advisable for us to hide from the local population the real excesses of this terrible war."⁴¹ Although—or perhaps because—these excesses were difficult to hide from the soldiers at the front, propaganda sought above all to combat their fatigue and defeatism.⁴²

One might assume that these campaigns were successful because the ennoblement of one's own cause would understandably find ready response among populations confronted with the horrifying reality of war. The effects of this official propaganda are, however, difficult to estimate and would have required more sophisticated public opinion surveys than were available—or would have been allowed.⁴³ The voluntary recruitment campaign in Britain was accompanied by "the most concerted propaganda exercise of the first half of the war;" certainly volunteers poured in but not necessarily because of propaganda.⁴⁴ The effects of propaganda directed at front line troops seem to be marginal or even negative whenever they perceived it as "bourrage de crane ("brain-washing").⁴⁵ The most that can be said for this propaganda may be that it reassured believers but did not persuade skeptics. A German officer concluded during the summer of 1918 that "attempts to reach the mass of workers had been in vain" and that the effect of "patriotic instruction" on the mass of soldiers "was probably similar."[46]

At least as much effort was expended on propaganda abroad. Both sides sought to influence the behavior of the United States[47] and the other neutrals.[48] They likewise launched campaigns to encourage defeatism amongst enemy civilians and soldiers at the front.[49] Large claims were subsequently made for the efficacy of this propaganda, especially by the Allies against Germany.[50] Indeed, German General Erich Ludendorff asserted that "we were hypnotized by Allied propaganda as a rabbit is by a snake" and that it played a critical part in Germany's defeat; this claim is, however, suspect as a convenient excuse, shifting responsibility from his own to Allied shoulders.[51] But its assumption about the efficacy of propaganda is also difficult to verify. As a contemporary British critic of propaganda commented, there was "no adequate means for testing the efficacy of the various propaganda efforts abroad."[52] Second World War studies suggest that soldiers surrender less because of enemy propaganda than because of the collapse of their own unit.[53]

Whatever its efficacy, propaganda provides a useful window into wartime nationalism. Those who conducted it assumed that nationalism was insufficient but could be augmented by manipulating public opinion. Opinion was evidently malleable and propaganda tailored to its audience and purpose. To their own populations, governments presented their cause as defensive and noble, while the enemy was painted as threateningly nationalistic and annexationist. Meanwhile they sought to divide enemy populations and governments by emphasizing the populations' pacifism and their governments' bellicosity. Thus, nationalism was shaped to fit all purposes: at home policy was presented as defensive patriotism and enemy nations as nationalistic, while enemy populations were encouraged to be pacifist whereas their governments were presented as chauvinistic.

More revealing for our purposes are the implications of propaganda in general. If we accept governmental estimates that their populations needed to be made more nationalistic, then we have a gauge of the paucity of popular nationalism. If government efforts to fabricate nationalism were successful, then we must attribute any resulting popular nationalism less to the masses than to their handlers. Conversely, to the extent that propaganda was unsuccessful, nationalism played a minor role. In short, the whole propaganda enterprise constitutes an argument against the power of popular nationalism.

Compulsion

In addition to persuading their populations with propaganda, governments had the recourse of compulsion. In explaining the four years of popular acceptance of the war, obedience may be as important as conviction.

The rapid growth of state power during the war is generally acknowledged.[54] Total war implied total control which took many forms. Some were imposed directly, the most obvious being mobilization: soldiers had no effective choice but to obey and opposition to the war was subject to severe, even mortal, reprisal. Direct control of civilians was more negative in the sense of prohibiting resistance to the war effort by such measures as the Defense of the Realm Act (DORA) in England[55] which allowed governments to restrict pacifist activities.[56] The workplace was brought more directly under control through agreements among government, labor, and management such as the Auxiliary Service Law in Germany and the Munitions Act in Britain.[57] Other forms of compulsion were more indirect. Governmental control over food distribution and social welfare gave enormous powers to influence morale either positively (as in Britain) or negatively (as in Germany).[58] The early domestic political truces—the union sacree in France and the Burgfrieden in Germany—allowed government to elicit wartime support in exchange for the carrot of postwar reform.[59]

The existence of mass compulsion does not imply universal passive acquiescence or sullen obedience, nor does it exclude enthusiastic support for the war. But neither does the continued support of the war by the majority of populations necessarily demonstrate enthusiasm. For those who were unenthusiastic, there was, however, little recourse but obedience. To the extent that governments had the power to compel this obedience, nationalism became less necessary.

War Aims, Policy and Strategy

War aims, diplomatic policy, and military strategy have been interpreted as being driven by nationalism, as when "the national principle showed itself as aggressive 'war aims.'"[60] As self-evident as it may seem, this assertion should be scrutinized.

It is undeniable that the war aims of all the belligerents (excepting Belgium) were expansive.[61] Yet what is notable about official war aims is their secrecy. Certainly one motivation for this confidentiality was to avoid both the jealousy of allies and fears of enemies: as German Chancellor Theobald von Bethmann Hollweg commented, "we are keeping all the cards in our hands hidden from the enemy's eyes."[62] An equally powerful consideration was domestic public opinion. All governments had taken great pains to present the war as defensive on the assumption that doing so was necessary to win mass support; wartime propaganda continued on this tack to preserve the fragile domestic truce which might be destroyed by a public debate on war aims.[63] In short, governments recognized that there was no consensus for extreme nationalism and expansive war aims. Consequently, they not only concealed their own aims but simultaneously sought to prevent publication and discussion of expansive unofficial programs.[64] Even after these restraints were removed, governments continued to conceal expansionist aims out of the recognition that a significant part of their populations were unwilling to continue the war for annexations.[65]

While certainly expansive, official programs on the aims of war were not strictly speaking nationalistic so much as power-seeking in the tradition of Realpolitik and cabinet diplomacy; Napoleon and Louis XIV would have felt thoroughly at home with them. Furthermore, except for the irredentist aims of France for Alsace-Lorraine and Italy for the Trentino from Austria, these aims were multinational and imperial (whether European or colonial) in their envisaged acquisition of non-nationals. These official programs were driven in part by domestic considerations—above all, the notion of rewarding the public for its war effort and shifting the cost to the defeated enemy populations. But official aims of war were seldom a response to unofficial war aims proposals. Rather they reflected policy and strategic considerations, at once a wish list and—especially after the military deadlock emerged—a barometer of shifting battlefield prospects.

If wartime diplomacy is described as nationalistic in the sense of being expansionist, the role of nationalism in this formulation should be questioned. The crucial element for policy was less nationalistic considerations than winning the war—i.e., the traditional power objective of states. Specifically, statesmen sought to maintain their own alliances and to disrupt enemy alliances in what was essentially a coalition conflict.[66] The changing demands of this policy required flexibility above all in war aims, thus their secrecy and the need to prevent public discussion of them particularly by avid nationalists. Nor indeed were statesmen seriously affected by domestic pressures as they formulated policy largely without regard for public opinion: British Foreign Secretary Sir Edward Grey and his Foreign Office colleagues were typical in priding "themselves on their detachment from the changing moods of public opinion." Traditional cabinet diplomacy, not popular nationalism, was their guide.

In a limited sense, military strategy can also be seen as motivated by nationalism. There were specific instances of strategy's being driven by national reconquest, most notably, the French attack in Alsace-Lorraine. Normally war aims were, however, the consequence more than the cause of strategy. Germany had not invaded Belgium and France in order to annex territory so much as to defeat the French army, just as Alsace-Lorraine had been attacked by the French army primarily to defeat Germany, and Poland had been invaded by Russia above all to defeat Germany and Austria-Hungary. These and subsequent offensives had been motivated on the one hand by the wartime diplomatic concern to keep allies from or to force enemies into a separate peace. They had also been designed to reassure domestic opinion that the war could still be won; again, defeatism more than nationalism was the operative concern.

Nonetheless, the main strategic objective obviously remained victory. This self-evident fact was formulated with characteristically brutal succinctness by two of the war's dominant leaders, Britain's David Lloyd George, who advocated a "knockout blow," and France's Georges Clemenceau, who stated "I make war."[67] The central strategic irony of the war was, however, that it began with the assumption of a short war through rapid offensives but actually produced a long war characterized by tenacious defense. Indeed, the major successes and failures of the war were defensive: the two battles of the Marne, Verdun, the Somme, and Tannenberg were the great defensive successes, while the German defeat of the Bolsheviks in 1918 was a failure of Russian defense and the final Allied victory was a failure of German defense. In this sense, military strategy produced for much of the war the defense governments and populations claimed they wanted. Far from being the result of popular nationalism, however, military strategy largely determined morale much more than did propaganda. As one contemporary observed, "the real propaganda is facts and results" on the battlefield.[68]

Sub-nationalities

Nowhere would the role of nationalism seem more self-evident than amongst the subject nationalities. This appeared appropriate since the "vital contributory cause to World War I was the repression of nationalities."[69] The question of the sub-nationalities took several different forms. One was the defensive effort of multinational states to preserve themselves by pacifying their own subject nationalities. In a game of mutual deception, the rulers of the Habsburg Monarchy sought wartime support from their subject nationalities in order to preserve the old structure, whereas the subject peoples responded because they hoped for reforms.[70] This was, however, a game doomed from the start: the Monarchy would not give concessions when they might have been acceptable and granted them only when they were no longer relevant. A similar blind man's bluff occurred in German, British, and Russian policies toward their sub-nationalities.

There were, however, two fundamental flaws in the assertion that these defensive policies toward subject nationalities demonstrated the importance of nationalism. First, it pushes the definition of nationalism beyond the limits of semantic credibility to characterize the policies of these multinational empires as nationalism—as imperialism or supra-nationalism or perhaps best as anti-nationalism but surely not nationalism. Second, all parties to this game were aware that wartime policies were built on the shifting sands of battlefield fortunes: not disingenuous promises but the military outcome would determine the internal structure of these empires.

A second form of sub-nationalism is the obverse of these policies, namely, the aspirations of the subject peoples for self-determination which can be seen as an important factor during the war. Certainly the subject peoples had aspirations for change, though in quite varying degrees and generally for reform rather than independence.[71] The most notable and, indeed, most important fact is that, like all the belligerent populations, the vast majority of subject nationalities did not revolt and in fact continued to serve, most notably in the Habsburg army.[72] Only when the war's outcome was clear did the sub-nationalities opt for independence.[73] Until then, they influenced the course of events hardly at all.

A third form of sub-nationalism was irredentism, i.e., the aspirations of existing states for co-nationals in other countries. The cases are numerous: France for Alsace-Lorraine, Serbia for Bosnian Serbs,

Italy for the Trentino, Rumania for Transylvania, Bulgaria for Macedonia. In the case of France, for instance, there was a universal consensus on Alsace-Lorraine, though a notable lack of positive interest in it or in revenge among French troops.[74] Certainly all these states acknowledged that such irredentism could be used to arouse public support for war but it was not the prime motive. Serbia entered the war less to expand than to survive as an independent state, France to remain a great power, Italy to become one, and Rumania and Bulgaria to expand their power.

Yet another form of sub-nationalism was as a tool of great power war diplomacy. To a greater or lesser degree, all the belligerents sought to provoke rebellion among the sub-nationalities of their opponents. The Germans particularly and the Austro-Hungarians (understandably with more trepidation) encouraged revolt in Russia.[75] They thereby tested what one German diplomat described as the orange theory that Russia could be peeled apart into its constituent ethnic parts.[76] The actual peeling occurred, however, after the Treaty of Brest-Litovsk in 1918, i.e., only as a consequence not as a cause of military defeat. Playing on their role as leader of the Slavs, the Russians pursued the same objective in Poland and the Habsburg Monarchy but, lacking the necessary military victories, had only limited success.

Concerned at first about the possibility of creating a central European power vacuum over which Germany and Russia would contend, the French and British were more cautious at first about encouraging revolt among Habsburg sub-nationalities. They did so only when military desperation required it in 1918.[77] But precisely these parlous military prospects limited the policy's success: central Europeans realized that their future depended on military events not ephemeral promises. As it turned out, political revolt—the Russian revolution—overshadowed sub-national revolts and the single most successful operation was the German facilitation of Lenin's return to Russia.

Thus, sub-nationalism was more a tool of great power policies than a factor in itself. Great power flirtation with this form of revolution bore fruit only at the end of the war and then because of military events rather than the nationalism of the subject nationalities. Great power diplomacy was governed primarily by Realpolitik, which had always prescribed that smaller political entities would serve great power objectives. Given this precedent, the powers necessarily had to deal practically, even cynically, with the sub-nationalities. It is revealing perhaps that the most convinced devotee of the sub-nationalities was Woodrow Wilson, who was least motivated by expansive war aims.

Finally, the colonial peoples can be regarded as a special case of sub-nationalities. Not regarded as a direct cause of the war, colonial nationalism was nonetheless evident, though not widespread, before the war. The colonial peoples were, however, indirectly implicated in the great power war: all the powers had colonial aspirations at their opponents' expense and the war almost unavoidably insured imperial diminution for the vanquished. The eventual redistribution of colonial booty at Versailles reaffirmed—however much it could not insure—the passive status of colonial peoples. As in central Europe, the extra-European subject nationalities were close to a non-factor.

Conclusions and Implications

Nationalism is widely viewed as a significant factor during the First World War. The above analysis suggests that this verdict should be reconsidered. Despite the widely touted enthusiasm of August 1914, public opinion in the belligerent states was more reserved than enthusiastic. We know only that the vast majority of populations accepted the war but not why: perhaps out of defensive patriotism, perhaps political passivity, perhaps repressed rebelliousness, but probably not widespread aggressive nationalism. Precisely this concern about insufficient nationalism was the basic impulse behind official and unofficial propaganda; while propaganda's efficacy is difficult to gauge, it seems clear that aggressive nationalism was not widely produced. The most critical players, soldiers at the front, appear to have been the least boisterous nationalists despite propaganda directed at them; dogged tenacity, desperate survival, and loyalty to comrades appear to be more typical of their sentiments. Although the war produced growing strains both at home and at the front, they were matched by the augmented powers of governmental control over information, the workplace, social welfare and food, and the individual. While expansive unofficial war-aims programs sometimes managed to evade the censors, official war aims were kept secret, adjusted to reflect battlefield events, and motivated more by traditional great power pursuit of power than by mass nationalism which was an anathema to cabinet diplomacy. Often seen as a central issue, sub-nationalism proves to be more tool than motor of great power policy. In short, nationalism's role during the war appears to be less central than it is often portrayed.

If this conclusion is persuasive, it has some revealing implications for our understanding of the war. The widely held view of nationalism's role suggests that the war was significantly influenced by it. Statesmen and generals became subject to this force and their individual responsibility was correspondingly less critical in explaining the war's course. It suggests likewise that the war's outbreak and outcome, being the consequence of such a force, were to that extent unavoidable. The present interpretation implies the reverse. If the role of nationalism is diminished, then one must look elsewhere for an understanding of the First World War. The traditional emphasis on decision-makers seems more persuasive and the course of the war is accordingly determined above all by their choices on the basis of prevailing assumptions about state relations—secret diplomacy, state power, the balance of power, and war as a valid tool of policy.

These observations can likewise be extended to the whole era of the world wars and, indeed, the twentieth century. The prominence of nationalism is widely seen in fascism, nazism, totalitarianism and the Second World War which followed from them. Thus, the Second World War is viewed as "even more of a national struggle than World War I,"[78] the era of the world wars marked nationalism's "flood tide,"[79] and, consequently, nationalism is "the most potent political force in the twentieth century."[80] This interpretation implies that nationalism significantly influenced, even determined, the course of events which statesmen could exploit but not alter. The present argument suggests that twentieth century nationalism may have been less an independent force than a tool in the hands of leaders.

The present analysis also influences our understanding of nationalism itself. Nationalism can be viewed as significant during the First World War only if it is embodied in public opinion, propaganda, the morale of soldiers at the front, war aims, statecraft, strategy, and the sub-nationalities, as examined above. Heretofore a definition of nationalism has been specifically eschewed in favor of accepting the conventional usage. It is, however, necessary to confront what might be called nationalism's definition dilemma.

Broadly defined to incorporate all wartime behavior, nationalism becomes a garment which fits all sizes. As such, it would seem to be represented in all the forms discussed above and to be highly significant. But, because it thereby homogenizes public opinion and all views become nationalism, nothing is explained. Conversely, nationalism can be defined narrowly as enthusiastic, mass aggressiveness and thereby distinguished from resigned, defensive patriotism. This distinction is in fact made in the literature between "national sentiment and nationalism," between "true nationalism" and "the will to defend,"[81] between "the true character of nationalism, [namely] 'warrior enthusiasm,'" as opposed to "resignation and resolution."[82]

Defined in this narrow sense, there is little evidence of nationalism: admittedly some is evidenced by the ruling classes (especially though not exclusively in Germany) but little by the vast majority of society. Even if it were seen as widely held, however, nationalism in this narrow sense was not influential because governments largely disregarded public opinion. The more aggressive government propaganda can be regarded as nationalism but in practice governments were less concerned with arousing mass aggressiveness than with insuring tenacity, i.e., maintaining defensive patriotism against the more serious danger of war fatigue. Whatever its success (which was probably marginal), seeing propaganda as nationalism makes nationalism essentially official policy rather than public opinion, a tool of government rather than a pressure on it.

Perceiving government policy in general (war aims, diplomacy, and strategy) as nationalism simply equates nationalism with aggressiveness. Nationalism in this sense is certainly important—indeed virtually universal and eternal—but explains nothing in particular. The definition dilemma can therefore be reduced to this: if nationalism is broadly defined, it is important but not useful as an explanation; if narrowly defined, it is useful but not important. Nationalism is best defined narrowly as mass aggressiveness but the masses were by and large not aggressive and the aggressors were not the masses.

The above analysis has some comparably awkward implications for the prevailing system of periodization. The history of Western civilization is structured as medieval, early modern, and modern. This construct is founded on the assumption that each of these periods is homogeneous within itself and distinctive relative to the others. Modern history is definable as such because it evidences characteristic features, including nationalism which is seen as being exclusively and distinctively modern. To the extent that this distinctiveness is accepted, modern civilization is validly demarcated from its predecessors. The prominence of nationalism is nowhere more widely claimed than in the First World War, itself a distinctive feature of modern civilization. The analysis suggested here, however, questions the assertion that the First World War is distinctively and significantly nationalistic. To that extent, the uniqueness of modern civilization is diminished and the prevailing system of periodization brought into question.

Notes to Chapter 6

1. D. Kaiser, Politics and War: European Conflict from Philip II to Hitler, Cambridge, MA, 1990, p. 334.
2. C.B. Hayes, Nationalism: A Religion, New York, 1960, p. 122.
3. M. Howard, War in European History, Oxford, 1976, p. 134.
4. J. Willms, Nationalismus ohne Nation: Deutsche Geschichte von 1789 bis 1914, Munich, 1983, p. 695.
5. J.-J. Becker, 1914: Comment les Francais sont entres dans la guerre, Paris, 1977. G. Krumeich, "L'entree en guerre en allemagne," in J.-J. Becker and S. Audouin-Rouzeau (eds.), Les societes europeennes et la guerre de 1914–1918, Nanterre, 1990, p. 66.
6. J.-B. Becker, Victoire et frustrations, 1914–1929, Paris, 1990, p. 26. P. Bouyoux, "La population de Toulouse et le sentiment national pendant la premiere guerre mondiale," J.-J. Becker and S. Audoin-Rouzeau (eds.), societes, p. 247. J.-J. Becker, "Voila le glas de nos gars qui sonne," in P. Fridenson, 1914–1918, L'autre front, Paris, 1977, p. 13.
7. Becker, Victoire, p. 26. See also: F. Caron, La France des patriotes, Paris, 1985, p. 10. P. J. Flood, France 1914–1918: Public Opinion and the War Effort, Baisingstoke, 1990, p. 32. D. Dahlmann, "Russia at the Outbreak of the First World War," J.-J. Becker and S. Audoin-Rouzeau, (eds.) Societes, pp. 58–59.
8. E. Demm, "Les intellectuels allemands et la guerre," in J.-J. Becker and S. Audoin-Rouzeau (eds.), Societes, pp.183–99. R.N. Stromberg, Redemption by War: The Intellectuals and 1914, Lawrence, 1982.
9. J. Williams, The Home Front: Britain, France and Germany, 1914–1918, London, 1972, p. 145. Flood, France, p. 32. S. Audoin-Rouzeau, 14–18, Les combattants des tranchees, Paris, 1986, p. 181. S. Audoin-Rouzeau, "The National Sentiment of the Soldiers during the Great War," in R. Tombs (ed.), Nationhood and Nationalism in France from Boulangism to the Great War 1889–1918, New York, 1991, p. 97. Krumeich, "L'entree," p. 66. Becker, Victoire, pp. 115, 121.
10. J. Kocka, Klassengesellschaft im Krieg, Gottingen, 1973, pp. 42–43. M.L. Sanders and P.M. Taylor, British Propaganda during the First World War, 1914–1918, London, 1982, pp. 11, 252. Audoin-Rouzeau, 1914, p. 181. B. Vigezzi, "L'Italie Liberale—gouvernement, partis, vie sociale—et l'interventon dans la premiere guerre mondiale," in J.-J. Becker and Audoin-Rouzeau (eds.), societes, pp. 104–6. Becker, Victoire, p. 129. C. Haste, Keep the Home Fires Burning: Propaganda in the First World War, London, 1977, pp. 40–41. Williams, Home, p. 145. P. Melograni, "Les soldats et la population civile italienne en 1917," in J.-J. Becker and S. Audoin-Rouzeau, societes, p. 335. J.-J. Becker, La France en guerre: 1914–1918, Bruxelles/Paris, 1988, pp. 118–22. Caron, France, pp. 577–80.
11. Kocka, Klassenkampf, pp. 42–43. W. Deist, "Censorship and Propaganda in

Germany during the First World War," in J.-J. Becker and S. Audoin-Rouzeau, (eds.) societes, pp. 203–4.
12. Becker, Victoire, p. 136. Bouyoux, "population," p. 254.
13. Becker, "Voila," p. 13, 27. J. B. Duroselle, "Preface," in J.-J. Becker and S. Audoin-Rouzeau, (eds.) societes, p. 21. Dahlmann, "Russia," p. 58. Vigezzi, "L'Italie," p. 94. Audoin-Rouzeau, "'Bourrage de crane,'" et information en France en 1914–1918," in J.-J. Becker and S. Audoin-Rouzeau (eds.), societes, pp.163–64.
14. S. Audoin-Rouzeau, 14, p. 98. Bouyoux, "population," pp. 246, 248. Krumeich, "L'entree," p. 71. Cochet, "Les soldats francais," in J.-J. Becker and S. Audoin-Rouzeau (eds.), pp. 357–58. Audoin-Rouzeau, "Bourrage," pp. 163–64.
15. Audoin-Rouzeau, "Sentiment," pp. 95–96.
16. Ibid., p. 91.
17. For prewar government fears about mobilization, see for instance: J.-J. Becker, Le Carnet B: les pouvoirs publics et l'anti-militarisme avant la guerre de 1914, Paris, 1973. For successful mobilization, see for instance: Dahlmann, "Russia," p. 59. Caron, France, p. 571. Flood, France, p. 13.
18. Becker, "Voila," p. 33. Becker, Victoire, p. 26. Krumeich, "L'entree," p. 71. Vigezzi, "L'Italie," pp. 111–12.
19. Audoin-Rouzeau, "Sentiment," p. 94. Krumeich "L'Entree," p. 66. Caron, France, pp. 565, 571–12. Flood, France, pp. 9–11. Dahlmann, "Russia," p. 59. Becker, "Voila," pp. 22–26, 33. Becker, Victoire, p. 26.
20. Audoin-Rouzeau, "Sentiment," p. 94.
21. Audoin-Rouzeau, 14, p. 202. Cochet, "soldats," pp. 112–17. Caron, France, pp. 357, 577–78. Becker, France, p. 112–17.
22. J. Delmas, "L'armee russe vue par les officiers francais affectes en Russie 1916–1917," J.-J. Becker and S. Audoin-Rouzeau (eds.), societes, pp. 379–83. Cochet, "soldats," pp. 359-60. Caron, France, pp. 577, 580–81. Audoin-Rouzeau, 14, pp. 203–4. Becker, Victoire, pp. 106–9. G. Pedroncini, Les mutineries de 1917, Paris, 1967. P. Melograni, "Les soldats et la poplulation civile italienne en 1917," J.-J. Becker and S. Audoin-Rouzeau, (eds.) societes, p. 333.
23. Audoin-Rouzeau, "sentiment," p. 96.
24. Cochet, "soldats," p. 361. Becker, France, pp. 39–40. Audoin-Rouzeau, 14, pp. 181, 195–99, 212.
25. G. Krumeich, "Le soldat allemand sur la Somme," J.-J. Becker and S. Audoin-Rouzeau (eds.), societes, pp. 367–74.
26. Cochet, "soldats," pp. 358–60, 364–65. Becker, France, p. 43. Audoin-Rouzeau, 14, pp. 199–204, 214. Audoin-Rouzeau, "sentiment," pp. 97–98. Duroselle, "Preface," p. 20.
27. Caron, France, p. 580.
28. Haste, Keep, p. 2 and also p. 1 ("The aim of propagandists is the direction and control of public opinion toward certain ends.") and pp. 20–21 ("creating and directing public opinion ... manipulating"). See also: Flood, France, p. 17. Deist, "Censorship," p. 200 ("manipulation of public opinion"). J.-C. Montant, "L'organisation centrale des services d'informations et de propagande du Quai d'Orsay pendant la grande guerre," in J.-J. Becker and S. Audoin-Rouzeau (eds.), societes, p. 135 ("mobilization of consciences"). Demm, "intellectuels," p. 184 ("mobilize the population intellectually and morally"). H.D. Lasswell, Propaganda Technique in World War I, Cambridge, MA, 1971.
29. Lasswell, Propaganda, p. 9. See also: Haste, Keep, p. 140 ("frenzy of hatred of the enemy"). Demm, "intellectuels," p. 183.
30. P. Buitenhuis, The Great War of Words: British, American and Canadian Propaganda and Fiction, Vancouver, 1987, p. 22.

31. Haste, Keep, p. 1. Deist, "Censorship," p. 200. Demm, "intellectuels," p. 183.
32. See works cited above: Haste, Flood, Lasswell, Williams, Montant, Audouin-Rouzeau ("Bourrage"), Hiley, Demm, Deist. See also: M.L. Sanders and P. M. Taylor, British Propaganda during the First World War, 1914–1918, London, 1982. F.P. Chambers, The War Behind the War: A History of the Political and Civilian Fronts, London, 1939. N. Hiley, "The News Media and British Propaganda 1914–1918," J.-J. Becker and S. Audoin-Rouzeau (eds.), societes.
33. Flood, France, pp. 84–96. Caron, France, p. 565.
34. Becker, France, pp. 44–48. Flood, France, pp. 96–106. G. Besier, "Les eglises protestantes en Allemagne, en Grand-Bretagne, en France, et le front interieur 1914–1918," in J.-J. Becker and S. Ausdoin-Rouzeau (eds.), societes, pp. 211–36.
35. Hiley, "News," pp. 175–81. Flood, France, p. 79.
36. M.S. Coetzee, "Popular Nationalism in Germany during World War I," History of European Ideas, vol. 15, No.1–3 (1992), pp. 369–75.
37. J.M. Winter, "Nationalism, the Visual Arts, and the Myth of War Enthusiasm in 1914," History of European Ideas, vol. 15, No. 1–3 (1992), pp. 357–62.
38. Buitenhuis, Great, pp. 16–20. Demm, "intellectuels," pp. 183–97. J.-F. Sirinelli, "Les intellectuels francais et la guerre," in J.-J. Becker and S. Audoin-Rouzeau (eds.) societes, pp. 145–61. F. Coetzee, "English Nationalism and the First World War," History of European Ideas, vol. 15, No. 1–3 (1992), pp. 363-68. L.L. Farrar, jr., "The Artist as Propagandist," in S.J. Stang (ed.), The Presence of Ford Maddox Ford, Philadelphia, 1981, pp. 145–60.
39. Haste, Keep, pp. 40–41.
40. Ibid., p. 31, pp. 29 and 34 ("bringing down the veil"). See also: Flood, France, pp. 24–32, 79–84. Buitenhuis, Great, pp. 79–80 ("the paper curtain"). Audoin-Rouzeau, "Bourrage," pp. 165, 169. Becker, Victoire, pp. 127–28. Williams, Home, pp. 24–25. Montant, "L'organisation," pp. 136–37. Deist, "Censorship," pp. 201, 203. Hiley, "News," pp. 176, 179. Sirinelli, "intellectuels," pp. 148–49, 155. For censorship of troops see: Becker, France, pp. 112–17. Flood, France, p. 108. Audoin-Rouzeau, 1914, pp. 191–92. Cochet, soldats, p. 358.
41. Flood, France, p. 80.
42. Audoin-Rouzeau, 14, p. 3. Sirinelli, "intellectuels," pp. 147–48.
43. Sanders and Taylor, Propaganda, p. 251.
44. Haste, Keep, p. 49.
45. Audoin-Rouzeau, 14, p. 214. Audoin-Rouzeau, "Bourrage," p. 172. Audoin-Rouzeau, "Sentiment," p. 92. Melograni, "soldats," p. 333.
46. Deist, "Censorship," p. 206.
47. Buitenhuis, Great, pp. xvii–iii, 54–79. Sanders and Taylor, British, pp. 200–8.
48. Haste, Keep, pp. 37–38, 40. Chambers, War, pp. 226–27. Williams, Home, p. 27. Montant, "organisation," p. 136.
49. Demm, "intellectuels," p. 184. Sanders and Taylor, British, pp. 208–9, 244–45. Chambers, War, pp. 227–28. G. G. Bruntz, Allied Propaganda and the Collapse of the German Empire in 1918, New York, 1938. G. Huber, Die franzosische Propaganda im Weltkrieg gegen Deutschland 1914 bis 1918, Munich, 1928.
50. Sanders and Taylor, British, pp. 244–45, 256–58. Haste, Keep, pp. 5–6.
51. Erich Ludendorff, My War Memoirs, London, 1922, p. 360.
52. Sanders and Taylor, British, p. 252 and p. 258 ("impossible to assess in any precise terms").
53. Ibid., p. 257.
54. K. Burk, Transformation of the British Government, 1914–1919, Boston, 1982. K. Burk (ed.), War and the State, London, 1985.
55. Sanders and Taylor, British, p. 9.

56. Haste, Keep, pp. 140–79. K. Robbins, The Abolition of War: The 'Peace Movement' in Britain 1914–1919, Cardiff, 1976. F.L. Carsten, War against War: British and German Radical Movements in the First World War, London, 1982.
57. F. Boll, "Le probleme ouvrier et les greves. L"Allemagne 1914–1918," in J.-J. Becker and S. Audoin-Rouzeau (eds.), pp. 265–66. G.D. Feldman, Army, Industry and Labor in Germany, 1914–1918, Princeton, 1966. Burk, Transformation. G. Hardach, "La mobilisation industrielle en 1914–1918: production, planification et ideologie," in P. Fridenson, 1914, pp. 81–110.
58. R. Wall and J.M. Winter (eds.), The Upheaval of War: Family, Work and Welfare in Europe 1914–1918, Cambridge, UK, 1988, pp. 453–67. P. Barral, "Le Paysannerie francaise a l'arriere," J.-J. Becker and S. Audoin-Rouzeau (eds.), societes, pp. 242–43. Melogrini, "soldats," pp. 334–35.
59. Kocka, Klassengesellschaft, pp. 37–40. Caron, France, pp. 586–88.
60. E. Holzle, Die Selbstentmachung Europas, Gottingen, 1975, p. 336.
61. F. Fischer, Germany's Aims in the First World War, New York, 1967. P. Renouvin, "Les buts de guerre du gouvernement francais, 1914–1918," Revue historique, 235 (1966), pp. 1–38. D. Stevenson, French War Aims against Germany, 1914–1919, Oxford, 1982. V.H. Rothwell, British War Aims and Peace Diplomacy 1914–1918, Oxford, 1971. C. J. Smith, The Russian Struggle for Power, 1914–1917, New York, 1956.
62. Fischer, Germany's, p. 98.
63. Ibid., p. 96. Deist,"Censorship," p. 204. Duroselle, "Preface," pp. 17–18.
64. On extreme unofficial aims, see: Fischer, Germany's, pp. 155–83, 164–73. On government efforts to avoid public discussion, see: ibid., pp. 165–66. Deist, "Censorship," pp. 202–3.
65. Becker, Victoire, pp. 115–16. Haste, Keep, pp. 174–75. Deist, "Censorship," p. 205.
66. L.L. Farrar, jr. Divide and Conquer: German Efforts to Conclude a Separate Peace, 1914–1918, Boulder, 1978.
67. Sanders and Taylor, British, p. 3 cites Steiner.
68. Haste, Keep, p. 41. Becker, Victoire, p. 120.
69. Sanders and Taylor, British, p. 252.
70. L.L. Snyder, The Making of Modern Man, Princeton, 1967, p. 592.
71. A.J.P. Taylor, The Habsburg Monarchy 1809–1918, New York, 1948, pp. 236–48. B. Jelavich, The Habsburg Empire in European Affairs, 1814–1918, Chicago, 1969, pp. 168–69.
72. Ibid.
73. Jelavich, Habsburg, p. 168. I. Deak, "The Ethnic Question in the Multinational Habsburg Army, 1848–1918," in N.F. Dreisziger (ed.), Ethnic Armies, Waterloo, Ontario, Canada, 1990, pp. 43–44.
74. Taylor, Habsburg, pp. 249–51. Jelavich, Habsburg, p. 170.
75. Becker, Victoire, pp. 115–16. Audoin-Rouzeau, 14, p. 204. Audoin-Rouzeau, "sentiment," p. 97.
76. Fischer, Germany's, pp. 120–26, 132-46.-Demm,"intellectuels,"pp. 191–92. E. Zechlin, "Friedensbestrebungen und Revolutionierungsversuche," in Aus Politik und Zeitgeschichte, Beilagen zur Wochenzeitung Das Parlament, 17 May 1961, 14 June 1961, 21 June 1961.
77. Farrar, Divide, p. 29.
78. D. Stevenson, The First World War and International Politics, Oxford, 1988, p. 217. Haste, Keep, p. 175. Chambers, War, p. 495. Taylor, Habsburg, p. 236.
79. Hayes, Religion, p. 151.
80. C.B. Hayes, Essays on Nationalism, New York, 1926, p. 29.

81. L.L. Snyder, Varieties of Nationalism: A Comparative Study, Hinsdale, 1976, p. 46.
82. Audoin-Rouzeau, "sentiment," pp. 89, 96.
83. Krumeich, "L'entree," p. 66.

Select Bibliography

Audoin-Rouzeau, S., *14–18, Les combattants des tranchees*, Paris, 1986. A revealing work based on soldiers' letters and military censors (English translation by Berg).

Becker, J.-J., and Audoin-Rouzeau, S. (eds.), *Les societes europeennes et la guerre de 1914–1918*, Nanterre, 1990. An outstanding collection of articles on the social, economic, and domestic political aspects of the war in most of the belligerent states (in French or English).

Fischer, F., *Germany's Aims in the First World War*, New York, 1967. The best study of German war aims and the standard for the question in general.

Flood, P.J., *France 1914–1918: Public Opinion and the War Effort*, Basingstoke, 1990. A straightforward account; the best in English.

Haste, C., *Keep the Home Fires Burning: Propaganda in the First World War*, London, 1977. Excellent study of British propaganda at home.

Sanders, M.L., and Taylor, P.M., *British Propaganda during the First World War, 1914–1918*, London, 1982. Focuses on British efforts abroad.

Stevenson, D., *The First World War and International Politics*, Oxford, 1988. The best general diplomatic history of the war.

Williams, J., *The Home Front: Britain, France and Germany, 1914–1918*, London, 1972. An able comparative study.

CHAPTER 7

LOVE AND DEATH
War and Gender in Britain, 1914–1918

Susan Kingsley Kent

The broken world[1] to which belligerents returned at the end of 1918 offered little solace to societies devastated by four years of unprecedented loss and destruction. Across Europe, soldiers and civilians, men and women, elites and commoners, victors and vanquished alike, faced disorder in every aspect of their lives.

The upheavals produced by the First World War provoked responses designed to recreate the social, political, and economic order that had prevailed prior to August of 1914. In recasting bourgeois Europe along corporatist economic and political lines, conservative forces sought to re-establish stability and to reassert their status in a world that looked and felt dramatically different from that of the prewar period.[2] In cultural terms, too, attempts to return to what was perceived to be a quieter, happier, more ordered time, were prodigious. Nowhere is this more evident than in the realm of gender identity and relations between men and women. Political and economic restructuring found their counterpart—indeed, their necessary corollary—in the reconstruction of gender after the Great War.

Sensitive and compelling studies detailing the impact of the war on masculinity and male identity have only recently been joined by similar work on femininity and female identity.[3] Historians who have tried to assess the impact of the war on the roles and position of

---

Notes for this chapter begin on page 172.

women in Britain have generally been limited by their approaches and methodologies to an exercise in measurement—of employment, wage levels, or rights.[4] Because such indices of change do not necessarily gauge shifts in the asymmetries of power that marked the relations of men and women in the interwar period, these studies can tell us little about how the Great War transformed the lives of men and women, their relationships with one another, and the cultural understandings of gender and sexuality that informed their consciousness and sense of identity.

This essay analyzes the impact of the war on the fashioning of gender identity as a means of helping to understand what happened to British feminism in the interwar years. The experiences of the Great War—articulated and represented in specific languages of gender and sexuality—forged dramatically different ideas about gender and sexual identity for many men and women from those prevailing in the late Victorian and Edwardian eras; these languages and the identities they spawned provide the context within which interwar feminism operated and by which it was constrained.

The outbreak of war in August 1914 brought to a halt the activities of both militant and constitutional suffragists in their efforts to gain votes for women. By that time, the suffrage campaign had attained the size and status of a mass movement, commanding the time, energies, and resources of thousands of men and women, and riveting the attention of the British public. In early 1918, in what it defined as a gesture of recognition for women's contribution to the war effort, Parliament granted the vote to women over the age of thirty. This measure, while welcome to feminists as a symbol of the fall of the sex barrier, failed to enfranchise some three million out of eleven million adult women. When war ended, feminists continued to agitate for votes for women on the same terms as they had been granted to men; but organized feminism, despite the fact that a considerable portion of the potential female electorate remained disenfranchised, never regained its prewar status as a mass movement. By the end of the 1920s, feminism as a distinct political and social movement had become insignificant. Feminists' understandings of masculinity and femininity—of gender and sexual identity—became transformed during the war and in the postwar period, until they were virtually indistinguishable from those of anti-feminists.

With the onset of the Great War, many feminists began to modify their understandings of masculinity and femininity. Their insistence upon equality with men, and the acknowledgment of the model of sex war that accompanied that demand, gradually gave way to an ideology that emphasized women's special sphere—a separate sphere, in fact—and carried with it an urgent belief in the relationship between the sexes as one of complementarity. Prewar feminists had vigorously attacked the notion of separate spheres and the medical and scientific discourses about gender and sexuality upon which those spheres rested. Many feminists after the First World War, by contrast, pursued a program that championed rather than challenged the prevailing ideas about masculinity and femininity that appeared in the literature of psychoanalysis and sexology. In embracing radically new—and seemingly liberating—views of women as human beings with sexual identities, many feminists within the mainstream National Union of Societies for Equal Citizenship (NUSEC) accepted theories of sexual difference that helped to advance notions of separate spheres for men and women. This shift did not take place suddenly, and was resisted throughout the 1920s by many other feminists who took themselves off to form such organizations as the Six Point Group and the Open Door Council, but the acceptance of the dominant discourse on sexuality represented a fundamental abandonment of prewar feminist ideology. By the end of the 1920s, so-called "new" feminists found themselves in a conceptual bind that trapped women in "traditional" domestic and maternal roles, and limited their ability to advocate equality and justice for women.

This fundamental change, this embracing of what amounted to an anti-feminist understanding of masculinity and femininity, came about as a consequence of the languages by means of which women's experiences and perceptions of the Great War were articulated. Those women who were able to hold on to prewar understandings about gender—who came to be called egalitarian or "old" feminists, though many were not old enough to have participated in the prewar suffrage campaign—were those who had experienced the war directly, at the front. Most "new" feminists, by contrast, saw the war from afar, from home. This difference of position vis à vis the war and its participants became manifested in differing sexualized languages by means of which the war was articulated, and accounts, at least in part, for old and new feminists holding fundamentally different understandings about masculinity, femininity, and as a consequence, feminism.

The sexual imagery utilized to represent the war changed over time, reflecting developments in the prosecution and fortunes of the war and the extent to which the home front was involved. During the first phase, lasting from August 1914 into 1915, the war was often depicted as a remasculinization of English culture, perceived to have become degenerate and effeminate in the years before August of 1914. This kind of representation relied upon a corresponding imagery of women as refemininized, especially in the aftermath of a widespread feminist movement that had challenged the dominant cultural norms of masculinity and femininity. Thus, an assertion of and emphasis on traditional notions of separate spheres for men and women characterized the first year of the war. It was accompanied by the notion of war as unleashed sexual desire, best exemplified by the gruesome tales of German atrocities committed against Belgian women that spread through the land.

The reassertion of separate spheres with its implied dichotomies of private and public, of different natures of women and men, of home and front, appeared very early, even among feminists. Merely cursory readings of *Common Cause*, the organ of the National Union of Women's Suffrage Societies, reveal a shift of focus from public, political affairs in July 1914 to more traditional women's concerns in August 1914. The National Union itself, in an unreflexive, almost knee-jerk reaction to war, turned to work that emphasized gender divisions, and declared its conviction that feminists' greatest and most obvious responsibilities in sustaining the vital strength of the nation were those pertaining to domesticity. "We ... very early arrived at the conclusion," Millicent Fawcett, longtime president of the National Union of Suffrage Societies, recalled after the war, "that the care of infant life, saving the children, and protecting their welfare was as true a service to the country as that which men were rendering by going into the armies to serve in the field." Indeed, it was the very corollary to men's service. "While the necessary, inevitable work of men as combatants is to spread death, destruction, red ruin, desolation and sorrow untold," she told a Kingsway Hall audience in October 1914, "the work of women is the exact opposite. It is ... to help, to assuage, to preserve, to build up the desolate home, to bind up the broken lives, to serve the State by saving life rather than destroying it." *Common Cause* regularly carried notices on the "Care of Maternity in Time of War," and articles and appeals for donations "To Save the Babies." The traditional cultural associations of men with war and death on the one hand, and women with home and the giving and preserving of life on the other, emerged with virtually no resistance from feminists; indeed, they were often fostered by feminist rhetoric. As S. Bulan put it in *The Englishwoman*, "at the call of war, the first thought of every man is to fight, of every woman to nurse."[5]

"We want to emphasize the vital part which women have to play in a crisis like the present," intoned *Common Cause* on 14 August 1914, offering schemes for relief forwarded by the local constituent societies in response to the NU's appeal. In a significant ordering of priorities, it listed the formation of Suffrage Sewing Guilds for the making of maternity outfits, children's and men's clothing; of committees to distribute clothing; of committees to look after the wives and children of the men who had joined the Reserves; and finally, of the formation of ambulance classes. When Sylvia Pankhurst set up a toy factory in the East End to give employment to women there, *Common Cause* responded with one of the more ludicrous representations of women and their work. "All women will rejoice to hear that women are taking up toy-making," it enthused in October 1914. "This meets what will soon be a real need (for nearly all our toys came from Germany) ... and it is truly 'women's work'!" Virtually nothing was said to contest the legal, economic, and institutional barriers that limited women's abilities to make a contribution to the war effort in any but the most traditional terms.[6]

"Mothering Our Soldiers" was another activity urged upon readers of *Common Cause*. In September 1914, it suggested that women set up laundry and mending stations in every district where Territorials were camped. In November 1914, Dr. Helen Wilson proposed and *Common Cause* endorsed, in what constituted a literal construction of the home front, the formation of a Women's Army to train in and teach the arts of homemaking. "The most precious national service that women can render, whether in peace or war, is the care of the home, the guardianship of the family. On this point Suffragists and Anti-suffragists are agreed. Cannot our young women be induced to 'enlist' for this national service[?] Can they not be shown that the most practical service they can render to the absent brother, or husband, or sweetheart, is to ensure him a more perfect home when he comes back to it? This means training." The Women's Army she envisaged would be organized along the lines of the Territorial Force.[7]

The reassertion of traditional norms of masculinity and femininity and of separate spheres for men and women found expression in the efforts to legitimate and justify the war itself. Much of the official propaganda presented the war as a fight for and on behalf of Belgium, which was usually depicted in the guise of womanhood. For Britons, Trevor Wilson has argued, "the Belgian issue ... defined the nature of the struggle."[8] "Little Belgium" evoked images of an innocent woman in need of protection from a paternal male. Such chivalric imagery became charged by and infused with sexual implications as accounts of the invasion of Belgium and rumors of German atrocities reached England and seared the collective British memory. Much of the atrocity propaganda that circulated throughout Britain focused on outrages committed against women. In May 1915, the government issued the Bryce Report, the findings of a commission charged with investigating stories of German atrocities in Belgium. For 1 penny, the cost of a daily newspaper, Britons could purchase the "summary of evidence" and an appendix of selected case histories. In what can only be described as a kind of pornographic orgy that fostered voyeurism and made war sexually "exciting," the report told of the following:

A Belgian soldier marching along outside Liege came upon "a woman, apparently of middle age, perhaps 28 to 30 years old, stark naked, tied to a tree. At her feet were two little children about three or four years old. All three were dead. I believe the woman had one of her breasts cut off, but I cannot be sure of this. Her whole bosom was covered with blood and her body was covered with blood and black marks. Both children had been killed by what appeared to be bayonet wounds. The woman's clothes were lying on the grass thrown all about the place." Another soldier watched Germans "going into the houses in the Place and bringing out the women and girls. About 20 were brought out. ... Each of them was held by the arms. They tried to get away. There were made to lie on tables which had been brought into the square. About 15 of them were then violated. Each of them was violated by about 12 soldiers. ... The ravishing went on for about 1 1/2 hours. I watched the whole time." A soldier retreating "saw a woman lying on her back inside a house; her skirt was pulled up over her head. There were no clothes on the lower part of the body. She had a wound extending from between her legs (private parts) to her breast." A Belgian officer testified that "a young girl of about 17 came up to me crying in the village; she was dressed only in a chemise: she told me that 17 girls including herself, had been dragged into a field and stripped quite naked and violated, and that twelve of them had been killed by being ripped up across the stomach with a bayonet." A soldier recounted coming across a girl of 14 at Weerde: "she was half mad when we found her. Her mother was there, and told us that seven Germans had violated her one after another." Another found a woman in a convent; she had been "pierced by a bayonet" and was dying. "The woman's stomach had been cut open right across, the wound being some foot or more long. The woman was with child as could clearly be seen from her size."[9] A litany of atrocities committed against women and children and civilian men by German soldiers continued for some 238 pages.

This kind of imagery linked sex and war in the conscious and unconscious minds of Britons. The Bryce Report "released into English imaginations a style, a language, and an imagery of violence and cruelty that would in time permeate imagined versions of the war, and become part of the record."[10] It needs to be emphasized that the images of violence and cruelty were images, primarily, of acts against women, so that the rape and sexual mutilation of women served as one of the major means by which the war was imagined and represented by contemporaries.

While the imagery of sexual violation of women served as a means of recruitment and justification for the war, it may well have acted, unconsciously at least, to reinforce the promises of sexual reward and release for enlisting that bombarded the British public. An advertisement for Mitchell's "Binnacle" Cigarettes showed a fashionable young woman making eyes at the man in uniform beside her, while pointedly ignoring the man in civilian clothes on her right. In one song that carried unmistakable undertones of prostitution, long the acknowledged avenue by which British men were first initiated into sexual activity, and by means of which they were expected to find relief from pent-up sexual tension, women urged men to "take the King's shilling"—to enlist—with the following: "On Sunday I walk out with a soldier,/On Monday I'm taken by a tar,/On Tuesday I'm out/With a baby Boy Scout,/On Wednesday with a Hussar./On Thursday I gang oot with a Kiltie,/On Friday the captain of the crew,/But on Saturday I'm willing, if only you'll take a shilling,/To make a man [out] of any ... of you."[11]

Feminists colluded in representing war as a form of unrepressed sexual desire. Much of the news carried by *Common Cause* dealt not with the war effort—casualty lists, battles, or troop movements, for example—but with instances of sexual misconduct on the part of (usually working-class) women. In what it decried as "a national shame," the paper carried a plea "for the protection of our young soldiers, many of them only nineteen, from the solicitations of women."

In October, *Common Cause* declared that the large numbers of women hanging around the training camps, behaving badly and creating "a real scandal," had become "a danger to themselves and others." In November 1914, an entire meeting at the Guildhall was devoted to addressing the problem of women drinking and loitering at the camps,[12] another indication of the near obsession with the display of overt sexuality preoccupying feminists and the general public.

These representations of the sexual imperatives of war were put forward within a framework of traditional gender and sexual relations and did not seriously threaten the bourgeois domestic ideology of separate spheres based upon belief in a single model of (insistent) sexuality for men and in the dual nature of female sexuality—that of purity and passionlessness ascribed to middle-class women and promiscuity and prostitution to working-class women. Images of sexual release, of loosening the sexual restraints between men and women in the depictions of khaki fever and stories of war babies, while containing hints of middle-class women adopting male sexual values and ignoring traditional standards of reticence and chastity, were nevertheless heavily weighted by class, and could thus adequately represent a war that was still thought about and presented in traditional terms. But by mid-1915 or so, as those on the home front began to understand that theirs was not a traditional war, this kind of sexual representation began to change too.

By 1916, boundaries between home and front could no longer be drawn with ease. Even before the monstrous casualties of the Somme battles forced Britons to face up to the realities of war in the twentieth century, the war experience on the home front was changing dramatically. Britons had to face the fact that this war involved everyone, not just the men who joined the ranks of the armed forces. A blurring of identities—of the distinctions between warriors and civilians, between men and women—was taking place, necessitating a different kind of sexual imagery to represent the war. Thus, in the second phase of war, from about late 1915 on, the representation of war as unleashed sexual desire gave way to visions of sexual disorder, a blurring of gender lines as women went off to factories and front to do war work and men found themselves immobilized in trenches. Toward the end of the war, sexual disorder came to be depicted as sexual conflict and polarization between the sexes, or sex war. Sexual conflict finally provided one of the few adequate means by which the political, economic, and social upheaval occasioned by the Great War could be represented.[13]

As men went off to war, women joined the workforce in unprecedented numbers, taking jobs as munitions workers, agricultural laborers, tram conductors, ambulance drivers, frontline nurses, and, finally, after the disasters of 1916, auxiliary soldiers. The exigencies of the war after mid-1915 dramatically upset the perceived gender system of the Victorian and Edwardian periods. Nina Boyle of the Women's Freedom League could rejoice that "woman's place, by universal consensus of opinion, is no longer the Home. It is the battlefield, the farm, the factory, the shop." The dismantling of barriers between men's and women's work fostered a blurring of distinctions that had helped to form gender identity. Rebecca West described her visit to a cordite factory in 1916 in terms that confounded the divisions of home and front. "It is of such vital importance to the State," she observed in "Hands That War," "that it is ringed with barbed-wire entanglements and patrolled by sentries, and its products must have sent tens of thousands of our enemies to their death. And it is inhabited chiefly by pretty young girls clad in Red-Riding-Hood fancy dress of khaki and scarlet." Slipping from war imagery to domestic imagery without drawing attention to any sense of incongruence, West highlighted the dramatic changes wrought by the war. "When one is made to put on rubber overshoes before entering a hut it might be the precaution of a persnickety housewife concerned about her floors, although actually it is to prevent the grit on one's outdoor shoes igniting a stray scrap of cordite and sending oneself and the hut up to the skies in a column of flame." The hard work, the long hours, the danger, and, indeed, the deaths of women resulting from munitions explosions, led West to declare that "surely, never before in modern history can women have lived a life so completely parallel to that of the regular Army." Mrs. Alec-Tweedie rejoiced in the fact that by the events of the war, "women have become soldiers." Moreover, she predicted, it might not be long before "we may have to have women fighters too. ... For ... the war has literally metamorphosed everything and everybody. To-day every man is a soldier, and every woman is a man." She argued for the formation of a Woman's Battalion, foreseeing the day when "rather than let the Old Country go under, the women of the Empire would be ... more than willing, to take a place in the firing line."[14] This is a far cry from knitting socks and rolling bandages or providing relief for Belgian refugees; the language of traditional femininity, of separate spheres for women and men could not adequately articulate the experiences and requirements of a war that failed to respect the boundaries between home and front, between civilian and soldier.

The association of sex and war carried potentially explosive implications for society when it became clear that this war would require the participation of all segments of the population; anxiety about the prosecution of the war frequently took shape as anxiety about sex, or was articulated in sexual terms. The charges of khaki fever and war babies that predominated in 1914 had contained a kind of patronizing and even good-hearted tone; as the war effort worsened, however, attacks on women's sexuality increased in virulence. Making no distinction between prostitutes on the one hand, and young women infected with khaki fever on the other, Arthur Conan Doyle wrote to *The Times* in February 1917 complaining about "vile women ... who prey upon and poison our soldiers ... these harpies carry off the lonely soldiers to their rooms ... and finally inoculate them ... with one of those diseases." In July 1918, delegates to an Imperial War Conference heard tales of infected women "lying in wait for clean young men who came to give their lives for their country." The Government, for its part, introduced regulation 40d of the Defense of the Realm Act in March 1918, at the height of worries about the German advance, declaring that "no woman suffering from venereal disease shall have sexual intercourse with any member of His Majesty's Forces." Clearly, in the minds of many, sex presented as great a threat to the survival and existence of Britain as did Germany; the two were, indeed, often conflated. Mrs. Alec-Tweedie made this connection abundantly clear when she warned that "every woman who lets herself 'go' is as bad as a German spy, and a traitor, not only to her sex, but to her country."[15]

By focusing on sex as one of the major issues of the war, contemporaries hit upon a means by which they could imagine, represent, and even narrate—that is, to make sense of—the war, which defied traditional terms and habits of thought. As women began to take up jobs previously held exclusively by men, and even to serve as auxiliaries in the armed forces, sexual representation utilizing traditional heterosexual terms and images was no longer adequate to the task of giving meaning to a war so completely out of line with all precedent. Visions of sexuality in which women had become fully as unrestrained as men, and/or that exposed sex as a drive towards violence, war, and death, began to predominate. For instance, although she understood the "bacchantic frenzy" that struck "hundreds of reputable women and girls round every camp," to be "the natural complement to the male frenzy of killing," drawing an analogy between sex and death that anticipated Freud, Helena Swanwick, "never learnt to tolerate this with an indifferent mind." It "revolted me almost as much as [the war's] more obvious brutalities," she recalled, in a remarkably bald illustration of the confusion of war and sex. In D.H. Lawrence's "Tickets, Please," women tram conductors, "fearless young hussies," set upon their inspector, John Thomas, whose amorous adventures with a number of women have infuriated them. Their assault is depicted in near-sexual terms, invoking the imagery of rape and castration. "Their blood was thoroughly up. He was their sport now. They were going to have their own back, out of him. ... His tunic was simply torn off his back, his shirt-sleeves were torn away, his arms were naked. ... Their faces were flushed, their hair wild, their eyes were all glittering strangely. He lay at last quite still, with face averted, as an animal lies when it is defeated and at the mercy of the captor." "You ought to be *killed*," the ringleader told John Thomas with "a terrifying lust in her voice." The prospect of women waging war against men was raised by H. G. Wells' *Mr. Britling Sees It Through* in the character of Letty, whose husband Teddy has been wounded and is missing in action. She proposes to form "The Women's Association for the Extirpation of the whole breed of War Lords," a band of women dedicated to ending all wars means of "killing the kind of people who make them. Rooting them out. By a campaign of pursuit and assassination that will go on for years and years after the war itself is over."[16]

For feminists, too, the connection between sex and war could easily give way to notions of sex war. In April 1915, Emmeline Pankhurst gave a speech infused with the imagery of sexual assault. "The men of Belgium, the men of France, the men of Serbia," she lamented to her Liverpool audience, "however willing they were to protect women from the things that are most horrible—and more horrible to women than death itself—[they] have not been able to do it. It is only by an accident, or a series of accidents, for which no man has the right to take credit that British women on British soil are not now enduring the horrors endured by the women of France, the women of Belgium, and the women of Serbia." Mary Lowndes wrote in *The Englishwoman* in October 1914 that the belief that men protect women had been proved false by the events on the continent. "And, indeed," she added, "we must remember that it is against themselves, against animal dominance and brute force, that men must learn to protect their women in days of peace, if there is to be any hope that in time of war they shall have the same immunity that (at any rate theoretically) is extended to peaceable non-combatants of the other sex." Nina Boyle reported to readers of *The Vote*, the official newspaper of the Women's Freedom League, in February 1915 that "British officers and officials are treating as gentlemen and soldiers, and not as criminals, men guilty of the foulest horrors;" she wrote "of a train full of school-girls ..., who were outraged by officers," and cited a statement in the medical journal, the *Lancet*, "that of a convent of sixty nuns, twenty-nine are expecting to be confined [by pregnancy] as the result of similar brutal treatment." The line between German soldier and British soldier was not very distinct in the rhetoric of these women, and Boyle very soon erased it entirely. "Greatest of all dangers to women," she wrote in August 1915, "is the unbridled passion of men ... even now, in war time, in our own land, from our own men, the danger stalks undiminished and unchecked."[17]

The picture of masculinity conjured up by such imagery was often that of "mechanical dolls who grin and kill and grin," "a grimacing phantom," "a creature at once ridiculous and disgusting," as R.H. Tawney described it resentfully in October 1916 while recuperating from wounds received on the Somme in July. He castigated the newspapers for "inventing a kind of conventional soldier" who revels in the "excitement" of war and finds "'sport' in killing other men," and hunts "Germans out of dug-outs as a terrier hunts rats." "We are depicted as merry assassins, rejoicing in the opportunity of a 'scrap' in which we know that more than three-quarters of our friends will be maimed or killed, careless of our own lives, exulting in the duty of turning human beings into lumps of disfigured clay." "The Happy Warrior" depicted by Herbert Read in 1916 in a poem dripping with contempt for those at home who continued to think of the war in chivalric terms, whose "aching jaws grip a hot parched tongue," and whose "wide eyes search unconsciously," gave readers a picture of a mute automaton dribbling bloody saliva down his shirtfront as he stabbed and stabbed again "a well-killed Boche." Moreover, the imagery of sexual assault raised by the Belgian atrocities continued to inform representations of the war. Valentine Wallop, in Ford Madox Ford's *Parade's End*, believed that "all manly men were lust-filled devils, desiring nothing better than to stride over battlefields, stabbing the wounded with long daggers in frenzies of sadism."[18] Such representations of masculinity bore little resemblance to the way men at the front perceived themselves or women at the front perceived them, but the power of these bloodthirsty images was lasting, and would have significant impact on the way women at home understood the nature of masculinity, femininity, and the relations between the sexes.

Feminists who spent some part of the war in arenas in which the war was actually prosecuted or where the direct consequences of the fighting were manifested experienced the war differently from those whose relationship to the war was one of distance and hearsay. Nurses, members of the Voluntary Aid Detachments or VADs, physicians at casualty clearing stations or base hospitals, or those who treated and cared for the wounded in hospitals in England; ambulance drivers transporting the wounded from battlefield to operating theater; individuals who served in auxiliary positions at the front or in support areas; YMCA and canteen volunteers in France; and those who underwent the traumas of war as victims of air raids or U-boat attacks; all represented their experiences of war in terms markedly dissimilar to those at home. While many of the images were also sexualized, the tone and content of the imagery conveyed a vastly different understanding of the relations of men and women in wartime, and this accounts, at least in part, for these individuals holding ideas about the nature of masculinity and femininity, and thus of feminism in the postwar period, that substantially differed from those of their colleagues.

Women in hospitals and at the front frequently commented upon the similarities they felt with the fighting men, evincing a solidarity or comradeship with them that overrode all distinctions. Upon taking up nursing, Vera Brittain constructed herself as in the same camp with fighting men, and as distinct from non-combatants. Her 12 May 1915 diary entry records her thoughts as she justified leaving Oxford to enter hospital training: "I ought not to put the speedy starting of my career forward as an excuse, any more than a man should against enlisting," she wrote. After her fiancée, Roland's, death, Brittain put in for foreign service, cognizant of the risks and dangers involved, but all the more adamant to go as a consequence. "If I had refused to put down my name I should despise myself as much as I would a regiment that wouldn't volunteer for foreign service," she explained. Once abroad, she shared with soldiers the sense of estrangement from the home front, "the uncomprehending remoteness of England from the tragic, profound freemasonry of those who accepted death together overseas," and spoke of those at home as "the uninitiated."[19]

Mary Dexter, describing her uniform to her mother, noted with satisfaction the resemblance she and her fellow ambulance drivers had to army officers. She recounted that a French *poilu* had mistaken one of the drivers for a soldier during an air raid. "In her greatcoat and cap and boots he had thought she was a man."[20]

Sometimes the blurring of sexual difference became so intense as to eliminate even the physical markings that distinguished men's and women's bodies, as when Mary Borden described her nursing tour in a base hospital in France. "There are no men here," she wrote of the patients she attended, "so why should I be a woman?" "I've never been so close before to human beings. We are locked together, the [orderlies] and I, and the wounded men; we are bound together. ... The same thing is throbbing in us, the single thing, the one life. We are one body, suffering and bleeding." After the war, Vera Brittain suffered from delusions that her face was changing; when she looked into a mirror, she believed she was "developing a beard."[21]

Women who encountered men at the front, whether they were wounded or not, experienced them in ways and formulated ideas about masculinity that differed markedly from those of the culture at home. In contrast to the image of the bloodthirsty soldiers who "grin and kill and grin," nurses and VADs described men in terms usually consigned to women and children, or in ways that denied them destructive power. An anonymous WAAC witnessed, in what she described as "one of the most distressing sights that I beheld during the war," a wounded man in her ambulance who "began crying for his mother—'Oh, mummy, mummy, come to me—mummy, I want you so. ... ' His voice was suddenly like a child's," she wrote. A member of the First Aid Nursing Yeomanry (FANY) recalled that wounded men would "burst into tears, refuse their food, beg to be allowed to stay," when evacuation orders came for them. In vivid sketches evoking a mother-child relationship, Irene Rathbone's autobiographical protagonist, Joan, spoke of men "unable to cut up their own food" who "had to be spoon-fed," of the patient to whom she brought a bed-pan, "settled him comfortably upon it, [and] wiped him—if he were unable to manage himself."[22]

Often the wounded were referred to not as men but as broken objects or body parts. Cicely Hamilton reported that during her stint in France she "grew quite accustomed to hearing human beings spoken of as if they were diseased or damaged portions of their bodies—as fractures or strangulated hernias." Helen Zenna Smith's ambulance driver referred to "these mangled things I drive night after night." Borden observed of her ward that "there are no men here. ... There are heads and knees and mangled testicles. There are chests with holes as big as your fist, and pulpy thighs, shapeless; and stumps where legs once were fastened. ... There are these things, but no men."[23] Of course, this phenomenon of detaching the individual human being from the horrible wounds from which he suffered was a function of the women's need to survive and remain effective, but it also had the effect of separating men from the destructive forces that had occasioned their wounds. Women at the front, unlike women at home, did not equate masculinity with brutality, aggression, and destruction. Rather, they perceived men as very much like children, or, indeed, like themselves.

Because the language used to express the experience of war at the front differed from that utilized to understand the war from the position of the home front, the sexual imagery necessarily differed as well. Rather than something to be feared or titillated by, sex, in the stories offered by the women at the front, offered pleasure, companionship, comfort, and love.

Women frequently narrated their war experiences as a sexual coming of age, as tales depicting an unfolding of sexual knowledge that led, if not to actual sexual experience, then to positive, relaxed attitudes about or openness towards sexuality. The stories all begin with an expression of more or less conventional Victorian attitudes toward and/or ignorance about sex. Vera Brittain's diary entries before the outbreak of war, for instance, reveal a sense of shame and even disgust about sex, what little she understood of it. When, in March 1913, on their way to play golf, she asked her mother "to disclose a few points on sexual matters which I thought I ought to know," she found the information so "distasteful" and "depressing" that it put her off her game. Joan, in *We That Were Young*, was also presented as a conventional middle-class Edwardian girl—earnest, innocent, and entirely ignorant about "that mysterious consummation of love of which she had ... on the whole kept resolutely from her thoughts."[24]

Through contact with men's bodies in the course of their nursing duties the authors became accustomed to and then appreciative of the physical aspects of men. Until Vera Brittain began nursing in June 1915, she had "never looked upon the nude body of an adult male." At first she feared she would be overcome with nervousness and embarrassment at the sight of a naked man but found she was not. "From the constant handling of their lean, muscular bodies, I came to understand the essential cleanliness, the innate nobility, of sexual love on its physical side," she wrote. "Although there was much to shock in Army hospital service, much to terrify, much, even, to disgust, this day-by-day contact with male anatomy was never part of the shame." Irene Rathbone was also quite aware of the initiation into sexual knowledge she received from the soldiers under her care, describing the eroticism her protagonist, Joan, experienced when she bathed her patients. "It gave her a peculiar soothing joy to take hold of a long white arm, to soap it, sponge it, and dry it; to wash a muscular young back, listening meanwhile to its owner talking desultorily about his sweetheart, his kids, or his 'mates' in the regiment. She was a nurse in uniform, and he was a wounded soldier; the gulf between them was fixed and rigid. And yet across that gulf, unrecognized and certainly unheeded by either, stretched the faint sweet fingers of sex." Brittain shared that experience of sexual introduction, and appreciated it. "Short of actually going to bed with them," she said of the wounded she nursed, "there was hardly an intimate service that I did not perform for one or another in the course of four years, and I still have reason to be thankful for the knowledge of masculine functioning which the care of them gave me, and for my early release from the sex-inhibitions that even to-day [in 1933] ... beset many of my female contemporaries, both married and single."[25]

The WAAC made the connection between the men she will nurse and sexual knowledge abundantly clear through a conversation with another nursing sister. "Have you many wounded?" she inquired. "Let me see—about twenty to-day," the sister replied. "Two died yesterday and one this morning. You'll see them all presently." Then, without a break, the sister continued. "Tell me, dear, have you ever had a man?" While the WAAC was shocked by this question, she would soon react to such suggestions with aplomb. When she sought a transfer from her unit, the medical officer urged her not to go, telling her of a "good-looking boy," shot, significantly, in the groin, who was in love with her and who would not recover if she left. The WAAC recalled having changed his bandages: "I had felt him tremble while I dressed his wound, but supposed his trembling to be due to pain." One day, the patient asked her to kiss him; she complied, kissing "him several times—on the lips. I felt his whole body thrill."[26]

Mary Borden utilized the sexual theme in a somewhat different way. Pain, "a lascivious monster," is portrayed in imagery usually associated with prostitution. She is "insatiable, greedily, vilely amorous, lustful, obscene—she lusts for the broken bodies we have here. Wherever I go I find her possessing the men in their beds, lying in bed with them." "She is a harlot in the pay of War, and she amuses herself with the wreckage of men. She consorts with decay, is addicted to blood, cohabits with mutilations, and her delight is the refuse of suffering bodies. ... You can watch her plying her trade here any day. She is shameless. She lies with the Heads and the Knees and the festering Abdomens. She never leaves them. ... At any hour of the day or night you can watch her deadly amours, and watch her victims struggling." This is also the kind of imagery utilized to portray the camp women enflamed by khaki fever at home, those furies preying upon the men in uniform, and whose licentious behavior is crippling the war effort and men's abilities to fulfill their masculine destiny. But for Borden the war itself is the whore, feeding on the once healthy bodies of men, rendering them grotesque and unnatural, and unfit for the "tender and lovely love for women" that "clean, normal, real men" seek. Having lost one of those "clean, normal, real men" to the effects of amputation—"she looked around her as if to find the man he had once been"—Borden turned to hospital work. Nurses and VADs, engaged in the battle that "now is going on over the helpless bodies of these men," "we who are doing the fighting now, with their real enemies," in this depiction are arrayed on the side of mutual, tender, loving, participatory sexual activity against a sexuality that is aggressive, predatory, diseased, and pecuniary. They do not win this fight, but Borden's story of her experience is none the less articulated in the same positive sexual terms as Brittain's, Rathbone's, and the WAAC's. The WAAC justified her kissing of the wounded man whom she did not love with a formulation that equated sex with life-giving. "From that day onward he was quite a different person," she explained. "He told me that now he had something to live for."[27] Women in these depictions are arrayed on the side of mutual, tender, loving, participatory sexual activity; at home, women's sexuality is portrayed as aggressive, predatory, diseased, and pecuniary.

Women at the front or in positions that proximated those of the frontsoldiers shared with the men experiences denied to those at home. Rather than construe men in fantastic terms, derived from a different construction of war given in patriotic journalistic accounts, government propaganda, and sanitized letters home, feminists at the front had an understanding of men's daily lives and of men that was far more in keeping with those of the men themselves. We have seen that the sexual violation and mutilation of women by men served as one of the chief means by which to represent the war at home. Women at the front, by contrast, saw not the mutilation of women by men but the mutilation of men by the weapons of mass destruction unleashed by industrialized nations. Their familiarity with what men suffered led them to think of the male of the species not as some barbaric, destructive creature who could not control his most violent instincts, but as a hurt, pathetic, vulnerable, child-like victim of circumstances far beyond his control. The sexual imagery utilized to depict or represent the war, consequently, involved a much greater sense of partnership, of participation on equal terms, of fellowship with men, than did that of the home front. Whereas aggression and conflict characterized the sexual relations that were mobilized to depict the war at home, stories of sexual initiation, of awakening, of a sexual coming of age, predominated among the women at the front. These were described as affirming encounters with life lived at its fullest, though passion was often invoked. Comfort, caring, and giving, as opposed to conflict, violence, and destruction characterized the relations of men and women who shared the horrors and exigencies of war. These differing understandings about the nature of masculinity, and thus, given the dichotomies of male/female, of femininity, had important consequences in the postwar period as feminists began to formulate policies that turned on their conceptions of gender and sexuality. "Old" feminists such as Winifred Holtby, Lady Rhondda, Cicely Hamilton, and Vera Brittain were able to hold on to understandings about masculinity and femininity, about male and female sexuality that characterized the prewar period. Their ability to contest the meanings about gender that were accepted not simply by the culture around them but by other feminists as well stems in part from the languages by means of which they articulated their experiences of the war.

While Hamilton, Brittain, and Borden viewed male aggression as largely a learned response, others—"New" feminists—saw in the war a lesson about the nature of masculinity, which led them to re-evaluate their beliefs about femininity as well. A number of feminists explicitly pointed to the war as the key event in effecting a transformation in their thinking. Catherine Gasquoine Hartley, for one, attributed her switch to what amounted to a "new" feminist position to the massive male aggression manifested by the war. Whereas once she had dreamed of "a golden age which was to come with the self-assertion of women," with the outbreak of war, she explained in 1917, "we women were brought back to the primitive conception of the relative position of the two sexes. ... Again man was the fighter, the protector of woman and the home. And at once his power became a reality." The aggression unleashed in the war, so unprecedented, so destructive, so horrifying in its effects, seems to have convinced Gasquoine Hartley that masculinity was essentially characterized by violence and brutality. Such an understanding necessitated that women, if they were ever to be really free, must accept "the responsibilities and limitations of their womanhood. And by this I mean a full and glad acceptance of those physical facts of their organic constitution which make them unlike men, and should limit their capacity for many kinds of work. It can never be anything but foolishness to attempt to break down the real differences between the two sexes." Christabel Pankhurst hinted of much the same fear when she wrote in 1924, "Some of us hoped [for] more from woman suffrage than is ever going to be accomplished. My own large anticipations were based upon ignorance (which the late war dispelled) of the magnitude of the task which we women reformers so confidently wished to undertake when the vote should be ours." Pankhurst's pre-war writings made it clear that she sought in the vote the means by which women would end the sexual abuse and degradation of women. The realization that this would not be possible came to her as a result of her observation of the massive destruction of the Great War, the manifestation, for her as for so many others, of an innate male aggression. As she put it, "war arises from passions and ambitions which do not yield to the influence of votes."[28]

In these constructions, the metaphors of war have come home: the military has placed Britain, or at least the women of Britain, under military occupation. Where they had once conceived masculinity and femininity to be the products of laws, attitudes, and institutions that encouraged an unfettered and aggressive male sexuality and a passive, even non-existent female sexuality, "new" feminists now took up a variation of the "drive-discharge" model that relied upon the notion of biological drives to explain male behavior. The social bases of masculinity and femininity gave way to a biologically determined, innate male and female sexuality, which in turn suggested that women must act differently in order to protect themselves and society from the aggression unleashed by war. The rhetoric of separate spheres had become infected with the rhetoric of war. In classic anti-feminist terms, these feminists gave voice to the cultural belief that the war had demonstrated the need for recreating barriers between men and women, for the recognition of sexual difference, if society were to return to a condition of normality, defined in biological or natural terms. But because many of the legal barriers barring women from public life were being dismantled, the institutional practices enforcing separate spheres came to be replaced by psychological ones. The power of psychologized separate spheres, the extent of the psychic and linguistic internalization of military occupation by the women of Britain, insured that all the parliamentary reforms in the world would be of little avail to those seeking equality with men.

Notes to Chapter 7

1. The phrase belongs to Raymond Sontag, who in turn borrowed it from Gabriel Marcel's play, *Le monde cassé*, of 1933. See Raymond J. Sontag, *A Broken World, 1919–1939* (New York, 1971), p. xv.
2. See Charles S. Maier, *Recasting Bourgeois Europe: Stabilization in France, Germany, and Italy in the Decade After World War I* (Princeton, New Jersey, 1975).
3. See Paul Fussell, *The Great War and Modern Memory* (New York, 1975); Victoria De Grazia, *How Fascism Ruled Women: Italy, 1922–1945* (Berkeley, 1992); Sandra Gilbert "Soldier's Heart: Literary Men, Literary Women, and the Great War," *Signs* 8 (3), Spring 1983, 422–50; Eric J. Leed, *No Man's Land: Combat and Identity in World War I* (Cambridge, 1979); Bonnie G. Smith, *Changing Lives: Women in European History since 1700* (Lexington, Mass., 1989).
4. See, for example, Arthur Marwick, *The Deluge: British Society and the First World War* (New York, 1965); Gail Braybon, *Women Workers in the First World War: The British Experience* (London, 1981).
5. Millicent Garrett Fawcett, *What I Remember* (1925, reprint. Westport, Conn., 1976), p. 218. S. Bulan, "The Untrained Nurse in National Emergency," *The Englishwoman* 69 (September 1914), p. 267.
6. *Common Cause* 14 August. 1914, pp. 386, 391; 21 August 1914, p. 398. E. Sylvia Pankhurst, *The Home Front* (1932, reprint. London, 1987), p. 72; *Common Cause* 9 October 1914, p. 470. Reported in "Our Active Service League," *Common Cause*, 11 September 1914, pp. 430–31.
7. "Mothering Our Soldiers," *Common Cause*, 18 September 1914, p. 438. "Woman's Part in War Time. Care of the Home," *Common Cause*, 20 November 1914, p. 551.
8. Trevor Wilson, *The Myriad Faces of War: Britain and the Great War, 1914-1918* (Cambridge, 1986), p. 25.
9. Committee on Alleged German Outrages, *Evidence and Documents Laid before the Committee on Alleged German Outrages* (Bryce Report appendix, 1915), pp. 14, 19, 107, 109, 111.
10. Samuel Hynes, *A War Imagined: The First World War and English Culture* (New York, 1991), p. 56.

11. Maurice Rickards and Michael Moody, eds., *The First World War: Ephemera, Mementoes, Documents* (London, 1975), item 101. Quoted in Wilson, *Myriad Faces of War*, p. 706.
12. "A National Shame," *Common Cause*, 28 August 1914, pp. 406–7. "Notes and News," *Common Cause*, 9 October 1914, p. 469; "A Way for Girls to Help," *Common Cause*, 23 October 1914, p. 494. Reported in *Common Cause*, 27 November 1914, p. 560.
13. See Fussell, *The Great War*, pp. 334, 174.
14. Rebecca West, "Hands That War: The Cordite Makers," *The Daily Chronicle*, 1916, quoted in Jane Marcus, ed., *The Young Rebecca* (New York, 1982), pp. 381–82. Mrs. Alec-Tweedie, *Women and Soldiers* (London, 1918), pp. 1–2, 26.
15. Quoted in Lucy Bland, "In the Name of Protection: The Policing of Women in the First World War," in Julia Brophy and Carol Smart, eds., *Women-in-Law: Explorations in Law, Family and Sexuality* (London, 1985), pp. 47, 32. Alec-Tweedie, *Women and Soldiers*, p. 85.
16. H.M. Swanwick, *I Have Been Young* (London, 1935), p. 252. D. H. Lawrence, "Tickets, Please," in *England, My England* (London, 1924), pp. 52, 62–63. H.G. Wells, *Mr. Britling Sees It Through* (New York, 1916), pp. 388, 386.
17. Emmeline Pankhrst, "What is Our Duty?" *The Suffragette*, 23 April 1915, pp. 25–26. Mary Lowndes, "The Recrudescence of Barbarism," *The Englishwoman* 70 (october 1914), P. 27. C. Nina Boyle, "We Present Our Bill," *The Vote*, 19 February 1915, p. 504. C. Nina Boyle, "The Male Peril," *The Vote*, 27 August 1915, p. 727.
18. R. H. Tawney, "Some Reflections of a Soldier," *Nation* 20 (October 21, 1916), pp. 104–6; see Hynes, *A War Imagined*, pp. 118, 117. Herbert Read, "The Scene of War: The Happy Warrior," in Peter Vansittart, *Voices from the Great War* (New York, 1981), p. 118. Ford Madox Ford, *Parade's End* (New York, 1979), p. 233.
19. Vera Brittain, May 12, 1915, *War Diary, 1913–1917: Chronicle of Youth* (London, 1981), p. 195; March 6, 1916, *War Diary*, p. 320. Vera Brittain, *Testament of Youth* (1933, reprint. London, 1978), pp. 360, 217.
20. Mary Dexter, January 1918, *In the Soldiers'Service: War Experiences of Mary Dexter, 1914–1918* (Boston, 1918), p. 166.
21. Mary Borden, *The Forbidden Zone* (London, 1929), pp. 60, 155–56. Brittain, *Testament of Youth*, pp. 496–97.
22. Anonymous, *WAAC: The Woman's Story of the War* (London, 1930), p. 222. A F.A.N.Y. in France, *Nursing Adventures* (London, 1917), pp. 121, 116. Irene Rathbone, *We That Were Young* (1932, reprint. New York, 1989), pp. 219, 236, 394.
23. Cicely Hamilton, *Life Errant* (London, 1935), p. 117. Helen Zenna Smith, *Not So Quiet... Stepdaughters of War* (1930, reprint. New York, 1989), p.57. Borden, *The Forbidden Zone*, p. 60.
24. Brittain, January 8, 1913, March 4, 1913, *War Diary*, pp. 26–27, 30-31. Rathbone, *We That Were Young*, pp. 139–40.
25. Brittain, *Testament of Youth*, pp. 165–66. Rathbone, *We That Were Young*, pp. 212–13.
26. Anonymous, *WAAC*, pp. 21, 33, 34, 35.
27. Borden, *The Forbidden Zone*, pp. 53–54, 61–62, 63, 49, 147. Anonymous, *WAAC*, pp. 35–36.
28. Catherine Gasquoine Hartley, *Motherhood and the Relationships of the Sexes* (London, 1917), pp. 14–15, 18. Christabel Pankhurst, *Pressing Problems of the Closing Age* (London, 1924), p. 40.

Select Bibliography

Paul Fussell, *The Great War and Modern Memory*. New York, 1975. A classic account of the war's role in the formation of modern literary thought and consciousness.

Eric Leed, *No Man's Land: Combat and Identity in World War I*. Cambridge, 1979. Compelling analysis of the "defensive" personality created by trench experiences of both German and British frontsoldiery.

Margaret Higonnet, Jane Jenson, Sonya Michel, Margaret Collins Weitz, editors. *Behind the Lines: Gender and the Two World Wars*. New Haven, 1987. A series of trailblazing essays exploring the impact of war on the construction of gender.

Susan Kingsley Kent, *Making Peace: The Reconstruction of Gender in Interwar Britain*. Princeton, 1993. Examines the use of sexual metaphors to represent the war and the consequences for postwar society.

Trevor Wilson, *The Myriad Faces of War: Britain and the Great War, 1914–1918*. Cambridge, 1986. A comprehensive political and social history of the war.

Samuel Hynes, *A War Imagined: The First World War and English Culture*. New York, 1991. A useful survey of cultural trends during and immediately after the war.

Vera Brittain, *Testament of Youth*. London, 1978 (reprint, originally published 1933). A poignant memoir of war experience.

J.M. Winter, *The Great War and the British People*. Cambridge, Ma., 1986. An innovative social history of the war's effects on those who stayed at home.

CHAPTER 8

ITALIAN WIDOWS OF THE FIRST WORLD WAR*

Francesca Lagorio

According to Joan Scott, the term *gender*, around which the numerous meanings attributed to sexual difference are concentrated, suggests that "relations between the sexes are a primary aspect of social organization (rather than following, say, from economic or demographic pressures); that the terms of male and female identities are in large part culturally determined (not produced by individuals or collectivities entirely on their own); and that differences between the sexes constitute and are constituted by hierarchical social structures."[1] Scott's definition constitutes a fundamental instrument of analysis for the identification of the way in which, according to specific contexts and in given periods, every human being fits into a complex network of family relationships, social hierarchies, cultural representations, and subjective fantasies concerning his or her sexual identity.

Historically, however, men and women have received differentiated treatment. Many studies by feminist anthropologists have argued that the majority of existing societies which present a male universalizing and comprehensive characterization are matched by a female universe which is divided into specific sub-categories. The classification of singles, mothers and widows in traditional societies has always involved very different roles, duties, privileges and attributes. Above all, however, it has been a formidable instrument for the social construction of a public identity.

Notes for this chapter begin on page 192.

What were a widow's characteristics in early twentieth-century Italian society and culture? An age-old Catholic tradition assigned her a very particular role, which could be termed both weak and strong, within the family and society. An adult woman and often a mother too, she found herself having to live without her husband who generally, if not always, was the principal source of economic revenue and, above all, the head of the family and the only custodian and person who knew about her sexuality. If the widow was young she was a potential threat to the social, familial, and sexual order of the community to which she belonged; if she was already middle-aged she could represent a source of authority. In 1953 a war widow still wrote, "diffidence towards a widow will end with the waning of the colors of her youth, her problems will be settled—if solitude is not one of them—when old age draws near." [2]

Under Italian law, until the end of the First World War widows shared exclusion from the exercise of civil rights with other women:[3] in accordance with the "Mediterranean code of honor it conceived non-domestic space as a constant menace to female purity and consequently to the integrity of the entire family clan."[4] With the death of her husband a woman reacquired by right the capacity for the acts which marriage had deprived her of (i.e., the free administration and disposal of her own property and the exercise of parental authority over her children).[5] At the same time, however, certain laws restricted her freedom of action, in particular in the presence of minors, with the manifest aim of maintaining control over her sexual freedom and enhancing the interests of the dead husband's family.[6] Fear of the loss of male power over the female body—caused, in the case of widows, by the death of the husband who had controlled it—accentuated the already unfavorable attitude towards second marriages which existed in Catholic and popular culture and prompted legislation[7] which imposed a ten month period of mourning upon all widows, even if they were not pregnant. Failure to comply entailed a pecuniary penalty for the woman and the forfeiture of every donation, dowry profit, and inheritance from her deceased husband.[8] The Senate Committee clarified the intention behind the law when it noted that in the case of "a widow who, forgetting the respect due to her lost husband and the prohibition of the law, does not feel disgust at remarrying ... it has been considered right to establish such severe penalties because an immodest act which brings such perturbation to the family needs to be severely punished."[9] As Segalen noted:

de la veuve on redoute ... une sexualité excessive: elle est celle qui a été initiée sexuellement et qui peut en faire profiter d'autres qu'un seul homme: elle risque d'avoir ici des rapports encore ambivalents mère/femme à l'égard d'un second mari plus jeune qu'elle, qu'elle initie et domine. La veuve est le type de femme le plus redouté car elle conjugue la crainte de rapports quasi incestueux et de domination au sein du ménage, tous deux sources de dangers pour l'ordre social.[10]

War widowhood amplified the sexual ambivalence resulting from the prospect of emancipation acquired at a husband's death through the assumption of the role of head of the family (while juridical and social minor status which was peculiar to being a woman persisted) and from the transition from full wifehood to the new possibility of freely disposing of one's own sexuality beyond the pale of social control. In this context the concern of governmental organs and the press over the assumed illegitimate unions of war widows is significant.[11] Postwar parliamentary debates on the extension of political representation to women offer a dual image of these widows: on the one hand, they are depicted as the miserable victims of the nation; on the other, as a potential danger to social stability.[12]

Recent historiography has enriched our appreciation of the subjective experience of men and women during the wartime and postwar era[13] and of the role filled by women during those years. In particular, a number of studies have offered important methodological and historiographical approaches to reassert the complexity of the male and female dimension, which has been hierarchically differentiated but remains intrinsically linked.[14]

In Italy the dramatic decision to intervene in the conflict on the side of the Allies, reached in May 1915 after a long internal dispute, set in motion the registering of more than six million mobilized citizens. According to official sources more than 650,000 men died in the war.[15] The data available, however, does not indicate the status of the fallen, nor does it distinguish between the various categories eligible for assistance, whether widows, orphans, parents, or collateral kin. This is why we can only indicate an estimated figure of over 200,000 Italian war widows.[16]

In view of the close material and moral link with the nation as a whole between widows and the state itself, a link which developed on the basis of the war experience, a study of widows during and after the First World War could be an excellent vantage point from which to observe the ways in which male and female identities were constructed and differentiated, and to illuminate the gap between official rhetoric and the individual or collective experiences of women who became widows during the war.

The story of these war widows involves a number of critical issues: it was a moment of dual fracture in their daily lives, for widowhood involved the disappearance of both an individual and a social point of reference. The radicalization of the economic and social condition of widows, which lasted well beyond the war, often kept the experience of widowhood suspended between the reappropriation of their own lives and the link with their past identity, which was kept alive by the war itself. The difficulty of constructing their own social identity appears to have been more acute for middle and upper-class widows and may have prompted them into associational activism in the postwar years.

It is important, therefore, to analyze how the cult of the fallen was organized, and the extent to which motivational factors such as honor, fatherland, and family re-emerged after 1918 as elements of continuity of the family model. Moreover, to what extent did the various widows' associations and their commemorative ceremonies, providing a new outlet for women as they did, nonetheless serve to reinscribe them into the imagery of the Mater dolorosa and into a role which re-emphasized their gendered status? The assistance provided by the Italian state for war victims and widows clearly indicates an effort to restore the prewar social and symbolic order. Total sacrifice, the death of the soldier, in fact obscured deep divisions in the social fabric and facilitated the recomposition of identity in the postwar years.

Widows were to fill an important and ambivalent social role in the ritual of the cult of the fallen—a role which was useful for the purification and new elaboration of the post-combat era. War widows in fact could represent the female ambivalence of the war experience. The role of suffering and mourning fit perfectly with the image of the passive and incomplete female who supposedly attained her identity as a citizen only through her union with a man. Yet it is also the case that the prominence of widows in veterans' associations and the persistence of their claims (the right to work and to obtaining pensions) presume a different conception of their own identity and of belonging to the body politic.

Widows' Social Identity

Collected testimonies of the war and postwar years indicate that women faced the issue of their membership in a community which required a profound modification of their own social identity, and that this question became central to their relationship with the state. The very fact of their husbands' going off to war initiated this redefinition of their persons and their activities.[17] In particular, the letters of two women (whose husbands had been called up) shed light upon many of the dilemmas which remained unresolved for widows even after the fighting had stopped. Maria Rosa was thirty years old in 1917 and had one daughter; she asked for their subsidy, which the government had revoked, to be reinstated: "My husband is fighting on the Carso for our holy cause; I hope that You, Illustrious Sir, will know how to assert my rights, as my husband is asserting those of an entire Nation....Your Excellency, grant me my rights."[18] When Giuseppina wrote the following letter she had been alone for two years. At first she had been granted a subsidy but this had been withdrawn because her husband's family was in a position to provide financially for her. The birth of a son also made her already precarious economic situation even more difficult. Giuseppina fought to recover her subsidy and, exasperated, finally wrote to the Prime Minister:

> In view of my unsuccessful efforts and my desperate financial situation, I find myself obliged to turn to Your Excellency to explain as follows: 1. because until the war broke out or, rather, Castaldo Andrea Antonio, my husband, was called up, we were not a part of his family and the only means of livelihood was the fruit of his work, and not as the documents included with this letter indicate. 2. I also want to point out that this Municipality did not acquire information which corresponds to the truth, because if the information had been acquired conscientiously, my subsidy would not have been suppressed. If late I moved to my husband's parents' house, it was so that I would not die of hunger, I and my little child. I, therefore, fervently pray, Your Excellency, in the hope that you may hear my petition and provide for my subsidy and obtain all the back payments which are rightfully due to an Italian citizen and soldier who is in the front line fighting for the honor and greatness of the Fatherland.[19]

Before "listening" to how the knowledge that their husbands would not return forced widows into the painful social, economic, and psychological readjustment of their lives necessary in a society which defined women on the basis of their relationship with men, one should note what another scholar has concluded regarding the numerous requests, applications, and petitions the widows addressed to the state:

> Husbands speak and write for wives of modern times; widows, on the contrary, take up their pens and start speaking about themselves in the first person because of the tensions, conflicts and claims of which they are

protagonists and objects ... It takes two people to converse and the tale—of oneself, one's own existence or some fragment of it—presumes a common code and a pact which amalgamates the other person's legitimacy as an interlocutor.[20]

Those petitions and requests, addressed to the king, the queen, the ministers, or the decentralized powers of the state (such as mayors, who often acted as mediators) suggest that the widows were not looking for state legitimation in matters of family conflicts. On the contrary, the war—in the sense that it was wanted and requested by the state—was to produce a sense of antagonism in the widows, a legitimate feeling of being creditors of the state.

Whether they returned or not, the mens' departure and absence disrupted an economic system in which the provision of the material foundations of existence was gendered. An analysis of the widows' petitions (whether complaining of delays in the granting of pensions and subsidies or seeking special assistance to deal with emergencies) indicates just how difficult was their situation. A widow's heart-rending words reveal her inability to overcome total indigence, especially in the presence of her children. Amelia Severo, mother of five small children, waited for two years for her pension and then turned in desperation to the Queen to intercede on her behalf. The woman describes her laborious journey through the bureaucracy:

> After some time instead of the longed for pension I was presented with a small bonus of 50 Lira which became 45 once income tax had been deducted. My petition must certainly have been interpreted in another way ... But I find myself unable to carry on in this atrocious way of life, which more often than not makes me want to end my cursed existence, though it is still sustained by my supreme love for my children.[21]

Many widows were forced to seek paid employment, having now to face life alone with full financial responsibility. Clementina de Lorenzi asked to be engaged as a servant in a village school; Emma Turchetto sought a license to open a tobacconist's shop.[22] These requests were sometimes perceived as a means of substituting for the role previously filled by men. A group of widows of railway workers killed in the war demanded to be employed themselves by the railways.[23] Perhaps the fact that applications for employment increased in the postwar years, once the husband's absence was now a psychological and economic reality, was not accidental.

Besides presenting an economic dilemma, the widows' appeals to the state complained about the state's refusal to admit its responsibility in the destruction of the family model. "Where do the high-sounding winged words of rhetoric go if this rhetoric is not sustained by more manageable facts of the life we live!" chided a colonel's widow. Another stressed that "we have a double, terrible sorrow that cannot be healed; first that of having sacrificed our love, our support, the father of our children, and then that of having lost him to no purpose. Since then I cannot rest."[24]

Matelda, the widow of naval lieutenant Pietro Pagni, complained of the treatment reserved by the state for the childless widows of career officers, one which was judged inequitable by many other widows in the same situation (as the Under-Secretary of State for Military Assistance and War Pensions pointed out). In her letter Matelda asked to be placed on a par with all the other categories of pensioners

> and granted a speedy and adequate increase after seven years of painful and undeserved neglect ... Childless widows have been forgotten ... They have not been granted the voucher which even prisoners received, or any increase in their pensions, or the two last cost of living allowances of L.40 each granted to civilian pensioners [a total of an extra L.80 a month]. According to the legislation proposed in Parliament it also appears that only widows of reserve officers will have a pension increase at the age of fifty. And must the war widows of career officers really die of hunger? We urge that the case be examined speedily because the widows of career officers who died childless in active service are awaiting consideration, because neither their dead consort nor they themselves have deserved to be so neglected in the new provisions! ... And yet there are so few childless widows compared to other widows that to tell [these childless widows] that the state finances are exhausted and cannot provide for them is not worthy of the immense sacrifice of the Great Dead.[25]

For bourgeois widows, economic impoverishment involved a downward slide in their social status, and their transformation from a family role as administrators and moral guardians to one which involved the assumption of real economic responsibility and which induced trauma and disorientation. As one widow explained:

> Excellency, we cannot say, like artisans' and peasants' children, that we have a right to financial support as orphans. Our dignity, the appearances we have to keep up because of our social rank, do not allow us to do this.... If she has no other income, a lieutenant colonel's wife has to live on 183 lire a month, whether or not she has children. A soldier's widow lives on 50 lire a month. The former has to live decorously and, never having worked for her livelihood, it would be very difficult for her to find an occupation. Since it is likely that in most cases the latter is used to working, she will always easily be able to earn 2 lire a day. Both positions are critical, but if one analyzes both situations, I do not know which is the most painful.[26]

State Provisions

In Italy state intervention in matters of public welfare was limited until the First World War to the regulation of the private sector. In 1904, during the parliamentary debate on the law on public charity, Prime Minister Giovanni stressed the state's circumscribed role: its only objective must remain that of filling in the deficiencies of private egoism.[27] The Great War brought to the fore the need for a profound modification of the state's functions in Italy as elsewhere, not only with regard to economic mobilization and the coordination of resources, but also with regard to society in general.[28] Thus, a progressive modification in the state's commitment occurred between 1915 and 1917: first, it supported the relief committees established in the first months of the war, then it promoted other new committees, next it advocated the creation in 1916 of the Commissariato Generale per l'Assistenza Civile e la Propaganda Interna (General Commissary for Civilian Relief and Internal Propaganda), and, finally, in 1917 it set up the new Ministero per l'Assistenza Militare e le Pensioni di Guerra (Ministry for Military Relief and War Pensions).

Thus, a new relationship developed between the state and its citizens: for men this relationship was determined by military service and for women by the shattering of the family nucleus. In addition, the demands of the conflict—which for the first time extended far beyond the battlefield—necessitated the redefinition of the relationship between citizens and the state; in practice this entailed that the juridical relationship grafted onto military service was superseded by the more extensive one predicated on damage suffered because of the war.

The first direct state provisions took the form of subsidies for the needy families of recalled servicemen (May 1915), subsequently extended to all draftees.[29] Soldiers' cohabitants (those who were not legally connected to the fighting men) were granted the right to state assistance. Although obtaining this status proved difficult, many people still feared that such provisions were too liberal and would endanger the role of women and the family in society: "in such a delicate matter in which the legislator, while allowing himself to be conquered by sentiments of compassion, moral considerations and the miserable conditions which the war had created in some cases, had to be principally concerned with keeping the juridical and moral bonds of the family intact, all provisions were extremely dangerous."[30]

Despite public reservations, the juridical figure of the assimilated widow was introduced in 1918: the unmarried companion of a fallen soldier had the right to a pension if the soldier's intentions had been publicly evident.[31] The provision, which was later suppressed by the fascist regime, gave rise to widespread protests and was criticized as being "in contrast with the fundamental principles of private law concerning the family."[32] This combination of moral experience and legislative intervention was not only symbolically important, it also carried considerable social weight. It was not by chance that one of the fundamental instruments of state aid developed from the introduction of war pensions, in spite of the fact that the government officials themselves stressed that "war pensions do not fulfill either the state's duties or those of society: they represent the minimum necessary to live on and must be integrated by subsidiary forms of assistance, which must serve to attest the Country's undying gratitude to the memory of those who have acquired the right to assistance from the state following on the death of a relative in the war, in the following descending order: widows, orphans, father, mother, brothers and sisters."[33]

In an effort to preserve order in the critical period following the defeat at Caporetto, the state established the Ministero per l'Assistenza Militare e le Pensioni di Guerra.[34] Contemporaries observed that:

> after holding its own ground for over two years because of the innate spontaneous virtues of the race, the country's resistance, both on the front line and behind the lines, underwent, not only through the wicked caprice of destiny, a sudden collapse ... The country should have been backed more efficiently, assiduously helped ... And so the concept of the need for a State organ of assistance took root.[35]

On leaving the Ministry he had directed since its inception, Leonida Bissolati, one of the protagonists of the state's response to the trauma of Caporetto, emphasized that:

> the effort accomplished, which statistics reveal as more intense than what I myself, you yourselves, could have imagined, was valuable on two accounts: it was the fulfillment of a holy and urgent duty towards all those who fought—whether they died, were invalided, or even remained unscathed, though always heroically, always usefully, for the great cause of the fatherland and of humanity; and it was also an internal trench from which we fought for the resistance when the (even involuntary) sluggishness and absence of public offices could have weakened and did weaken many among all those for whom the events of the war made the need for assistance more pressing. And this assistance was not so much and not only material: it was moral assistance on a very high level.[36]

Yet, if the size of the pensions (Table 1) is measured against the decrease of the purchasing power of 100 Italian Lire (Table 2), the economic condition of widows appears extremely critical.

It was reiterated after the war that it was necessary "to study every way in which to avoid creating a population on welfare"[37] but this professed goal contrasted, where widows were concerned, with the paucity and inadequacy of measures intended to provide employment for widows or otherwise alleviate their domestic difficulties.[38] Widows too were subjected to the generalized process of re-establishing gender divisions which had been disrupted by wartime conditions. The heated resumption of the debate on maternity and the active support given to the reintegration of men into the public and private sectors reduced the social assertiveness and new public role which women had forged during the war years.[39] The repair of the social fractures resulting from the war was consequently reflected in efforts to address the all-too-real problem of the rupture of the family nucleus.[40] The need to re-absorb men into the workplace accentuated the struggle between the sexes; the first state provisions for reintegrating demobilized men in the labor market ignored widows.[41] As the Treasury Minister pointed out:

> Where widows are concerned no special provisions exist for their preferential admission to public employment. It is a fact, however, that the personnel of the Administration of the postal, telegraph, and telephone services includes many women and this Presidency will see, within its competence, whether dispositions should be sent out or provisions put into effect so that the system which already exists without any specific dispositions in the State Railway Services may be generalized in favor of widows.[42]

This document was one of the responses to an inquiry distributed by the Office of the President of the Council of Ministers to all Ministries, a move designed to assuage pressure from a socialist association of veterans and widows, the Lega proletaria.[43] In October 1919 the Lega asked the Government to commit itself to giving preference to disabled ex-servicemen, war widows, and orphans for employment in the public administration. While some offices were unaware of the legislative deficiency or did not want an increase in employment categories, others complained of the absence of widows among the protected subjects.[44] The widows' situation was made even worse by the lack of lists of vacant posts in the ministries that made it difficult to know what was available.

The Association of War Mothers and Widows: Continuity and Breakdown

The hardships and difficulties of war widows were not expressed only through individual initiatives. The various veterans' associations, which were formed at the end of the war, not only provided effective material assistance to widows but also appeared to present a collective identity which offered its supporters opportunities with which to interpret the war experience. Where widows were concerned in particular, the associations either emphasized continuity with the prewar social order or stressed the need to face the modification of life necessitated by the loss of a spouse. In other words, greater stress was placed upon the need for increased war pensions to keep pace with the rising cost of living, or upon guaranteed employment. One association, exclusively female, the Associazione Madri e Vedove dei Caduti in Guerra (Association of Mothers and Widows of the Fallen), remained suspended between obtaining "compensation" for the loss of the head of the family and demanding new legislation. The Association managed to express a distinctive identity, based on consolation and the bond of "victims," but it also represented the expression of a new social role and, potentially, a restatement of citizenship.

On the one hand the organization expressed a kind of modernity in the articulation of an interest. The "processing" of mourning within this associative channel presumed a measure of social continuity, yet the widows' associations efforts were directed, even if only as mediators between the state and their own members, toward the recognition of a right to rather than a dependence upon charity. In July 1921 the board of the Association presented a memorandum to the relevant state institutions outlining their requests, which included a decree on lotteries to the Ministry of Finance, the concession of war surplus, free circulation on public transport, and new regulations concerning pensions. The closing lines of the communication are emblematic of the ambivalence of the strategy adopted: "we consider it our duty to remind you that, after having been forced to form an action committee for the Association itself, this Central Presidency is finding it difficult to hold back the union-oriented tendencies which the long wait imposed by the Government is accentuating more and more in the families of the fallen."[45]

Consequently, the Association appears to have been caught paradoxically between its new role as an instrument of pressure and its more conservative or traditional position, given its reference point of a female universe with individual and social values which corresponded to the reactionary climate in the postwar period. The Association's refusal to declare any political affiliation and its idealization of the Fatherland were indicative of its strongly conservative orientation, as suggested in its program:

> The Associazione Nazionale Madri e Vedove dei Caduti, founded in Milan in 1917 by hearts which were broken and comforted by the light of Faith and love for the Fatherland, proposes, above and beyond any political party, to organize all the Mothers and Widows of the Men who fell in the War and, as supporters, the fathers, brothers, sisters and orphans of the Fallen into one single, large family which, while daily renewing its struggle for the triumph of the Church and the greatness of Italy on God's Altars, cooperates with every healthy force in the country toward national reconstruction, defends the rights of the families of the fallen, promotes mutual brotherly assistance in their needs and the pious and active remembrance of those who died for their Country.[46]

The Association also stressed that its establishment was "inspired in all its activities by the supreme ideals of Religion and the Fatherland above every political party and in memory of the Valiant Dead."[47] This sentiment was echoed by one of its leaders, who wrote that the Association

> calls on all good Italians in order to offer them an occasion for accomplishing a dutiful act of gratitude ... to stop, for a moment, the race to attain egotistical targets, in the pressing events of this tormented postwar period, and "bring to mind" those who through their sacrifice have left the Country the inheritance of their sacred affections ... Through its Secretariat for Assistance, it embraces all the families of the Fallen.[48]

The ideological struggle present in the Association could also be attributed to the process of female emancipation embodied in nineteenth-century philanthropism, which marked the transition from charitable to welfare activities and which tended to give women instrumental opportunities rather than alms.[49]

The Association was founded in Milan on 26 November 1917, in a memorial crypt of Milanese who had fallen in the conflict. It was promoted by a group of bourgeois and noble women, themselves the mothers or widows of war victims, with the assistance of a priest, Father Enrico Mauri.[50] Its initial concern was to develop the organization of mourning.[51] Meanwhile, mothers and widows of the fallen were also organizing an Assistance League, which received the immediate support of the authorities, and collaborating with the Comitato d'Azione tra Mutilati, Invalidi e Feriti di Guerra (Action Committee of the War Maimed, Disabled and Wounded.)[52]

These organizations defended the validity of the war and of the sacrifice it involved, and engaged in the activity always defined as "patriotic" in support of combatants and their families. The Association remained in the foreground, participating in assemblies and demonstrations in favor of internal mobilization, but its principal focus remained the organization of mourning.[53] After all, there was a general "need for reintegration and recovery of the soldier's death, of transfer of the individual, obscene and unspeakable death to collective living, which is sustained and no longer contradicted by it."[54]

The rhetoric concerning the fallen, with the consequent mythicization of their sacrifice,[55] undoubtedly meant (among other things) concealing the difficulties faced by the grieving families.[56] That rhetoric also fulfilled another contradictory function in the definition of collective and individual identity, which may help explain why widows were able to present themselves as moral defenders of the entire nation.[57] The first national meeting of the Association of Widows and Mothers pronounced that "Mothers and wives who with proud and Christian sorrow have promised on the beloved tombs of their fallen to consecrate themselves to the generous ideal for which they died."[58] As George Mosse pointed out, the fallen and the way in which they were commemorated formed a decisive part of the myth of the war experience, which, in turn, played a fundamental role in guaranteeing a measure of continuity in the transition from war to peace.[59]

The Association's statutes were discussed at a 14 April 1918 congress attended by local secretaries representing nearly all the regions of Italy. The cult of the fallen was given pride of place. Article two of the constitution specified this:

> to profess the importance of religious-moral values in the supreme hours of sorrow and in the trials of the Fatherland ...,to cooperate so that all may accomplish their duty towards the Fatherland and towards the advent of a greater Italy in harmony with her glorious traditions ...,to promote and foster initiatives and provisions destined to give moral relief to the families of the fallen and the recognition of their rights, through forming and fostering secretariats for the assistance of war orphans, mothers and widows, ... to promote honors and prayers for those who have fallen for the Fatherland.

The next article of the statute underscored the work of the relief secretariats:

to favor, together with similar pro-orphan organizations, their education within their families and their placement when necessary in institutions ..., to visit and bring help to needy families of fallen soldiers, and also to help them legally in procedures and controversies concerning their pensions, the assignment of subsidies and their share in the public provisions ..., to represent the mothers and widows of fallen soldiers ..., to adhere to and cooperate with all those initiatives which are aimed at alleviating the hard contingencies of war.

The statutory document clearly revealed the link between the modernity of the organization in setting itself up as an instrument of pressure on the one hand and the continuity of social values and identities it embodied on the other. Article four of the statutes established that only mothers and widows—classified according to their financial contribution—could be effective members; the sisters of fallen soldiers could only be supporters. While being considered, this article was emended to invite the fathers of fallen soldiers to belong to the Association as supporting members. They were organized in a separate group which would "give precious encouragement, advice and support" and "avoid the formation of other associations which ... could produce a division in the sorrowful family, a division which must be avoided."[60] The Association applied to the government to be listed as a non-profit organization. This was granted in 1920.[61]

One can trace the Association's early activities through the recollections of Elena Chiavellati, the widow of an officer killed in the Second World War and an executive member:

> It is both dutiful and evocative to remember its romantic origins in times of calamity and offer the example of the small group of strong Italian women who built the moral edifice which was soon to spread to the very confines of the fatherland on the foundation of their mourning ... Thus the first nucleus of smitten women grew under an exquisitely moral sign; it was the eternal commandment of the sacrifice which, as yet unfulfilled, drew on itself for the necessary strength to revive that of others.[62]

Her reminiscences illustrate the association's importance in organizing grief and memory, the opportunities it afforded for civic participation, and its conservative bent with regard to basic social values, the same ones which had contributed to the combatants' deaths in the first place. These themes are echoed in a letter from another widow, herself a noblewoman, to the king:

> The thought of that peace, the fruit of the sacrifice of our dear ones and our own sacrifice, is not only a comfort but a stimulus to continue being, within the bosom of the country, not a suffering mass but an ever-living

member, vibrant with intense love, always ready, in the tenacity of our intentions, to devote all our energies and ourselves in order to see Italy freer and greater under the coordinating paternal authority of the State, the attainment of the dream for which our sons and spouses die ... The solution of social problems through class collaboration and the moral and intellectual elevation of the workers, the development and freedom of culture, the assertion of the need for concord to bring to an end the painful situation of settling down, will be most actively reciprocated in the hearts of the Mothers and Widows of the Fallen.[63]

But the "painful situation" did not allow them autonomy of action once they had embraced the traditional values, and it was not by chance that the Association was able to develop considerably under fascism.

In its defense of national unity, the Association was actively involved in the selection of the tomb of the "Unknown Soldier" (1921) for Italy's war commemoration and in the criticism of "the bolshevik insanity which denies all the most values."[64] The fascist regime, which consolidated and utilized the myth of the Great War and understood the importance of the Association's apotheosis of the fallen,[65] merged the Association with two other similarly oriented groups, the one of the fathers and the other one of the relatives (Associazione dei Padri dei Caduti, Associazione dei congiunti dei Caduti), in 1923. In 1924 these three associations were renamed the Associaiiazione Nazionale Famiglie Caduti in Guerra, a non-profit agency. The fascist regime, however, practiced a policy of rigid control of the new Association, especially after 1926, placing it under the guidance of a commissary.[66] This process of reorganization met with minimal opposition, in part because of divisions within the Association, but also because it led to the availability of more funding, an increase in membership and a more functional system of social control.[67]

For example, the number of its executive members who visited the houses of indigent widows and who had been active since the Association's inception actually increased to produce a more efficient control of the widows being assisted. In fact, when a visitor found that a widow had not "behaved" (that is, conformed to the association's precepts), assistance was suspended. From 1921 onwards the work of the Association regarding the employment of war widows was merely carried out through the dispensation of individual subsidies, the establishment of health services and rest homes for disabled or elderly mothers and widows, and the distribution of food and clothing. More ambitious or innovatory initiatives, however, were absent. Labor cooperatives for war widows were instituted only in Milan. Thus, preference was given to the strategy of maintaining the value of housework, with the intention of defending the maternal role of women.[68]

The war widow emphasizes sexual ambivalence in a system where marriage is the ultimate social status. Patriotism and family overlap can get confused, but it was the war itself which made returning to traditional life more difficult. For the widows, in fact, the war was a double fracture of their daily existence. War widowhood brought a loss of security on both an individual and social level for women. It is important to underline both the war's radicalizing economic and social impact, and the very contradictory function of the widow's experience, swinging as it did between a desire to control her own life and to remain attached to her past life which was kept alive by the memories of the war. For the middle- and upper-class widows this status alteration was more difficult to accept.

The war experience established a close material and moral link between widows and the state. In the postwar era widows found themselves, on the one hand, as protagonists of their new-found citizenship. On the other hand, the social role of mourning continued to link them to their deceased husbands.

Postwar Italian welfare policy reflected a clear effort to restore the symbolic and social prewar world: widows were a fundamental social instrument in the effort to rebuild the postwar order. The total sacrifice involved in the death of the soldiers masked the deep lacerations of the social order and, once invoked, made the restoration easier. The remembrance of those killed and the motives which emerged in war as connections between the battle front and the home front—honor, patriotism, family—re-emerged once the war was over as a constant of family life. Even the organization of mourning—ceremonies, commemorations, honors—by the various widows' organizations resulted in a constant redefinition of personal identity. This female association managed to express a distinctive identity, and played a double role. It represented the expression of a new social role and a restatement of citizenship, but it also based its identity on consolation and the bond of "victims."

TABLE 1 Yearly allowances to widows by period, husband's rank, and children (Italian Lire)

Period	1915–21	1915–18	1919–20	1921	
No. of Children	0	1 to 5	1 to 5	1 to 5	
Children's Age		All Ages	All Ages	14 Years	14 Years
Military Rank					
Soldier	630	630–780	730–955	1400–2025	830–1455
Corporal	840	840–990	940–1165	1640–2265	1040–1665
Sergeant	1120	1120–1270	1220–1445	1700–2325	1320–1945
Warrant Officer	1500	1500–1650	1600–1825	1900–2525	1700–2325
Sub Lieutenant	1500	1500–1650	1600–1825	2135–2940	1700–2325
Lieutenant	1500	1500–1650	1600–1825	2315–2940	1700–2325
Captain	1720	1720–1870	1820–2045	3215–3840	1920–2545
Major	2000	2000–2150	2100–2325	4070–4695	2200–2825
Lieut. Colonel	2400	2400–2550	2500–2725	4340–4965	2600–3225
Colonel	3200	3200–3350	3300–3525	4925–5550	3400–4025
Brigadier Gen.	3600	3600–3750	3700–3925	5375–6000	3800–4425
Senior Gen.	4000	4000–4150	4100–4325	6200–6825	4200–4825

TABLE 2 Purchasing power of 100 Lire for the years from 1914 to 1921*

Year	According to Cost of Living Index	According to Wholesale Price Index
1914	100	100
1915	93.5	73.3
1916	74.7	51.9
1917	52.8	34.0
1918	37.9	23.2
1919	37.3	21.3
1920	28.4	16.2
1921	24.0	17.7

* I would like to thank Agostino Bistarelli and Claudio Pavone for many long and stimulating hours of discussion and debate over the issues aired in this essay. I owe particular debts of gratitude to Paola di Cori who bravely endured several drafts of this piece and offered wise advice on how to reshape each successive incarnation.

Notes to Chapter 8

1. J. Wallach Scott, *Women's History,* in idem, *Gender and the Politics of History* (New York, Columbia University Press, 1988), pp. 15–27, p.25.
2. Elena Chiavellati, *Le vedove,* in "Vivi tra i Vivi," National Organ of the Associazione nazionale famiglie dei caduti in guerra, February 1958, p.10.
3. The post-unitary Civil Code of 1865 provided for the enjoyment of civil rights by all citizens but at the same time it excluded certain categories from their complete or partial exercise. Women were debarred from guardianship, from being part of a Family Council, and from witnessing the registration of deeds and wills (cf. respectively arts. 268 c.c and 236 c.c.; arts. 351 and 788 c.c). According to the Code of Penal Procedure women could not act as arbitrators in agreements (art.10). Neither did they have the right of either active or passive representation. Besides, without any legislative declaration, they were debarred from the practise of certain professions (cf. the sentence of the Court of Cassation of Turin of April 18, 1884 which confirmed the decision of the Court of Appeal of November 14, 1883 which struck off the lawyers' rolls the first woman to obtain a degree in Jurisprudence, Lidia Poet, thus establishing the preclusion of the lawyer's profession to women).
4. P. di Cori, *The Double Gaze: Visibility of Sexual Gender in Photographic Representations (1908–1918),* in M. Cioni-N. Prunster, *Visions and Revisions, Women in Italian Culture* (Berg Publishers, Ltd., Oxford, 1993): first ed.; idem, *Il doppio sguardo. Visibilità dei generi sessuali nella rappresentazione fotografica (1908–1918),* in *La Grande Guerra. Esperienza, memoria, immagini* (Bologna, 1986). On this subject we refer the readers to G. Fiume (ed. by) *Onore e storia nelle società mediterranee* (Palermo, 1989) in particular cf. the essay included in L. Scaraffia's *Riflessioni ai margini del convegno.*
5. We should remember that in Italy, until 1970, the only cause for the annulment of marriage was the death of one of the spouses. the matrimonial régime involved a further limitation of the female juridical capacity. The husband was declared the unquestioned head of the family (art. 131 c.c.) in personal relationships, in patrimonial aspects and in relations with the offspring—patria potestas was in fact attributed to both spouses, but only the man could practise it (art. 220 c.c.)—above all, the woman was subjected to the necessary marital authorization (arts. 134, 135, 136, 137 c.c.) to "donate, alienate real estate, subject it to mortgage, obtain loans, to cede or collect capital, to act as guarantee or compound or be a party in court proceedings relating to such acts." The husband forbid her to receive certain persons, thus definitively completing the circle of family subjection (cf. M. Sasso, *Autorità maritale,* in *Nuovo Digesto Italiano* (Torino, 1937–40).
6. According to the dictum established by art. 235 c.c: "By will or by an authentic act the father can impose conditions on the surviving mother concerning the education of the children and the administration of property." The dispositions laid

down by the deceased person carried the authority of an order, but the woman could ask for a dispensation from the Family Council or, in the case of its negative opinion, from the state institutions: she could have recourse to the court and the Court of Appeal. Besides, if at the moment of her husband's death the woman was pregnant, the court, on request of an interested person, could appoint a curator of the womb (art. 236 c.c.) whose duty it was to watch over the birth. After the birth full patria potestas reverted to the mother. In case of remarriage the widow had to summon the Family Council to whose authority she was still subject.

7. J. A. McNamara, *Wives and Widows in Early Christian Tought*, in "International Journal of Women's Studies," November-December, 1979, pp. 575–92; L. Siciliano Villanuova, *Le seconde nozze della vedova "intra tempus luctus." Il valore derogatorio del diritto canonico*, in *Studi giuridici in onore di Carlo Fadda* (Napoli, 1906, pp.141–43); E. P. Thompson, *Rough Music: le charivari anglais*, in "Annales ESC," 2, 1972; E. Raseri, *Sulla frequenza delle seconde nozze e sulle durata di vedovanza in Italia ed altri stati* (Milano, 1888); G. Gabrielli, *La "Scampanata" o "Cocciata" nelle nozze della vedova*, in "Lares," II, 1931, pp.58–61.

8. Cf. Civil Code arts. no. 570 which defined and regulated a widow's mourning, and art. 128 which established the sanctions in cases of non-observance of the set period. Besides, a husband could make widowhood a condition for a testamentary legacy or bequest. On this subject cf. L. Gallavresi, *I diritti della vedova durante l'anno di lutto* (Milano, 1882); and V. Scialoja, *I diritti della vedova durante l'anno del lutto secondo l'art. 1415 del Codice Civile* (Roma, 1886); C. Nencha, *Della condicione di vedovanza. Studio sull'ultimo capoverso dell'art, 850 c.c.* (Trani, 1886); L. Ramponi, *La condizione del celibato e di vedovanza nei testamenti e nei contratti* (Firenze, 1893); M. Marucchi, *Della condizione di vedovanza apposta in un testamento*, in "Giornale della Legge," fasc. 18, 19, 20, vol. I, 1887.

9. Report by Vigliani, a member of the Senate Committee, quoted in L. Ramponi, *Le condizioni del celibato e di vedovanza nei testamenti e nei contratti* (Firenze, 1893), p. 96.

10. M. Segalen, *Quelques réflexions pour l'étude de la condition féminine*, in "Annales de démographie historique," 1981, p. 18.

11. We will give as an example what Luzzatti—a professor of constitutional law and able economist who was elected member of parliament a number of times and was Prime Minister in 1910—wrote in an important Italian newspaper on the importance of an early reform of war pensions in order to "remove the excuse widows have against contracting legitimate marriage in order not to lose their pension. The proposals here are legitimate. They must all be pondered with the idea of reconciling finances with morals (...). But we have heard no one say that the present state of things must persist, because it only generates illegitimate families, spurious children, and the ill-treatment of legitimate children; it represents nothing other than shameless and remorseless permanent sin; it breaks the backbone of honest families, which are the glory and fortune of the states which are destined to stand out in the civilized world." L. Luzzatti, *La riforma della legge sulle pensioni di guerra*, "Corriere della Sera, " November 10, 1916. We quote, as another example, the words of the Commander of an Army Corps to the Prime Minister's Office on September 14, 1920: "We feel that attention should be brought to the situation of many widows who, in order not to lose their war pensions, remarry only in the church, with considerable juridical consequences for the children born of these marriages which are not legally valid," in Archivio Centrale dello Stato, Presidenza del Consiglio dei Ministri, 1920, f 1/2.

12. The rhetoric of family sacrifices gave many parliamentary members the opportunity, in the course of the first postwar debates—during which the vote was granted to women in one of the two chambers in 1919, but was not ratified by the senate because the government fell—to allow widows at least to vote. The Catholic member of parliament Micheli, who was in favor of women's vote, declared: "I am certain that if tomorrow (...) the mothers and widows of the men who fell in the war could participate in the elections these elections would acquire almost the solemnity of a rite. The memory of the sacrafice accomplished would certainly bring weight to bear on making the electoral competition more serious and considered," in Camera dei Deputati, Atti Parlamentari, Doc. no. 2121, session 1919–1923.

However, all compromise on women's votes was rejected and the House approved the integral text which provided for the concession of administrative suffrage to all women while putting off political suffrage to the next legislature. We have quoted Micheli's words because they show how it was not the assumption of the role of head of the family which suggested the concession of electorship to widows and mothers, as "single mothers," but rather the substitution of the woman for the combatant. Where widows, unlike the combatants' mothers, were concerned, the two social representations we have tried to highlight—of "mutilated" wives and of their possible sexual freedom—coincide. Where this is concerned, we have the example of the exclusion of widows—mothers on the contrary were included—from the bill for the concession of administrative voting limited to certain categories of "worthy" women, because of the difficulty of identifying "those who live notoriously in concubinage" as B. Mussolini, who was Prime Minister at the time maintained. The bill fell through again because of the end of the legislature and was presented again—and once again modified—a few months later. This time widows were included, but with the significant exception of "those for whom personal separation had torn asunder all bonds of sentiment and affection with the heroic fallen spouse." The bill was approved on 22 November, 1925, but with the fascist regime's "podestarile" reform of the following year which suppressed the electivity of local administration no one—neither men nor women—had in fact the right to vote.

For an overall picture of the history of the vote for women, cf. M. P. Bigaran, *Progetti e dibattiti parlamentari sul suffragio femminile: da Peruzzi a Giolitti*, in "Rivista di Storia Contemporanea," 1, 1985; idem, *Il voto alle donne in Italia dal 1912 al fascismo*, in "Rivista di Storia Contemporanea," 2, 1987.

13. For contributions on these aspects cf. in particular P. Fussell, *The Great War and Modern Memory* (Oxford, 1975); E. Leed, *No Man's Land* (Cambridge, 1979).

14. M. Randolph Higonnet, J. Jenson, S. Michel, M. Collins Weitz, eds., *Behind the Lines. Gender and the Two World Wars* (New Haven and London, 1987); for Italy see, P. di Cori, *The Double Gaze ...*, quoted; M. De Giorgio, *Dalla "Donna Nuova" alla donna della "nuova" Italia*, in D. Leoni-C. Zadra, *La Grande Guerre ...*, quoted, pp. 307–31; A. Bravo, ed, *Donne e Uomini in guerra* (Roma-Bari, 1991).

15. The data we have developed is based on the estimates presented in: Ministero della Guerra-Ufficio Statistico, *La forza dell'esercito. Statistica dello sforzoa militare italiano alla guerra mondiale* (Roma, 1927); Ministero per l'Assistenza militare e le pensioni di guerra, *L'assistenza di guerra in Italia. Assistenza Militare—Pensioni di guerra. III Conferenza Interalleata per la protezione degli Invalidi di Guerra*, presentation and comments by L. Pavoni and D. Avarelli (Roma, 1919); Presidenza del Consiglio-Istituto Centrale di Statistica, *Censimento del Regno d'Italia*, years 1911 e 1921; *Albo d'oro dei Caduti* (Roma, 1927); Minisatero dell'economia

nazionale-Direzione Generale della Statistica, *Annuario Statistico italiano*, years 1919-1921 (Roma, 1921); F. Zugaro, *L'albo d'oro dei caduti per l'Italia nella guerra mondiale*, extract from n.4 of the *Bollettino dell'Ufficio Storico dello Stato Maggiore del Regio Esercito* (Roma, 1926); Ufficio Centrale Notizie-Bologna, *I morti della Provincia di Bologna nella guerra MCMXV-MCMXVIII per elenco alfabetico* (Bologna, 1927).

16. On the basis of the only complete data, concerning the fallen of the province of Bologna, we have calculated the percentage of married persons as compared to the total losses (32.30%). The data thus obtained, applied to the national total of the fallen (680.071), gives a figure of 219.662 married dead and consequently of widows.

    In order to get closer to the exact figures we then divided the Bologna data by years of birth thus obtaining the rate of deceased married soldiers by age. We obtained two further indexes which, when applied to the total of the national figure of fallen soldiers, leads to the respective figures of 208.711 and 206.360. A third projection was made analyzing the data of the composition by civil status and relative age groups of the Italian population. Comparing this last data with the make-up by age group of the Italian army, the rate of married men came to 38.2%. If we were to apply this index to the universe of the fallen we would have 259,923 widows.

17. From the beginning of the war there was a constant proliferation of women's agitations against the war throughout the peninsula as well as their immediate registration in the files of the Central Police Offices. These agitations were caused by the upset to economic-family equilibrium produced by the men's departure for the front line; cf. Archivio Centrale dello Stato (ACS), Direzione Generale di Pubblica Sicurezza (DGPS), I Guerra Mondiale 1915-1918.

18. ACS, Presidenza del Consiglio dei Ministri (PCM), 1917, f. 1.2.

19. Idem.

20. G. Calvi, *Dal margine al centro. Soggettività femminile, famiglia, stato moderno in Toscana (XVI-XVIII sec.)*, in *Discutendo di storia. Soggettività ricerca, biografia*, pp. 103-12, 105.

21. ACS, PCM, 1992, f. 2.1.

22. ACS, PCM, 1920, f. 2, n. 853 and PCM 1916, f. 2.

23. Statement transmitted to the PCM by the DGPS on July 10th 1920, in ACS, PCM, 1920, f. 2, n. 1429.

24. The two letters are preserved in ACS, PCM, 1918, f.2 and f.1.2.

25. ACS, PCM, 1922, f. 2/10.4.

26. Letter written by Elody Tarchetti Perelli in ACS, PCM, 1917, f.1/2.

27. Giolitti report on the law on charity read in the Chamber of Deputies on 18.7.1904 n. 390.

28. As an example of the enormous legislation, we should remember that between 1914 and 1918 over 2,500 economic provisions were enforced in Italy (a quarter of these between '14 and '16); for a detailed reconstruction cf. R. Tremelloni, *Aspetti economici della guerra*, in Presidenza del Consiglio dei Ministri, *1915-1918. L'Italia nella grande guerra* (Roma, 1970), pp.265-98.

29. The Bill 13 may, 1915 n.620 regulates the concession of daily help to the needy families of rank and file soldiers. Some extensions and adjustments of the sums are contained in the following provisions: dlgt. 6.10.'15; dlgt. 2.10.'16; dlgt. 30.4.'17; dlgt. 10.9.'17; dlgt. 16.11.'18.

30. Ministero per l'Assistenza ..., *L'Assistenza* ..., quoted, p.125.

31. Decreto Luogotenenziale of 27.10.1918 n. 1726 arts. 11 and 12.

32. R.Cao Pinna, *Pensioni di guerra*, in *Nuovo Digesto*, quoted p.773.

33. Ministero per l'Assistenza ..., *L'Assistenza* ...,quoted, p.275.
34. On 24 October 1917 the Austrians broke through the Italian lines. The retreat of the Italian troops, which became a disorderly rout, had serious repercussions on the government and on the Supreme Command. The Boselli government fell and was replaced by Emanuele Orlando's. General Cadorna was replaced by General Diaz.
35. Ministero per l'Assistenza militare ..., *L'Assistenza Militare* ..., op.cit. p.622.
36. Leonida Bissolati's farewell speech to civilian and military officials in idem. p.31.
37. S. Nitti, speech to the Chamber of Deputies, 19.12.1917.
38. Legge 20.4.1920, n.512.
39. F. Pieroni Bortolotti's two volumes, *Socialismo e questione femminile in Italia 1892–1922* (Milano, 1974), and *Femminismo e partiti politici in Italia 1919–1926* (Roma, 1978), are still indispensable for the history of women during this period; see also A. Bravo, *Donne contadine e prima guerra mondiale*, in "Società e Storia," II (1980), n. 10; D. Leoni-C. Zadra, *I ruoli sconvolti: donne e famiglia a Volano nel Trentino durante la guerra del Quindici*, in "Movimento operaio e socialista," V (1982), n. 3; for changes in the legislation during this period, A. Galoppini, *Il lungo viaggio verso la parità*, Bologna, 1980.
40. Cf. Karen Hausen, *The German* ... quot.
41. L. 25.3.1917 n. 481 for the employment of disabled servicemen; L. 18.7.1917 for war orphans.
42. ACS, PCM, 1919, f. 3, n. 44.
43. For a complete history of this association see G. Isola, *Guerra al regno della guerra? Storia della Lega proletaria mutilati, invalidi, reduci, orfani e vedove di guerra (1918–1924), (Le lettere, Firenze, 1990)*.
44. ACS, PCM, 1919, f.3.
45. Letter from the Associazione Nazionale Madri e Vedove Caduti in Guerra (ANMVCG) to Prime Minister Bonomi, 8.7.1921, in ACS, PCM, 1921, f. 2.10 n.648.
46. Membership Card preserved in the Archives of the Associazione Nazionale Famiglie Caduti e Dispersi in Guerra (AANFCDG), Documenti e Circolari, Roma.
47. Curriculum vitae sent by the Associazione to the king on 23.3.1922, in ACS, Ufficio del Primo Aiutante di Campo del Re 1921–25 (UPACR), B.404, n.478.
48. Letter from the widow R. Vercelli Lolli to General Cittadini, aide-de-camp to the King, on 30.5.1922, in ACS, UPACR, B.404.
49. A. Buttafuoco, *Straniere in patria. Temi e momenti dell'emancipazione femminile italiana dalle Repubbliche giacobine al fascismo*, in A. M. Crispino, (ed. by), *Esperienza storica femminile nell'età moderna e contemporanea, Parte prima*, La Goccia (Roma, 1988), pp. 91–123, p. 99.
50. For an account of the manifestation cf. "Vivi tra i Vivi," quot., July 1959.
51. Manifesto of the ANMVCG of 23 May 1918, signed by the National President, Emilia Salvi, in AAFCDG, Doc.e Circ., Roma.
52. A. Morelli, *Storia dell'Associazione*, 7th issue, in "Vivi tra i Vivi," July 1959. Pieroni Bortolotti gives a different reconstruction, see, *Femminismo e Partiti politici in Italia 1919–1926* (Roma, 1978), maintaining that the Lega and the Associazione were alternatives. The material preserved in the archives of the association appears however to confirm Morelli's reconstruction.
53. "Religious and civil honors to our Heroes and their venerated Tombs and Cemeteries inspired with equal fervor by the memory of our beloved fallen and the sacred ideals of Religion and the Fatherland." This explicit reference is to be found in the declaration *Il nostro programma*, ANMVCG, printed on the membership cards.

54. C. Canal, *La retorica della morte. I monumenti ai caduti della Grande Guerra*, in "Rivista di Storia Contemporanea," 1982, n.4, pp. 659–69, p. 660. On overcoming the "disagreeable past" see also G. L. Mosse, *Le Guerre mondiali. Dalla tragedia al mito dei caduti* (Roma-Bari, 1990); idem, *Two World Wars and the Myth of War Experience*, in "The Journal of Contemporary History," n. 21, 1986, pp. 491–513.
55. Concerning the postwar rites in which the "Mater" appears see L. Scaraffia, *Bemerkungen zur Geschichte der Mater dolorosa der Schmerzensmutter, vorsuglich in Suditalian*, in "L'homme. Zeitschriften fur Feministiche Geschichtszissenschaft," n. 1, 1990. See also A. Bravo, *Simboli del materno*, in idem., *Donne e Uomini* ..., quoted, pp. 196–234.

   In a pamphlet distributed in the parishes in 1916 widows were admonished as follows: "the souls of your husbands, oh piteous widows, also insist on this union of hearts as that which guarantees your faithfulness to their love and best provides for their needs through suffrages which hasten their entry into heaven." The union it referred to was the union between the widow and the Sacred Heart of Jesus, *La vedova e gli orfani a causa della guerra* (Tolentino, 1916, Tipografica Fidelio). On this subject, cf. Paola di Cori, *Rosso e bianco. La devozione al Sacro Cuore di Gesù nel primo dopoguerra*, in "Memoria," n. 5, 1982; A. Zambardieri, *Per la storia della devozione al Sacro Cuore in Italia tra '800 e '900*, in "Rivista di storia della Chiesa in Italia," XLI, 1987; L. Scaraffia, *Devozioni di guerra. Identità femminile e simboli religiosi negli anni quaranta*, in A. Bravo, *Donne e Uomini* ..., quoted, pp. 135–60.
56. K. Hausen, *The German* ..., in *Behind* ..., quoted.
57. On this subject, cf. M. Isnenghi, *Le guerre degli italiani. Parole, immagini, ricordi, 1848–1945* (Milano, 1989).
58. Manifesto to the citizens on the occasion of the religious opening ceremony of the Congress of 14 April 1918, quoted in "Vivi tra i Vivi," April 1960.
59. G. L. Mosse, *Le guerre* ..., quot.
60. The document is quoted in "Vivi tra i Vivi," quot., December 1959. According to Morelli's reconstruction, *La storia* ..., quot., some fathers of fallen men were dissatisfied with the qualification of supporting members which the Associazione Madri e Vedove dei Caduti had assigned to them and created their own association: the Associazione Nazionale Padri dei Caduti in Guerra, with its seat in Milan. No document concerning this Association is preserved in ANFCDG, Doc.e Circ., Roma.
61. DR, 19 February 1920.
62. E. Chiavellati, *Anniversario*, in "Vivi tra i Vivi," January 1958.
63. M. Gotti Bonaparte, Letter to the King, in ACS, UPACR, B.404, n.478.
64. Immediately after the war the winning nation rendered sovereign honors to a symbol: the unknown hero. Within two or three years of the end of hostilities France and Great Britain (in 1920), the United States and Italy (in 1921), and the other countries later all returned to the sites of the conflict to "elect" the body of the unknown soldier; then, after a solemn journey and funeral rite the unknown soldier found a new tomb; the Arch of Triumph in Paris, Westminster in London, and the Arlington National Cemetery in Washington.
65. cf. G. Rochat, *L'Italia nella prima guerra mondiale. Mito e storiografia fino al 1943*, in "Rivista di storia contemporanea," fasc.1, 1976, pp.1–27; G.L. Mosse, *La guerra* ...,quot; L. Passerini, *Mussolini immaginario* (Roma-Bari, 1991).
66. This operation was concluded in November 1926 and a member of parliament, count Valentino Orsolini Cencelli, was placed at the head of the Association as General Commissary of the state. He discontinued all section and provincial

assemblies and as an executive member of the association recalled, "no more meetings were held." *Report of the Comitato di Venezia*, preserved in AANFCDG, Doc.e Circ., Roma.
67. In 1927 the new Administration of the Association asked the executive members for an increase in the number of associates and sections to make a capillary territorial control possible. We would like to stress how this action was developed through the use of the diffusion and rooting of the Catholic religion. The report of the Provincial Committee of Venice is crudely explanatory: the task "was carried out relatively easily, because it was considered suitable to entrust it to the Presidents of the district Sections who received the specific mandate to form sections in all the communes belonging to their districts; they were ordered to choose as secretary of the Section in formation the delegate of the 'charitable institution in favor of orphans.' Since the Delegate was in fact in most cases the Parish Priest of the village he had not only the moral prestige and necessary technical ability, but also a knowledge of the individuals and the possibility of weighing and controlling every circumstance," in *Relazione del Comitato provinciale e della sezione provinciale di Venezia*, quot. The dual function of relief and control was practised in Germany too, cf. K. Hausen, *The German ...*, in *Behind the Line ...*, quot.
68. Cf. the discussion of the executives of the Association, in AFCDG, Verbali, Roma.

Select Bibliography

F. Bettio, *The Sexual Division of Labour: the Italian Case* (New York: Oxford University Press, 1988).

A. Bravo, ed., *Donne e Uomini nelle Guerre Mondiali* (Bari: Laterza, 1991).

M. De Giorgio, *Le italiane dall'Unità ad oggi* (Roma/Bari: Laterza, 1992).

P. Di Cori, "The Double Gaze: Visibility of Sexual Gender in Photographic Representations (1908–1918)," in M. Cioni and N. Punster, eds., *Visions and Revisions. Women in Italian Culture* (Oxford: Berg, 1993).

D. Leoni and C. Zadra, *La Grande Guerra: Esperienza, Memoria, Immagini* (Bologna: Il Mulino, 1986).

CHAPTER 9

FOR FATHERLAND AND JEWISH PEOPLE
Jewish Women in Austria During The First World War

Marsha L. Rozenblit

The First World War presented Austrian Jewry[1] with several major crises. Jews faced all the normal problems of a society at war—mobilized men, slaughter at the front, food shortages, hunger, and poverty at home. They also coped with all of the challenges of Austria-Hungary at war: several Russian invasions of the Austrian provinces of Galicia and Bukovina, the reality of the Eastern Front positioned on Austrian territory, and the contentiousness of nationality politics in a supra-national, dynastic state. Jews, however, also suffered during the war simply because they were Jews. The Russian invasions of Galicia and Bukovina caused hundreds of thousands of Jews to flee, because of either real or feared Russian persecution or because they lived in the battle zone and had to leave. Moreover, Jews suffered from rising anti-Semitism, especially in 1917 and 1918 when extreme food shortages caused many to blame the situation on "Jewish" profiteering.[2] Finally, the collapse of the Monarchy in 1918 created a grave crisis of identity for the Jews. Previously loyal to the supra-national state, and having asserted that they were "Austrians," they now had to construct new national identities in successor states which mostly denied that they could belong to the dominant nationalities of those states.[3]

Notes for this chapter begin on page 213.

Jewish women[4] in Austria experienced all these crises—the Russian invasions, rising anti-Semitism, and the identity crisis generated by the collapse of the Monarchy—both as Jews and as women. In particular, the problem of Galician refugees became a Jewish women's issue. Because so many men were mobilized, most of the refugees were women or children. Moreover, middle-class Jewish women in Vienna, Bohemia, and Moravia rallied to the cause of the Galician Jewish refugees and devoted themselves to helping these unfortunate Jews. Refugee aid allowed them to participate in work on the home front, and thus to contribute to the Austrian war effort, in a way that was socially acceptable for middle-class women. More important, refugee aid provided them with the opportunity to assert both their loyalty to Austria and their solidarity with the Jewish people. Thus, by helping poor suffering Jews, most of them women and children, middle-class Jewish women felt secure in an identity which allowed for supra-national Austrianism and Jewish folk loyalty at the same time.

With the outbreak of war in 1914, most Jewish women, like Jews generally, were caught up in the general excitement of the war. One Jewish woman in Vienna—21 years old in 1914—recalled in her memoirs over 30 years later:

> For the first time in their lives many people felt themselves transported above their narrow personal drives; no more selfish interests! Victory for the nation was the only dominant thought in most of us, for the moment at least. We had been struck by lightning and our very souls were left burning .... I was in a state of constant ecstasy, hardly able to concentrate on anything.[5]

Like most other Austrians, she assumed "that we would come out victorious and within a few months at that."[6] For men, war might have been, in the words of the Viennese Jewish writer Stefan Zweig, "a rapid excursion into the romantic, a wild, manly adventure,"[7] but conventional notions of women and war permitted women to weep over the potential loss of husbands, sons, and brothers, even in August 1914. Bertha Landre from Moravia, 12 years old in 1914, recalled in her memoirs the shame she felt because her mother cried when Austria declared war on Serbia. Her mother could not understand how people could celebrate when young men were going to the slaughter.[8]

Jewish women in Austria immediately mobilized to do their share for the Austrian war effort. As early as 26 July 1914, Clothilde Benedikt, an activist in Vienna, called on (obviously middle-class) Jewish women to help the war effort by raising and contributing money to help the families of called-up soldiers and to establish soup kitchens. She asked the women of Vienna to sacrifice, that is to serve less expensive food, to dress less well, and to abstain from vacations, in order to have extra money to help the less fortunate. Finally, she called on Jewish girls to volunteer to care for the children of mothers who had to work when their husbands were called up. Her appeal to Jewish women did not yet presuppose Jewish recipients of this charity, but assumed, in the spirit of the brotherhood of the early months of the war, that Jewish women would simply participate in the larger Austrian effort.[9]

Jewish women participated eagerly in war work. Many individuals donated their money, time, and energy to the Red Cross, making bandages or arranging for gifts for soldiers, or volunteering as aides in Red Cross hospitals.[10] Esti Freud, who was later to become Freud's daughter-in-law, became a volunteer nurse at the suggestion of her father, "a good Austrian patriot," who, she noted dryly in her memoirs, "had no son to sacrifice on the altar of the Fatherland."[11] Jewish organizations even set up special courses and homes to train such aides and to care for them.[12] Jewish women perceived this work as demonstrating the same loyalty to the Fatherland as men enacted on the battlefield. In a letter from a mother to her soldier son, reprinted in the Viennese Jewish newspaper, *Oesterreichische Wochenschrift*, the mother intersperses descriptions of her work for the Red Cross with statements about his loyalty to the Fatherland, and concludes that "everyone fights, loyal to the dear Fatherland."[13]

The Red Cross was not the only institution through which individual Jewish women helped the war effort. In Jamnitz, Moravia, for example, Berta Schwarzbart gathered girls and women together in her home to knit scarves, vests, and socks for soldiers, which they sent to the War Welfare Office.[14] In Pohrlitz, Moravia, a group of Jewish women donated fruit, juice, wine, and hundreds of scarves and pairs of socks to the National Organization of Austrian Housewives to distribute to soldiers.[15] Throughout the war Jewish women also used the Jewish tradition of making charitable contributions on important occasions to donate money to help war invalids as well as to the wives, widows, and orphans of soldiers.[16]

Jewish women's charitable organizations all over the Austrian half of the Monarchy hurried to do their share for the war effort. They donated their buildings to the Red Cross for wounded soldiers, and they provided food and linens to mobilized soldiers and their families, especially their children.[17] The *Frauenwohltätigkeitsverein Providentia* in Vienna, for example, which under normal times ran a home for feeble-minded children, opened an all-day kindergarten in August 1914 for children whose fathers were in the army and whose mothers needed to work.[18] Similarly, the women of the *Verein Kaiser Franz Josephs-Kinderhort zur Ausspeisung armer israelitischer Schulkinder des XII., XIII., XIV., und XV. Bezirkes in Wien* proudly reported at the end of 1914 that once the war began they fed and ran a day care center for children of all religions whose parents were rendered unemployed by the war. At the day care center, the girls knitted warm wool socks for soldiers. Many women had joined the organization since August, presumably to do their duty for Austria.[19] By the end of the following year the organization had served over 120,000 dinners and 20,000 liters of milk to 300 children.[20]

Like all Austrian Zionists, Zionist women's groups eagerly rushed to prove their Austrian patriotism by contributing to the war effort. In Prague, the Zionist Club of Jewish Women and Girls established a soup kitchen for the children of called-up soldiers and worked hard throughout the war at trying to feed such children. Similarly, girls (and boys) in the Zionist youth group *Blau-Weiss* in Bohemia did railroad station service, providing food for called-up soldiers in the train stations.[21]

Serious about their desire to provide effective help on the home front, at the beginning of the war Jewish women understood the need to centralize their efforts. In Vienna, for example, many female Jewish charitable organizations banded together to form *Weibliche Fürsorge*, which provided information, assistance, and food to those in need, especially the families of soldiers and those thrown out of work because of the war.[22] Throughout the war, *Weibliche Fürsorge* and its constituent organizations worked tirelessly to help poor women and children, the dependents of still living or already dead soldiers. They ran soup kitchens, day care centers, kindergartens, trade schools, and sewing rooms. All this effort sprang from the simple desire to participate in the war effort as Austrians for Austria.

Throughout the war Jewish women's groups continued to work on behalf of soldiers and their families in need. To celebrate its 100th anniversary in 1916, for example, the *Erster Israelitische Frauen-Wohltätigkeitsverein* of Vienna created a special fund to ease the plight of war widows and orphans.[23] Many organizations created orphanages to care for war orphans,[24] and some worked especially to solve the special problems of mothers who had lost their financial support when their sons were drafted.[25] Jewish women's organizations also held fundraisers for such noble causes as blind and invalid soldiers.[26]

Recognizing the special needs of Jewish soldiers, Jewish women's groups labored on their behalf. In Vienna, Margarethe Grunwald, the wife of one of Vienna's prominent rabbis, coordinated regular drives to provide Jewish soldiers with gift packages at Chanukah and Purim time.[27] Jewish women's groups organized Chanukah and Purim parties for soldiers. In Prague, for example, the *Jüdischer Frauenverein* celebrated both Chanukah and the Kaiser's 67th jubilee in 1915 with a party for Jewish soldiers in the Prague garrison. The soldiers enjoyed a concert, coffee, cake, and cigarettes.[28] The Viennese *Zionistischer Mädchenverein Moriah* collected money to provide wounded Jewish soldiers in Viennese hospitals with newspapers, cigarettes, books, and refreshments, and the members took it upon themselves to visit the soldiers.[29] All over the Monarchy, Jewish women organized or helped organize Passover seders and kosher food for Passover for soldiers.[30]

Jewish women who contributed to the war effort on the home front generally justified their efforts in terms of both general humanitarianism and duty to the Fatherland. Like the men who enjoined them to their task, they too used male, military language to describe their activities. In a speech celebrating the 100th anniversary of the Israelite Women's Philanthropic Organization in January 1916, Rabbi Moritz Güdemann of Vienna spoke about women battling the "quadruple alliance" of hunger, need, sickness, and death.[31] Female Jewish spokesmen used the same language. In a passionate article in December 1914, Rahel Edelstein made a direct analogy between the home-front service of Jewish women and Moses keeping his hands outstretched while Joshua and the children of Israel fought the Amalekites, thus ensuring an Israelite victory.[32] In a report on female work in early 1915, Clothilde Benedikt called these activist women "a second, female army in the service of philanthropy."[33] Similarly, Lina Weiss noted in 1915 that "women also want to seize their weapons, but the weapons they use are of a different sort."[34] In using such male language Jewish women sought to gain parity for their work on the home front, even if the battlefield always remained more significant.[35] By making charity work at least verbally analogous to the battlefield, these women asserted that they too possessed the same patriotism as men, the same civic virtue in defense of the just cause. Men and women alike were Austrians doing battle for Austria.

Such behavior and attitudes were typical of middle-class women in all the combatant nations during the war.[36] They were also typical of Jewish women elsewhere, although in Germany Jewish women—like Jewish men—also hoped that their war work would silence anti-Semitism. In Austria, although male spokesmen hoped that Jewish blood spilled on the battlefield would end anti-Semitism, Jewish women seemed not to concern themselves with this issue.[37]

For their parts, the organized Jewish communities in Austria tried to solve the special problems that the war posed for Jewish women in the Monarchy. As early as 1914, Rabbi Max Grunwald prepared a special prayerbook for women and girls to satisfy the special needs of wartime, and he pledged the proceeds from its sale to Jewish war charity.[38] Much more pressing than devotions was the problem of obtaining government financial support for women who were religiously but not civilly married to soldiers. This problem was most acute in Galicia and Bukovina and among Galician and Bukovinian Jews elsewhere in the Monarchy. Rabbis all over performed special marriage services to legitimize these marriages, and Jewish communities urged women to arrange for such legitimations.[39] Even the Zionists, normally unconcerned about such religious matters, complained that the state did not automatically recognize religious marriages for the purpose of supporting the wives of soldiers, and various Jewish groups—including the Zionist Executive Committee for West Austria—registered a formal complaint with the Minister for the Defense of the Realm.[40] In November 1916 the Minister decreed that henceforth the fathers, wives, and children of "religious" marriages could receive state financial support for the families of soldiers.[41]

At the beginning of the war Rabbi Moritz Güdemann, the chief rabbi of Vienna, worried about the potential plight of Jewish women whose husbands were missing in action and presumed dead. Without actual proof of death, Jewish law refused to consider these women widows and prevented them from re-marrying. He proposed a solution, known in Jewish tradition, in which called-up soldiers could issue legally binding statements granting divorces to their wives in the event that they were missing in action and the state declared them dead. In 1914, the organized Jewish community of Vienna rejected such a proposal.[42] Later in the war, however, rabbis working for the Jewish chaplaincy division of the Red Cross did help women obtain death certificates for husbands missing in action and presumed dead.[43]

The influx of Galician and Bukovinian refugees into Vienna, Bohemia, and Moravia, beginning in September 1914, provided Jews generally, and especially Jewish women, with the opportunity to participate in the war effort while helping fellow Jews. Huge numbers of refugees arrived. By the end of 1915 altogether 385,645 refugees had fled Galicia and Bukovina, of which 157,630 were Jews. Half of the Jewish refugees fled to Vienna: at the end of 1915 Vienna housed 77,090 Jewish refugees (out of a total of 137,000 refugees of all religions). Bohemia provided temporary shelter to 57,159 Jewish refugees (out of a total of 96,607 there), and Moravia 18,429 Jewish refugees (out of 57,501).[44] The number of refugees fluctuated during the war. Many refugees returned home, especially to western Galicia, when the German and Austrian armies liberated Galicia from the Russians, but others fled before the Russian offensives in Galicia in 1916. Because of widespread devastation in Galicia and Bukovina during the war, many refugees could not return home even when the war on the Eastern Front ended. At the end of the war, large numbers of Jewish refugees still lived in Vienna, Bohemia, and Moravia.

The plight of these refugees was horrific. Not only had they fled the dreaded Russian army, but they lived in abysmal conditions in the regions in which they sought refuge. The press was filled with heartwrenching stories of families living in foul places, sleeping in filthy straw, having almost nothing to eat, and freezing cold. One particularly moving report about Galician refugees in Karlsbad described a dark, evil-smelling cellar in which 80 refugees crowded on straw, including a woman who had just given birth and someone with dysentery.[45] The Austrian government assumed responsibility for the refugees, as they were Austrian citizens suffering because of Austria's war. The central government and local communes provided basic financial support for them, and in Moravia the government established huge refugee barracks in Nikolsburg, Gaya, Pohrlitz, and elsewhere.[46] But the need was greater than the government, strapped for money during wartime, could possibly afford. Refugees in Vienna and Bohemia required housing, and all of the refugees needed money, food, clothing, schooling, and work. Jews—and especially Jewish women—stepped in to help the refugees.

Jews perceived their help for the refugees both as a contribution to the Austrian war effort and as an act of Jewish charity and solidarity. Galician Jews had fled, Austrian Jews argued, because they were Austrians, fleeing from the hated Russian enemy, who persecuted them in particular because of their loyalty to Austria. Through their suffering, Galician refugees had shown themselves to be "steadfast and loyal protectors of the Fatherland and the dynasty," indeed, the truest Austrians.[47] One report about the refugees concluded: "They pray daily for the old, good Emperor, whom they love with every fiber of their being. They pray for the victory of our arms. And God will hear the prayers of these poor [souls]."[48] Even the Zionists, who were more sensitive to the anti-Semitic underpinnings of Russian persecution than others, argued that Russians hated the Galician Jews "because of their unshakeable love of the Fatherland and their adamant loyalty to the state."[49] Helping the refugees, therefore, constituted a patriotic act; providing food, clothing, and shelter to weary refugees contributed to the Austrian war effort. It was, in the words of the Prague Zionist newspaper *Selbstwehr*, "a huge, eminently patriotic labor."[50]

Helping the large number of refugees was also an act of human kindness and traditional Jewish charity. Jews mobilized quickly to provide money, food, clothing, and religious articles to the refugees, and to create schools, soup kitchens, and other institutions for them. This effort transcended the usual political and religious conflicts within the community. The organized Jewish religious communities in Vienna, Prague, and all over Bohemia and Moravia eagerly contributed to the effort to help the refugees. The Zionists, who normally eschewed traditional philanthropy and focused on raising Jewish national consciousness and working for the establishment of a Jewish state, devoted considerable energy to helping the refugees. Major Jewish charitable organizations like the *Israelitische Allianz* worked tirelessly on behalf of the refugees.[51] Orthodox Jews also aided the refugees, most of whom were traditional, observant Jews. All these groups managed to work together on behalf of the refugees, even if they each took credit for being the most important, or the most tireless.

Because of the enormous needs of the Galician Jewish refugees, most of the "war work" done by Jews was for other Jews. This reality confirmed in Jewish minds their conviction that they could be Austrians and Jews at the same time. It also heightened Jewish solidarity and a sense of Jewish ethnic separateness in Austria. Liberal and Orthodox Jews had previously asserted that the Jews formed merely a religious confession, not a nationality in Austria. The Zionists had argued the opposite, that the Jews were a nation, and deserved the same status as other nationalities in Austria. The war and work on behalf of Jewish refugees did not make all Jews into Jewish nationalists, but it did contribute to a growing conviction that the Jews were a *Volksgemeinschaft*, an ethnic community, in a society composed of many national groups.

Jewish women did not reflect a great deal on why they labored on behalf of the refugees, but they certainly worked tirelessly for them. Presumably they were comfortable combining Austrian and Jewish war work. They could alleviate the plight of their fellow Jews while they contributed to the larger Austrian war effort. Working with a Jewish clientele certainly eliminated any problems of anti-Semitism they might have experienced in the larger war effort, and indeed may even explain why Austrian Jewish women, unlike their co-religionists in Germany, did not focus on how their war work would lessen anti-Semitism. Moreover, the fact that most of the refugees were women and children added a specific female imperative to their task.

There are no statistics on the gender or age breakdown of the refugees. It stands to reason, however, that most of them were women, children, or old people. Most men from 18 to 50, including even the ultra-orthodox Jews of Galicia, had been called into military service. Reports about the refugees which filled the Jewish press usually talk about women, children, and old men. A report on 359 Galician refugees in Reichenberg in December 1914 simply stated that they were mostly women, children, and old men.[52] Similarly, a report on refugees in Upper Austria in 1917 noted that there were very few men among the refugees.[53] An appeal for money and clothing from a women's committee in Strassnitz, Moravia, noted that it was Galician refugee women and children who were in terrible need in the barracks there.[54] Stories abound about women, whose husbands were either in military service or had been killed in action, caring for their children and elderly parents. Alternatively, older parents had to take in their adult daughters and daughters-in-law, whose husbands were in military service, and their grandchildren. One description of a refugee family in Brünn noted that the father was 62, the mother 59, the two daughters were in their 30s, and the five grandchildren were all under 12. One son had been missing since November 1915 on the Eastern Front; both sons-in-law were in the army, one having been wounded in Italy. Three grandchildren had died since they arrived in Brünn. The family had fled with their Ruthenian maid, herself an elderly woman.[55] Thus, there was a feminization of the refugee population, which rendered them a natural object for female Jewish charity.

Jewish women's organizations and ad hoc committees all over the Monarchy rallied to provide food, blankets, clothing, and shoes to the refugees.⁵⁶ In Vienna, for example, Sophie Grünfeld worked tirelessly on several committees to provide food to poor refugees. She chaired the Viennese Auxiliary Committee for Refugees from Galicia and Bukovina, which operated a kosher soup kitchen in Vienna's twentieth district, where many refugees resided. This soup kitchen provided cheap meals for very poor refugees, and a slightly more expensive meal for the "upper classes" among the refugees. Flora Kohn, who worked closely with Grünfeld, reported that the soup kitchen fed 1,000 refugees soup, sausage, meat dumplings, beans, and potatoes (this in 1914 before food shortages rendered such a diet impossible) every day.⁵⁷ Similarly, Hermine Kadisch ran the soup kitchens of the *Verein zur Errichtung von Volksküchen (nach isr. Ritus)* in Vienna's Leopoldstadt and Brigittenau districts, where most of the refugees lived. By the end of the war, despite excrutiating problems finding food in 1917 and 1918, her organization had served 16 million portions, of which 3 million were free. Kadisch also ran a special soup kitchen for the middle class, which had fallen on hard times during the war. Interestingly, Kadisch never formally served as president of the organization, but the Jewish press regularly accorded her that status. Most of the people who helped her run the soup kitchens were female volunteers.⁵⁸ *Weibliche Fürsorge* was also extremely active trying to provide food to the refugees. Before Passover, 1915, Margarethe Grunwald, wife of one of Vienna's prominent rabbis, headed a *Weibliche Fürsorge* campaign to distribute potatoes to the refugees, who could not eat bread during the holiday. She raised over 22,000 crowns and distributed over 360,000 kilos of potatoes to 60,000 people.⁵⁹

Jewish women's groups provided clothing to poor refugees, especially refugee children. In Prague, for example, the Zionist Club of Jewish Women and Girls volunteered to sort through the large number of donated clothes so that they could distribute them to the refugees both in Prague and in the refugee camps in Moravia.⁶⁰ Bnai Brith women in Prague also distributed linen and clothing to refugees.⁶¹ Jewish women's groups organized clothing collections for refugees elsewhere as well.⁶²

Women tried to enliven Jewish holiday celebrations for the refugees. In 1914 in particular, before food shortages became acute, they organized Chanukah parties for refugee children.⁶³ Women also arranged seders for the refugees; the women of *Machzike Hadath*, for example, an organization of Orthodox Jews, worked hard providing Passover food to refugees. In Vienna, the First Zionist Women's

Organization raised money before Passover in 1915 to provide 2,000 refugees with potatoes for the holidays.[64]

Since most middle-class women who entered the public arena in this period justified their behavior in terms of extending their nurturing roles as mothers,[65] it is not surprising that Jewish women's groups worked especially hard to alleviate the special problems faced by refugee children. Viennese Zionist activist Erna Patak, for example, established a day care center at the beginning of the war "for the poorest of the poor, the Jewish refugee children in Vienna." In her 1916 request for subvention aid from the Jewish community, she noted that her day care center provided four kosher meals a day, clothes and shoes, education, and vocational training. At that point that center had 50 children, 20 of whom had fathers in the army. The Jewish community deemed her center "extraordinarily worthy," and provided her with a monthly subvention.[66] Patak also headed campaigns to distribute clothing, shoes, underwear, bedding, and kitchen utensils to poor refugees.[67] In Prague as well, the Zionist Club of Jewish Women and Girls established a day care center for refugee children which provided clothing, food, baths, and play, supervised by Galician refugee girls.[68]

Women's organizations wanted to provide not only charity but also occupational training and work for refugee girls and women. In Vienna, *Weibliche Fürsorge*, for example, set up "sewing rooms" for refugee women and courses to teach girls sewing and embroidery.[69] Similarly, in Marienbad, Bohemia a group established a sewing and knitting school, and in the winter of 1915/16 refugee women there knitted thousands of socks and hats for soldiers.[70] By far the largest organizer of "sewing rooms" and courses was the (male-run) *Hilfsverein für die notleidende jüdische Bevölkerung in Galizien*. In peacetime, the organization had helped poor Jews in Galicia. During the war, it established sewing rooms in Vienna, Bohemia, and Moravia so that refugee girls could earn money making underwear and linen for soldiers and other refugees. It also arranged for courses in net-making (*Filettechnik*). Bnai Brith Women assisted the *Hilfsverein* by collecting sewing machines and fabric for use by the refugee girls.[71] In Vienna *Weibliche Fürsorge* organized business courses for girls, teaching them typing and office work, presumably to train them for careers in the newly growing field of female office work.[72]

By far the most important effort on behalf of Galician refugee women and girls in Vienna was undertaken by Anitta Müller and the host of organizations that this indefatigable woman created. With financial aid both from the Vienna city refugee aid agency and from Jewish organizations, she created a series of clinics, homes, day care centers, and schools which targeted aid specifically at Jewish refugee women and children. Already by November 1914 she created an agency that dispensed advice, diapers, and food to refugee mothers and a home for refugee women who had just given birth so that they could spend a week resting before they returned to the dirty refugee quarters.[73] Similarly, she established a kindergarten in the Prater for refugee children so that they could be clean, well-fed, receive medical attention, and learn Polish and German songs and games.[74] In 1915 she opened a tea room to serve bread and tea to 1,600 people a day, a clinic to care for refugee infants that fed about 700 babies a day and encouraged mothers to nurse, and a school to teach refugee girls sewing and office skills that had 800 students. Müller wanted to provide good care, employable skills, and Western culture to the poor Galician refugees.[75] In 1918 her organizations, by then organized under the umbrella organization *Soziale Hilfsgemeinschaft Anitta Müller*, helped 3,239 new mothers, 1,377 infants, 3,037 girls learning a trade, and had served four million portions of soup and tea.[76]

The Jewish press was filled with praise for this "tireless organizer," this "organizational genius" who could recognize problems and know the right way to solve them, and for her "colossal field of work *(Arbeitsfeld),*" an obvious complement to the battlefield. Even the Orthodox newspaper proudly called her "the most popular Jewish woman in Vienna." The *Oesterreichische Wochenschrift* asserted that her work, and that of her colleagues, resulted from a very stong consciousness of Jewish national solidarity. The newspaper also credited her with transforming traditional Jewish female philanthropy into modern, professional social work.[77]

Indeed, Müller saw her own work not as charity but as a duty. This duty had two imperatives. On the one hand, she viewed her "social war work" as an obligation to her Fatherland in war and as analogous to the efforts of soldiers on the battlefield.[78] On the other hand, she felt a duty to provide the kind of aid that would help people become independent, productive members of society.[79] In the process, she not only sought to professionalize social work but to make it a woman's profession, with women helping other women in need. Torn by the terrible suffering that Jews, and especially Jewish children, experienced during the war, both as pogrom victims and as refugees,

Müller felt compelled to intervene to save these children and their mothers. She did so by eschewing the traditional methods of female philanthropy—fundraising luncheons and the like—and instead opened clinics to help mothers and chidren and mobilized an army of female volunteers and office personnel to staff these clinics. This staff was proud of the fact that female Jewish refugees could find women helping them in the clinics, women answering their questions, women giving them diapers and food. One of the pamphlets describing her work pointed out that refugee women in the clinics "encounter women in whose eyes they read the sympathy of those who understand them, to whom they may also reveal their secret sufferings, and who deal with everything with dependable tact, with female tenderness, and expeditiously."[80] Müller was also an ardent Zionist who after the war combined a career in Jewish social work with one as a Zionist activist, and who urged women to vote for the new Jewish National Party, ran as a candidate of the party for the Vienna City Council and Lower Austrian diet, and worked to inculcate Jewish national consciousness among Jewish women in Austria.[81] Much of her work for refugee women and children therefore also derived from her very strong Jewish ethnic consciousness.[82]

Jewish women who mobilized to help Jewish refugees in the Dual Monarchy during the First World War did not leave a large legacy of written works defending their actions. What few articles and reprinted speeches exist point to several motives for such an outpouring of support. In the early months of the war some Jewish women's groups explained their actions in terms of general humanity.[83] Sofie Grünfeld, for example, very active in creating soup kitchens for refugees, ascribed her activity to love of humanity, and apologized for the food shortages that limited her hospitality.[84] She also clearly saw her work as an Austrian patriotic act. In her speech at a seder for refugees in 1915, she told them that she had organized the seder because of the pain she felt that the evil enemy—"our evil enemy"— had made them flee. The Jews of Vienna had sent their sons to fight in their land, and Galician Jews had fled to Vienna seeking protection and help from Jews in the capital. This woman who had already lost her son and son-in-law in the fighting declared refugee behavior in the face of adversity to be an act of heroism.[85] The men who descibed her work in the press used military language, thus equating it with the war effort itself. The woman who ran the soup kitchen was a "field marshall " who commanded "auxiliary troops of the cooking and serving *Mannschaft*."[86] The women who helped refugees, another writer claimed, were "soldiers against need and misery."[87]

Jewish liberals like Sophie Grünfeld who helped the refugees did not justify their actions in terms of Jewish ethnic solidarity, but did emphasize that work for Galician refugees had deepened their sense of the unity of all Jews. At that 1915 seder Grünfeld concluded: "We have learned that we are all children of one religion."[88] Other Jewish women who worked tirelessly to help the refugees did become involved primarily out of a sense of Jewish ethnic solidarity. At the very beginning of the war, Malvine Friedmann, for example, appealed to all Jews with a deep Jewish feeling, and even to those Jews who were indifferent to the Jewish religion but still possessed a sense of belonging to the Jewish people, to help the Jewish refugees.[89] Certainly the Zionist Anitta Müller and her colleagues responded to the crisis posed by the refugees by asserting their Jewish solidarity and helping them.

Such solidarity did not preclude a strong sense of social distance between the refugees and the women who assisted them. The Viennese Jewish women who volunteered to aid refugees did not always understand the Eastern European Jewish women whom they helped. Grünfeld articulated a typical Viennese Jewish distaste for Galician Jews when she told the refugees in 1915: "You were foreign and your culture seemed not to be our own. You had other customs, and we came to you not with the love that brothers should bring to each other in need."[90] Even the Zionist women around Anitta Müller who believed in Jewish ethnic solidarity shared this view. After all, the refugee women came from "a peculiar (*eigenartig*) cultural area" which was indeed quite foreign.[91] Nevertheless, Müller and her colleagues felt an Austrian, a Jewish, and a female obligation to help the refugees; indeed, helping the refugees awoke in them a stong feeling of Jewish solidarity.[92]

Jewish women in different regions of the Monarchy seem to have viewed the Galician refugees somewhat differently. In Prague, which had a relatively homogeneous Jewish population identified as German by culture, there seems to have been more discomfort with the refugees, a greater sense of superiority, and a desire to "improve" and Westernize them.[93] In Vienna, on the other hand, one senses somewhat less distance, less superiority, and less of a desire to remake the refugees in the image of Western Jews. Undoubtedly the fact that about a quarter of all Viennese Jews themselves came from Galicia at least partially accounts for this difference.[94]

When Jewish women in Austria helped the Galician refugees, therefore, they did so to assert female, Austrian, and Jewish loyalties all at the same time. Refugee aid was the perfect cause for Jewish women in the Monarchy. By helping those who had fled the Eastern Front they were helping suffering fellow Jews. Because these Jews suffered on account of the Austrian war and for their Austrian loyalties, such Jewish charity was part of the Austrian war effort and served to demonstrate the Austrian loyalties of all Jews. Because so many of the refugees were women and children, the women who helped them were merely extending their mothering roles into the public sphere and thus this work which took them outside the home was socially acceptable. Such work for the cause of Galician refugees strengthened both the Austrian identity and the Jewish folk consciousness of middle-class Jewish women in Vienna and Prague, and in smaller cities and towns in Bohemia and Moravia.

Unfortunately for them, and for Jewish men as well, the dissolution of the Monarchy at the end of the war rendered their supranational Austrian identity obsolete. They now had to create new identities for themselves in the successor states. The lasting legacy of the war, however, was a heightened sense of Jewish solidarity and this heightened solidarity—generated in no small measure by the efforts on behalf of the Galician refugees—was to prove central to the reconstruction of Jewish identity in the interwar period.

Notes to Chapter 9

1. This article deals only with events in the Austrian half of the Monarchy. The situation in Hungary—both in general and with respect to the Jews—was vastly different and deserves a separate study. According to the census of 1910, 1,313,687 Jews lived in the Austrian half of the monarchy, three-quarters of them in Galicia and Bukovina. In addition, over 150,000 Jews lived in the mixed Czech and German provinces of Bohemia and Moravia, and 175,000 lived in the capital, Vienna (*Oesterreichische Statistik*, N.F., 2:2).
2. Jews in Germany faced even greater anti-Semitism during the war, and the government there even conducted a census of the military to ascertain if Jews were shirking or fulfilling their military responsibility. See Werner Jochmann, "Die Ausbreitung des Antisemitismus," in Werner E. Mosse and Arnold Paucker, *Deutsches Judentum in Krieg und Revolution 1916–1923* (Tübingen: J.C.B. Mohr, 1971), pp. 409–510; and Werner T. Angress, "The German Army's 'Judenzählung' of 1916. Genesis—Consequences—Significance," *Leo Baeck Institute Yearbook* 23 (1978), pp. 117–37.
3. See Marsha L. Rozenblit, "The Dilemma of Identity: The Impact of the First World War on Habsburg Jewry," in *The Habsburg Legacy: National Identity in*

Historical Perspective, Austrian Studies 5, Ritchie Robertson and Edward Timms, eds. (Edinburgh: Edinburgh University Press, 1994), pp. 144–57.

4. There is a growing body of literature on women during the First World War. Unfortunately, most of this scholarly literature deals either with images of women in literature, or with working-class women, or with constructions of gender identity during the war, and was therefore not especially helpful for this essay. Among the most important of the new books are M. Higonnet, J. Jensen, S. Michel, and M. Weitz, eds., *Behind the Lines: Gender and the Two World Wars* (New Haven: Yale University Press, 1987); Ute Daniel, *Arbeiterfrauen in der Kriegsgesellschaft: Beruf, Familie und Politik im Ersten Weltkrieg* (Göttingen: Vandenhoeck & Ruprecht, 1989); Jean Bethke Elshtain, *Women and War* (New York: Basic Books, 1987); and Carol Berkin and Clara Lovett, eds., *Women, War and Revolution* (New York: Holmes and Meier, 1980).

5. Lillian M. Bader, "One Life is Not Enough," Unpublished Memoir, Leo Baeck Institute, pp. 75–76. In her study of German women during the First World War, Ute Daniel, *Arbeiterfrauen in der Kriegsgesellschaft*, p. 24, argues that women shared equally with men in the euphoria of August 1914, which transcended class, status, generation, and gender in Germany.

6. Bader, p. 77.

7. Stefan Zweig, *The World of Yesterday* (New York: Viking Press, 1943), p. 226.

8. Bertha Landre, "Durch's Sieb der Zeit gefallen. Jedes Menschenleben ist ein Roman," Unpublished Memoir, Leo Baeck Institute, pp. 97, 99. According to theorist Jean Bethke Elshtain, during war, men fight and women "work and weep and sometimes protest"(*Women and War* [New York: Basic Books, 1987], p. 3).

9. *Oesterreichische Wochenschrift*, 31 July 1914, p. 530.

10. See for example, *Oesterreichische Wochenschrift*, 16 October 1914, p. 703; 19 February 1915, p. 145; *Jüdische Volksstimme* (Brünn), 3 September 1914, p. 3; 10 September 1914, p. 4.

11. Esti D. Freud, "Vignettes of My Life," Unpublished Memoir, 1979, Leo Baeck Institute, p. 14.

12. Central Archives for the History of the Jewish People, Jerusalem (hereinafter CAHJP), AW 372, AW 356. *Oesterreichische Wochenschrift*, 29 January 1915, p. 91; *Zweimonats-Bericht für die Mitglieder der ... Bnai Brith*, vol. 18, #2 (1915), p. 73.

13. *Oesterreichische Wochenschrift*, 16 October 1914, p. 703.

14. *Oesterreichische Wochenschrift*, 1 January 1915, p. 7.

15. *Jüdische Volksstimme*, 10 September 1914, p. 4.

16. See lists of contributions for such purposes in Vienna in CAHJP, AW 246/5, AW 247/4, AW 248/4, AW 249/4, AW 250/4.

17. See, for example, *Oesterreichische Wochenschrift* (Vienna), 14 August 1914, pp. 565, 571; 21 August 1914, pp. 585, 587; 4 September 1914, p. 620; 18 September 1914, p. 647; 23 April 1915, p. 318; 25 June 1915, p. 480; *Selbstwehr* (Prague), 27 August 1914, pp. 2-3; 20 September 1914, p. 3; 13 November 1914, p. 2; 7 May 1915, p. 6; *Jüdische Volksstimme* (Brünn), 10 September 1914, p. 4; 17 September 1914, p. 3; *Zweimonats-Bericht für die Mitglieder der ... Bnai Brith*, vol. 18, #1 (1915), p. 24; vol. 20, #1/2 (1917), pp. 17, 32. See also CAHJP, AW 247/4, Letter from Kaiserin Elisabeth Lehrmädchenheim. Of course not only Jewish women's organizations, but the larger Jewish community as well, participated in providing assistance to soldiers and their families.

18. CAHJP, AW 356.

19. "Bericht des Vereines Kaiser Franz Josephs-Kinderhort ... über das Vereinsjahr 1913-1914," CAHJP, AW 2355/10.

20. "Bericht des Vereines Kaiser Franz Josephs-Kinderhort ... über das Vereinsjahr

1914-1915," CAHJP, AW 2355/11. Many of these organizations received subvention aid from the organized Jewish community for this war work.
21. *Selbstwehr*, 27 August 1914, p. 2; 20 September 1914, p. 6; 29 October 1915, p. 6.
22. *Oesterreichische Wochenschrift*, 7 August, 1914, pp. 551-52.
23. *Oesterreichische Wochenschrift*, 1 January 1916, p. 10.
24. The Kaiserin Elisabeth Lehrmädchenheim, for example, created a war orphanage for 80 children in the second district of Vienna in 1916, and by 1917 it had 150 orphans. See *Oesterreichische Wochenschrift*, 28 April 1916, p. 283; 29 June 1917, p. 415; 13 September 1918, p. 584. See also 24 November 1916, p. 768.
25. For example, in Vienna the Verein Franz Josephs Kinderhort worked on behalf of these mothers and Jeanette Feuchtwang chaired a fund to help the mothers of fallen soldiers. See *Oesterreichische Wochenschrift*, 17 November 1916, p. 753; 9 February 1917; 7 September 1917, p. 571; 12 September 1917, p. 644; *Jüdische Volksstimme*, 10 January 1917, p. 5.
26. See, for example, *Oesterreichische Wochenschrift*, 5 February 1915, p. 111; 25 February 1916, p. 148; 12 May 1916, p. 329.
27. *Oesterreichische Wochenschrift*, 5 November 1915, pp. 823-24; 12 November 1915, p. 838; 24 December 1915, p. 949; 28 April 1916, p. 287; 29 December 1916, p. 854; 5 January 1917, p. 9; 16 February 1917, p. 108; 2 November 1917, p. 696; 28 December 1917, p. 826. Similar activities took place elsewhere in Austria, see *Oesterreichische Wochenschrift*, 18 February 1916, p. 129; 27 October 1916, p. 706; *Zweimonats-Bericht für die Mitglieder der ... Bnai Brith*, vol. 18, #1 (1915), p. 36.
28. *Selbstwehr*, 10 December 1915, p. 6. See also *Oesterreichische Wochenschrift*, 25 December 1914, p. 908; 10 December 1915, pp. 903-4, 908, 910; 17 December 1915, p. 928; 29 December 1916, p. 854; 28 December 1917, pp. 824–25, 827; 18 January 1918, pp. 40–41; *Jüdische Zeitung*, 4 May 1917, p. 5.
29. *Oesterreichische Wochenschrift*, 23 April 1915, p. 321; *Jüdische Zeitung*, 23 April 1915, p. 3. Such activities were common elsewhere as well. See *Selbstwehr*, 19 May 1916, p. 6.
30. *Oesterreichische Wochenschrift*, 16 April 1915, p. 303; 23 April 1915, p. 319; 17 March 1916, p. 195; 14 April 1916, p. 266; 28 April 1916, p. 288; 5 May 1916, pp. 305, 309; 12 May 1916, p. 326; 20 April 1917, pp. 240, 244; 19 April 1918, p. 242; *Selbstwehr*, 12 May 1916, p. 7; CAHJP, AW 248/4, Referatsbogen, probably April 1916.
31. *Israelitischer Frauen Wohltätigkeits Verein in Wien. 100. Vereinsjahr Jubiläums- und Jahres-Bericht für das Jahr 1915* (Vienna, 1916), p. 4, in CAHJP, AW 2232/28.
32. *Oesterreichische Wochenschrift*, 4 December 1914, p. 835.
33. *Oesterreichische Wochenschrift*, 19 March 1915, p. 225.
34. *Oesterreichische Wochenschrift*, 28 September 1915, p. 723.
35. On the continued primacy of the battle front, despite the emphasis on women's work on the home front, see Margaret Higonnet and Patrice Higonnet, "The Double Helix," in Higonnet, pp. 34–35; Elshtain, p. 22.
36. See especially Elshtain, *Women and War*, who traces the history of this concept of civic virtue in war for both men and women. In general, however, Elshtain creates a dichotomy between men as "just warriors" and women as "beautiful souls" who do war work and sacrifice their sons to war. Such a dichotomy, based as it is largely on evidence from Britain and America, does not work so neatly in the case of the Central Powers, whose women suffered a great deal in the later part of the war. For how women coped with the terrible privations at the end of the war, see Daniel, *Arbeiterfrauen in der Kriegsgesellschaft*, pp. 183-232.

37. On German Jewish women during the war see Marion Kaplan, *The Making of the Jewish Middle Class: Women, Family, and Identity in Imperial Germany* (New York: Oxford University Press, 1991), pp. 219–27.
38. Max Grunwald, *Gebete in Kriegszeit für israelitische Frauen und Mädchen* (Vienna: Jos. Schlesinger, 1914). See also correspondence in CAHJP, AW 357/1; *Oesterreichische Wochenschrift*, 18 September 1914.
39. *Oesterreichische Wochenschrift*, 7 July 1916, p. 447; 2 November 1917, p. 700; *Zweimonatsbericht für die Mitglieder der ... Bnai Brith*, vol. 17, #5/6 (1914), p. 186; *Selbstwehr*, 26 November 1915, p. 7. In western Austria, the government recognized marriages performed by rabbis to be binding civil marriages, but such was not the case in Galicia, where Jews had to obtain a separate civil marriage and many religious Jews did not bother.
40. *Jüdische Zeitung*, 31 March 1916, p. 1.
41. *Oesterreichische Wochenschrift*, 12 January 1917, p. 25.
42. Letter from Rabbi Güdemann to Board of the Jewish Community, 8 December 1914, CAHJP, AW 357/1.
43. *Oesterreichische Wochenschrift*, 1 March 1918, p. 144; *Selbstwehr*, 26 April 1918, p. 7; *Jüdische Zeitung*, 19 April 1918, p. 4.
44. *LXIII. Jahresbericht der Israelitischen Allianz zu Wien erstattet an die XLIII. ordentliche Generalversammlung am 5. Juni 1916* (Vienna, 1916), in CAHJP, AW 2828/35, p. 7.
45. See, for examples, *Oesterreichische Wochenschrift*, 18 December 1914, p. 886; *Jüdische Volksstimme*, 8 October 1914, pp. 2–3; 13 January 1915, p. 5; 20 January 1915, p. 1.
46. See yearly reports of the Vienna based *Israelitische Allianz* in CAHJP, AW 2828/34, 2828/35, 2828/36, and 2828/37. The city of Vienna, for example, established the Central Office for Aid to Refugees from Galicia and Bukovina, headed by Dr. Rudolf Schwarz-Hiller, to provide assistance to refugees in Vienna. See *Oesterreichishce Wochenschrift*, 6 November 1914, p. 765; 1 January 1916, pp. 17–19.
47. *Oesterreichische Wochenschrift*, 26 February 1915, p. 154. See also 4 September 1914, pp. 609–10; 18 September 1914, pp. 643, 655; 18 December 1914, p. 878; 25 December 1914, pp. 893–95; 29 January 1915, p. 86; 30 April 1915, p. 326; 8 October 1915, p. 748.
48. *Oesterreichische Wochenschrift*, 18 December 1914, p. 886.
49. *Selbstwehr*, 20 August 1915, p. 3.
50. *Selbstwehr*, 22 January 1915, p. 4.
51. The Jewish press was filled with reports on Jewish assistance to the refugees. For the work of the *Israelitische Allianz*, see its yearly reports for 1915, 1916, 1917, and 1918 in CAHJP, AW 2828/34, 2828/35, 2828/36, and 2828/37. In Prague in particular Zionists and liberal Jews worked together to assist refugees. See *Selbstwehr*, 30 October 1914, pp. 1-2.
52. *Oesterreichische Wochenschrift*, 18 December 1914, p. 886.
53. *Oesterreichische Wochenschrift*, 20 July 1917, p. 467.
54. *Jüdische Volksstimme*, 27 July 1916, p. 3.
55. *Jüdische Volksstimme*, 24 May 1917, p. 5.
56. See, for example, *Oesterreichische Wochenschrift*, 18 September 1914, pp. 647-48; 23 October 1914, p. 732; 8 January 1915, p. 31; 22 January 1915, p. 68; 5 Feburary 1915, p. 110; 26 March 1915, p. 244; 9 April 1915, p. 283; 5 November 1915, p. 822; 10 December 1915, p. 909; 1 January 1916, p. 12; 18 August 1916, p. 549; 27 August 1916, p. 704; 20 March 1917, p. 207; 15 June 1917, pp. 383, 386; *Selbstwehr*, 5 February 1915, p. 6; 26 February 1915, p. 6; 12

March 1915, p. 6; 25 June 1915, p. 4; 27 August 1915, p. 7; *Jüdische Volksstimme*, 28 May 1915, p. 4; *Jüdische Zeitung*, 23 February 1917, p. 3. See also CAHJP, AW 356, Protocoll, 22 October 1914.
57. *Oesterreichische Wochenschrift*, 5 February 1915, p. 111; 19 February 1915, p. 143; CAHJP, AW 247/4, letter from Flora Kohn to the Viennese Jewish community, 17 February 1915.
58. *Oesterreichische Wochenschrift*, 19 March 1915, p. 227; 16 February 1917, p. 105; 1 February 1918, p. 74; 14 June 1918, p. 366. See the formal printed reports of the *Verein zur Errichtung von Volksküchen (nach israelitischem Ritus)* for 1914, 1915, 1917, and 1918 in CAHJP, AW 2286/26, 2286/27, 2286/28, and 2286/29 and the article on the Verein in *Hickls Wiener Jüdischer Volkskalender für das Jahr 5678 (1917-1918)*, pp. 86-87. This article notes that the middle-class soup kitchen was largely for women. Women were active in soup kitchen work in Bohemia and Moravia as well. See, for example, *Selbstwehr*, 11 June 1915, p. 6; 3 November 1916, p. 6; *Jüdische Volksstimme*, 7 September 1915.
59. *Oesterreichische Wochenschrift*, 12 February 1915, p. 124; 19 February 1915, p. 142; 26 February 1915, p. 163; 12 March 1915, pp. 201-2; 2 April 1915, p. 260; 9 April 1915, p. 281. On other efforts of *Weibliche Fürsorge* for refugees, see report on activities of Charlotte Freifrau von Königswarter, its honorary president, in CAHJP, AW 357/2.
60. *Selbstwehr*, 30 October 1914, p. 2; 8 January 1915, p. 5; 15 January 1915, p. 3; 5 February 1915, p. 7. The clothing was collected by the boys and girls of the youth group, Blau-Weiss.
61. *Zweimonats-Bericht für die Mitglieder der ... Bnai Brith*, vol. 19, #2 (1916), p. 83.
62. *Selbstwehr*, 22 January 1915, p. 5; 29 January 1915, p. 6; 5 February 1915, p. 6; *Jüdische Zeitung*, 5 March 1915, p. 2; *Zweimonats-Bericht für die Mitglieder der ... Bnai Brith*, vol. 19, #2 (1916), p. 94.
63. *Oesterreichische Wochenschrift*, 11 December 1914, p. 863; 18 December 1914, pp. 884, 887; 25 December 1914, p. 901; 8 January 1915, p. 35. See also 21 December 1917, p. 809; 28 December 1917, p. 824.
64. *Oesterreichische Wochenschrift*, 5 March 1915, p. 182; 2 April 1915, pp. 261-62; 9 April 1915, pp. 282, 287; 19 April 1918, p. 238; *Jüdische Zeitung*, 12 March 1915, p. 4; 16 April 1915, p. 2.
65. On the ideology of "nurturant motherhood" and how it was used to defend the role of American women during the First World War see Barbara Steinson, "'The Mother Half of Humanity': American Women in the Peace and Preparedness Movement in World War I," in Berkin and Lovett, pp. 259–81.
66. Letter of Erna Patak, 5 April 1916, CAHJP, AW 248/4; *Jüdische Zeitung*, 26 February 1915, p. 2; 14 April 1916, p. 9. The Jewish community provided subvention aid to many groups that helped the refugees. See, for example, correspondence in AW 247/4, 248/4.
67. Pamphlet describing Zionist work for refugees 1914–1916 in CAHJP, AW 248/5; *Jüdische Zeitung*, 26 February 1915, p. 2; 14 April 1916, p. 7.
68. *Selbstwehr*, 19 March 1915, p. 3; 29 October 1915, p. 6; 20 July 1917, p. 6; *Das jüdische Prag* (Prague: Verlag der *Selbstwehr*, 1917), pp. 54–55. For similar efforts elsewhere in Bohemia, see *Selbstwehr*, 11 January 1918, pp. 5–6.
69. *Oesterreichische Wochenschrift*, 30 October 1914, p. 750; 10 September 1915, p. 685.
70. *Oesterreichische Wochenschrift*, 4 August 1916, p. 518.
71. *Oesterreichische Wochenschrift*, 23 October 1914, p. 728; 1 September 1916, p. 584; 17 October 1916, p. 689; 1 December 1916, p. 806; 26 January 1917, p. 58; 17 May 1917, p. 301; *Jüdische Zeitung*, 15 September 1916, pp. 4–5; *Zwei-*

monats-Bericht für die Mitglieder der ... Bnai Brith, vol. 17, #5/6 (1914), pp. 194–99; vol. 18, #6 (1915), pp. 173–75; vol. 21, #1/2 (1918), pp. 56–57; letter from *Hilfsverein* to Vienna Jewish community in CAHJP, AW 250/4.
72. *Oesterreichische Wochenschrift*, 23 October 1914, p. 728; 30 October 1914, p. 750. During the war years, virtually all of the applicants for clerical work at the Vienna Jewish community were women. See, for examples, applications for such jobs in CAHJP, AW 246/5, 247/5, 248/5, 249/5, 250/5. Many Jewish women must have become office workers for the army because in 1918 the Austrian army allowed its female clerical staff in Vienna to take Saturday off instead of Sunday (*Jüdische Korrespondent*, 2 May 1918, p. 4). Studies of women in the First World War all agree that the only lasting change in female employment patterns caused by the war was in the field of office work. See, for example, Jean-Louis Robert, "Women and Work in France during the First World War," in Richard Wall and Jay Winter, eds., *The Upheaval of War: Family, Work and Welfare in Europe, 1914–1918* (Cambridge: Cambridge University Press, 1988), pp. 257, 264; Deborah Thom, "Women and Work in Wartime Britain," in Wall and Winter, pp. 302, 306.
73. *Oesterreichische Wochenschrift*, 6 November 1914, p. 765; 20 November 1914, pp. 803–4; *Ein Jahr Flüchtlingsfürsorge der Frau Anitta Müller, 1914–1915* (Vienna: R. Löwit, 1915?) in CAHJP, AW 2318, pp. 5–7; on financial aid, pp. 59–62.
74. *Oesterreichische Wochenschrift*, 11 December 1914, p. 862; 22 January 1915, p. 65; *Ein Jahr Flüchtlingsfürsorge der Frau Anitta Müller*, CAHJP, AW 2318, pp. 10–11.
75. *Oesterreichische Wochenschrift*, 22 January 1915, p. 67; 13 August 1915, p. 614; 19 November 1915, pp. 855–56; 19 May 1916, pp. 340–41; *Ein Jahr Flüchtlingsfürsorge der Frau Anitta Müller*, CAHJP, AW 2318, pp. 9, 11–12.
76. *Oesterreichische Wochenschrift*, 6 September 1918, p. 559; "Referat über die Institutionen, welche von Frau Anitta Mueller geleitet und aus von ihr gesammelten Mitteln erhalten werden," 25 June 1918, in CAHJP, AW 250/5.
77. *Oesterreichische Wochenschrift*, 22 January 1915, p. 67; 13 August 1915, p. 614; 8 June 1917, p. 359; 6 September 1918, pp. 558–59; *Jüdische Korrespondent*, 28 November 1918, p. 4; *Jüdische Volksstimme*, 23 May 1919, p. 3; *Zweimonats-Bericht für die Mitglieder der ... Bnai Brith*, vol. 21, #3/4 (1918), p. 99.
78. *Ein Jahr Flüchtlingsfürsorge der Frau Anitta Müller*, CAHJP, AW 2318, p. 16.
79. "Zehn Jahre Arbeit des Vereines Soziale-Hilfsgemeinschaft Anitta Müller, 1914-1924" (printed pamphlet), pp. 3–4, in CAHJP, AW 2317.
80. *Ein Jahr Flüchtlingfürsorge der Frau Anitta Müller*, CAHJP, AW 2318, pp. 4–7; quotation on p. 7. Not only were the social workers women, but a majority of the members of the Board of the *Soziale Hilfsgemeinschaft Anitta Müller* were women. See "Zehn Jahre Arbeit," CAHJP, AW 2317, p. 29. All over Western Europe and America, women extended traditional female nurturing roles to the public sphere by creating professional social work. For similar developments among German Jews, for example, see Marion Kaplan, *The Jewish Feminist Movement in Germany: The Campaigns of the Jüdischer Frauenbund, 1904–1938* (Westport, Conn.: Greenwood Press, 1979).
81. *Jüdische Zeitung*, 8 November 1918, p. 2; 15 November 1918, p. 6; 20 December 1918, p. 6; 24 January 1919, pp. 4–5; 25 April 1919, p. 1; *Wiener Morgenzeitung*, 22 April 1919, p. 3. Her Zionist colleague Erna Patak also ran for parliament, provincial assembly, and city council on the Jewish national ticket, *Jüdische Zeitung*, 24 January 1919, p. 1; 25 April 1919, p. 1; *Wiener Morgenzeitung*, 19 January 1919, p. 3. For Müller's views on inculcating Jewish nationalism in Jewish women, see *Oesterreichische Wochenschrift*, 17 January 1919, pp. 34–36, and the women's page she edited for the Zionist *Wiener Morgenzeitung* in 1919.

82. Certainly the Jewish press credited her strong Jewish ethnic consciousness for her work on behalf of the refugees. See, for example, *Oesterreichische Wochenschrift*, 8 June 1917, pp. 358-60; 6 September 1918, pp. 558-59.
83. See appeal of *Weibliche Fürsorge* and several other organizations in *Oesterreichische Wochenschrift*, 18 September 1914, p. 647; or articles in 27 November 1914, p. 824; 8 January 1915, pp. 30–31.
84. *Oesterreichische Wochenschrift*, 2 April 1915, p. 262.
85. *Oesterreichische Wochenschrift*, 2 April 1915, pp. 261–62.
86. Ibid., p. 261.
87. *Oesterreichische Wochenschrift*, 4 February 1916, pp. 86–87.
88. *Oesterreichische Wochenschrift*, 2 April 1915, pp. 261–62.
89. *Oesterreichische Wochenschrift*, 28 September 1914, pp. 669–70.
90. *Oesterreichische Wochenschrift*, 2 April 1915, p. 262.
91. *Ein Jahr Flüchtlingsfürsorge der Frau Anitta Müller*, CAHJP, AW 2318, p. 4.
92. Anitta Müller, "Mein Bestand für die Flüchlinge," *Hickls Wiener jüdischer Volkskalender für das Jahr 5677 (1916–1917)*, p. 70.
93. *Das jüdische Prag*, pp. 54–55.
94. Conflict between western and eastern Jews in Europe has been studied a great deal. For Vienna, where the conflict was considerably less than in Germany, see Marsha Rozenblit, *The Jews of Vienna, 1867–1914: Assimilation and Identity* (Albany: State University of New York Press, 1984), pp. 43–44, 97; idem, "The Jews of Germany and Austria: A Comparative Perspective," in Robert Wistrich, ed., *Austrians and Jews in the Twentieth Century* (New York: St. Martin's Press, 1992), pp. 12–14; Robert Wistrich, *The Jews of Vienna in the Age of Franz Joseph* (Oxford: Oxford University Press, 1989), pp. 62–97. For Germany, see Jack Wertheimer, *Unwelcome Strangers: East European Jews in Imperial Germany* (New York: Oxford University Press, 1987) and Steven Aschheim, *Brothers and Strangers: The East European Jew in German and German Jewish Consciousness, 1800–1923* (Madison: University of Wisconsin Press, 1982). The role of Galician refugees in changing or modifying western Austrian attitudes to Galician Jews needs further study.

Select Bibliography

Daniel, Ute. *Arbeiterfrauen in der Kriegsgesellschaft* (Göttingen: Vandenhoeck and Ruprecht, 1989). This book does an excellent job of detailing the work experiences of German working-class women during the war.

Kaplan, Marion. *The Making of the Jewish Middle Class: Women, Family and Identity in Imperial Germany* (New York: Oxford University Press, 1991). This fine book also includes a good summary of the situation of Jewish women in Germany during the conflict (pp. 219—27).

Kieval, Hillel J. *The Making of Czech Jewry: National Conflict and Jewish Society in Bohemia, 1870—1918* (New York: Oxford Universoity Press, 1988). Kieval argues that Bohemian Jews adopted a Czech identity long before the Monarchy's dissolution in 1918. His chapters on the war are good, but deal primarily with the activities of Jewish nationalists.

McCagg, William O., Jr. *A History of Habsburg Jews, 1670—1918* (Bloomington: Indiana University Press, 1989). An idiosyncratic treatment of Jewish modernization in the Hapsburg Monarchy with an interesting, but not particularly satisfying, chapter on the Monarchy's dissolution.

Mosse, Werner E., and Arnold Paucker. *Deutsches Judentum in Krieg und Revolution 1916—1923* (Tübingen: J.C.B. Mohr, 1971). A collection of essays dealing with the problem of rising anti-Semitism and the Jewish response.

III

REPRESENTATIONS: IMAGES OF THE SOLDIER

CHAPTER 10

SOLDIERS, CIVILIANS AND THE WARFARE OF ATTRITION
Representations of Combat in France, 1914–1918

John Horne

> "You are not a hero, Fumat. You are only a martyr. And we are going to lay you in the earth of France, which has engulfed an innumerable army of martyrs."
>
> (Georges Duhamel, *Vie des martyrs*, 1918)[1]

Hero, martyr, victim—many are the ways in which the ordinary soldiers and officers of the Great War saw themselves and were seen by contemporaries. Traditionally, much of the analysis of combat experience has turned on attempts to distinguish between the "reality" of that experience and the inflated patriotism or literary romanticism used by civilians (as well as some soldiers) to portray warfare on the Western Front, where the French army was mainly engaged.[2] Recent studies, however, have underlined the relativity of combat experience. They have insisted on the need to see the soldier in relationship to a complex world rather than as one term of a polarized opposition between "front" and "rear". That world included the considerable diversity of the Western Front (active or quiet sectors, front as opposed to rear) and the soldier's connection with his own family and milieu as well as with a more negative "home front" of

---

Notes for this chapter begin on page 244.

"shirkers", "profiteers," and armchair patriots. It also encompassed a range of more political factors, such as national sentiment and the "contract" by which citizen soldiers accepted military discipline.[3] A further implication of recent works is the importance of disentangling the soldiers' experience from its retrospective mythologization, not least by veterans.[4]

This essay takes up a related but separate question to that of overall combat experience and identity. It asks how the industrialized warfare which was the central revelation of the Great War was portrayed by the soldiers themselves, and also how civilians understood it. It is a question which arguably lay at the heart of the relationship between front and rear. Recent work on the "high" military history of the war has identified the central drama of the Western Front in the discrepancy between a "technological" and a "mental" battlefield.[5] The technological battlefield was shaped not only by the enormously destructive capacity of modern firepower but also by the overwhelming advantage which in 1914 (as opposed to 1939) it conferred on the defensive. Lightly-armed attacking infantry were repeatedly shown to be no match for artillery, barbed wire, and machine guns.

The "mental" battlefield derived from the prewar belief of military hierarchies in the doctrine of the offensive. This did not ignore firepower, but was informed by cultural values which found the antidote to firepower in the human qualities of command (élan, discipline, morale) and in the lingering model of the Napoleonic set-piece battle. The failure of industrialized siege warfare to coincide with this imaginary battlefield produced the military reality of the Western Front. At unprecedented human cost, successive offensives were launched which were designed to restore the war of movement and achieve a decisive military victory, but which degenerated ineluctably into the brutal logic of attrition and an apparently interminable conflict.

The implications of this analysis extend far beyond military history "from above". Society as a whole experienced the same discrepancy between imaginary preconceptions of warfare and the realities of the Western Front. Public opinion before 1914 paralleled military thinking in its assumptions about the potency of the offensive. The images of warfare thus conjured up were in turn linked to the codes of masculine behavior considered appropriate to combat (heroism, action, movement, conquest) and to the nature of a future war, which was usually imagined to be short and settled by a decisive military engagement. Soldiers and civilians no less than high commands faced a bitter "learning experience" during the war in which the imagery of combat, assumptions about the duration of the war, and the appropriate models of behavior for home and fighting fronts, all required radical readjustment. A disjunction between prediction and actuality doubtless marks all wars but it dominated the Great War. Our concern here is how this disjunction was expressed, and whether or not it was resolved, by the wartime systems of "representation" which formulated and transmitted the soldiers' experience from front to rear—systems which were both official and "public" (i.e., promoted by the censured media) and personal and "private."

Establishing the changing representations of combat during the war among both soldiers and civilians opens a potentially vast field of cultural history. One relatively focused approach, however, is to consider the correspondence of soldiers. The French were largely literate by 1914.[6] During the war, they wrote letters on an unprecedented scale and, from 1916, the surveillance (on a sampling basis) of most soldiers' and some civilians' letters by the state for the purpose of monitoring opinion and morale provides a copious record of popular attitudes which historians have already used in the reconstruction of soldiers' experience.[7] Despite the problems posed by military censorship and authorial self-censorship, the archives of the postal control provide valuable evidence, among much else, on how soldiers and to a lesser extent civilians understood the nature of warfare in the last three years of the war.[8]

But correspondence was more than a private affair. Some soldiers' letters were accorded public status as privileged testimony to the national spirit of resistance and as an exemplification of the ideal virtues of the warrior. Published collections of letters became a flourishing sub-genre of wartime literature—and one which allows the publicly acceptable view of combat, and of model comportments by both soldiers and civilians in relation to it, to be compared with the views expressed in the postal control archives. Correspondence, in other words, provides a means of exploring representations of combat and of mapping both public and private responses to the disparity between anticipated modes of battle and the realities of trench warfare.

The first year of the war saw the clear public definition of a soldierly ideal inspired by traditional images of combat. One of its principal expressions was the profusion of letters published in the press and subsequently anthologized.[9] Within a month of the outbreak of hostilities, the popular novelist Victor Margueritte summed up the essential message of the phenomenon in the ultra-official *Bulletin des Armées de la République,* distributed to all French troops. The letters, he maintained, expressed the *Union sacrée* in arms and re-established the chain of national history connecting 1914 to the French revolution. But they did so because they bore witness to a particularly French form of heroism, a kind of insouciant courage which guaranteed victory.

> These envelopes without stamps, ... these pages written truly on the wing where in a few words you tell your tales—confident, simple, boyish, doubly heroic in their bravura and their gaiety *à la française* —these are the balm for our worries and the cordial of hope! ... This communion of all France, animated by the spirit of [17]92, is the pledge of our forthcoming victory."[10]

The ideal of heroism was overtly stated in numerous published letters, as by the soldier who wrote on tenth August 1914 (before seeing action) that "I leave full of ardour ... I wish to die a hero, thinking of God and of France." Other letters told of wounded soldiers making light of their injuries in order to return to battle.[11] Death was sometimes portrayed as a heroic *tableau vivant*—as in the letter recounting the end of the poet, Charles Péguy, killed while standing "upright, insanely glorious in his bravery."[12] More often it was consecrated with simple professions of duty, as in the last letter written by a married man to his wife and two children in the event of his death, assuring them that he died "a true Frenchman, a good Frenchman."[13]

A studied gaiety under fire emerged as a peculiarly French refinement of the heroic ideal. One soldier described a bloody encounter to his parents, concluding; "I like these little skirmishes, *c'est rigolo* (they are amusing); *Vive la France!*" An officer found his men to be "stylish" *(chic)*.

> Ah! the *chics soldats!* They are these *agents de liaison* who come to communicate an order in the midst of the bullets, pipe in hand, who have to be made to take shelter in the trenches while they speak to you; it is the priest who, in order to give absolution to the section under cover stands on the parapet ...; it is one of my soldiers who, mortally wounded in the retreat [to the Marne], said to one of his comrades 'Tell the lieutenant to write to my mother that I died facing the enemy'."[14]

All the anthologies took this "heroism of our soldiers ... [with] their fine humour under fire" to be a fundamental characteristic of French combatants.[15]

The war of movement in 1914, despite extremely high French casualties, reinforced conventional representations of combat, with epic tales such as "the capture of German flags" and "the bayonet charge."[16]

This does not mean that the published letters failed to register the shock of siege warfare from October. "Modern war surprises us all," confided a military chaplain; "No more episodic combats, no more hand to hand fighting, no more assaults as there used to be, but men bent over the ground digging trenches and awaiting the hour of death under salvoes of machine-gun fire."[17] A soldier wrote that: "Instead of the classic battle lasting a day, followed by marches and maneuvers ... we fight every day and every night, and then go to earth like badgers, remaining opposite each other indefinitely." And another warned his correspondent not to imagine serried ranks of soldiers engaging the enemy at close quarters "according to the traditional civilian clichés," because it needed a trained eye even to see the enemy during a battle.[18] But despite this perplexing new form of warfare, and ample evidence of the destructive power of machine guns and artillery, the conventional assumptions about battle went unquestioned.

For the dominance of the defensive was presented as troubling only to the enemy. Sometimes an imagined technical superiority was seen as the key to French offensive superiority. This was notably the case with the 75mm light field gun, endowed by the popular press with quasi-magical properties, and which emerged as a panacea to the warfare of attrition in some letters ("The 75 is truly a terrifying weapon. In less than three minutes the position was literally wiped out. We threw ourselves on it, heads down, but the work was already done. A score of Bavarian survivors surrendered"). In other cases, the withering effect of French defensive fire on advancing Germans was noted triumphantly but the reciprocal conclusion for French offensives was not drawn; "Once [the Germans] had come within a thousand meters of us, our numerous machine guns and forty seventy-fives immediately opened up, and there was the most frightful butchery one can imagine."[19]

As with the high command, the public representation of combat at the beginning of the war placed its faith in the superior moral qualities of French soldiers, and hence of the nation, to overcome enemy firepower. As one officer wrote: "We shall win, logically we must, for each day we deserve outright victory a little more by our will, our utter disregard of death, and by the smile with which we greet each one of our miseries."[20] Conversely, the morale of German soldiers was assumed to be low, negating the effect of their firepower. One letter recounted Germans "dying of fright" under a French heavy artillery bombardment, many of them in a posture of prayer, while captured German letters were published selectively to suggest the collapse of enemy morale.[21]

The public image of combat in 1914–1915 thus portrayed a distinctively French form of heroism in order to claim the inevitability of a victorious offensive, despite the initial retreat to the Marne and the subsequent stalemate of trench warfare. As a cultural construct, the image was fed by various sources. An elite ideal of *panache* or *crânerie*—of elegance and gaiety in the face of danger—was seen well before the war as a distinctive feature of the French code of male conduct, even compensating for demographic weakness.[22] Chivalry, which in France as elsewhere contributed to the invention of a canon of national literature in the 19th century, supplied literary models for modern heroism. Educated soldiers invoked figures like Bayard, the knight without fear and reproach, while the anthologists cited medieval chivalry as a source of the "France [which] in this duel without mercy ... holds the sword of Du Guesclin, of Jeanne d'Arc, and of Bayard."[23] Tales of military prowess in the revolutionary and Napoleonic wars, widely disseminated in the primary school text books of the Third Republic, supplied other models of heroism. One editor described the epistolary tale of prostrate, wounded Frenchmen staggering up to repel German soldiers with cries of "Arise the dead!" as being the equal of "the great epics of the Revolution and Empire."[24]

In fact, the public image of warfare was part of a wider "war culture" in 1914–1915, which saw the significance of the conflict in unilateral German aggression, in the "atrocities" and sense of violation occasioned by the German invasion, and in the rapid victory which alone could repair these outrages.[25] The associated tendency to give the war universal meaning (characteristic of national mobilization in all the combatant societies) turned it, from the French point of view, into a Manichaean struggle of "civilization" and justice against "barbarism" and immorality—"barbarism" which became all the more sinister by being harnessed to the most advanced bureaucratic and industrial capacities. The published soldiers' letters exemplified this language in which French heroism became the logical opposite of the demonized enemy. The larger political and ethical meaning attributed to the conflict by this "war culture," as well as popular belief in the offensive, thus obscured the significance of the dawning warfare of attrition.

How the first year of the war was viewed in *unpublished* soldiers' letters is not easy to establish, as it pre-dates the postal control records. The peasant writer, antimilitarist, and trade union activist, Emile Guillaumin, who helped administer the mail service of his regiment in the autumn of 1914, became highly skeptical of the public imagery of combat. He found no evidence of wounded soldiers chafing to return to battle and, indeed, one corporal who had shown real heroism under fire dreaded his return to the front. Guillaumin considered Péguy to have died heroically but ultimately as victim rather than martyr. And the two popular reactions to the war discerned by Guillaumin—pessimism, often accompanied by alcoholism, or resignation—were a far cry from the public ideal.[26]

Yet if we turn to the unpublished letters of two middle-class soldiers, one a left-wing Catholic (Anatole Castex), the other a Jewish atheist (André Kahn), a more ambiguous relationship with the public representation of warfare emerges.[27] In both cases, the terrible nature of war is made explicit, including the nightmarish quality (due to extreme fatigue) of the war of movement, the impartial destructiveness of machine guns and artillery, and gruesome details of combat. No epic here. André Kahn, in particular, talked of this aspect of the war in terms of "stupidity" *(bêtise)* and "pity" for all the combatants, friend and foe. But Kahn also condemned the *Boches,* not the war, for the "barbaric" destruction of the historic town of Ypres, while Castex denounced the enemy as criminals and readily believed tales of their "atrocities."[28] Castex repeated many of the tropes about the demoralization of the enemy and praised the magically destructive power of a new French explosive, "turpinite"—mythical in every sense of the word.[29] And both men referred to the mocking "gaiety" of the French soldiers and to the inevitability of French victory due to superior moral qualities.[30] These are the letters of educated young men, but a recent collection of previously unpublished soldiers' correspondence from the *Midi,* spanning all social classes, confirms this mixture of views which were both characteristic of, and rigorously excluded from, the public ideal of warfare in 1914–1915.[31] Nor should this surprise us, for the ideal was by definition prescriptive, and thus a caricature, while also forming part of a "war culture" in which soldiers as well as civilians participated.

It might be supposed that the tension between public and private representations of combat already evident in 1914–1915, as well as that between the initial "war culture" and the wider experience of the war, increased as the conflict lengthened and casualties rose. But before examining private depictions of the warfare of attrition, it must first be asked whether the public image itself was modified. This can be explored by considering the published correspondence of individual soldiers which, from 1915, tended to replace the patriotic anthologies.[32] Although these volumes appeared for the remainder of the war, they typically concerned soldiers who died between autumn 1914 and the end of 1916, that is, during the period when prior expectations of warfare confronted the defeat of the French offensives of 1915, the costly defense of Verdun in 1916, and the failure of the Franco-British offensive on the Somme. Without exception, they were intended as a posthumous memorial, a few being printed privately but most being issued by major publishers, sometimes running into several editions.[33]

Superficially, the heroic ideal remained prevalent. Patriotic ardor, self-conscious insouciance under fire, and faith in victory recur throughout the texts. "War is a light and easy thing," wrote Robert Dubarle, captain in the elite Chasseurs Alpins and parliamentary deputy for Grenoble, shortly before he was killed leading his company against an enemy trench in June 1915, "and death, though tearing me from my loved ones, frightens me less than ever. The *Boches* may come, I shall oppose them in the front line until the end."[34] Roger Cahen, graduate of the Ecole Normale Supérieure, teacher and free-thinker, who was killed in January 1916 after barely three months at the front, declared breezily that "I'm sure I shall miss these months. I was made for this adventurous life where I enjoy admirable spectacles and comradeship."[35] Ferdinand Belmont, from the Grenoble bourgeoisie (like Dubarle) and a medical student who volunteered while under age for the Chasseurs Alpins, epitomized warlike resolve when writing in mid-June 1915:

> Splendid weather: a day made for victory. Since yesterday, the cannon roar ceaselessly on all sides. The concert is infernal. Periodically, machine-guns and volleys of rifle-fire burst out ... I am fine. I want to kill some *Boches. Vive la France!*"[36]

Mentioned in dispatches and awarded the Légion d'Honneur, he was killed by a shell six months later.

The heroic model was spelled out even more clearly for the home front readership by the editorial presentation of these volumes. "Written with lighthearted pluck *(crânerie enjouée)* by the young officer," commented the introduction to the letters of J. Saleilles, graduate of the Ecole des Sciences-Politiques in Paris, who was killed leading an attack in the Champagne offensive in September 1915.[37] Robert

Dubarle's colonel described him as the "Bayard of the 68th regiment," and a camp was named in his honor with a plaque recording the citation of his Légion d'Honneur: "He was a model of energy and of moral force."[38] Marcel Etévé, the brilliant *normalien* killed in July 1916 on the Somme, was presented by Ernest Lavisse (director of the Ecole Normale Supérieure and doyen of official Republican historical scholarship) as the ideal type of young French intellectual–sensitive, modest, brave and endowed with a natural moral and intellectual ascendancy over his comrades.[39] In many respects, what emerges from these volumes is a composite, model portrait of the middle- and upper-class junior officer, spanning the divide between Catholic and secular republican cultures with the same traits of selfless service, confident patriotism, romantic sensibility, and physical courage.

It is all the more striking, therefore, to find this explicit and public ideal undermined by reference to the horror of combat, the scale of casualties, and the apparent impossibility of a victorious breakthrough. Nowhere is this clearer than in the case of Augustin Cochin. At forty, Cochin was an established historian from a distinguished Catholic and monarchist family. He viewed the death in action of his brother Jacques in February 1915 in quintessentially heroic terms. Jacques had been killed leading a charge, thus symbolizing the offensive will of the French, and had "entered eternity through the wide gate of heroes and martyrs."[40] Cochin also interpreted Jacques' death by the light of his own reactionary values, seeing him as the epitome of the "Catholic bourgeoisie" galvanized into action by the war in defense of an elitist individualism against the crushing "human machinery" of the modern state, typified by Germany. The ideal of *crânerie* became a political affirmation of the traditional elites' social supremacy in the face of modernity.

> The officer is to the fore, like my poor brother, who was found without any weapon other than his cane and gloves, his arm outstretched in the gesture of attack, several paces in front, the first among his men to be killed. That is the French manner."[41]

But the ideal foundered under his own experience of the front. Describing artillery bombardments, Cochin admitted to his mother in September 1915 that he was terrified, "not heroic for tuppence," while on hill 304 at Verdun, in April 1916, he described men going mad with the enforced passivity of ten hours under heavy bombardment.[42] He twice evoked the "joy and emotion" of a "magnificent charge" which evaporated as the stalemate of attrition re-established itself. On the first occasion, the Germans counter-attacked ("massacre ... no-one behind, two kilometers of plain strewn with dead"), until Cochin helped re-stabilize the line ("the *sales têtes* could go no further. But neither could we"). On the second occasion, the Germans drove them out with an artillery barrage ("Massacre, we lost more men than the assault troops").[43] This is not to suggest that Cochin became demoralized. But as the Catholic novelist Paul Bourget observed in his introduction, Cochin lost his "illusions about the poetry of war" when faced with the "sinister realities" of the battlefield. "What an odious war, days and days spent in holes," wrote Cochin in his last letter to his mother, the day before he was killed by machine-gun fire on the Somme while, like his brother Jacques, leading an assault.[44]

The tension between the idealized representation of combat and the "sinister realities" of warfare characterized the other published correspondents too, except where they died early in the war or soon after reaching the front. The young painter E. Lemercier wrote letters of lyrical intensity and elevated patriotism to his mother. In December 1914, he reassuringly described the heroism of the ordinary soldiers: "The general good humour is admirable. However much they wish to return home, the comrades accept heroically all the vicissitudes of their calling. Their courage, though infinitely less literary than mine, is all the more pragmatic and adaptable."[45] But heroism and horror co-existed in unresolved tension in his account of an offensive the following February:

> You cannot imagine, my beloved mother, what men are capable of. For five days my shoes have been grey with human brains, I have been walking on human torsos, I have stumbled on entrails. The men eat the little they have alongside corpses. The regiment has been heroic; we have lost all our officers. They died bravely .... At last, after five days of horror which cost us twelve hundred victims, we were withdrawn from this place of abomination."[46]

Lemercier's was the most popular of all the wartime volumes of published correspondence, going through 23 editions.[47]

Robert Dubarle unburdened himself of his frustration with the warfare of attrition to his wife in February 1915: "But when will the truly decisive victory come, which will end these massacres?" Following the death in action of his brother and brother-in-law, he admitted that "in my life so stricken with sorrows, there is no longer any place for the gay banter of [the beginning of the war]."[48] Marcel Etévé reproached a close friend from the Ecole Normale Supérieure in a home front job who was being drawn to pacifist ideas for having imagined that those fighting would not share such views: "You speak to me of the 'war against war' and you seem to imagine that I couldn't share your opinion. What kind of brute do you take me for? Did you think that the soldiers ... were anything other than men like you and me, submitting to this war as the worst of catastrophes ...?"[49] And expressing the same doubt over the meaning of the conflict in a different ideological register, Pierre-Maurice Masson, a Catholic *normalien* and academic who was killed by a shell in Lorraine in April 1916, wrote the previous October to friends who had two sons killed in action:

> One needs to have an almost religious faith in one's country to accept such an immolation without revolt and moral disarray. There are moments when, faced with the death of all these young men ... one has doubts which strangle one. Is the game worth the sacrifice? Will these millions of men, willing or passive victims, really bring in a better humanity, one closer to the kingdom of God?"[50]

Such tension in the published correspondence between imagined and real combat, between the expected victorious offensive and the murderous immobility of the Western Front, necessitated a shift in the understanding of warfare on the part of combatant and civilian alike. This evolution did not take the form of overt criticism of military tactics or of calls for a negotiated peace. Of the published letters, only those of Jules-Emile Henches, a career artillery officer who was killed on the Somme in October 1916, came close to condemning the high command for failing to understand the true causes of the military stalemate and for indifference to casualty levels.[51] What did characterize the published correspondence was the emergence of a discourse of "sacrifice."

Marcel Etévé, when sent the yearbook of the Ecole Normale Supérieure with the list of those already killed, concluded that the salutary example of their ultimate sacrifice prepared him to accept his own. Shortly before his death, Robert Dubarle wrote of "the glorious privilege of sacrificing oneself, voluntarily ...," though in more somber tone, following the death of his brother in action, he counseled his wife: "Let us try, without complaining too much, to offer our sacrifice to our country and to place the love of fatherland above our own grief."[52] Almost all of the published volumes referred to the example of sacrifice given by the ordinary soldiers, "these humble men," as Dubarle wrote, "who without question sacrifice their lives to their country and accept with laughter the privations and fatigue of war." Ferdinand Belmont, with a sharp eye on the social hierarchy of the army, considered that the "real heroes" were those who "renew their admirable sacrifice every day, without making a fuss," even though others favored by chance or rank received the recognition of this collective heroism by being decorated.[53]

Religious faith (which in the French case largely meant Catholicism) provided a ready repository of language and gesture for accepting the war in terms of sacrifice. The central role of sacrifice in conferring meaning on suffering by redemption and renewal undoubtedly contributed to the revival of religious practice widely observed on the Western Front, something that emerged as a distinct current in the published letters. Thus, J. Saleilles wondered of the dead whether "their sacrifice, the gift of their blood, is not the supernatural source of the renewal of life which must be given to our country ... That is why we must not wail and lament like pagans in the face of all these dead." And Ferdinand Belmont, moved by attending a field mass with 500 soldiers, wrote that "the war, like all great sacrifices, at least has a purifying role. It is by sacrifice and suffering that regeneration occurs."[54] Several anthologies of letters by Catholic priests serving as soldiers or ambulance men on the western front made the same point, though with the additional motive of using the war to reintegrate Catholicism into the nation, if not to rechristianize France. "We await the decisive all-out assault," wrote one. "So many sacrifices! May they help bring the resurrection of a greater, more beautiful and truly Christian France."[55]

Other creeds (particularly secular ones) may not have enjoyed the same ritual and psychological advantages as Catholicism in expressing sacrifice and its vital corollary, consolation. But the need to develop a language and symbolism of sacrifice which could reconcile the scale of loss on the Western Front with the purpose and meaning of the war as expressed through the "war culture" of 1914–1915, had arguably become central to the public representation of combat by the middle phase of the war. And the published volumes of letters had an exemplary role in this process. For, as on the outbreak of war, the letter was both private communication linking soldier and rear and, when published, a didactic message from the collective figure of the *poilu* to the home front (albeit one monopolized by middle-class junior officers). And that message, by 1916–1917, was the need to adapt the heroic ideal and the conventional imagery of combat to an acceptance of the realities of the battlefield without any loss of commitment to ultimate victory. A study of the forces of moral resistance of the French people entitled *The Third France*, which was published in 1917 by Victor Giraud, a republican intellectual, drew centrally on the published soldiers' letters to show how the sacrifice of the soldier at the front and that of the civilian, especially the woman, in mourning at home, linked a nation confronted by "the monotonous and sordid and perilous existence of the trenches" in an attitude of "stoicism, resignation, bravery [and] of the spontaneous gift of oneself."[56] The nationalist writer, Maurice Barrès, in his book of April 1917, *Les Diverses Familles spirituelles de la France*, made a similar point about a new depth of national unity achieved through the experience of combat as revealed by the soldiers' correspondence. He saw the different cultural and ideological currents of the country—Protestant, Jewish, republican free-thinking, socialist, conservative, and Catholic—each redeeming through its sacrifice a particular vision of France which was part of a larger whole ("oh miracle, they are all right"). Barrès' final chapter argued that the soldiers' sacrifice gave the war its meaning, for themselves and society as a whole, and the reciprocal duty of the civilians was not to betray the collective national renewal for which, in different ways, the soldiers' correspondence called ("the France of tomorrow will need the close collaboration of the priest, the free-thinking officer, and the [republican] primary school teacher").[57]

The public representation of warfare, of course, remained highly selective, censored and, whether in published correspondence or in the media more generally, dominated by the educated middle and upper middle class. The archives of the postal control allow this semi-official image to be compared with that of the ordinary soldiers. This is a comparison both of the publicly acceptable face of combat with the plethora of private views conveyed from front to rear and also of elite attitudes with those of the peasants, workers and lower middle-class men who composed the bulk of the armies on the Western Front. A vast archival source, the postal control is here used in a limited and exploratory way through the mail reports for six regiments from three infantry divisions, the 19th (recruited from eastern Brittany and western Normandy), the 25th, and the 120th (both from the Auvergne).[58] The year examined is 1917 when French morale was tested most severely, especially by the failure of the April offensive and the mutinies in May and June.[59]

If published correspondence was part of a controlled public representation of warfare, private letters were not the completely free expression of personal opinion. Correspondents were well aware of the postal control which had a repressive as well as a monitoring function. Although typically only 20 to 25 percent of letters were checked, this might rise to the totality (in cases of collective disobedience, for example), and this resulted in a certain self-censorship. From 40 to 70 percent of the letters home from the 25th division were unsigned in the spring of 1917, and after a severe crisis of morale in the 70th regiment (19th Division), the authorities insisted that the sender's name and unit be inscribed on the envelope.[60] Criticism of the military command was comparatively rare and couched in general terms. Where the war was excoriated, the tendency (as we shall see) was to use a common, almost ritual language of denunciation.

Most letters ignored military matters, though not necessarily for reasons of self-censorship. As the postal controllers make clear, they concerned themselves with "family questions and personal affairs." This should not surprise us as the relationship between home and fighting front was at root concerned with the material and moral well-being of loved ones and with individual survival. But the nature of warfare was hardly extraneous to that relationship, and a minority of letters in any given mail control commented (positively or negatively) on the fighting, the length of the war, the prospects for victory, and on more general relations between the front and rear and between the fighting soldier and the rest of society. Thus 15 percent of the 500 letters read for the 98th Regiment on 15 June, in the traumatic aftershock of the April offensive, expressed a "very marked discouragement", though the percentage of letters with opinions was generally smaller than this. It is impossible to know the exact relationship between such letters and opinion within the regiment concerned. But given that the soldiers expressing opinions in each mail control seem to vary, it is reasonable to assume that the different discourses on the war discernible in the letters, and the changing balance between them, reflected soldiers' attitudes more broadly and formed a private representation of warfare communicated to the home front.[61]

The discordance between the technological determinants of siege warfare and the commitment to the victorious offensive was perhaps at its most acute for ordinary soldiers as well as the high command in the spring of 1917. The endlessness of the conflict and the continuous strain of trench life had produced an understandable preoccupation with peace—in the sense of an end to the fighting. In a minority of cases, this took the form of what the postal controllers called *lassitude*, or weariness and disgust at the thought of continuing. "As for the end of the war," wrote one soldier, "I think it'll begin to be talked about towards 1925," while another, contemplating the approaching spring offensive, lamented that "we are going to resume this martyr's life; let's hope that it ceases."[62] Yet by and large, morale appeared to be good. If there was fairly frequent reference to the soldiers' "sacrifice," many anticipated that peace would be won by a victorious spring offensive. "Are we on the point of seeing the end?," wrote a soldier of the 48th Regiment to his godfather in mid-March. "I like to think that soon we'll have peace. A little more courage and we'll beat (the Germans)," while one of his comrades tried to stiffen his mother's morale by telling her to "get it into your head that [the war] cannot go on much longer."[63]

Not only was faith in the offensive an antidote to *lassitude* but the spring also saw a revival of the more overtly warlike and antiGerman language of the initial phase of the war. In March, all three divisions traversed the region devastated by the enemy in their retreat to the fortified Hindenburg line. The postal control commissions noted for both the 19th and 25th Divisions that the ruins and ravages left by the Germans had increased the soldiers' hatred and desire for revenge.[64] Tales of rape, defiled churches and other "atrocities," when added to the evidence of physical destruction, reawakened charges of "barbarism." "The *boche* bandits have left ruin and misery behind them," wrote a soldier of the 71st, while a sapper who had been told by a girl of her gang rape swore that "if ever we get to Germany, I'll take pity on the civilians, but as for the soldiers, I'll shoot the lot of them and I'll burn all the houses."[65] A soldier of the 38th Regiment (120th Division) called the Germans "barbarians" and "criminals" as he described to a friend their deliberate destruction of fruit trees, promising to "make them pay." A fellow soldier informed his fiancée that before seeing her on leave he wanted to kill a few *boches*, without taking any prisoners, in order to revenge himself for German "barbarism."[66]

The impending Franco-British offensive reinforced these "optimistic and warlike sentiments" in all three Divisions, according to the postal control commission, which even referred to the "gaiety" of the men. "Our valiant Breton corps is more aggressive than ever and only asks to chase out the *Boche*, " wrote an artillery n.c.o. from the 19th Division in one of a number of such letters.[67] The language of patriotic resolve disappeared in the aftermath of the spring offensive, but was capable of being reactivated subsequently (e.g., by a gas attack or heavy bombardment). This suggests that the "war culture" of 1914–1915 did not simply wither in contact with the reality of trench warfare but remained a frame of reference for ordinary soldiers when the conduct of the enemy or the turn of events raised the moral or political meaning of the conflict.

On the eve of the April offensive, then, morale was high and the belief that the French army stood on the brink of a decisive breakthrough (fostered by the press) was widespread among soldiers as well as civilians. Yet seasoned troops were also apprehensive in the light of their past exposure to the tactics of attrition. The 19th Division held the record for the longest tour of duty at Verdun in 1916 (lasting the entire campaign), while both the 25th and 120th Divisions had seen action at Verdun and on the Somme. "There is uncertainty on the operations to come," noted the postal control commission of the 16th Regiment in late March. "'If only they could bring the longed-for end. What would the sacrifices matter so long as they brought a result?,' is the dominant note."[68]

The last batch of mail sent by the 19th Division before it attacked Mont Cornillet in the Champagne region on 30 April, on the extreme right of the Nivelle offensive, fully conveyed this ambivalence. Overall morale was "excellent," with many hoping, like Nivelle, that they were on the brink of victory. "We are going to attack along the whole line. The *Boches* are lost," wrote one soldier, while another hoped that "this time we'll succeed in making them leave." Also, like the high command, ordinary soldiers drew great comfort from the French bombardment, which seemed to reverse the advantage of firepower and make it impossible for the German defenders to resist the eventual attack. "I've never seen such a formidable bombardment," wrote one soldier of the 48th Regiment (19th Division), in one of many such letters. "It roars constantly, day and night, [and] the *Boches* will have to quit their lairs, for nothing could resist." The 25th Division, attacking a fortnight earlier on the opposite (northern) end of the offensive, next to the British at Saint-Quentin, had been similarly impressed by the massive British artillery barrage. Yet doubts persisted. A soldier of the 70th Regiment wrote that "we shall attack in the first wave, we have to make it across fifteen hundred meters if we can, but there's no point in getting steamed up, what is meant to happen will happen, that's all," and a comrade explained that "it's tough, I assure you, to make [the Germans] withdraw."[69]

The failure of the offensive and the reassertion of the warfare of attrition was traumatic and graphically conveyed to civilians. Letters home from the 19th Division the day after its attack registered a state of shock, yet managed to suggest the essential reasons for the débâcle—the failure of French artillery to break the German defensive positions, the withering effect of enemy machine gun fire, and the devastation caused by the French "creeping" artillery barrage as it fell on its own advancing soldiers. "Yesterday, the thirtieth of April, was not a happy day for us. Lots of officers and half the men in the regiment fell. All this destruction was carried out ... by our own artillery," reported one soldier, while another commented laconically: "we couldn't advance because the [enemy] machine guns mowed us down." "We advanced a little," commented another, "but alas! how many losses."[70] The 25th Division, attacking near Saint Quentin on 13 April, left home correspondents in no doubt about the uncut barbed wire which had kept it from its target of a sugar refinery, or about the resultant "big losses" and collapse of morale: "I assure you that I have the most frightful depression from this terrible, endless massacre," stated one letter; "you need your head screwed on not to go mad."[71]

But the full impact of the disintegration of the offensive and of hopes for a rapid end to the war came in the succeeding weeks. War weariness proliferated and the war was condemned by many soldiers as morally repugnant. "We cannot hold out any longer, we've been through terrible moments and the men cannot go on," wrote one man in the 19th Division, and several referred to the recent offensive as "a second Verdun."[72] Losses were communicated either by precise examples of sections or companies decimated in the attack or in sweeping visions of demographic annihilation ("all the Bretons will be killed if this continues," wrote one man from the 71st Regiment).[73] Numerous letters described the implacable logic of attrition:

> The great offensive, the one which was meant to be decisive and expel the *Boches* was a total failure like all the others ... what a butchery. I hope they realize this time that ... only diplomacy can settle the matter."[74]

And the vocabulary of impersonalized death—"butchery," "carnage," "slaughter," "hell"—became commonplace.

The spring offensive of 1917 thus marked for the French the point at which the imaginary battlefield of the victorious offensive, relating courage and effort to strategic result, finally withered in the face of the obdurate reality of the warfare of attrition. The language of necessary "sacrifice" had been relatively common in the correspondence highlighted by the postal controllers in early 1917, albeit in a less exalted form than in the published letters of educated officers. But the language of depression and repudiation which became so much stronger in reaction to the failed offensive (though never universal) was its exact opposite. Where the public discourse of "sacrifice" made sense of the warfare of attrition by reference to the ultimate purpose of the war and to the virtue of resignation, the private discourse of moral repudiation proclaimed the *absence* of meaning. It was the language not of "sacrifice" but of the "sacrificed." Sometimes it directly subverted the vocabulary of the heroic ideal and the meaning given the war by the cultural mobilization of 1914–1915. "We have machine guns and [poison] gas into the bargain," wrote a soldier of the 71st Regiment in September; "that's what they call the war for civilization." A drum-major in the 70th commented that "the days, the weeks, the months go by and we still endure our martyrdom ... Suffering mounts up ... I wonder what goal we are pursuing."[75] And a soldier commenting on the death in action of the son of mutual friends (unlike Robert Dubarle) found no consolation in the idea of sacrifice: "when one has taken such trouble to raise a child, who costs the eyes in one's head, and then loses it at this age, it is frightful; I tell you, this war plunges everyone into misery and the most appalling suffering."[76]

If moral repudiation of the warfare of attrition negated the language of necessary sacrifice, it was logical to replace the resignation implied by sacrifice with the gesture of refusal. This is precisely what occurred to varying degrees in all three Divisions in early to mid-June, when they were at rest in the rear. The soldiers' correspondence was naturally veiled in its references to mutinies, which overall involved some 40,000 troops on the Western Front, but enough filtered through to confirm that these were above all a protest against the warfare of attrition. In the 19th Division, men of the 71st Regiment smashed their tools rather than engage in routine laboring work, while soldiers from the 70th Regiment "wandered through the streets with the red flag ... and fired revolvers." As one letter noted, "the soldiers are not pleased. ... For three years they've been dying without knowing why or for whom; it's scandalous."[77] In the 25th Division, the 98th Regiment was particularly affected. One battalion refused to work in the trenches, with the letters making it clear that the soldiers were protesting at a "butchery" whose responsibility lay firmly with the high command.[78] The 16th Regiment, which escaped the mutinies in June, revolted in August to cries of "we want peace," "what's the point in getting your head shot off?," and "enough of the slaughter."[79] In the 120th Division, the 38th Regiment was sympathetic to the mutinies of other units and, according to one correspondent, when the colonel addressed the men in the language of heroism and high morale ("he said that the 38th was still light-hearted ... and that in the midst of danger, sadness had to be chased away so the *Boche* could be beaten"), he was given short shrift.[80]

Nor was the mood of revulsion or the gesture of refusal one which isolated the front from the rear. The letters themselves acted as a private information network conveying news of the military débâcle and thus of the essential reality of the warfare of attrition to family and friends, despite the heavily censored press (which was virtually silent over the outcome of the offensive) and the public discourse of resignation and sacrifice.[81] The reports of the prefects for the departments from which the three divisions were principally drawn make it quite clear that in June 1917, the crisis of morale among the civilian population was due in substantial measure to the impact of the soldiers' letters, reinforced by furloughs which were often marked by uninhibited protests in the trains from the front and in the main stations. The prefect of the Ille-et-Vilaine, for example, noted that the devastation of French troops by their own artillery had adversely affected civilian morale (a reference to the débâcle of the 19th Division's attack on the 30 April), while the sub-prefect of Roanne (from which the 98th Regiment was recruited) considered that hostility to the war by the town's workers had been accentuated by the soldiers "who tell their relations that they are being 'butchered,' that they are killed by our own cannons, and that they are 'made to advance without the protection of our artillery'."[82] At least some soldiers took the strikes which broke out (principally from economic rather than political motives) in May and June 1917, as signals of solidarity between rear and front: "I'm glad to see the women workers of my district refusing to make shells to crush us with," wrote a soldier from the Ille-et-Vilaine, referring to industrial unrest in the state arsenal at Rennes; "this business is frightening for the whole French population and ... we want an end to the scourge [of war]."[83]

Moral protest against the warfare of attrition and gestures of refusal to fight were fundamentally political on the part of the soldiers concerned because they pointed to the gulf between the mental and technological battlefields, and challenged the authority of a high command which had been unable to bridge it. The crisis of morale signaled that substantial elements of military and civilian opinion found the reality of the warfare of attrition unacceptable in its failure to relate sacrifice to achievement, in its indifference to the human cost of the offensive, and in its inability to end the conflict. Yet it was a large step from protest against a particular form of warfare to rejection of the war. Once morale had been restored (under Nivelle's successor Pétain) by a variety of means, including the elimination of future mass offensives on the Nivelle model, the meaning attributed to the conflict by the "war culture" of 1914–1915 and the language of acceptable sacrifice and resignation could reassert themselves.[84] After the summer of 1917, despite fluctuations in the morale of all three Divisions, there was no major resurgence of the discourse of repudiation or acts of refusal for the remainder of the year. And despite the absence of a major study of military morale for 1918, the indications are that the German spring offensive renewed the sense of urgency of 1914, stiffening the mood of military resistance, until it became clear in the late summer, despite the absence of a triumphant Allied breakthrough, that the Germans were definitively in retreat.

Several conclusions and further questions are suggested by this study of the representation of warfare in French soldiers' correspondence during the Great War. The vision of combat with which the French went to war, and the heroic ideal associated with it, could not survive prolonged exposure to the passive immobility and costly offensives of the Western Front. Although the cult of the air aces, such as Guynemer, can be understood as an attempt to salvage these conventional ideas of combat and manly conduct, the published letters of junior officers show that by 1915–1916 the ideal was being undermined even as it was expressed.[85] In order to reconcile faith in victory with bloody stalemate (or the "mental" with the "technological" battlefield), triumphant heroism perforce gave way to the ideal of "sacrifice".

It remains an open question as to how much this mutation was a largely upper- and middle-class affair, the cultural construct of educated junior officers and home-front propagandists. At the level of visual representation, in the illustrated press, it was as likely to be the image of the hirsute *poilu* as that of the officer which barred the way to the brutal invader and incarnated the national will to resist. But as far as the published correspondence is concerned—and the same is true of soldiers' diaries and memoirs—the voice of the front soldier was monopolized by the junior officer. One explanation of the popular success of fictional works like Henri Barbusse's *Le Feu* and Georges Duhamel's *Civilisation* and *Vie des Martyrs* (the first two winning the Prix Goncourt during the war) is that they gave public expression to the suffering and sacrifice of the ordinary soldier.

Nevertheless, the subalterns themselves frequently referred to the courage, heroism and self-abnegation of the men, in both published and unpublished correspondence, while commenting on its less "literary" and self-conscious register, as we have seen. Granted that both heroism and self-sacrifice were ideals, model comportments, there is no reason to suppose that they did not have a demotic variant. The references to "sacrifice" in the ordinary soldiers' letters read by the postal controllers tend to support this suggestion, although the language and content of the popular sense of self-sacrifice differed from that of the officer elite, with resignation and even fatalism playing a part. But the terms and extent of this more popular understanding of "sacrifice" require further exploration.

The depiction of combat through the discourse of "sacrifice" (whether public or private) was ultimately ambiguous, a combination of duty and horror in which duty prevailed. The moral condemnation of the warfare of attrition by word and deed, following the April 1917 offensive, directly challenged the language of "sacrifice" and resignation. The authorities were naturally alarmed about the potential radicalization of this response. But its immediate significance lay less in its challenge to the consensus on the meaning of the war (few soldiers advocated German victory as the price of peace) than in the breakdown of a representation of warfare derived from prewar values and images, and hence in the threat to model comportments and male codes of conduct which derived from this. When soldiers refused to attack and challenged the symbols of military authority, or civilians demanded the return of the men from the front, they rejected the reciprocal models of military self-sacrifice and civilian stoicism which constituted the public ideal.

Ultimately, the outright rejection of the warfare of attrition was countered and contained by a variety of forces, not least of which was the continuing, widespread perception that basic political questions and moral issues turned on the military outcome of the war. But the sense of horror at the nature of combat on the Western Front, which generated both public and private languages of "sacrifice," and also provoked overt dissidence and revolt after the 1917 offensive, remained a haunting vision. Its force would become, if anything, more compelling for the French as the issues for which the war had been fought and won lost their urgency in the postwar years.

Notes to Chapter 10

1. G. Duhamel, *Vie des martyrs* (Paris: Mercure de France, 1966), p. 177.
2. Most notably in that unique classification of combat literature according to the criterion of its "realism," J. Norton Cru, *Témoins* (Paris: Les Etincelles, 1929; new ed., Nancy: Presses Universitaires de Nancy, 1993), but also in a host of studies (often by those with personal experience) seeking to render faithfully the life of the soldier. Amongst the best of the latter are J. Meyer, *La Biffe* (Paris: Albin Michel, 1928) and *La Vie quotidienne des soldats pendant la grande guerre* (Paris: Hachette, 1966).
3. Foremost in the new approach must be cited G. Pedroncini, *Les Mutineries de 1917* (Paris: Presses Universitaires de France, 1967); J. Maurin, *Armées, guerre société: soldats languedociens, 1889–1919* (Paris: Publications de la Sorbonne, 1982); A. Cochet, *L'Opinion et le moral des soldats en 1916 d'après les archives du contrôle postal* (*troisième cycle* thesis, University of Paris X-Nanterre, 1985, 2 vols); S. Audoin-Rouzeau, *Men at War 1914–1918. National Sentiment and Trench Journalism in France during the First World War* (Paris: Colin, 1986; English translation, Oxford: Berg, 1993); and L. Smith, *Between Mutiny and Obedience. The Case of the French Fifth Infantry Division during World War I* (Princeton: Princeton University Press, 1994).
4. Exemplary and exhaustive on the relationship between combatant experience and veteran memory is A. Prost, *Les Anciens Combattants et la société française 1918–1939* (Paris: Presses de l'Institut National des Sciences Politiques, 1977, 3 vols). A shorter version is available in English as *In the Wake of War. "Les Anciens Combattants" and French Society* (Oxford: Berg, 1992).
5. D. Porch, "The French Army and the Spirit of the Offensive, 1900–1914," in B. Bond and I. Roy (eds.), *War and Society. A Yearbook of Military History* (London: Croom Helm, 1975), pp. 117–43; and, above all, the conceptually pathbreaking study by T. Travers, *The Killing Ground. The British Army, the Western Front and the Emergence of Modern Warfare, 1900–1918* (London: Unwin Hyman, 1987).
6. F. Furet and J. Ozouf, *Lire et écrire. L'alphabétisation des français de Calvin à Jules Ferry* (Paris: Editions de Minuit, 1977), vol. 1, pp. 57–58.
7. P. Renouvin, "L'Opinion publique et la guerre en 1917," *Revue d'Histoire Moderne et Contemporaine*, 1968, pp. 4-23; J. Jeanneney, "Les Archives des commissions de contrôle postal aux armées (1916-1918): une source précieuse pour l'histoire contemporaine de l'opinion et des mentalités," ibid., pp. 209–33; G. Lien, "La Commission de censure et la commission de contrôle postal à Marseille pendant la première guerre mondiale," *Revue d'Histoire Moderne et Contemporaine*, 1971, pp. 649-67; and above all, the work of Annick Cochet which makes sustained and imaginative use of this source. See in particular, Cochet, *L'Opinion et le moral des soldats en 1916*, op. cit.; "Les Paysans sur le front en 1916," *Bulletin du Centre d'Histoire de la France Contemporaine*,

3, 1982, pp. 37-41; and "Les Soldats français," in J.-J. Becker and S. Audoin-Rouzeau (eds.), *Les Sociétés européennes et la guerre de 1914–1918* (Université de Paris X-Nanterre: Centre d'Histoire de la France Contemporaine), pp. 357–66.

8. The postal control archives are in the Service Historique de l'Armée de Terre in the Château de Vincennes, Paris (hereafter SHV).

9. Four anthologies are used here to analyze this phenomenon; E. Daudet (ed.), *L'Ame française et l'âme allemande. Lettres de soldats* (Paris: Attinger Frères, n.d., but 1915); C. Foleÿ (ed.), *La Vie de guerre contée par les soldats* (Paris: Berger-Lavrault, 1915); R. Lestrange (ed.), *Lettres de héros* (Paris: Société anonyme de l'imprimerie Kugelmann, 1915); R. Narsy (ed.), *La France au-dessus de tout. Lettres de combattants* (Paris: Bloud et Gay, 1915).

10. V. Margueritte, "Vos Lettres," *Bulletin des Armées de la République*, 31 August 1914, p. 1.

11. Foley, *La Vie de guerre*, pp. 1–2, 16.

12. Narsy, *La France au-dessus de tout*, p. 60

13. Ibid., p. 67, which also cites a badly-wounded soldier's last letter, "I leave without regret, conscious of having done my duty."

14. Daudet, *L'Ame française*, p. 40

15. Introduction to Daudet, *L'Ame française*, p. 3.

16. Narsy, op. cit., pp. 33–4, 36.

17. Foleÿ, *La Vie de guerre*, p. 60.

18. Narsy, *La France au-dessus de tout*, pp. 7, 21.

19. Daudet, *L'Ame française*, pp. 9, 29.

20. Foley, *La Vie de guerre*, p. 147.

21. Daudet, *L'Ame française*, pp. 40 and 65 ff.

22. R. A. Nye, *Masculinity and Male Codes of Honor in Modern France* (New York: Oxford University Press, 1993), p. 226.

23. Lestrange, *Lettres de héros*, pp. 10–11. Likewise, Narsy considered that the virtues revealed by the soldiers' letters were not just those of the current moment but of "France, chivalrous, far-seeing, generous; of France always the same ... from the companions of Joinville to the soldiers of Joffre" (*La France au-dessus de tout*, p. 4).

24. Lestrange, *Lettres de héros*, p. 179. For revolutionary antecedents of heroic ideals in the Great War in a slightly different context, see S. Audoin-Rouzeau, *La Guerre des enfants* (Paris: Colin, 1993).

25. For the concept of a "war culture," see Audoin-Rouzeau, op. cit., passim. For the invasion and "German atrocities" in the same context, see J. Horne, "Les Mains coupées: <atrocités allemandes> et opinion française en 1914," *Guerres mondiales et conflits contemporains*, 171, 1993, pp. 29–45, and R. Harris, "'The Child of the Barbarian': Rape, Race and Nationalism in World War I," *Past and Present*, 141, 1993, pp. 170–206.

26. "Emile Guillaumin à trois amis," in *L'Actualité de l'histoire*, 31, 1960, pp. 37-40 (letters of 10 November 1914 and 10 March 1915).

27. H. Castex (ed.), *Verdun, années infernales. Journal d'un soldat au front d'août 1914 à septembre 1916* (Paris: Editions Albatros, 1980); J.-F. Kahn (ed.), *Journal de guerre d'un juif patriote 1914–1918* (Paris: Editions Jean-Claude Simoën, 1978). The titles are misleading since both books are in reality collections of war letters written by the editors' father and grandfather respectively.

28. Kahn, *Journal de guerre*, p. 67 (1 December 1914), and Castex, *Verdun*, pp. 76, 92.

29. Castex, *Verdun*, p. 93. For the "turpinite" myth, see A. Dauzat, *Légendes, prophéties et superstitions de la guerre* (Paris: La Renaissance du Livre, n.d.), pp. 99-102.

30. Kahn, *Journal de guerre*, p. 92, and p. 103 for his faith in the French commander-in-chief, "Joffre-the-phlegmatic"; Castex, *Verdun*, pp. 80-1, for his New Year hopes in 1915.
31. G. Baconnier, A. Minet and L. Soler (eds.), *La Plume au fusil. Les poilus du Midi à travers leur correspondence* (Toulouse: Privat, 1985), pp.127–78.
32. Twelve volumes of letters by individual soldiers are used for the purpose of this analysis; F. Belmont, *Lettres d'un officier de chasseurs alpins (2 août 1914–28 décembre 1915* (Paris: Plon, 1916); V. Boudon, *Avec Charles Péguy de la Lorraine à la Marne, août-septembre 1914. Correspondance de guerre de Charles Péguy* (Paris: Hachette, 1916); R. Cahen, *Lettres de l'Argonne*, in "Entretiens des non-combattants pendant la guerre," *Union pour la Vérité*, April 1916; A. Cochin, *Quelques lettres d'Augustin Cochin à sa famille et à ses amis* (Paris: Imprimerie Louis de Soye, 1916; new ed., as *Le Capitaine Augustin Cochin. Lettres de guerre* {Paris: Bloud et Gay, 1917); L. Delourme, *Lettres de Louis Delourme écrites à ses parents pendant la campagne de mil neuf cent quinze* (Toulouse: Imprimerie J.-M. Caussé, n.d., but 1916); R. Dubarle, *Lettres de guerre de Capitaine R. Dubarle au 68e Bataillon de Chasseurs Alpins* (Paris: Perrin, 1918); M. Etévé, *Lieutenant Marcel Etévé. Lettres d'un combattant, août 1914-juillet 1916* (Paris: Hachette, 1917); J.-E. Henches, *Lettres de guerre. Extraits de la correspondance du chef d'escadron Jules-Emile Henches (14e septembre 1875–16 octobre 1916)*, (Cahors: Imprimerie Coulesant, 1917; a smaller selection was published as *Lettres d'un artilleur* by Hachette in 1918); n.a., but E. .E. Lemercier, *Lettres d'un soldat, 1914–1915* (Paris: Librairie Chapelot, 1916); P.-M. Masson, *Lettres de guerre, août 1914-avril 1916* (Paris: Hachette, 1917); Jules Portes, *Souvenirs et correspondance de guerre* (Paris: Eclaireurs-Unionistes de France, 1915); and J. Saleilles, *Lettres de guerre* (Dijon: Imprimerie Darantière, 1916). This list tallies approximately with that of Norton Cru, *Témoins*, for volumes of correspondence published during the war, but adds several which he does not mention. Without being exhaustive, it represents the essence of the genre.
33. Thus Delourme and Saleilles were published privately. Cochin and Henches were published by their families but were taken up by major commercial publishers, in the case of Cochin following the appearance of extracts in the Catholic paper, *Le Correspondant* (10 Nov. 1916). Cahen was published in the review of a republican free-thinking organisation, the Union pour la Vérité, and Portes was published by the protestant youth organisation of which he was a leading militant, the Eclaireurs-Unionistes de France. The remainder appeared with leading publishing houses, in the cases of Lemercier and Etévé following extracts in the literary and political periodical, the *Revue de Paris* (1 and 15 August 1915 and 1 August 1917 respectively). For Lemercier, see also note 47 below.
34. Dubarle, *Lettres de guerre*, p. xxiv.
35. Cahen, *Lettres de l'Argonne*, pp. 32–33.
36. Belmont, *Lettres d'un officier de chasseurs alpins.*
37. Saleilles, *Lettres de guerre*, p. 6.
38. Dubarle, *Lettres de guerre*, pp. xxv, 251.
39. M. Etévé, "Lettres (1915-1916)," *Revue de Paris*, 1 August 1917, p. 565
40. A. Cochin, *Le Capitaine Augustin Cochin*, p. 15, letter of 19 February 1915 to a family friend.
41. Cochin, op. cit., p. 20.
42. Cochin, op. cit., pp. 29, 45–46.
43. Cochin, op. cit., pp. 37, 54.
44. Cochin, op. cit., p. 56.
45. E. Lemercier, *Lettres d'un soldat*, p. 80.

46. Lemercier, op. cit., pp. 135–36.
47. Lemercier was also published in English as *Letters of a Soldier* (London: Constable, 1917) and *Soldier of France to his Mother* (New York : McClure, 1917) (J. Norton Cru, *Témoins*, p. 530).
48. Dubarle, *Lettres de guerre*, pp. 142, 220.
49. M. Etévé, "Lettres (1915–1916)," p. 580 (letter of 27 September 1915).
50. P.-M. Masson, *Lettres de guerre*, p. 140.
51. J.-E. Henches, *Lettres de guerre*, (12 January 1916). This was privately published and distributed in Cahors and, in a severely expurgated version, commercially by Hachette in 1918.
52. Etévé, "Lettres (1915-1916)," p.590; Dubarle, *Lettres de guerre*, pp. xxiv, 168.
53. Dubarle, *Lettres de guerre*, p. xx; Belmont, *Lettres d'un officier de chasseurs alpins*, pp. 171–72.
54. J. Saleilles, *Lettres de guerre*, p. 143; F. Belmont, *Lettres d'un officier de chasseurs alpins*, p. 70.
55. V. Bucaille, *Lettres de prêtres aux armées* (Paris: Payot, 1916), p. 86. On the broader question of faith and the soldiers' experience, see A. Becker, *La Guerre et la foi. De la mort à la mémoire 1914–1930* (Paris: Colin, 1994).
56. V. Giraud, "La France jugée par elle-même. Les lettres du front," in *Revue des Deux Mondes* , 15 February 1917, and in idem, *La Troisième France* (Paris: Hachette, 1917), pp. 140, 148.
57. M. Barrès, *Les Diverses Familles spirituelles de la France* (Paris: Emile-Paul, 1917), pp. 194, 268. Translated into English as *The Faith of France* (Boston: Houghton Miflin, 1918).
58. The principal infantry regiments of the 19th Division were the 48th (Guingamp), the 70th (Vitré), and the 71st (Saint-Brieuc). From the 25th and 120th Divisions, three regiments have been examined, all from the Loire–the 16th (Montbrison), the 38th (Saint-Etienne) and the 98th (Roanne).
59. P. Renouvin, "L'Opinion publique et la guerre en 1917," op. cit.; J.-J. Becker, *Les Français dans la grande guerre* (1980; English translation, *The Great War and the French People* [Leamington Spa: Berg, 1985], part 3).
60. SHV 16N 1398, 25e Division d'Infanterie (DI), all regiments, 5 April 1917 and SHV 16N 1399, 16e Régiment d'Infanterie (RI), 5 June 1917 (but the comment applied to all units in the 25e DI); SHV 16N 1393, 71e RI, 10 July 1917.
61. For further discussion of this crucial point, see J.-N. Jeanneney, "Les Archives des commissions de contrôle postal aux armées," op. cit., and A. Cochet, *L'Opinion et le moral des soldats en 1916*, op. cit., vol. 1, pp. 14–24.
62. SHV 16N 1398, 270e RI, 10–16 March 1917 (a reserve regiment of the 70th).
63. SHV 16N 1398, 48e RI, 10–16 March 1917.
64. SHV 16N 1398, 19e DI, 24–30 March 1917; SHV 16N 1398, 25e DI, 5 April 1917.
65. SHV 16N 1398, 19e DI, 24–30 March 1917.
66. SHV 16N 1398, 120e DI, 38e RI, 9 April 1917. The highly personalized language of insult was also used, notably "les salauds" (the bastards) and "cette sale race de Boches" (this filthy race of *Boches*).
67. SHV 16N 1398, 19e DI, 24–30 March 1917; SHV 16N 1398, 25e DI, 5 April 1917, which considered that the "the men remain gay and confident of success"; SHV 16N 1398, 120e DI, 38e RI, 7–13 April 1917, which noted "many optimistic and warlike sentiments."
68. SHV 16N 1398, 16e RI, 24 March 1917.
69. SHV 16N 1406, 19e DI, 1 May 1917; 19e DI, 48e RI, 1 May 1917; 19e DI, 70e RI, 2 May 1917.

70. SHV16N 1406, 19e DI, 2 May 1917.
71. SHV, 16N 1398, 98e RI, 25e DI, 21 April 1917 and 4 May 1917.
72. SHV 16N 1406, 270e RI, 19e DI, 9 May 1917.
73. SHV 16N 1406, 71e RI, 19e DI, 10 May 1917.
74. SHV, 16N 1406, 270e RI, 19e DI, 9 May 1917.
75. SHV, 16N 1494, 71e RI and 70e RI, 19e DI, 27 September 1917.
76. SHV, 16N 1399, 98e RI, 25e DI, 15 June 1917.
77. SHV, 16N 1393, 19e DI, 70e RI, 12, 13, and 14 June 1917.
78. SHV, 16N 1399, 25e DI, 98e RI, 15 June 1917.
79. SHV, 16N 1393, 25e DI, 16e DI, 20 August 1917; P. Belot, *Trente ans de baroud. Histoire militaire du Général Colombat* (Paris: Arthaud, 1945), p. 156. Colombat was the commander of the 16th Regiment from August 1917.
80. SHV, 16N 1399, 120e DI, 38e RI, 4 June 1917.
81. J. Horne, "Information, opinion publique, et l'offensive Nivelle," in L. Gervereau (ed.), *Images de 1917* (Paris: Musée d'Histoire Contemporaine/ Bibliothèque de Documentation Internationale Contemporaine, 1987), pp. 72–79.
82. SHV, 16N 1538, reports of the prefects for June 1917.
83. SHV, 16N 1393, 19e DI, 70e DI, 13 June 1917.
84. G. Pedroncini, *Les Mutineries de 1917*, op. cit., pp.232–78.
85. L. Kennett, *The First Air War, 1914–1918* (New York: The Free Press, 1991), pp. 151–74.

Select Bibliography

Audoin-Rouzeau, S., *Men at War 1914–1918. National Sentiment and Trench Journalism in France during the First World War* (1986; English translation, Oxford: Berg, 1993). A major study of ordinary soldiers and their cultural world from newspapers produced in the trenches.

Becker, A., *La Guerre et la foi. De la mort à la mémoire 1914–1930* (Paris: Colin, 1994). A pioneering exploration of faith (essentially in its religious varieties) as one of the principal cultural forms through which the war was experienced, especially by soldiers.

Becker, J.-J., *The Great War and the French People* (1980; English translation, Leamington Spa: Berg, 1985). The best general introduction to public opinion and morale in France, with samplings of documents from local and national archives.

Cochet, A., "L'Opinion et le moral des soldats en 1916 d'après les archives du contrôle postal" (troisième cycle thesis, University of Paris X-Nanterre, 1985), 2 vols. The fundamental study of the postal control archives, which uses these to reconstruct the broad currents of soldiers' opinion via retrospectively applied sampling techniques. Regrettably, a version has not been published in French or English.

Norton Cru, J, *Témoins* (1929; new ed., Nancy, Presses Universitaires de Nancy, 1993). Comprehensive analytical listing of autobiographical soldiers' writing (memoirs, diaries, letters) classified according to rather simplistic and subjective criteria of "realism." This work itself played a significant part in the creation of a retrospective literary canon of front-line experience in the interwar years.

Pedroncini, G., *Les Mutineries de 1917* (Paris: Presses Universitaires de France, 1967). The first work to use military archives to study the mutinies. It remains fundamental.

Prost, A., *In the Wake of War. Les 'Anciens Combattants' and French Society* (1977; English translation, Oxford: Berg, 1992). Translation of the small volume of documents accompanying the same author's magisterial thesis on the structure, politics and anthropology of the French veterans' movement in the interwar period, which was published in French in three volumes. The introduction outlines the main ideas of the larger work.

Smith, L., *Between Mutiny and Obedience. The Case of the French Fifth Infantry Division during World War I* (Princeton, Princeton University Press, 1994). A detailed and methodologically innovative study using a wide variety of sources which argues for the culturally constructed, and ultimately negotiated, nature of military discipline in an army of soldier-citizens.

CHAPTER 11

MASCULINITY, MEMORY, AND THE FRENCH FIRST WORLD WAR NOVEL
Henri Barbusse and Roland Dorgelès[1]

Leonard V. Smith

The study of how war transforms identity has led historians to consider the relationship between war and gender. "Gender" here is used as a term distinct from "sex." Whereas "sex" refers to agreed-upon biological distinctions between male and female, "gender" refers to behavioral, cultural, even epistemological expectations proceeding from sexual difference.[2] In wartime, historians have argued, gender is disrupted even as it is employed to mobilize members of the male and female sexes. For example, soldiers in the First World War were called upon as men to defend their mothers, wives, and daughters from the barbarous enemy, only to find a type of warfare that can be interpreted as emasculating. And the very weapons in their hands were often produced by women called from traditional female spheres of home and nursery to take up jobs previously monopolized by men. The stories of transformed gender roles, a growing and sophisticated body of historical literature has argued, constitute a major theme of the story of war itself.[3]

The transformation of the male gender sphere in the First World War has most often been interpreted in terms of a "crisis of masculinity."[4] Most simply stated, a gender crisis ensued within the male self

---

Notes for this chapter begin on page 269.

when the irresistible force of conventional martial courage ran up against the unmovable object of the stalemated war. The stalemate produced by the trench system and superior defensive firepower meant that behavioral expectations such as "courage" or "manliness" resulted simply in getting maimed or killed to no military effect.[5] In its most extreme form, as Elaine Showalter memorably argued, the First World War crisis of masculinity resulted in shell shock, a male appropriation of what psychiatry construed previously as the singularly female condition of hysteria.[6] Yet though it is still useful as a starting point, the concept of a "masculinity crisis" remains slippery in definition and even more in delineation. Certainly, shell shock was not the only or even the most prevalent response to dysfunctional male courage. Analytical attention here will thus shift toward other forms of resolution through transformed ways of understanding masculinity itself.

The war novel affords unique insights into the recasting of gender roles. Anthropologists and literary theorists have alerted historians to the ways narratives of all varieties not only record historical "reality," but play vital roles in creating it.[7] Despite the growing influence of still photography and motion pictures, stories about the First World War were told principally through the written word. Novels provided the most artfully produced and complex narratives about the war. Practices of writing and reading these novels played major roles in establishing the boundaries of imagination and memory of the First World War. If masculinity indeed fell into crisis and was recast, the novel is a good place to look for the particulars.

This essay will explore the "crisis of masculinity" and its resolution in two of the best-known French war novels, both written by veterans: Henri Barbusse's *Le Feu* (Under Fire, 1916); and Roland Dorgelès's *Les Croix de bois* (Wooden Crosses, 1919).[8] Both novels proved tremendous commercial successes, and are still considered the pinnacles of their authors' artistic careers. As will be explored further below, the two books also appeared at different but strategic moments in the formation of civilian understanding of the war. Specifically, the essay explores two aspects of how Barbusse and Dorgelès sought to resolve the "crisis of masculinity" of the First World War by retooling gender, by restoring masculinity to the male sex.

As Roger Chartier has noted, books function historically not just as texts, but as events in the history of mentalities.[9] He has called historians' attention to establishing historical readings of books, and to the ways in which producers of books prescribed these readings. This task requires looking both inside and outside the literary texts. This essay will first describe representations of masculinity in the two novels, in a section that will concentrate on how the victimized, emasculated soldier was first created then rescued by the author. In so doing, the author restored to the soldier his masculinity. Second, the essay will explore how Barbusse and Dorgelès sought to inscribe messages of restored masculinity through prescribing a particular practice of reading. The result in both cases, the essay will conclude, was a closed system of understanding soldiers' experience, in which all posterity needed to know was provided by the author. This "Truth" of soldiers' experience thus became itself a gendered concept in the literary resolution of the crisis of masculinity.

The Texts: Creating and Rescuing the Victimized Soldier

Despite their celebrity in the interwar years, neither Barbusse nor Dorgelès is very well known today, particularly in the English-speaking world. Most late twentieth-century readers would likely find both *Le Feu* or *Les Croix des bois* quite heavy-handed. But much in both books would prove familiar to anyone who has read what became the definitive First World War novel, Erich Marie Remarque's *All Quiet on the Western Front* (1929). Graphic, often gory, description dominates fairly simple plots, as innocent and sensitive narrators witness most of their comrades die gruesome deaths. Certainly, an important component in the celebrity enjoyed by both Barbusse and Dorgelès at the time was their success in contradicting wartime propaganda. Rather than the officially cheerful, good-natured, obedient *poilu*[10] who did his duty without complaint or even much reflection, the soldier created by Barbusse and Dorgelès confronts unmitigated helplessness in the face of unlimited terror. He is a victim living an unlivable situation, his very self as much at risk as his body. His battle experience inverts his prewar understanding of war as a contest or aggressiveness and courage. In the trenches, he passively awaits falling artillery shells or snipers' bullets. In No Man's Land, he is completely exposed. The soldier is emasculated in the trenches by being controlled into passivity, by capricious authority figures who condemn him and his comrades to squalor, pain, dismemberment, and death.

In today's terminology of sex versus gender, these victims can be understood as men without masculinity, as sexed male bodies with the prewar norms of the male gender sphere torn asunder by the war. Otherwise stated, the victimized soldiers are emasculated, but not really effeminized. Indeed, Barbusse explicitly situates the male self in the trenches about midway on a spectrum ranging from the completely aggressive "soldier" to the effeminized staffers and shirkers. Early in the novel, this "man" is defined principally in terms of these two "Others." In one of the passages from the book least flattering to Barbusse, he describes Black African colonials as archetypical "real soldiers," characterized by "their ferocity in attack, their devouring passion to be in with the bayonet, and their predilection for 'no quarter.'"[11] "*We* are not soldiers," responds a white Frenchman, "we are men." At the other end of the spectrum were staff officers, no better than shirkers who managed to avoid military service entirely. They delight in brutalizing subordinates from positions of safety, and in "making believe down there, all spruced up with their fine caps and officers' coats and shameful boots, … and wash[ing] themselves oftener twice than once. …"[12]

A 1929 study by a team of sexologists led by Magnus Hirschfeld described emasculation in the First World War in terms of heterosexual frustration. Certainly, both novels lend themselves to such a reading.[13] The opening scene of *Les Croix de bois* portrays the arrival of three new soldiers to the unit. The veterans "took stock of them wonderingly, enviously, as though they had been travelers disembarking from strange legendary lands." The narrator reflects that "yesterday they had still been walking along real streets seeing women, trams, shops; yesterday they were still living the lives of men."[14] Dorgelès re-emphasizes sexual frustration later in the book, when a group of soldiers prowls behind the lines looking for a reputed house of prostitution, to be marked by a bouquet of white flowers.[15] They finally find the house, and make a huge commotion in order to gain admittance. Finally, the beautiful dark-haired woman they expect to gratify them opens the door, to reveal the corpse of a child laid out for burial. It turns out that a local custom calls for the display of a white bouquet at the door in such tragic situations. Humiliation is thus added to sexual frustration.

But both authors portray thwarted heterosexuality even more graphically. The only woman to figure prominently in *Le Feu* is a beautiful young peasant refugee named Euxodie. One soldier describes her other-worldly presence, at once ubiquitous and unattainable:

> You don't know when you've got her. You see her here, there, with her fair hair on top, then—off! Nobody about. And you know, she doesn't know

what danger is; marching about sometimes, almost in the front line, and she's been seen knocking about in No Man's Land.[16]

Later, a soldier named Lameuse makes a desperate and unsuccessful attempt to kiss her. She coldly rebuffs him, as if intentionally to maintain herself as an exclusively metaphysical object of desire. But her physicality is dramatically brought home later, as her (month-old) dead body is discovered by Lameuse while he is digging a trench:

> She was trying to fall on me with all her weight. Old man, she wanted to kiss me, and I didn't want—it was terrible. She seemed to be saying to me, "You wanted to kiss me, well then, come, come *now!*"[17]

Les Croix de bois takes emasculation and victimization through denied heterosexuality to its limit, in a scene representing a homoerotic encounter produced by an accident of war. During a battle, a soldier named Sulphart leaps into a hole occupied by an older soldier from the territorials:

> Crammed together, face to face, their breath mingling, the two men stared at one another, neither able to see anything of the other beyond his fixed eyes, and the old man's hard mustache pricked Sulphart's lips. They said not a word to one another, they were simply stupefied, and their intermingled legs timidly tried to find their way in farther, seeking to hide themselves still better.[18]

An explosion kills the older man, "and Sulphart took upon his own lips the last breath of the dying man, a horrible moan, as if he had actually given up his life in that last convulsive hiccough."[19] This quasi-kiss joining two male bodies, one at the moment of death, becomes Dorgelès's symbol of the perversity of the war itself.

But having created the victimized and emasculated soldier, the author must then proceed to rescue him. The first step involves presenting an alternative construction of masculinity that restores to men what the war took away. Otherwise stated, the author constructs a retooled male self that restores gender to sex. Although sexuality figures prominently in the ways emasculation is represented in both novels, the reconstituted male self actually transcends sexuality.[20] But beyond this similarity, the bases of retooled masculinity differ significantly between the two authors, for reasons that can be explained partly by differences in artistic careers and partly by the fact that the two books appeared at two distinct moments in the construction of the memory of the war.

Henri Barbusse was 41 years old in 1914. Before the war, he had a gradually rising literary career, though he supplemented his earnings with civil service employment and journalism. Before the war, he had published two books of verse and a novel.[21] He also had links to some well-established leftist pacifist organizations. But as was the case for many of similar political views, Barbusse's pacifism was transformed virtually overnight in August 1914. "This war is a social war," he wrote to the director of *L'Humanité* on 9 August, "that is going to make a great step—perhaps the definitive step—toward realizing our cause."[22] He proudly announced that despite his age, which would have permitted him to serve in the auxiliary forces, he had volunteered for active duty as a private. "If I make the sacrifice of my life and if I go with joy to war," Barbusse concluded, "it is not only as a Frenchman, but above all as a man."[23] Herein, I would argue, lies the essence of Barbusse's retooled construct of masculinity as it would evolve in *Le Feu*—the Socialist Just Warrior.

When *Le Feu* was published in late 1916, the French war effort had entered a precarious stage.[24] At the time, the French were completing their pyrrhic victory at Verdun, and planning the desperate, ill-fated Chemin des Dames offensive that provoked the 1917 army mutinies. With over one million Frenchmen already dead, weakening allies, and final victory far from certain, many in France began to seek new reasons for carrying on. Barbusse certainly sought to remobilize French soldiers, though hardly toward official ends.

Barbusse turned to the one of the oldest male symbols in Western thought, identified by political scientist Jean Bethke Elshtain as the Just Warrior.[25] The Just Warrior is a man who can behave both violently and virtuously because of the absolute righteousness of his cause. A peace-loving man can thus become a ferocious (if most often reluctant) aggressor in the name of the Just Cause. This unquestionable moral foundation constitutes an integral part of the Just Warrior's masculinity. In Barbusse, the emasculated male self proceeds directly from the ambiguous moral foundations of the war. Relocating absolute morality thus automatically reconstitutes the masculinity of the men fighting it. Barbusse finds this morality in socialism. Viewed in this way, *Le Feu* recounts the spiritual journey of the protagonists from emasculated men to Socialist Just Warriors.

One such man fully formed emerges from *Le Feu* in the one authority figure portrayed sympathetically in the novel, Corporal Bertrand. During a group conversation after a particularly bloody battle, Bertrand observes without pride—but also without shame—that he personally killed three Germans. But he adds without a trace of doubt that "it was necessary, for the future's sake. ... The work of the future will be to wipe out the present, to wipe it out more than we can imagine, to wipe it out like something abominable and shameful."[26] Bertrand unmistakably identifies this future as socialist by identifying German socialist Karl Liebknecht as "one figure that has risen above the war and will blaze with the beauty and strength of his courage. ..."[27] The narrator worships Bertrand as an ideal, among those men "who are destined, however little their paths may run through a splendor of events, to dominate their time."[28] For his part, Bertrand is too fine an exemplar not to die a martyr's death. Some ten pages later, the reader learns that "by virtue of always doing his duty, he has at last got killed."[29] The description of his body leaves little to imagine as to Barbusse's point: "his arms are outstretched in the form of a cross; the hands open, the fingers separated."

But Barbusse is too good a collectivist to link male redemption through socialism to any specific individual. The concluding chapter, titled "The Dawn," involves a group discussion of the war, in which this message is extended among the survivors. One soldier growls that there will be no more war "when there is no more Germany."[30] Another retorts that Germany is simply the current incarnation of militarism and that others have preceded and will follow; while yet another soldier responds that "there'll be no more war when the spirit of war is defeated." Still another soldier concludes that "we're fighting for progress, not for a country; against error, not against a country."[31]

As the conversation continues, it emerges that the war is actually a continuation of the French Revolution. The narrator instructs the assembled soldiers that equality must at last take precedence over liberty and fraternity.[32] The war thus becomes a crusade against capitalism as well as nationalism. In fact, it is not difficult to establish a similarity between the "financiers, speculators great and small, armor-plated in their banks and houses" and the staff officers and colonial soldiers described earlier in the novel:

> There are those who admire the exchange of flashing blows, who hail like women the bright colors of uniforms; those whom military ballads poured upon the public intoxicate as with brandy; the dizzy-brained, the feeble-minded, the superstitious, the savages.[33]

But by the end of the discussion, the survivors emerge well along the path toward becoming Just Warriors through encountering the Truth, a term that in Barbusse's essays as well as his fiction amounts to a code word for socialist ideology: "Truth not only invests them with a dawn of hope, but raises on it a renewal of strength and courage."[34] Because this Truth now justifies any sacrifice, men can appropriately draw courage from it. Courage justified results in masculinity restored. Truth itself thus becomes an essential component of masculinity, a notion Barbusse considered crucial to his prescribed reading of *Le Feu*, as will be elaborated further below.

Roland Dorgelès was 13 years younger than Barbusse in 1914, (that is, 28 years old). He had had a far more diverse artistic career than Barbusse, lived among the literary and artistic bohemians of Montmartre. His prewar 15 minutes of fame came in 1910, when he masterminded a scheme to enter in a Salon des Indépendants competition a painting by a donkey with a brush tied to its tail.[35] Although he left this sort of youthful exuberance behind later in life, Dorgelès never exhibited Barbusse's deep attachment to any political ideology. Rather, I would argue, art, apparently for art's sake, played the role in Dorgelès's retooled version of masculinity played by socialist ideology in Barbusse. In Dorgelès, art restored to the man what the stalemated war of the trenches had taken away.

Les Croix de bois was published in April 1919, very much in the shadow of *Le Feu*. But the end of wartime censorship and the beginning of the demobilization of the French army made it possible for Dorgelès's book to make its own imprint on the memory of the war. *Les Croix de bois* was the first major French First World War novel actually to carry the story to the end of the war, and to suggest that veterans would be as helpless and alienated in civilian life as he believed they had been in the trenches. The end of the war also meant that recasting masculinity could be separated from remobilizing it to finish the war. The rescuing of the victimized soldier is thus more oblique in *Les Croix de bois* than in *Le Feu*, and more clearly based in the novelist himself.

Dorgelès recasts masculinity in aesthetic rather than in overtly political terms. He links masculinity to the act of narration itself, to the capacity to convey experience correctly. Masculinity is thus as hierarchical in *Les Croix de bois* as it is egalitarian in *Le Feu*. Narration demarcates power and status in Dorgelès, and the hierarchies of masculinity shift as the novel proceeds. Like *Le Feu*, *Les Croix de bois* employs a peculiar first-person narrative technique. The narrator is present but omniscient; he recounts far more than any individual present could possibly know. I would argue that this technique, while basically a means to a socialist end in Barbusse, is central to the rescue of the victimized soldier in Dorgelès. The theme of rescue through artistic narration helps explain three central characters in *Les Croix de bois*: Larcher, the narrator; Demachy, a young and sensitive law student; and Sulphart, a crude and somewhat dim but good-natured working-class conscript.

The novel begins with a male initiation ritual revolving around narration, as Demachy and two other neophytes arrive with the unit at the front. The grimy veterans stare at them, as Sulphart makes fun of Demachy's moleskin satchel. He suggests that "if you had a stray idea that the Boches wouldn't mark you down as much as you wanted, you might perhaps have brought along a little flag and tootled on a trumpet."[36] But having ritually humiliated the outsider, Sulphart immediately proceeds to make him an insider by narrating to him the "real" war by showing him how to camouflage the offending satchel. He plays the same instructive role later in the conversation, when it emerges that Demachy has brought with him an inordinately large number of cartridges in the apparently absurd belief that they might be attacked.[37] Sulphart reaffirms his role as master narrator as the scene comes to a close, when the group discusses previous battle experience. Demachy announces that he would like to have been at the Battle of the Marne of September 1914, because it constituted a French victory. Sulphart asserts the retreat after the Battle of the Frontiers of August 1914 "was where you got to know a man." He closes the discussion with the definitive statement that the Marne was nothing more than "a show that brought in fifteen sous to the lads that pulled it off."[38] Sulphart has by now taken the novice under his wing, and the two become fast friends for the rest of the novel.

The theme of narration restoring masculinity to the victimized soldier (or failing do to so) helps explain the fate of these three characters. In the climactic battle of the novel, Sulphart loses part of one hand. He is invalided out of the war, just as it is coming to a close. The victimization and the emasculation of the war of the trenches follows him into civilian society. His wife abandons him (thus perpetuating his sexual frustration), and he ambles his way to Paris to find consolation in drink. No less significantly, once out of the trenches Sulphart loses his ability to provide true narration. The author/narrator observes, not without condescension:

> Like all the wounded men, Sulphart was stuffed with reminiscences of the war that he was very fain to narrate, he had his cheeks, so to say,

bulging with them, and they dribbled quite as a matter of course from his lips like the milk out of the mouth of a baby that has sucked too much.[39]

The relevant chapter concludes with Sulphart in a café debating the outcome of the war with a civilian. He insists lamely that the war is concluding in victory, "because I have come out of it with my life."[40] Sulphart's fundamental inability to convey the cultural meaning of the war means that he remains a permanent invalid in a gendered sense, as well as in a physical sense. The end of the war finds him a man without masculinity.

The fate of Demachy is closely linked to that of the narrator Larcher. The two had become close friends at the beginning of the novel, though on a completely different basis from Demachy and Sulphart. Class and education unite them; their first words to each other announce their respective professions of law student and writer.[41] Almost immediately, they use the bourgeois, even aristocratic, *vous* to each other, and Larcher rejoices that he had found someone with whom he could talk of "our books, our theatres, our cafés, and of pretty girls breathing perfume." But like Corporal Bertrand in *Le Feu*, Demachy has too much Dickensian purity to survive to the end of the novel. (Indeed, all of the important characters are killed except for Sulphart and Larcher.) Demachy dies a slow, solitary death from a stomach wound in No Man's Land. He remains conscious to the end, trying to dress his wound while crying hopelessly for help. Larcher narrates his death in truly poignant detail, although he was not there himself or even apparently within earshot. Indeed, the tragedy of a sensitive young man dying, not just in agony but alone, is part of the point.

With the end of the war, the uniquely masculine authority to narrate the meaning of the war falls to the author himself. The last chapter depicts Larcher in his study, struggling to come to terms with his own grief and how to represent it. He laments that, ironically, the dead must be victimized a second time, as all mourning must come to an end. This happens in part through forgetting:

> The image of the soldier who is disappeared for ever will slowly fade in the consoled hearts of those he loved so much. And all the dead men will die for a second time.[42]

Memory may inevitably efface part of what happened, but the correct meaning can still emerge if it is expressed by the right voice. Consequently, the narrative approach in *Les Croix de bois* becomes far more than a curiosity or a mere appropriation of artistic license. The author not only can but must establish himself as the arbiter of the meaning of the war, lest that meaning disappear entirely. This end justifies any literary means. Larcher has not only the right but the obligation to narrate inner thoughts and events he could not possibly have witnessed first hand. Indeed, by its last paragraphs, the book has not only largely effaced the lines demarcating Larcher from the other characters, but the line demarcating Larcher from Dorgelès. Larcher/Dorgelès confesses that "in a strange confusion, I can no longer distinguish between those whom in the flesh and blood and bone I knew out there, and those I have created to be the humble heroes of a book."[43] The result, as I will explain more closely in the next section, is a stunningly individualistic restoration of gender to sex based on artistic voice. Dorgelès can reclaim masculinity through writing. The Sulpharts of the world can do the same only through reading and believing without question in the unconstructed Truth of what they have read.

The Prescribed Reading: Gendering "The Truth"

One might think that little actually connects Barbusse and Dorgelès on questions of gender. Indeed, in many respects the Socialist Just Warrior bears little resemblance to the passive veteran/reader who escapes victimization and emasculation only through ennoblement by the artist. Certainly, Barbusse and Dorgelès pursued very different literary careers after the war, as will be explored further below. Relations between the two seem to have been cordial, but they were apparently not close friends. A congratulatory letter from Barbusse to Dorgelès after the appearance of *Les Croix de bois* praised him for having "evoked the war with enormous power."[44] But only a handful of letters from Dorgelès to Barbusse survive in the large collection of Barbusse's correspondence now at the Bibliothèque Nationale in Paris.[45] Many of these simply convey polite greetings or do not concern writing about the war at all.

Rather, what Barbusse and Dorgelès share is advocacy of a cultural practice of reading, in which authors and readers share an identical understanding of the literary text. Both authors shared a near fixation on the unconstructed Truth of the text, claiming all the while simply to write as mere scribes of that Truth, as if it had an existence wholly separable from themselves. The Truth of the victimized and emasculated soldier and his rescue by the war novelist depended on a reading practice in which the reader simply accepts the single reading prescribed by the author. Barbusse and Dorgelès asserted an identity between the written and read text. As Roger Chartier described this practice, "reading is thought of as inscribed in the text, an effect automatically produced by the very strategy of writing peculiar to the work or its genre."[46] The concern of Barbusse and Dorgelès with a single "Truth" and the resulting prescribed practice of reading became part of the process of retooling masculinity, and of restoring masculinity to French society at large.

In Barbusse, writing and reading the Truth are complementary acts in the on-going political mobilization of the Socialist Just Warrior. *Le Feu* proved a stunning success among a reading public starved for a narrative that questioned information coming from official channels.[47] By the spring of 1917, Barbusse had become a major public figure—precisely at the moment when the revolution in Russia, the entry into the war of the United States, and the mutinies in the French army put the politics of the war at all levels up for grabs. Barbusse's implausible claim by 1925 that "I am not a militant, I am a man of letters,"[48] reflects perhaps an understandable effort to distance himself from the dilemmas of interwar socialism. But writing and reading correctly remained for him keenly political acts.

Opinions will always differ as to whether men writing and reading about "politics" amounts to their writing and reading about "masculinity." At stake ultimately is perhaps a question of belief—whether or not one believes in the existence of "politics" devoid of gender. But whatever one's views on this larger question, a strong case can be made linking "politics" and masculinity in Barbusse's writings and his prescribed reading of them. Barbusse wrote to mobilize other men as veterans, citizens, and proletarians in a public domain whose essential maleness he did little to question. His letters from the front to his wife are nearly silent on public politics.[49] His collection of essays written between 1917 and 1920 maintains a deafening silence on women in the new world the war was supposed to make possible, even on so fundamental an issue as the franchise.[50] Soldiers, veterans, and Socialist Just Warriors constitute the politically conscious vanguard. They are not genderless political human beings, they are political men.

In the shortest chapter in *Le Feu* (two pages), a soldier discovers the narrator writing the text. He asks the narrator whether he will use all soldiers' "big words" (colloquialisms, most obscene), that "printers wouldn't like much to print." The narrator makes the cultural contract with the reader by assuring him that "I shall put the big words in their place, dadda, for they're the truth."[51] Barbusse explained the role of the reader in this contract in a preface to the September 1917 edition of *Le Feu* titled "To the Soldiers still Living." He provided the prescribed reading by describing how he was sure soldiers were already reading the book.[52] The very success of *Le Feu* proclaimed it the master narrative: "Comrades, whose lives and thoughts I shared, ... you have loved my book because it is a book of truth [*vérité*]."[53] Indeed, the words *vrai* (true) or *vérité* appear no fewer than nine times in three pages of prose. The identity among author, reader, and experience already exists; the text simply describes it: "At least—you have told me so and I believe you—I will help you to recall what you have been. I will help you keep inside you the hell that you have hated. ..."[54] In this system of meaning, only soldiers can interpret soldiers' experience and the political messages to be drawn therefrom: "Soldiers of the war, soldiers of audacious and immortal progress, soldiers of the truth, we will always be together and they will not separate us."[55] The man needs only to read, believe, and act accordingly.

Barbusse's subsequent activism suggests that he saw the alliance between the author and readers of *Le Feu* as the beginning of a broader alliance between male intellectuals and the male masses that would continue to mobilize Socialist Just Warriors after the war. Barbusse called on his brother veterans to become "soldiers of thought" in a July 1917 appeal that led to the formation of the Association Républicaine des Anciens Combattants (Republican Association of Veterans, or ARAC).[56] In his speech to the first ARAC congress in September 1919, he assured his listeners that "we will lift our eyes up above, and we will guide ourselves toward the truth."[57] In May 1919, Barbusse helped found a corresponding organization for writers, *Clarté*, named for his 1919 novel of that name (translated as *Light*).[58] Barbusse assured his brother writers that "the movement we place ourselves at the head of deliberately would come to pass without us. Democracy is invincible. But the inevitable resurrection of humanity will bloom in a more calm and beautiful manner if it is lit up by thought, if the world is peopled with lucid consciences as well as wills."[59]

Dorgelès made his major statement about how he expected to be read in a series of articles published in November and December

1928, and reprinted in 1929 as *Souvenirs sur les croix de bois*.[60] Interest in the war was beginning to revive with the tenth anniversary of the Armistice, a development that became much more pronounced after the publication of *All Quiet on the Western Front* in German in January 1929. By that time, Dorgelès had become a literary notable of some stature. *Les Croix de bois* had sold 150,000 copies within 18 months of its publication[61] and had won the Prix Fémina, probably the second most prestigious literary prize after the Prix Goncourt. In 1929, Dorgelès was elected one of ten members of the Académie Goncourt, which brought him considerable authority in the arbitration of literary taste.

Paradoxically, Dorgelès explained his prescribed reading of *Les Croix de bois* through a description of how the book was written. As with Barbusse, the reading of the text is inscribed in the writing. The reader (particularly the veteran) simply accepts the Truth of the literary text as the definitive narrative:

> Not for an instant did I think of keeping the history of my regiment. I had a higher ambition; not to recount *my* war, but *the* war. To renounce dates, erase the names of the sectors, to forget the numbers of the armies, and to draw out of myself affirmed memories so nourished with truth that each combatant would cry out "These also were mine."[62]

As in Barbusse, the author describes a collective but unitary experience whose Truth is verified by a plebiscite of readers. But this gendered Truth in Dorgelès has distinct origins and functions.

Barbusse wrote to mobilize the living, in the name of an ideology that he believed had an objective reality far beyond himself. Dorgelès wrote to memorialize the dead, to find the correct artistic language of commemoration. The distinction, then, concerns ideological versus literary Truth. Literary Truth transcends conventions implicit in the idea of an objective reality. This truth can have its origins only in the author. Dorgelès paraphrased closely in *Souvenirs* his confession in *Les Croix de bois* that he had effaced the line between fact and fiction:

> I distorted, imagined, recast, and there was made, in my mind, such a tragic combination that today I no longer know how to distinguish between the fiction and the reality.[63]

Only an artist can narrate in this way and still convey the Truth. Consequently, Dorgelès must represent himself as having gifts denied to ordinary men, gifts that make his work worthy of incorporation into the culture of commemoration. In other words, to represent literary Truth, he must represent himself as an extraordinary and gifted witness. This is precisely what Dorgelès does in his *Souvenirs*, in highly gendered terms. Just as opinions will probably always differ about the relationship between "politics" and masculinity in Barbusse, so they will about the relationship between art and masculinity in Dorgelès. The argument here is based on the proposition that when a man writes to explain his self-esteem while wearing a uniform in wartime, he is at least in part explaining his masculinity. In his *Souvenirs*, Dorgelès tells an autobiographical tale recounting how he employs art to restore gender to sex by recounting how he enters the war a would-be heroic solider and emerges from it a heroic artist. His own triumph over emasculation renders him a valid witness, and legitimizes his representation and rescue of the victimized soldier.

Although he had not done military service before the war because of a pulmonary condition, Dorgelès rushed to the colors at the mobilization. "I was so impatient to go see the battle," he recalled.[64] Indeed, Dorgelès expressed more interest in witnessing the war than in being prepared to fight it. He claimed that he and some friends managed to browbeat their commandant into sending them to the front with the first reinforcements, without any even such rudimentary training as existed at the time.[65] But by the time Dorgelès actually arrived at the front, the Battle of the Marne had come to an end, and the stalemated war of the trenches had begun. The changed war reaffirmed Dorgelès's determination to distinguish himself as a witness. "What was necessary," he wrote, "was to assimilate the war in all its poisons. And out of two beings to make only one, the writer and the soldier."[66]

Once at the front, Dorgelès recalled admiring the classless character of the army, as a world in which there were "no more barriers, no more social rank."[67] But he draws hierarchies based on the right to narrate just as severe as those in *Les Croix de bois*. Dorgelès described with ill-concealed condescension a *ferblantier* (a tinsmith or a salesman of tin products) who scrupulously wrote in a notebook the names of the stations through which their train to the front passed. Dorgelès perhaps protested too much that "I cannot think of making fun of the poor relics that these aging survivors will one day take out of the drawer," though he added that "they offer interest only to those whose names are on them."[68] Dorgelès saw himself as made of different stuff. "The meditative ones certainly suffered more than the others," he wrote, "but they had in them the means better to resist."[69] Those cursed but also blessed with special contemplative powers had a corresponding responsibility in the literary Society of Orders: "I learned to suffer in order to witness in the name of those who suffered so much."[70]

On the battlefield, narration restores masculinity to the man. Dorgelès took part in the French offensive at Neuville-St. Vaast in the Artois May-June 1915, and indeed was cited in regimental orders for his bravery.[71] With his company pinned down in a ferocious artillery barrage, Dorgelès recalled, "I felt myself weaken."[72] To regain control over himself, he forced himself to read a Protestant religious tract that he happened to have on him, then to write a passage that later appeared in *Les Croix de bois*. He described his state of mind during the episode: "The soldier perhaps was going to die, the man feel himself a coward, but someone was still resisting—the writer."[73] The parallel to the three characters in the novel described earlier is striking. Demachy (the sensitive soldier/law student who nevertheless does not narrate) dies. Sulphart, who provides inappropriate narration, becomes a coward through his dissipated existence. Larcher, the writer, resists.[74]

This restored masculinity proves highly durable as the heroic soldier continues his metamorphosis to heroic artist. Despite the centrality of his experience on the battlefield, Dorgelès found it very difficult to write in the trenches: "I know nothing more incompatible with the duties of a novelist than those of a corporal machine-gunner."[75] A transfer to aviation in September 1915 afforded a bit more time, but not enough to complete his novel. Fate intervened in June 1916 when his plane crashed during a training flight. Thereafter, he became a mechanics instructor, which he remained until the end of the war. He admitted himself so ill-suited to his duties that his superiors simply left him alone most of the time to write. But his self-esteem continued to strengthen. He described the time he spent writing *Les Croix de bois* as "happiness, absolute happiness. ... To be able to wash, eat, sleep. To live at last like a man. But also, and above all, to be able to write."[76]

Dorgelès's narrative in the *Souvenirs* brings to completion the novel, the war, and the construction of the heroic artist all simultaneously. The value of his testimony was affirmed early on by his publisher, Albin Michel. Dorgelès visited the publishing house in Paris during a leave, and emerged within five minutes with a contract and a one thousand-franc advance, with the novel unfinished and apparently without anyone at the house having read a word.[77] Michel personally decided that the house would print 10,000 copies, though Dorgelès claimed certainty at the time that they could not sell half that many.[78] The last intrusion of the military occurred when the book had to pass before the censors. (The war was not actually over when the novel reached its penultimate form.) Dorgelès, still technically a corporal in uniform, compared his interview with the military censor to a court martial.[79] His recast masculinity came under attack when the censor insisted he remove a scene describing the execution of a French soldier. After some soul-searching, Dorgelès complied, though he recalled that "I had a feeling of committing an act of cowardice in suppressing the episode of the man shot. Too bad! I will do my duty." He was rescued by the Armistice; the accompanying relaxation of censorship meant that the chapter could be restored. The postwar heroic writer completely replaced the would-be heroic soldier the day the novel appeared—the day of Dorgelès's discharge, 1 April 1919.[80]

Conclusion

The complexities behind the creation of memory are such that only a few salient issues can be addressed here. I have intentionally avoided the key issue of prescribed versus "actual" readings of the literary texts as being too involved and too problematic in terms of source material to be appropriately addressed in this format. Certainly, not all readers read as they were told. Public conflicts over the verisimilitude of Barbusse's and Dorgelès's work were few but ferocious.[81] This essay has also carefully avoided the question of whether the essential experience of French soldiers in the First World War actually *was* victimization, though I have argued elsewhere that such a categorization is at best simplistic.[82] My focus here has been not on soldiers' "real" experience, rather on the cultural construction of the memory of that experience through the war novel. Carolyn Walker Bynum's observation concerning miracles recorded in the lives of medieval holy persons applies equally well to representations of combat in First World War novels. The historian's task in analyzing some sources lies not in trying scientifically to determine their veracity, but in exploring why contemporaries believed certain elements important enough to write down in certain ways.[83] In this context, it is appropriate not to take the victimized soldier as a given, rather as a cultural creation that had origins and functions.

Issues of gender, particularly masculinity, help explain the historical construction of the victimized soldier. My argument here has used as a starting point the "crisis of masculinity" of First World War, and has pointed to ways two war authors employed the victimized soldier and his rescue by the novelist as a means of resolving it. Barbusse and Dorgelès constructed retooled discourses of masculinity to restore meaning in the male gender sphere to the male sex. Barbusse developed a discourse of the Socialist Just Warrior, in which ideology restored masculinity to the emasculated soldier. Dorgelès developed a more oblique and aesthetically oriented discourse, in which masculinity is relocated through ennoblement by the artist of the victimization of the soldier. Both Barbusse and Dorgelès assumed a reading practice based on the acceptance by the reader of the unconstructed Truth presented by the author. The result, I would argue, was a closed system of meaning centered on the novelist.

But despite the role played by *Le Feu* and *Les Croix de bois* in shaping memory in the first years after the war, one cannot help but be struck by how poorly both books—and for that matter, their authors—have withstood the test of time. Barbusse remained an important figure within leftist literary circles, he never wrote another book as successful as *Le Feu*. His inevitable involvement in the internecine bloodlettings of interwar socialism limited his impact on the political mainstream in France before his death in 1935. He antagonized critics left and right with two late works, which cast so unlikely a pair as Jesus Christ and Joseph Stalin as Socialist Just Warriors.[84] Dorgelès likewise never matched the success of *Les Croix de bois*, despite longevity and an extended term as president of the Académie Goncourt. The most durable cultural artifact he produced later in life proved to be not a book but a phrase; he is generally credited with having coined the term *drôle de guerre* (most often translated as "phony war") to describe the front before the German invasion of France in 1940. Until recently, only *Le Feu* remained in print even in French. Barbusse has attracted interest from historians of the literary left in France, who nevertheless go to some trouble to distinguish between the politics of the message and its aesthetic qualities.[85] Dorgelès has attracted little attention from either literary critics or historians.[86]

Ironically, the memory of the victimized soldier of the First World War outlasted the memory of his rescue or, to a great degree in the cases of Barbusse or Dorgelès, the memory of the authors who created him. Only a piece of the puzzle constructed here survived. Plainly, additional cultural processes were at work that merit more exploration. Gender, I would suggest, figured prominently in these processes. Certainly, struggles over recasting gender roles continued throughout the interwar period, as Louise Roberts has shown in a fine examination of womens' hairstyles and fashions in interwar France.[87] These struggles took place on the printed page as well as in the beauty parlor, and no doubt in still less likely settings. And masculinity was contested right alongside femininity. Something in these interwar struggles over masculinity helps explain how the victimized soldier not only survived in the form he did, but acquired the status of a historical truism.

Notes to Chapter 11

1. An early version of this essay was presented at the Annual Meeting of the Western Society for French History at Orcas Island, Washington, on 23 October 1992, and a revised version at the Newberry Library Colloquium in Chicago, Illinois, on 14 July 1993. Revision of the essay was supported by a John N. Stern Fellowship at the Newberry Library and a Mellon Fellowship at the National Humanities Center. I wish to thank Mr. Stern, the Mellon Foundation, and those who attended the earlier presentations.
2. A thoughtful exposition of this distinction appears in Joan Wallach Scott, *Gender and the Politics of History* (New York: Columbia University Press, 1988). The limitations of demarcating sex from gender are explored in Thomas Laqueur, *Making Sex: Body and Gender from the Greeks to Freud* (Cambridge: Harvard University Press, 1990).
3. The best overall survey of the subject remains Margaret Higonnet, et al., eds., *Behind the Lines: Gender and the Two World Wars* (New Haven: Yale University Press, 1987).
4. See, for example, Theodore Roszak, "The Hard and the Soft: The Force of Feminism in Modern Times," in Betty Roszak and Theodore Roszak, eds., *Masculine/Feminine: Readings in Sexual Mythology and the Liberation of Women* (New York: Harper & Row, 1969); Annelise Maugue, *L'Identité masculine en crise au tournant du siècle, 1871–1914* (Paris: Rivages, 1987). Unlike Roszak, Maugue maintained that the war ultimately ended the "masculinity crisis" through a rejuvenated cult of the hero.
5. This minimal definition comes from Leonard V. Smith, "The 'Crisis of Masculinity' of World War I in the Fifth Infantry Division," *Proceedings of the Annual Meeting of the Western Society for French History*, 17 (1990): 447–54. See also the thoughtful (if not very complementary) response by Patricia J. Hilden, "Commentary on Papers by Fishman and Smith," ibid., 457–58.
6. Elaine Showalter, *The Female Malady: Women, Madness and English Culture* (New York: Penguin Books, 1985), Chapter 7.
7. See particularly Clifford Geertz, *The Interpretation of Cultures* (New York: Basic

Books, 1973); and Dominick LaCapra, *History, Politics, and the Novel* (Ithaca: Cornell University Press, 1987).
8. Henri Barbusse, *Le Feu (Journal d'une escouade)* (Paris: Flammarion, 1916); Roland Dorgelès, *Les Croix de bois* (Paris: Albin Michel, 1919). For convenience, I have used here the only English translations: *Under Fire: The Story of a Squad*, Fitzwater Wray, trans., (New York: E.P. Dutton & Co., 1917); and *Wooden Crosses* [no translator noted], (New York: G.P. Putnam's Sons, 1921).
9. For a short but very thoughtful exposition, see Roger Chartier, "Texts, Printing, Readings," in Lynn Hunt, ed., *The New Cultural History* (Berkeley: University of California Press, 1989), 154-75.
10. This diminutive term for a French infantryman means literally "hairy one," who, like Samson, allegedly drew his strength from his long hair.
11. *Under Fire*, 45.
12. Ibid., 114.
13. The team concluded: "In the trenches, the common soldier ceased to be a human being; but what is much worse, is that through the altered circumstances of life he was compelled to stop being a man. In the trenches, there was no place for sexual life, at least not a normal one." Magnus Hirschfeld, et al., *The Sexual History of the Great War* (New York: Falstaff Press, 1937 [originally published in German in 1929]), 77.
14. *Wooden Crosses*, 3.
15. Ibid., Ch. 8.
16. *Under Fire*, 58.
17. Ibid., 204–5.
18. *Wooden Crosses*, 359–60.
19. Ibid., 360.
20. The themes of chastity and transcended sexuality in retooled masculinity are explored in George Mosse, *Nationalism and Sexuality: Middle Class Morality and Sexual Norms in Modern Europe* (Madison: University of Wisconsin Press, 1988).
21. These works are respectively *Pleureuses* (1895), *Les Suppliants* (1903), and *L'Enfer* (1908). For a competent summary of Barbusse's career, see the entry by J.E. Flower in *Dictionary of Literary Biography, vol.65, French Novelists, 1900–1930* (Detroit: Bruccoli, Clark, Layman, 1988), 15–19.
22. Reprinted in Henri Barbusse, *Paroles d'un combattant: articles et discours (1917–1920)* (Paris: Flammarion, 1920), 7.All translations from French citations are my own.
23. Ibid., p. 8.
24. The novel was first published in serial form in *L'Oeuvre* in August through November 1916, and then as a whole that December. It doubtful that the authorities would have allowed it to appear even six months later, in the wake of the fall of the Tsar in Russia and the 1917 mutinies in the French army.
25. Jean Bethke Elshtain, *Women and War* (New York: Basic Books, 1987).
26. *Under Fire*, 265–66.
27. Ibid., 266.
28. Ibid., 266–67.
29. Ibid., 276.
30. Ibid., 344.
31. Ibid., 344–45.
32. Ibid., 349–50.
33. Ibid., 353–54.
34. Ibid., 357–58.

35. See Micheline Dupray, *Ronald Dorgelès: un siècle de la vie littéraire française* (Paris: Presses de la Renaissance, 1986), 73.
36. *Wooden Crosses*, 4–5.
37. Ibid., 6–7.
38. Ibid., 15, 17.
39. Ibid., 378–79.
40. Ibid., 395.
41. Ibid., 8.
42. Ibid., 397.
43. Ibid., 399.
44. Quoted in Dupray, *Roland Dorgelès*, 193.
45. See Bibliothèque Nationale, N.a.Fr. 16533, Numbers 398-415.
46. Chartier, "Texts, Printings, Readings," 156.
47. According to publicity from the publisher, *Le Feu* sold 300,000 copies within two years of its publication. It also won the Prix Goncourt, the most prestigious French literary prize. See Henri-Jean Martin, Roger Chartier, and Jean-Pierre Vivet, eds., *Histoire de l'édition française: Tome IV, le livre concurrencé, 1900–1950* (Paris: Promodis, 1986), 196.
48. Quoted in J.E. Flower, *Literature and the Left in France: Society, Politics and the Novel since the Late Nineteenth Century* (Totowa, N.J.: Barnes & Noble Books, 1983), 25.
49. *Lettres de Henri Barbusse à sa femme, 1914–1917* (Paris: Ernest Flammarion, 1937).
50. *Paroles d'un combattant: Articles et discours (1917–1920)* (Paris: Ernest Flammarion, 1920).
51. *Le Feu*, 174–75.
52. "Aux Soldats vivants," in *Paroles*, 43–45.
53. Ibid., 42.
54. Ibid., 44.
55. Ibid., 45.
56. "Aux anciens Combattants," *L'Œuvre*, July 1917, reprinted in *Paroles*, 24.
57. "Ce qui veulent les anciens combattants," ibid., 129.
58. See Nicole Racine, "The Clarté Movement in France, 1919–21," *Journal of Contemporary History* 2 (1967): 195–208.
59. "Le Groupe 'Clarté'," *L'Humanité*, 1 May 1919, in *Paroles*, 103.
60. (Paris: À la Cité des Livres, 1929). The articles were originally published in *Les Nouvelles Littéraires*.
61. Martin, et al., *Histoire de l'édition française*, 196.
62. *Souvenirs*, 33–34.
63. Ibid., 35.
64. Ibid., 10.
65. Ibid., 11.
66. Ibid., 26.
67. Ibid., 7.
68. Ibid., 14–15.
69. Ibid., 16–17.
70. Ibid., 25.
71. See the catalogue for a 1978 exhibition on Dorgelès at the Bibliothèque Nationale, *Roland Dorgelès: de Montmartre à l'Academie Française* (Paris: Bibliothèque Nationale, 1978), 54.
72. Dorgelès, *Souvenirs*, 30–31.
73. Ibid., 31.
74. A few months before his death in March 1973, Dorgelès described resisting death in exactly the same terms, as he scrawled on a piece of paper with his hand barely

functioning: "I want to try / to write / To write was my joy /...I resist / resist [illegible] / I can't anymore...." Bibliothèque Nationale, *Roland Dorgelès*, 229.
75. *Souvenirs*, 39.
76. Ibid., 45.
77. Ibid., 51.
78. Ibid., 61.
79. Ibid., 55–60.
80. Ibid., 61–62.
81. The most famous involved the challenge posed by Jean Norton Cru in *Témoins: Essai d'analyse et de critique des souvenirs de combattants édités en français de 1915 à 1928* (Paris: Les Etincelles, 1929).
82. Leonard V. Smith, *Between Mutiny and Obedience: The Case of the French Fifth Infantry Division during World War I* (Princeton: Princeton University Press, 1994).
83. Carolyn Walker Bynum, *Holy Feast and Holy Fast: The Religious Significance of Food to Medieval Women* (Berkeley: University of California Press, 1987), 8.
84. *Jésus* (Paris: Flammarion, 1927); *Staline: Un Monde nouveau à travers l'homme* (Paris: Flammarion, 1935).
85. See, for example, Flower, *Literature and the Left*, and Frank Field, *Three French Writers and the Great War: Studies in the Rise of Communism and Fascism* (Cambridge: Cambridge University Press, 1975).
86. After the 1978 exhibition at the Bibliothèque Nationale, the major exception is Dupray, *Dorgelès*, a highly hagiographic biography written in close association with Dorgelès's widow.
87. Louise Roberts, "Samson and Delilah Revisited: The Politics of Fashion in 1920s France," *American Historical Review* 98 (June 1993): 657–84.

Select Bibliography

Cru, Jean Norton. *Témoins: Essay d'analyse et de critique des souvenirs de combattants édités en français de 1915 à 1928*. Paris: Les Étincelles, 1929. Still the most important study of French war books. No less fixated on "truth" than Barbusse or Dorgelès, but provides a scathing critique of distortions and factual errors in some of the most famous war texts. Abridged English version published as *War Books: A Study in Historical Criticism*, Stanley J. Pincetl, Jr., editor and translator. San Diego: San Diego State University Press, 1976.

Dupray, Micheline. *Roland Dorgelès: un siècle de la vie littéraire française*. Paris: Presses de la Renaissance, 1986. Very comprehensive, with many excerpts from unpublished correspondance. But written in close association with Dorgelès's widow, and highly hagiographic.

Flower, J.E. *Literature and the Left in France*. London: Macmillian, 1983. Comprehensive if unadventurous exposition of political context in which Barbusse wrote.

Fields, Frank. *Three French Writers and the Great War: Studies in the Rise of Communism and Fascism*. Cambridge: Cambridge University Press, 1975. More aesthetically oriented than Flower (and not very complementary). But expounds similar theme.

Fussell, Paul. *The Great War and Modern Memory*. London: Oxford University Pres, 1975. Still a classic, though 20 years after its publication it is probably more useful as literary criticism than as history.

Hynes, Samuel. *A War Imagined: The First World War and English Culture.* New York: Atheneum, 1991. More comprehensive than Leed or Fussell, and more interested in memory and civilian society. Most recent exposition of the soldier-as-victim theme.

Higonnet, Margaret Randolph, Jane Jenson, Sonya Michel, and Margaret Collings Weitz, eds., *Behind the Lines: Gender and the World Wars.* New Haven: Yale University Press, 1987. Essays not of uniform quality, but the best survey of the subject.

Leed, Eric. *No Man's Land: Combat and Identity in First World War.* New York: Cambridge University Press, 1979. More focused on Britain and Germany than on France, but the best overall exposition of the soldier-as-victim theme.

CHAPTER 12

RUSSIAN GENERAL STAFF TRAINING AND THE APPROACH OF WAR

John W. Steinberg

Introduction

As the Great Powers mobilized for the First World War, each nation's military establishment depended on the professional abilities of its General Staff to lead their country to victory. The quality of military leadership throughout Europe represented one of the decisive factors in the ability of nations to wage war on the early twentieth-century battlefield.[1] During this time European military professionals believed that the basic aim of the General Staff was to plan for the next war while simultaneously developing the skills needed to maintain order in the midst of a chaotic situation, specifically, battle. To accomplish this goal, the careers of General Staff Officers in the years prior to the First World War focused on continued education and training designed to teach them to think and react in similar terms to any problem they might encounter on the battlefield.

Progressive thinkers within the Russian military establishment had been seeking to adopt such standards in order to improve the quality of their leadership since the disastrous Crimean War.[2] The most significant nineteenth-century officer who provided not only the intellectual under-

---

Notes for this chapter begin on page 298.

pinning but also the motivation for reform was the enlightened D.A. Miliutin, who served as Alexander II's War Minister from 1861 to 1881. During his tenure as War Minister, Miliutin completely reorganized Russia's military establishment. Through the creation of military districts, the streamlining of the War Ministry, and the implementation of the 1874 universal conscription law, Miliutin laid the foundation for the creation of a modern nation at arms. More important for the purposes of this article, he strove to create a system of officer training that would prepare soldiers for service on the Imperial General Staff. Thus, Miliutin envisioned the creation of an elite cohort of military leaders who achieved rank and status based on qualification and job performance rather than birthright. The distribution of appointments based on merit as opposed to personal connections within the Russian High Command continued to be the goal of reform-minded military leaders after Miliutin was ousted from power in the wake of the assassination of Alexander II.[3]

To understand the level of military professionalism that existed at the apex of the Russian High Command in August 1914, this article seeks to measure the progress achieved by Russia's reform-minded military thinkers and leaders in their efforts to create the meritocracy envisioned by Miliutin. The topics that will be examined include the careers and performance of selected elements which comprised a part of the Russian General Staff at the outbreak of the First World War. First, the background of General Staff Officers will be observed through a study of their careers, that is, the type of military education they received, the rate at which they were promoted, and the tasks they performed when assigned to units within the army. Then, the capabilities of staff officers to perform their duties on the battlefield will be studied through an examination of their performance during peacetime maneuvers in general, and specifically one exercise that occurred in May/June 1914. Finally, this article will present some overall conclusions about the level of military professionalism that existed in Russia as the guns of August, 1914 sounded and the armies of Europe marched onto the modern battlefield.

Education, Social Status, and Rates of Promotion— A Study in Career Patterns

The careers of the General Staff Officers who commanded the Russian Army at the outbreak of the First World War can best be characterized as a process in which they alternated between different stages of formal education and extended periods of service in the ranks or in the army's administration. One of the primary issues in terms of the modernization of the army's cadre was whether non-aristocrats could earn appointments to the General Staff based on their knowledge and performance as officers in the Imperial Army. The officers who formed the ranks of the Imperial Guard Regiments had traditionally gained access to the high command as a result of their aristocratic pedigree and subsequent connections. With the Tsar's tacit support, guards officers resisted the rise of soldiers of humble origin into the commanding ranks of the army. But officers of lesser social origin did indeed make notable inroads into the power structure of the armed forces. The cause for this transformation rested with the educational reforms that Miliutin initiated in the 1860s.

Miliutin's efforts to create educational opportunities for future military leaders were designed to accomplish two goals. First, the adoption of the universal conscription act of 1874 increased the size of the army thereby necessitating the training of a larger number of men to fill the ranks of the officer corps. The other problem Miliutin addressed through his reforms was the level of overall training and education received by the officers who would eventually become members of the army's high command. In this fashion the War Minister intended to provide Russia with an officer corps that met both the size and the intellectual requirements needed to fight on the modern battlefield.

Miliutin's educational reforms began with what was traditionally the first stepping stone toward a military career—the Cadet Corps Academy. Established during the reign of Empress Anne (1730–1740) to reward the aristocrats who supported her political ascent, the Cadet Corps was redefined by Miliutin to become accessible to a broader base of the population.[4] For those students who could not afford to attend the Cadet Corps Academies yet still aspired to careers in the Imperial Officer Corps, Miliutin institutionalized Iunker Schools—a training organization that had existed haphazardly throughout the army at the regimental level since the beginning of the nineteenth-century. By 1914, these schools provided both a secondary and branch-training education to volunteers from any social class. With the regularization of their role in the military establishment, Iunker schools became not only the schools that trained the majority of line officers within the army, but also one of the most important avenues for aspirants of lesser social origin to enter the Tsarist officer corps and, in some cases, eventually gain appointment to the General Staff.[5]

The rank given to students upon joining the field army depended on which type of military school they attended first. For example, graduates of Iunker schools had to spend a period of time as a warrant officers, usually in infantry units, before formally being commissioned as officers. After graduating from a Cadet Corps Academy, students joined the army as sub-Lieutenants unless they went directly into a Guards regiment. Those students—almost exclusively of noble origin—who went into the Imperial Guard immediately enjoyed the higher rank of Lieutenant, thus maintaining the initial advantage of the aristocracy in the Imperial Officer Corps. After a period of service and examination elapsed, the officers who aspired to be appointed to the General Staff had the opportunity to attend one of the Empire's seven formal branch-training institutions. With the notable exception of the Corps of Pages, which was created in the early eighteenth-century exclusively for the education and preparation of the children of the high aristocracy for both civilian and military service to the Tsar, these schools were the product of Miliutin's reforming efforts.[6]

The last step in the education of future staff officers was admission to and graduation from the Imperial Nicholas Military Academy. Formerly called the Nicholas Academy of the General Staff, it had been established in 1832 under the supervision of Baron Antoine-Henri Jomini at the command of Nicholas I. Himself a graduate of the academy, Miliutin upgraded both the academic and training standards of the Empire's premier military educational institution.[7] Admission to and retention within the academy depended on students passing a rigorous battery of examinations that began at the regimental level and culminated with students/officers having to defend thesis-length research on military history before a board of staff officers at the academy. While the bulk of their work occured in the classroom, officers who attended the academy prior to the First World War increasingly benefited from additional field exercises designed to enhance the effectiveness of peacetime training. But the emphasis of staff training was on the development of the skills needed for administering as opposed to commanding troops in the field. Thus, it was often the case that General Staff officers were better prepared to be regimental clerks than battlefield commanders.[8]

Given full license by Alexander II, Education Minister D.A. Tolstoy systematically strove to counter-reform civilian education while

Miliutin's reforms continued to move military education forward.[9] Even with the counter-reforming policies enacted throughout the reign of Alexander III, the purpose and worthiness of a military education was never in doubt. Although there were efforts to limit admissions to students of lower social origins, Miliutin's institutional reforms at military schools remained largely intact.[10] As a result, by 1914 educational levels in the military academies approached those that existed throughout Europe.

In an effort to ascertain the extent of Miliutin's intended meritocracy a data set was compiled that consisted of biographical information on each general who appeared on the list of the General Staff in 1914.[11] The data analyzed includes: type of military or civilian education, rate of promotion, and guard status. The primary source used to quantify the careers of Russian General Staff Officers was *Spisok general'nago shtaba*, a list annually published under the auspices of the War Ministry. This book provided brief biographical profiles of each member of the Imperial General Staff. Every officer had a record that listed his name, rank, current appointments, date of all promotions, military schools attended, each duty assignment since joining the General Staff, and all military decorations. The sample in this analysis is composed of the 82 generals, 115 lieutenant generals, and 225 major generals who appeared in the 1914 edition of this source. With the exception of 33 generals who graduated from the General Staff Academy in the 1860s and 1870s, these officers all attended the Nicholas Academy during the 1880s and 1890s. This group of 422 officers formed the core of the Russian high command at the beginning of the First World War. They had been exposed to the education and training which Miliutin had conceptualized and implemented in his attempt to modernize Russian military society.

The information was coded and analyzed with the assistance of SPSSX, a statistical software package commonly used in social science research. The purpose of this exercise was to determine the relationship, if any, between an officer's education and rate of promotion through the ranks of the Imperial Russian Army. To this goal, the number of months were tabulated that it took for each general to be promoted through the army's ranks. Specifically, the following variables received examination: number of months from enlistment to lieutenant (hereafter referred to as: METOL), enlistment to colonel (METOC), and enlistment to major-general (METOM). The intervals between lieutenant and colonel (MLTOC), and colonel and major general (MCTOM), were also measured in this program. The rank of captain was intentionally omitted because of the various levels of captaincy that existed in the Russian Army.[12] After completing this exercise, the information on promotion rates and their relationship to the following variables were examined: type of secondary schools, branch-training institution, and guard versus non-guard status. Through this method of investigation, this article seeks to identify the composition and career patterns of the Russian General Staff in the summer of 1914.

At the beginning of 1914, 1,229 men held the rank of major general or above in the Russian Army. Of these military leaders 422, or 34 percent, were officers of the Imperial General Staff. Table 1.1 reveals the specific number of generals at each rank for the entire army and the General Staff.

TABLE 1.1

	Officer Corps	General Staff	% of GSO at each rank
General of the Army	100	82	82%
Lieutenant General	277	115	42%
Major General	851	225	26%

Sources: D.O. "Dolzhnosti, zanimaemyia generalami nashei armii," *Ofitserskaia zhizn'*, 48 (15 December 1913) p. 698, and *Spisok general'nago shtaba, 1914*.

Since the *spisok* did not clearly label the social status of a General Staff Officer at birth, the type of unit that he served in after receiving his commission represents the best available indicator of class division in the Russian high command in the winter of 1913-1914.[13] By 1914 more non-guard officers, 231 (54.7 percent) served on the General Staff than officers who had originally received commissions in guard's regiments, 191 (45.3 percent).[14] These statistics alone indicate that officers who did not originate from the landed nobility—the traditional source of military elites—had by 1914 become a majority within the army's high command, primarily as a result of Miliutin's efforts to create a meritocracy.

The data on advancement rates revealed that guards officers were on the fast track until they reached the rank of colonel. While the average was 332 months for all officers to reach the rank of colonel from their date of enlistment, the guards officers needed only 319 months compared to the 342 months for the non-guards officers. But the gap between the two types of servitors narrowed considerably for promotions from colonel to major-general—105 for the guards and six fewer months for the non-guards who took only 99 months to reach this rank.

TABLE 1.2
Rate of promotion by Guard/Non-Guard Status

Status	METOL	METOC	METOM	MLTOC	MLTOM	MCTOM
Guard	76.3	214.6	319.5	138.2	243.2	104.9
Non-Guard	63.4	243.4	342.7	178.1	278.3	99.3
Avg. Months	69.4	230.4	332.2	159.5	261.0	101.8

METOL = number of months from enlistment to lieutenant.
METOC = number of months from enlistment to colonel.
METOM = number of months from enlistment to major general.
MLTOC = number of months between promotion from lieutenant to colonel.
MLTOM = number of months between promotion from lieutenant to major general.
MCTOM = number of months between promotion from colonel to major general.

While not offering much evidence about promotion rates, cross tabulating the data gathered between guards status and type of initial military education, helps illustrate the overall impact of the Miliutin reforms. For example, the majority of generals under study attended the prestigious Cadet Corps Academies but of the 299 who went to these institutions only 146 joined guards regiments. Before the Miliutin reforms, most officers who attended Cadet Corps Academies would have joined guards regiments. Because of Miliutin's efforts to open educational institutions to anyone qualified, officers who did not have the money or connections to join guards regiments comprised better than 50 percent of the 1914 General Staff.

TABLE 1.3
Guard/Non-Guard Status by Secondary Schools

Type of school	Guard Students / %	Non-Guard Students / %
Cadet Corps	146 / 34.6	153 / 36.3
Civilian Schools	24 / 5.7	57 / 13.5
None	21 / 5.0	1 / 5.0
Total No./Total %	191 / 45.3	231 / 54.7

More insight can be gained about the impact of Miliutin's reforms on the General Staff in the early twentieth-century if these numbers are broken down according to where students received their branch training. While the Corps of Pages and Nicholas Cavalry schools were not surprisingly dominated by guards officers, the composition of the rest of the Empire's branch-training institutions was split between the guards and non-guards officers.[15] But it is important to note that the number of guards officers verses the number of non-guards officers at the Pavlov and Konstantine Infantry Military Schools remained close to equal, while a majority of non-guards officers attended the more technically oriented Mikhailovski Artillery and Nicholas Engineering schools. As expected, non-guards officers dominated the student population at Iunker Schools, (see Table 1.4).

TABLE 1.4
Guards vs Non-Guards officers by branch training institutions

School	No. of Guard / %	Non-Guard / %
Corps of Pages	33 / 7.8	1 / .2
Nik Cav	20 / 4.7	7 / 1.7
Pav Mil	31 / 7.3	42 / 10.0
Alek Mil	20 / 4.7	40 / 9.5
Kon Mil	31 / 7.3	33 / 7.8
Mik Ar	26 / 6.2	51 / 12.1
Nik Eng	9 / 2.1	22 / 5.2
Iunker	2 / .5	30 / 7.1
Other*	19 / 4.5	5 / 1.2
Total/Average	191 /45.3	231 / 54.7

Corps of Pages = His Imperial Majesty's Corps of Pages
Nik Cav = Nicholas Cavalry School
Pav Mil = Pavlov Infantry Military School
Alek Mil = Aleksandr Infantry Military School
Kon Mil = Konstantine Infantry Military School
Mik Art = Mikhailovski Artillery School
Nik Eng = Nicholas Engineering School
Iunker = Iunker Schools

* In 24 profiles the officers attended a civilian university or had no higher education noted on their service records.

These trends are further evident when examining the promotion rates of officers in relation to the branch-training institution they attended. Once again, students who graduated from the Corps of Pages or the Nicholas Cavalry school usually reached the rank of colonel faster than the soldiers who attended the other branch-training institutions. After the rank of colonel, however, those students who attended the more technically oriented Nicholas

Engineering or Mikhail Artillery schools moved through the ranks at a slightly more rapid pace. More significantly, students who received their specialized military training at one of the Empire's Iunker Schools also moved from the rank of colonel to major general (95) at a rate faster than even those students who attended the Corps of Pages (102).

TABLE 1.5
Promotion rates by branch training schools

School	METOL	METOC	METOM	MLTOC	MLTOM	MCTOM
C. of Pages	72.2	206.8	309.2	134.6	237.0	102.3
Nik Cav	69.9	213.9	323.7	147.4	258.8	109.7
Pav Mil	68.9	231.4	336.2	162.1	267.3	104.8
Alek Mil	71.8	232.3	340.7	160.7	269.0	108.3
Kon Mil	69.2	230.6	332.3	161.3	263.0	101.7
Mik Art	65.8	242.7	342.1	171.4	271.3	99.3
Nik Eng	69.2	235.5	330.2	165.9	262.3	94.5
Iunker	80.5	247.6	43.9	165.5	264.8	95.2
Other	63.9	202.7	295.1	138.7	231.2	92.4
Overall Avg.	69.4	230.4	332.2	159.5	261.9	101.8

Thus, as indicated when examining guard verses non-guard status, the rank of Colonel became an important turning point in the careers of Russian Staff Officers. Officers who were either in a highly specialized branch of service (engineering or artillery) or who had worked their way up through the ranks, as was often the case with graduates of Iunker Schools, usually needed more time to reach the rank of Colonel. Upon their appointment as Colonels, however, officers who attended Iunker schools or the artillery or engineering schools had every opportunity to emerge at the top of the army's high command by the time of their retirement from active service (see Table 1.5).

Difficult problems remained for future General Staff Officers after they completed their branch training. First and foremost, graduation from the General Staff Academy became mandatory to attain higher rank and receive an appointment to the General Staff. After completing their formal education, those officers who obtained appointment to the General Staff faced four career possibilities: they could spend the balance of their careers as field commanders; they could rotate from troop command to bureaucratic positions within the army's administration; or they could spend the rest of their careers as functionaries within the War Ministry. The truly gifted officers usually seemed to find their way, after a period of service in the ranks, into educational institutions, ultimately as professors. As the emphasis of reformers shifted the focus of military education from administrative to field training, staff officers, including academy professors, sought to rotate in and out of the ranks of field regiments. Following such a career path allowed staff officers to remain current with training routines while maintaining their connections within the army's administrative apparatus.

According to the statistics generated by this data base, officers of higher-class origin clearly had the early advantage over the rest of the soldiers who aspired to reach the commanding heights of the army. Wealth bought better education and the value of aristocratic connections remained a significant factor in determining who received appointments to guard units. But regardless of any personal connections or prior education, promotion rates reveal that a leveling occurred at the rank of colonel among the officers of the Imperial Russian General Staff. In each of the paradigms examined in this study, officers who had started their careers in the Imperial Guard benefited from the most rapid promotion rates on the General Staff. At the rank of Colonel, this trend would for the most part reverse itself, thus producing a leveling between those who had the advantages of wealth and connections and those who did not.

Seeking to understand exactly why the rank of colonel was a turning point in General Staff careers remains an elusive task. Presently, the best explanations for this phenomenon are hypothetical. The most common explanation is related to class origin. Officers of the Imperial Guard did not wish to endure the hardship of field duty nor learn about the sophisticated weapons needed to conduct modern warfare, thereby disqualifying themselves from consideration for positions of high command. In addition, poor pay, combined with progressively difficult competition within the army, resulted in members of the landed nobility searching for other career options. Another explanation for the rise of soldiers of humble origins to the top of the army's command structure, of course, is that Miliutin's military system had created the semblance of a meritocracy which recognized the best and the brightest officers through advancement. Thus, while still maintaining considerable influence within the military establishment, by the outbreak of the First World War, the grip that the traditional service elite once held had lost some of its strength.

Military Training and Peacetime Maneuvers in Late Imperial Russia

General Staff Officers had risen to prominence within the army and Russian society in the late nineteenth century because of their education and training as well as two international events. Most important were the three wars of German unification. Every clear-minded military thinker in Russia became interested in how the Prussian General Staff orchestrated the rapid defeat of France.[16] Then, in the wake of victory at Plevna and the defeat of the Ottoman empire in the Russo-Turkish War of 1877/78, the general public and Russia's military leaders believed that Miliutin's reforms had been instrumental in restoring the luster to the Empire's armed forces. While military success enhanced the image of the General Staff throughout Russian society, many problems still existed within the armed forces that centered around the vital issues of organization, training, and planning that were not acknowledged until the disasters of 1904/05.[17]

Regardless of whether they believed in reform or tradition, Tsarist military leaders had to ascertain the cause of the Manchurian disaster to regain their credibility. As a result, in the period between the Russo-Japanese War and the First World War, ideas were exchanged and attempts made to correct perceived military deficiencies. The basic tenants of the educational system remained intact as reformers focused on continued officer and soldier training. The goal of this initiative was to stop reliving the glorious past and confront the pressing issues of the day, to repair the damage resulting from the Far Eastern debacle, and to prepare for the next war. The method suggested to address the problems that officers encountered on the modern battlefield, as discussed in the writings of such luminaries as N.P. Mikhnevich, A.A. Neznamov, and N.N. Golovin, was to devote more energy to the practical application of theoretical ideas. Thus, General Staff Officers who advocated modernization now focused their energy on making peacetime maneuvers more effective as instructive training drills for the army's rank and file.[18]

Exercises of this nature, however, introduced a host of new challenges to the commanders of the Russian Army. Major questions were raised about the goals of such maneuvers—should they train soldiers and lower-ranking officers for battlefield duties? Or should they intentionally simulate a Clausewitzian fog of confusion in which colonels could demonstrate to generals that they knew how to command a regiment under battlefield conditions? Finally, military reformers favored integrating both functions thereby fostering a unified approach to the conduct of maneuvers. Little consensus existed throughout the army on this issue.[19]

Despite progress toward transforming the conduct of maneuvers, memoirs feature passages describing the beauty and pageantry of the Imperial Guard Regiments as they received the ultimate honor—the opportunity to pass and review before the Tsar.[20] The officers in the Imperial Guards Regiments frequently enjoyed this privilege, viewed it as their birthright to have such access to the Tsar and, not wishing to compromise their traditional role as the primary defenders of the crown, resisted all efforts to change a standing military tradition.[21] The adoption of Miliutin's meritocratic system that rewarded people regardless of social origin had by the 1907–1914 period resulted in the addition of non-aristocratic officers into the ranks of both the officer corps and the General Staff. Simply put, capturing the Tsar's attention on the parade ground was but one possible route to an optimal service appointment at any level or within any branch of the state bureaucracy. In this way, Miliutin had redressed the power of the guards officers but after his 1881 ouster from power, the Ministry of War fell into the hands of the capable but conservative P.A. Vannovski. Annual maneuvers continued, but now they fell more heavily under the influence of the tactical ideas of M.I. Dragomirov who remained fascinated with the power of the bayonet in the hands of a properly trained soldier.[22] Maneuvers as a valuable training exercise for higher staff officers were resurrected only after the 1898 appointment of A.N. Kuropatkin as Minister of War. His appointment stemmed from his reputation as a modern thinker possessing the knowledge and skills to lead the Russian military establishment into the twentieth century.

Kuropatkin's career represented the perfect model for the successful Tsarist General Staff Officer at the beginning of the twentieth century. Born into the lower nobility in Pskov, Kuropatkin gained admission into the 1st Cadet Corps Academy, obtained his branch training at the 1st Pavlov military infantry school, and graduated from the General Staff Academy in 1874. Without an independent source of income, Kuropatkin did not join a guard's regiment upon the completion of his military education. He went on to distinguish himself while serving on the staff of General Skobelev in the Russo-Turkish War of 1877/78. His reward for this service was an appointment to the Department of Statistics at the General Staff Academy. During the next twenty years he would rotate between his position at the Academy and various field and administrative positions in the army. He was an educator who understood the army's administrative apparatus and had commanded troops in the field during war and peace. But on the Manchurian battlefield, Kuropatkin lost his nerve, fought battles to a stalemate, and then withdrew to preserve the integrity of his army for the day when it would reign supreme. His failure as a military leader put all modernizing elements in the Tsar's military establishment on the defensive because conservative opinion now blamed the General Staff and officers like Kuropatkin for the humiliating defeat in the Japanese War.[23]

Nevertheless, during his six-year tenure as Minister of War (1898–1904), Kuropatkin paid particular attention to the problem of upgrading training standards—maintaining the firm belief that the army could no longer afford the luxury of largely ceremonial exercises or training routines that did not give proper attention to the needs of officers. Nothing symbolized his efforts more than the 1902 Kursk maneuver. In 1902, Kuropatkin, along with students and instructors from the Nicholas Academy, formulated the idea of mobilizing the Moscow, Kiev, and some elements of the Warsaw Military Districts. Under the leadership of Grand Duke Sergei Aleksandrovich, the troops of the Moscow Military District were charged with the task of defending the city of Kursk from an attack by the troops of the Kiev and Warsaw Military Districts, or the "southern army." Since Tsar Nicholas II was the Commander of the "southern army," the outcome of this maneuver was pre-determined—Imperial participation would hinder Kuropatkin's professionalizing efforts right up to the outbreak of the Russo-Japanese War. To the Minister of War's credit, however, he did manage to mobilize three military districts, send soldiers into the field, and require Staff Officers to compose exercise books that consisted of written reports about their daily activities.[24] Thus, a formula emerged that progressive General Staff officers would seek to adopt in the post-1905 period.

The ingredients of this formula consisted of Kuropatkin's idea for providing the army's rank and file with a training exercise that would simulate battlefield conditions. The goal was to make soldiers perform their task in the mud with little sleep, while equally exhausted officers groped through the confusion of operational conditions to maintain their command. Perhaps more important, the key to measuring the success or failure of the maneuver rested with the information contained in the allegedly unbiased report about the activities that occurred during the period of mobilization within each military district. In general terms, these reports were supposed to discuss both the positive and negative aspects of the performance of commanding officers during the period of the exercise. More specifically, they were intended to address questions such as: how well did officers perform their assignments? Did they understand and follow the orders of their superiors? What factors prevented them from achieving the goals of the exercise?[25]

To accomplish this task, Kuropatkin envisioned using the students of the Nicholas Academy of the General Staff to write the reports. In the 1902 maneuver, students from the academy were given the title of military observer and charged with the task of writing reports based on the events they witnessed in the exercise. Despite this effort to professionalize the reporting component of the maneuver, the main observer in 1902, Grand Duke Mikhail Nikolaevich, was once again a member of the Imperial Family and controlled a critical position within the command structure of this exercise—thereby compromising the instructive aspect of the maneuver.[26]

The interference of the Imperial family with the operation of the army, therefore, represented the single most powerful counter-reform voice within the military establishment. If the Tsar had to win every training exercise, and if the observers had to consistently patronize the Royal family in their post-maneuver report, then the overall effectiveness of the exercise would always be hampered. The Romanovs, with the exception of Grand Duke Nikolai Nikolaevich, who was a graduate of the General Staff Academy, did not seek to become military professionals.[27] Instead, Nicholas II's relatives expected to be awarded high rank and the most important positions within the army simply based on their pedigree. As a result, in the waning years of the dynasty most of the Romanovs never grasped the professional needs of the institution that legitimized and maintained their power.

Another problem that confronted professionalizing elements were the teachings and then the legacy of General M.I. Dragomirov. As a hero of the 1877/78 war, commandant of the Nicholas Academy of the General Staff from 1878 to 1889, and then commander of the Kiev Military District until his death in 1905, Dragomirov had been highly critical of Kuropatkin both as Minister of War and Commander in Chief of the Manchurian Army. Having been recognized as the foremost authority on tactics in the Empire, Dragomirov believed that the emphasis of military education should be placed on teaching officers how to train peasants into soldiers.[28] While such training was essential to the well-being of the Imperial army, this type of thinking did not encourage the development of unified training technique.[29] Dragomirov's ideas on training, therefore, stood in direct contrast to Kuropotkin's. After the 1905 death of Dragomirov, his ideas remained dominant within the army while Kuropatkin's star fell in disgrace in the aftermath of the Manchurian defeat. Progressive elements within the Russian General Staff, therefore, always had to appease the Dragomirov cohort of the officer corps in most training exercises if they expected to have the chance to test any of their ideas.[30]

Ironically, after 1905 the biggest ally and worst enemy of reform elements was the Manchurian legacy which had demonstrated that the entire Russian Army was not prepared to fight on the modern battlefield. As a result, in the 1905-1914 period, much attention was devoted to the peacetime practice of large-scale war games as first envisioned by Kuropatkin.[31] But this did not change the fact that conservative military elements blamed Kuropatkin for defeat in the Far East, thereby rendering suspect the value of even his best ideas. Not surprisingly, at the exercises held every July and August, the Royal family and Imperial Guard, in all of their splendor and regalia, dominated the event and turned it into everything from a fashion show to a sacred ceremony.

While such exercises represented annual summer maneuvers on a grand scale, and suffered from more Imperial than professional influence, much could still be accomplished with this type of undertaking. First, it gave the General Staff the opportunity to judge how much time was needed to mobilize a military district. They could thereby estimate transportation and supply requirements of the troops within a given district. Military school students, as well, had the opportunity to command troops in the field; peasant/soldiers received some practical drill, and everyone had a chance to see his Tsar. But in the end, a stigma remained that condemned these exercises to be little more than elaborate shows for the Tsar, various state officials, and foreign military observers.

The Maneuver between Helsinki and St. Petersburg, May, 1914

Unable to transform the grand maneuver into an instructive training exercise of the caliber desired, the General Staff undertook a new initiative that was designed to execute a maneuver on a smaller scale—an intra-military district maneuver.[32] An example of this type of exercise occurred in the region between Helsinki and St. Petersburg in May 1914. The most important factor in this maneuver was its geographical setting. The area between Helsinki and St. Petersburg was of vital strategic significance for a variety of reasons. The Russians envisioned, and subsequently prepared for, a German attempt to seize control of the eastern shores of the Gulf of Finland, drive across the Karelian Isthmus to the western shore of Lake Ladoga, and then attempt to encircle St. Petersburg from the north while the rest of the Tsar's army was campaigning in East Prussia or Galicia. Besides this legitimate strategic concern, another and perhaps more significant reason for a maneuver in this region rested with the complement of General Staff Officers who were stationed in the Helsinki/Vyborg area. In the period after the Russo-Japanese War, when a new emphasis was placed on the practical application of theoretical concepts, General Staff bureaucrats sought field assignments with the army in Finland. From Helsinki or Vyborg they could gain valuable field experience and test their ideas on training while remaining in close contact with their colleagues and activities in St. Petersburg. Thus, in the spring of 1914, a mere three months before the outbreak of the First World War, an intra-military district maneuver commenced that was designed to provide an instructive training exercise for both the rank and file of the Imperial Army.

The invading army, or "Red Army," consisted of the 1st and 18th Army Corps along with a reserve of one Guard Corps. In total the Red Army had 7 infantry divisions representing an invading German army. Artillery support was supposed to come from ships in the Gulf of Finland.[33] The forces defending the Karelian Isthmus consisted of the 22nd Army Corps which was stationed at the Vyborg fortress. Its complement consisted of 14 Finnish rifle regiments, one cavalry regiment, one cossack division, one artillery division, and a sapper battalion.[34] The main test of this exercise was to determine how well a solitary military district could respond to the emergency of an invasion from a numerically superior enemy force before reinforcements arrived from other elements of the Russian army.

The composition of the staff of each participating army exhibits the typical alignment of General Staff verses non-General Staff officers within the command structure of the Imperial Army as it prepared for the First World War. Army corps in the Russian Army usually were not commanded by General Staff Officers. Instead, General Staff Officers settled for the placement of their personnel in the position of Chief of Staff. For example, the commander of the Blue force, Lt. General Petrov, was not a member of the General Staff. His Chief of Staff, however, was Colonel Fedor Vasil'vich Stepanov who graduated from the General Staff Academy in 1902 and had been serving in the St. Petersburg Military District since August 1905. The Commander of the invading Red Force, Lt. General Avgusteishii, likewise had no affiliation with the General Staff, but his Chief of Staff, Lt. General Arsenii Atanol'evich Gulevich, held appointments to both the General Staff and the Finland Lifeguard Regiment. He had held various positions in and around the Imperial Capital since his graduation from the General Staff Academy in 1892.[35]

More important to the success of these exercises, both armies had staffs of military observers who sent representatives to each military unit in order to write reports on their activities. Both of these staffs were commanded by General Staff Officers. In the Blue army, the position was filled by Lt. General Aleksandr Fedorovich Bauer, and in the Red army the senior military observer was Major General Aleksandr Nikolaevich Apukhtin. Bauer was a fortress artillery specialist with little prior experience in the St. Petersburg military district until he was given command of the Sveaborg Fortress in November 1913. Apukhtin was an infantry general who had been serving in St. Petersburg since the Russo-Japanese War as both a field commander and administrator.[36] Several other military observers went into the field and submitted reports to commanders who did not have to protect any other officer's reputation. Through the use of a scaled-down maneuver, the General Staff was able to conduct a field exercise that did not attract the direct attention of the Tsar or any other Romanov. While it is safe to assume that the members of the royal family were aware of this exercise, their lack of interest resulted in a field maneuver that was closer to the goal that Kuropatkin strove to achieve when he was Minister of War.

On the evening of April 30th, the commander of the 22nd Army Corps, Lt. General Petrov, received a telegram at his headquarters in the Vyborg fortress from the mobilization section of the Main Administration of the General Staff. The message informed him that the "Red Forces" had declared war on his "Blue Forces" and that he should prepare for the imminent invasion of the Karelian isthmus. Along with this report, Petrov received special instructions about the objective of the exercise. Noting that he would have a vastly inferior but better equipped army, Colonel Kaminski of the General Staff's mobilization section informed Petrov that: "The goal of the 22nd Army Corps in the forthcoming games is to study the conditions in which troops would have to operate in the Finnish military theater."[37] Working from the assumption that there would not be any feasible method for containing the invasion, Petrov was instructed to order his Cossacks to practice their reconnaissance skills, and to utilize other service branches to enact a series of delaying tactics designed to safeguard the Imperial Capital.[38] Even more important, the General Staff ordered that every commander above the company level, along with every military observer, produce an exercise notebook that recorded all of their respective activities on a daily basis.[39]

With the task of the maneuver clearly defined, the next communication that Petrov received stated that on May 5th a naval engagement had occurred between the Red and Blue fleets near the Baltic port of Revel. The Blue fleet could not withstand the pressure of the Red fleet's firepower and had to retreat to the protection of Kronstadt. In response to the Blue fleet's withdrawal from operations, the Red fleet successfully imposed a blockade on the island fortress. Subsequently, the "Blue Forces" could not expect reinforcement from the sea. Petrov now had to assume that an invasion of the territory under his command was imminent. The critical problem then became identifying the location of the enemy's invasion force. General Staff briefings led Petrov to believe that the key to the operation would be the fortresses at Vyborg and Sveaborg—the points commanding the Karelian isthmus. As a result, Petrov issued the following order to his regimental commanders:

> Keep the enemy in a position to assault them with the fortress artillery at Vyborg and Sveaborg, but do not let them gain access to the railway that connects the two. Since we cannot expect any reinforcements before the end of May, do not let enemy forces penetrate the area south of the Vyborg fortress. The key to our success in this campaign rests with our ability to avoid losing the advantage of these fortresses in the first days of the next war.[40]

Petrov, therefore, made clear to his subordinates that they were all charged with the task of containing enemy forces with an inferior number of troops for a 30-day period. The only way he could envision accomplishing this task was to use the firepower of the forts that were under his command.

After ten days of mini-raids or false landings, the anticipated invasion of the "Red Force" occurred on the morning of May 15th at a beachhead between the cities of Kotka and Fridrikhstam (halfway between Helsinki and Vyborg).[41] In response to this development, six Finnish rifle regiments, three from Vyborg under the command of Major General Notbek and three from Sveaborg under the command of Major General Stel'nitskii, marched toward the landing zone. Both of these newly formed divisions included motorized artillery regiments.[42] The objective of the "Red Forces" became clear on the night of May 15th/16th when another landing occurred in the region south of the Vyborg Fortress. Petrov responded to this new crisis by taking the balance of his Finnish rifle regiments onto the field under his personal command. But the Red Forces were not going to stop at anything less than attempting to isolate the Vyborg Fortress while seizing control of the northern and eastern shores of the Gulf of Finland. After the initial stages of the operation, the "Red Forces" were supposed to unify under the command of Lt. General Avgusteishii, march to the railroad that connected Helsinki to St. Petersburg, and finally attempt to surround, if not capture, the Imperial Capital.[43]

Petrov did succeed in executing delaying tactics that prevented a breakthrough of the Red Army in its drive to the Imperial Capital. In this sense, the Blue Army won the maneuver, but the goal of this exercise was not to determine a winner or loser. Instead, the General Staff wanted to develop a response to any German attempt to invade the Capital from the north. Daily written reports on the maneuvers provided the best resource for developing a strategy to counter a tactical threat from the north. The quality of the daily reports required a level of detail that would allow Russian military planners to formulate a rational and manageable reaction to an invasion. This, in turn, would allow any commander to obtain the same result that Petrov accomplished in May 1914.

The submission of one anonymous military observer indicates that at least some elements within the General Staff understood the significance of these reports.[44] The principle cause for the success of the Blue army, according to this report, rested with the outstanding reconnaissance work of its Cossack and Cavalry brigades. While the basic scenario was revealed in telegrams from St. Petersburg, the Cossacks of the 22nd Army Corps (the Blue Force) carefully scouted the activities of the Red Army as soon as it landed on the Karelian isthmus. In addition, this report focused both on the daily disposition of the Red Army as it advanced toward St. Petersburg and the effectiveness of communications in the midst of crisis. Petrov always had current information at his disposal. As a result, the commander of the "Blue Army" knew the best time and most expedient route to use while moving and resupplying troops. Without question, the most important conclusion that the General Staff could draw from this exercise was that intelligence was invaluable, indeed, the key to success on the battlefield—know every move of your enemy to avoid surprises in moments of confusion.

Overall, the maneuver between Helsinki and St. Petersburg represented a victory for reformist elements in the Russian General Staff. After years of agitating for the implementation of instructive as opposed to ceremonial field drills, they had finally found a model that worked. If the exercise was small in regard to the number of troops deployed, then the Imperial family did not participate. When the Tsar and his various relatives stayed at home, the General Staff could pay attention to the lessons of the exercise. But the success of these maneuvers was limited to the number of soldiers and officers who could learn from the experience of the exercise. General Staff officers could write reports and disseminate information about the maneuver under these conditions. Nothing, however, replaces practical experience. After all, one of General Samsonov's most pressing problems in August 1914 was a lack of intelligence about his enemy. This type of enigma epitomized the Russian military establishment—even when properly trained officers knew how to solve problems, the anachronistic autocratic form of government could not accommodate their efforts.

CONCLUSION: The First World War and Catastrophe

As a result of the reform process that started with Miliutin, Russian General Staff Officers by the beginning of the First World War had received a quality education which was reinforced with constant attempts to upgrade training standards. The efforts of reform-minded officers to create a meritocracy fostered the emergence of General Staff officers who had skill levels comparable to their peers in other European armies. Higher military education combined with an increased awareness of the necessity for meaningful peacetime training indicates that professional standards did exist in the Russian army by the outbreak of the First World War. The performance of Russian General Staff officers in the First World War, however, demonstrated that the presence of military professionalism did not guarantee the existence of an all-powerful command cadre that could control the army and the Empire during wartime emergency. In the opening stages of the war, the conflict between reformers and traditionalists still existed and had a strong impact on the relationship that developed between the high command at the front and the military establishment in the Imperial capital. Since the 1904/05 debacle, there had been much debate over the drafting of a new Law on the Field Administration of the Army in Wartime. On 16 July 1914 the Tsar signed this new Law and simultaneously made himself the Supreme Commander-in-Chief. Nicholas II intended to be the unifying element in an administrative system based on creating a command organization (*Stavka*) to control all of the military action, while using the War Ministry in St. Petersburg to manage the enormous questions of supplies and logistics. Another facet of the law was that the Supreme Commander-in-Chief would have complete military and civilian control over the entire theater of military operations. But on July 19th, Nicholas II, bowing to political pressure and military advice, appointed Grand Duke Nicholai Nicholaevich to the position of Supreme Commander-in-Chief.[45]

The Grand Duke's ascent to such lofty heights within the Army revived the post-1905 antagonisms that had emerged when he created and chaired the Council of State Defense.[46] One of his prime opponents in the military debates of the immediate Japanese War period was the Minister of War in 1914, V.A. Sukhomlinov. While much has been written about the differences that existed between these two individuals, the fact remains that the two most powerful and influential officers in the Imperial Army never cooperated with each other in matters of planning or problem solving.[47] Not surprisingly, the wartime command structure of the army inherited the same conflict that had prevented reformers from influencing the direction of military policy in the prewar period.

The tenacious prewar struggle between reformers and traditionalists within the General Staff over the issue of military professionalism would fade into the background as the Russian war effort became an acute struggle to maintain the army on the field of battle. As the emergency intensified, Russia's best hope for prevailing rested with the capabilities of its High Command to manage both the battle front, as well as the home front. As a result of their education and training, Russian General Staff officers were conceptually prepared for the modern battlefield, but not for all of the complicating factors that confronted them because of the First World War. While the cause for overall failure can in part be attributed to the lack of homogeneity in the Russian General Staff, of equal if not greater significance were other factors such as an industrial complex that was totally insufficient for the demands of the war, an antiquated transportation and communication network, and a political leadership that failed to understand the grave peril in which the war had placed it.

The military system as a whole, therefore, was not prepared to wage a war on the scale of the First World War. In August/September 1914 the three top generals in the East Prussian theater of operation were the front commander Ia G. Zhilinsky, commander of 1st army P.K. von Rennenkampf, and the ill-fated commander of 2nd army, A.V. Samsonov. All three were senior General Staff officers who had benefited from the impact of Miliutin's reforms throughout their military careers. At the very least they were exposed to reform ideas yet none of the three had taken a leading role in the process. In 1914, therefore, Samsonov and Von Rennenkampf were experienced troop commanders and Zhilinsky was a career functionary of the War Ministry. Regardless of the efficiency of all three officers, they were given command of an impossible situation because of a host of other reasons, thus dooming the East Prussian Campaign as soon as the front went into operation.

Problems such as poor communications resulted in a lack of coordination between units which allowed for Rennenkampf to call a halt after Gumbinnen, Samsonov to march blindly into East Prussia, and Zhilinsky to lose control of the situation. Such communication difficulties permeated the entire operation, from the company level to the Stavka of the Imperial Army. The lack of a signal code, particularly between units at the front, was a professional failing that compromised the operation. But shortages of key materials ranging from the signal wires to the food, uniforms, and weapons needed to fight a modern war were usually the result of factors beyond the control of the General Staff. While many ascribe failure on the Eastern Front to the lack of coordination, cooperation, and the competence of Russia's commanding generals, the East Prussian catastrophe was likely as soon as Colonel Max Hoffman designed and the German Army executed a plan in response to the invasion.[48] Victory on the South-

Western Front provided the Tsarist government with the good news that it needed to downplay the devastating news from the East Prussian Front. By the summer of 1915, however, all of the gains from the previous year's campaigns were lost and the Imperial Russian Army engaged in what proved to be a fight to its death. The one exception to repeated setbacks in the field, the Brusilov offensive in the summer of 1916, was the work of a traditionally trained guard's general who acted without informing his superiors of his intentions until shortly before operations commenced. Nonetheless, that the Army's defensive capabilities did not collapse until the 1917 Revolution remains an indicator of the level of military professionalism that existed in Russia during the First World War; the Army did not disintegrate as an effective fighting force because of punishment inflicted on it by the German or Austro-Hungarian army.[49]

The conclusion can be drawn, therefore, that in the late nineteenth and early twentieth centuries the raising of military educational standards enhanced the ability of officers, regardless of social origin, to earn appointment to the command staff of the army. Military schools had been either reformed or established specifically to create opportunities through better access for a broader base of society. The result of the opening of military schools to lower and non-aristocratic Russians was recognition that service through promotion occurred due to individual merit as well as pedigree. While the General Staff strove to adopt professional standards, it still remained a part of the Tsarist military establishment which, as a reflection of Imperial society, was a conflict-ridden institution.

Nevertheless, by August 1914 the Russians had learned how to sort through the ranks of their army and to allow some of the most capable officers to reach the high command regardless of their social origins. Developing a suitable method for conducting peacetime training exercises became an important part of this equation. While the Imperial Army still subscribed to the pageantry and ceremony of its parade ground drill, by the early twentieth century the focus was shifting from satisfying the whims of the Imperial family to creating instructive exercises. A meritocracy, therefore, had taken root within the General Staff because of the combination of a new type of training system that focused on sharpening the knowledge and skills of officers after they had completed their military education.

While the professionals could sort through their own ranks and identify meritorious officers, such recognition did not guarantee their rise to the top of the command structure. Regardless of the cause, be it the politics of the military/economic alliance with France, the shortcomings of the national infrastructure, or the divisions that existed at the apex of Russia's military leadership, the Imperial Army blindly marched onto the battlefield in August 1914. A relatively small cohort of highly trained professionals, whose overall effectiveness as First World War military leaders is still unclear, did not have the power or authority to overcome the combination of factors that prevented them from controlling the chaos and confusion that are the natural partners of warfare in any age. The end result was a Russian army that occasionally achieved tactical success yet never strategic victory on the First World War battlefield.

Notes to Chapter 12

1. Most efforts to define the concept of military professionalism have focused on contemporary affairs and resulted in multi-faceted paradigms that range from studies of professional consciousness to the existence of corporate identity to the role of military leaders in politics. Examples of the literature on military professionalism include: S.E. Finer, *The Man on Horseback: The Role of the Military in Politics* (New York, 1962); Samuel Huntington, *The Soldier and the State: The Theory and Politics of Civil-Military Relations* (New York, 1957); Morris Janowitz, *The Professional Soldier: A Social and Political Portrait* (New York, 1971); John Johnson, *The Role of the Military in Underdeveloped Countries* (Princeton, 1962); V.R. Leikina-Svirskaia, *Intelligentsiia v Rossii vo votoroi polovine XIX veka* (Moscow, 1971). An outstanding essay on this topic can be found in the introduction to Allan R. Millett, *The General: Robert L. Bullard and Officership in the United States Army 1881–1925* (Westport, CT, 1975); G.Teitler, *The Genesis of the Professional Officers' Corps* (Beverly Hills, 1977); Stephen D. Wesbrook, ed. *The Political Education of Soldiers* (Beverly Hills, 1983).
2. For books and articles that focus specifically on Russia see: L.G. Beskrovnyi, *Armiia i flot rossii v nachale XXv* (Moscow, 1986); John Bushnell, *Mutiny amid Repression: Russian Soldiers in the Revolution of 1905–1906* (Bloomington, 1985). Two essential books are by William C. Fuller Jr., *Civil-Military Conflict in Imperial Russia 1881–1914* (Princeton, 1985) and *Strategy and Power in Russia 1600–1914* (New York, 1992). A recent and important addition to this literature is Bruce W. Menning, *Bayonets before Bullets: The Imperial Russian Army, 1861–1914* (Bloomington, 1992); Norman Stone, *The Eastern Front* (London, 1975). A valuable book due to its comparative analysis of Germany, France, and Russia in 1914 is Jack Synder, *The Ideology of the Offensive: Military Decision Making and the Disasters of 1914* (Ithaca, 1984); see also Allan K. Wildman, *The End of The Russian Imperial Army: The Old Army and the Soldiers' Revolt (March-April 1917)* (Princeton, 1980); P.A. Zaionchkovskii, *Samoderzhavie i russkaia armiia na rubezhe XIX-XX stoletiia* (Moscow, 1973). Two articles that discuss this topic are: John Bushnell, "The Tsarist Officer Corps, 1881–1914: Customs, Duties, Inefficiency," *American Historical Review* 86, No. 4 (October, 1981):

753–80 and Peter Kenez, "A Profile of the Pre-revolutionary Officer Corps," *California Slavic Studies* 7 (1973): 121–58.

3. For an inside view of the military during this period, see D.A. Miliutin, *Dnevnik D.A. Miliutin*, edited by P.A. Zaionchkovskii, 4 vols. (Moscow, 1947–1950). Important secondary sources on the Great Reforms are Forrest A. Miller, *Dmitrii Miliutin and the Reform Era in Russia* (Nashville, 1968) and P.A. Zaionchkovskii, *Voennye reformy 1860–1870 godov v rossii* (Moscow, 1952).

4. It is important to note that social origin still had an important role in determining who gained admissions into any Tsarist educational institution. The element of Russian society that truly benefited from the Miliutin efforts were the *raznochintsy* (people born to families without any social classification or rank) and the limited members of an emerging bourgeois class. For more details on this, see Chapter Two of my dissertation: John W. Steinberg, "The Education and Training of the Russian General Staff: A History of the Imperial Nicholas Military Academy, 1832–1914" (Ph.D. Dissertation, The Ohio State University, 1990) pp. 74–149.

5. The best English source on these institutions is J.E.O. Screen, *The Helsinki Yunker School, 1846–1879: A Case Study of Officer Training in the Russian Army* (Helsinki, 1986). For the reform of Iunker Schools, see P.A. Zaionchkovskii, *Voennye reformy 1860–1870 godov v Rossii* (Moscow, 1952) pp. 240–46.

6. Two guides to military educational institutions in Russia at the turn of the century are M.S. Lalaev, *Istoricheskii ocherk voenno-uchebnykh zavedenii nodvedomstvennykh glavnomu ikh upravleniiu, 1881–1891* (St. Petersburg, 1892); and *Obzor deiat'nosti voennogo ministerstva v tsarstvovanie Imperatora Aleksandra III-ogo 1881–1894* (St. Petersburg, 1903). In English, see Thomas Darlington, *Education in Russia* (London, 1909).

7. More reading on this process can be located in my dissertation, "The Education and Training of the Russian General Staff: A History of the Imperial Nicholas Military Academy,1832–1914," pp. 150–203; and Carl Van Dyke, *Russian Imperial Military Doctrine and Education, 1832–1914* (Westport, CT, 1990). For the Russian explanation of this process, see N.P. Glinoetskii, *Istoricheskii ocherk nikolaevskoi akademii general'nago shtaba* (St. Petersburg, 1882).

8. Students who completed the course work at the academy were not guaranteed appointment to the General Staff. Appointment was then based on the overall academic performance of the students. Still, however, accusations would be made that appointments to the General Staff depended on an undefined level of favoritism. For such claims and a useful account of life at the General Staff Staff Academy, see A.I. Denikin, *The Career of a Tsarist Officer: Memoirs, 1872-1916*, translated by Margaret Patoski, (Minneapolis, 1975) pp. 55–64.

9. A good source on this topic is Allen Sinel, *The Classroom and the Chancellery: State Educational Reform in Russia under Count Dmitry Tolstoy* (Cambridge, MA 1973).

10. Obraz, pp.212–34.

11. Clearly this issue has been examined by Zaionchkovski and Kenez for the entire officer corps. Their conclusion is that within line regiments the majority of officers were of bourgeois origins. The point of this investigation is now to determine how widespread this trend affected the composition of the Imperial General Staff.

12. Three different types of Captain existed in the Russian Army: first, Staff Captain, then full Captain, and finally, Captain of the General Staff. The problem with compiling data for statistical analysis rests with the nature of each position. Captain of the General Staff was a position only for officers who came from Guard

Regiments whereas non-guard officers had to pass through the two other Captain ranks. This, of course, gave Guards officers an inherent advantage in passing through the ranks. Since not all of the officers passed through an identical Captaincy, compiling data for these purposes became too cumbersome, hence the reluctant decision to pass over Captain's rank all together when counting the number of months it took for each General Staff Officer to pass through the ranks of the army.

13. In order to be an officer in an Imperial guards regiment the young officer needed some type of personal connection (ideally a legacy) to receive an appointment to these prestigous positions. In addition, the future Guards officer needed some independent source of income since his military pay would not meet his expenses for uniforms or the extravagant lifestyle maintained by officers in these regiments. Since most of the officers in this study graduated from the General Staff Academy in the 1870s and 1880s, I am working from the assumption that the relationship between the Cadet Corps Academies and guard service remained firm. It should be noted, however, that this situation dramatically changed as the twentieth century approached because of the progressive impoverishment of Russia's landed nobility. Simply put, between poor pay and high expenses the nobility could no longer afford to finance the beauty and pagentry of the guards regiments. The result was an increasing number of merchants' sons going to the Cadet Corps and joining guard regiments in the twentieth century. Roberta T. Manning, *The Crisis of the Old Order in Russia* (Princeton, 1982) pp. 30–32, and Seymour Becker, *Nobility and Privilege in Late Imperial Russia* (Dekalb, IL, 1985) pp. 120–23.

14. Unless otherwise noted, all statistics that appear in the text and tables of this chapter were calculated from the biographical profiles in *Spisok general'nago shtaba*, (Petrograd, 1914).

15. Students could only attend the Corps of Pages after receiving an Imperial appointment. These appointments were only granted to the sons and grandsons of aristocrats who achieved one of the three highest classes in the Table of Ranks–military or civilian. See Becker, pp. 120–23. The Cavalry, as was the case in all European armies of this period, was traditionally dominated by the nobility.

16. The best analysis on the Franco-Prussian War written by a Russian Staff Officer is by N.P. Mikhnevich, *Voina mezhdy germaniei i frantsiei, 1870–1871* (St. Petersburg, 1897).

17. See Fuller, *Strategy*, pp. 323–27.

18. The most forceful advocate of reforming the army's system of training was Golovin. His ideas on this subject can be found in N.N. Golovin, *Vysshaia voennaia shkola* (St. Petersburg, 1909). Kuropatkin discusses this topic in some detail in his *Prilozheniia k otchetu general-ad'iutanta Kuropatkina*. (Warsaw, 1906).

19. Two representative articles that discuss this trend are D. Balanin, "Voennaia igra v pole," *Razvedchik* 1000 (1909): 746–49; I. Beliavskii, "Nashi Manevry," *Bratskaia pomoshch* 1 (1910): 12–28.

20. This would be the case until and well after the fall of the Romanov's. Although a work of fiction, P.N. Krasnov's, *From Double Eagle to the Red Flag*, vol. I, Part 1 (New York, 1928), pp. 3–255, provides a splendid illustration of this type of mentality.

21. It should be noted that this tradition dates back to the reign of Peter the Great.

22. A short biography that sums up the lessons of his teachings is M.D. Bonch-Bruevich, "Mikhail Ivanovich Dragomirov," *Izvestiia imperatorskoi nikolaevskoi voennoi akademii* 25 (1912): 80–100. Also see Menning, *Bayonets before Bullets*, Chapter 1 and 3.

23. I have compiled this information on Kuropatkin's life from two sources: K.I. Velichko, et al., "Aleksei Nikolaevich Kuropatkin," *Voennaia Entsiklopediia* vol. K, (St. Petersburg, 1914) pp.410–16; *Spisok general'nago shtaba* (St. Petersburg, 1914), p. 5.
24. The best articles that describe this event include: L.L. Drake, "V period bol'shikh Kurskikh manevrov 1902 g," *Voenno-istoricheskii vestnik* 3–4 (1911): pp. 31–38; (no author) "Moskovskaia armiia na bol'shikh' manevrakh' pod' Kurskom," *Razvedchik* 626 (1902): 925–29, 627 (1902): 948–53; (no author) "Deistviia iuzhnoi armii na Kurskikh' manevrakh' v Vysochaishem' prisutstvii v 1902 rodu," *Razvedchik* 637 (1903): 4-9, 638 (1903): 30–35.
25. See: N.A. Lokhvitskii, *O posrednikakh na manervrakh* (St. Petersburg, 1911) pp.4–12; V. Grigor'ev, "Rol' posrednika na manev,." *Voennyi sbornik* 4 (1910) pp. 89–106, 5 (1910) pp. 55–70.
26. Drake, p.33.
27. For the Grand Duke's biography, see *Spisok*, p.8.
28. Dragomirov developed this reputation after the publication of his textbook which all officers read as a part of their education. See M.I. Dragomirov, *Uchebnik taktiki podgotovka voisk v mirnoe vremia upotreblenie voisk*, 3rd ed. (Kiev, 1906). His ideas on training were constantly reiterated in the articles that he wrote in a variety of newspapers, magazines, and journals that comprised the Imperial military press. For a published collection of these articles, see M.I. Dragomirov, *Sbornik original'nykh i perevodnykh statei M. Dragomirova 1858–1880*, vol. 2 (St.Petersburg, 1881).
29. A good article that discusses the teachings of Dragomirov is M.D. Bonch-Bruevich, "Dragomirov o boevoi podgotovke ofitserov," *Voennaia mysl'*, 7 (1944): 63–73. For Dragomirov's own words, see M.I. Dragomirov, "Konspekt lektsii po taktik," *Voennyi Sbornik* 9 (1912): 1–25.
30. A good example of this type of opinion is M.D. Bonch-Bruevich, "K nastupaiushchemu periodu manevrov," *Razvedchik* 1085 (1911): 510–13.
31. L.G. Beskrovnyi, *Russkaia armiia i flot XIX veke* (Moscow, 1973) pp. 26–27.
32. I am basing this assumption on the evidence offered in documents that were sent through the General Staff to the Commander of the 22nd Army Corp which was based in Helsinki in the spring of 1914. These documents consisted of the orders that resulted in the war game that is discussed below. A solid book that provides a suitable outline about the growth and practice of maneuvers in this period is M.A. Gareev, *Obshchevoiskobye ucheniia* (Moscow, 1990), pp. 53–82. Finally, it should be noted that the interwar period, 1905–1914, was the period when, under the leadership of the Grand Duke Nicholas Nicholaevich, the Chief of the General Staff was given the same type of autonomy, at least in principle, as his German counterpart. While there is a large amount of literature on the reforms of this period, I recommend Michael Perrins, "The Council for State Defense 1905–1909: A Study in Russian Bureaucratic Politics," *Slavonic and East European Review* 58 (1980).
33. All archival research for this paper was conducted at the National Archives of Finland. The Finns, not surprisingly, have not devoted much time to organizing these materials. I worked exclusively in one archive entitled *Venalaiset sotilasasiakirjat* (Russian military records–hereafter cited as "Rmr"). The best means of identification was a file name and number, hence: Voennaia igr #3035.
34. Rmr, Voennaia igr #3031.
35. Rmr, voennaia igr #3035 for information on personal and *spisok* for biographical data.

36. Ibid.
37. Voennaia igr #3035.
38. Ibid.
39. Ibid.
40. Ibid.
41. Ibid.
42. Voennaia igr #3031.
43. Voennaia igr #11414.
44. Voennaia igr #3035.
45. For the details on the administrative structure of the Imperial Army as it marched to war, see David R. Jones, "Imperial Russia's Forces at War," p. 290 in Allan R. Millett and Williamson Murray, *Military Effectiveness: The First World War*, vol. 1 (Boston:Allen & Unwin, 1988), pp.249–328. On military control over civilians in wartime Russia, see Dan Graf, "The Reign of the Generals: Military Government in Western Russia, 1914–1915," (Ph.D. Dissertation, The University of Nebraska, 1972).
46. See Steinberg, pp. 215–20; John D. Walz, "State Defense and Russian Politics under the Last Tsar" (Unpublished Ph.D. dissertation, Syracuse University, 1967).
47. I personally do not believe that, as Norman Stone suggests, the Imperial Officers Corps was split into two large bodies in which reformers were loyal patrons of the Grand Duke and traditionalists were dependent on Sukhomlinov. While there may be an element of truth to this formulation, I think it oversimplifies a complex network of relationships that officers established over the course of their careers. See Chapter One of Stone's book for his explanation of the divisions within the officer corps of the Imperial army. For a detailed examination of the stormy relationship that existed between the Grand Duke and Sukhomlinov see, Dan Graf, "The Reign of the Generals: Military Government in Western Russia, 1914–1915" (unpublished Ph.D. dissertation, The University of Nebraska, 1972), pp. 156–80.
48. The most recent study of the East Prussian Campaign of August 1914 is Dennis E. Showalter, *Tannenberg: Clash of Empires* (Hamden, CT, 1991). These facts are supported in all of the classic secondary studies of this campaign, for example: N.N. Golovin, *The Russian Campaign of 1914*, tr. A.G.S. Muntz (Ft. Leavenworth, KS, 1933); Sir Edmund Ironside, *Tannenberg: The First Thirty Days in East Prussia* (Edinburgh, 1933); I.I. Rostunov, *Russkii front pervoi mirovoi voiny* (Moscow, 1976); Ia. K. Tsikhovich,ed., *Strategicheskii ocherk voiny, 1914–1918* Chast' 1, (Moscow, 1922); A.M. Zaionchkovskii, *Mirovaia voina: manevrennyi period 1914–1915 godov na russkom (evropeiskom) teatre* (Moscow, 1929).
49. Norman Stone will make the claim that during the winter of 1917 the Imperial Army possessed a superiority in men and materials causing great optimism—a belief that in the upcoming 1917 campaign Russia would have forces needed to finally turn the tide and throw the German invaders off of Russian soil, see pp. 211–15. For the complete analysis of the army in the revolution, see Wildman's two-volume study of this topic.

Select Bibliography

Fuller, Wiliam C., Jr. *Civil-Military Conflict in Imperial Russia, 1881-1914* Princeton: Princeton University Press, 1985. A study of military professionalism which examines the status of the army in Russian society and places special emphasis on the interaction between the army and the Tsar's government.

Menning, Bruce W. *Bayonets before Bullets: The Imperial Russian Army, 1861–1914* Bloomington: Indianan University Press, 1992. The most comprehensive analysis of the Russian army at the turn of the century, focusing on both its institutional and operational history.

Showalter, Dennis E. *Tannenberg: Clash of Empires.* Hamden, CT: Archon Books, 1991. The most recent book to be published on this critial first campaign of the First World War.

Solzhenitsyn, Aleksandr. *August 1914.* New York: Farrar. Straus and Giroux, 1989. First published in Russian in 1971, this novel provides a relatively accurate view of the state of the Russian Army on the war's eve.

Snyder, Jack. *The Ideology of the Offensive: Military Decision Making and the Disasters of 1914.* Ithaca: Cornell University Press, 1984. Provides a comparative analysis of German, French, and Russian military establishments as they prepared for war.

Stone, Norman. *The Eastern Front 1914–1917.* New York: Charles Scribner's Sons, 1975. The only book in English focusing on the Eastern Front.

Wildman, Allan K. *The End of the Russian Imperial Army.* 2 vols. Princeton: Princeton University Press, 1980 & 1987. A systematic study of the collapse of the Imperial Army in the course of the Revolution.

CHAPTER 13

KNIGHTS OF THE SKY
The Rise of Military Aviation

John H. Morrow, Jr.

Understanding the social and cultural impact of the First World War in any realm presumes an understanding of the prewar circumstances as a point of departure. With the creation of the dirigible in 1884 and the invention of the airplane in 1903, powered flight was a new phenomenon at the dawn of the twentieth century. Military aviation was consequently in its infancy when the First World War began in August 1914, as the oldest air services had only begun in 1909. Dreams of flight embodied in the myths of Daedalus and Icarus long antedated the actual achievement of powered flight, just as visions of aerial warfare preceded the formation of air arms, and from its very beginning military aviation captured the rapt attention of civilians. Historian Peter Fritszche, in his work on German aviation and popular imagination, points out that achievements in aviation served as measures of the greatness of nations at the beginning of the twentieth century.[1] The popular fascination with aeronautics indicates just how important these accomplishments were to the public. Understanding the dimensions of this attraction is fundamental to understanding the social and cultural significance of military aviation before, during, and after the Great War in England, France, and Germany, the major combatant powers of the first total war of the century.

Notes for this chapter begin on page 321.

In France and Germany the popular clamor for aviation, particularly military aviation, surged in 1908 with the 12 hour flight by the Zeppelin LZ4 and the first cross-country flight in an airplane by Henri Farman. Aviation became a "universal preoccupation" in France, and aviators popular heroes. The circumstances surrounding the German army's acquiring of its first Zeppelin in 1908 indicated that governments would have to contend with a new factor in their decisions on military aviation—public opinion. The LZ4's flight in July unleashed such a press campaign that the War Ministry awarded Zeppelin more funds. Its crash in August spurred a popular campaign that raised seven million marks for Zeppelin construction and ultimately generated such enthusiasm that the War Ministry accepted its first Zeppelin early in 1909, before it met the army's performance stipulations. The public and press had clearly been instrumental in promoting the Zeppelin to the army.[2]

Peter Fritzsche observed that the Zeppelin served a multitude of purposes for middle-class nationalist associations and interest groups: it affirmed the power of German industry to dominate nature and to create prospective vehicles for *Weltpolitik*; and it became the focal point of a popular nationalism inclusive of all classes. Its achievements occasioned a popular response that, while essentially urban and middle class, included aristocrats and even socialists among those praising the achievements of the Zeppelin as proof of the superiority of German culture and technology.[3]

By the end of 1908, flight generated increasingly bellicose popular attitudes encouraging militarization, and these formed the context for European aviation's development in the five-and-one-half years left before the war. Because the flights of airships and airplanes impressed the public, military aviation leagues formed in Germany and France. The German Air Fleet League, modeled after the German Navy League, formed in the summer of 1908 to promote military aviation. By 1909 it had 3,000 members and a board of prominent military, industrial, and political figures including Ernst Bassermann, parliamentary leader of the National Liberal Party.

In France the propagandist René Quinton formed the National Aviation League in September 1908, whose vice president was Paul Painlevé, a future Prime Minister and War Minister. By February 1909 the French Senate and Chamber of Deputies had formed committees on aerial locomotion, the latter having 82 members. Farsighted civilians began to envisage the possibilities of military aviation. In late 1908 Prince Pierre d'Arenberg, president of a provincial automobile club in the department of Cher, conceived of making the department an aviation center. From this seed, through civil-military cooperation, would grow France's largest prewar flying school and famous wartime training field at Avord.[4]

French aerial meetings attracted gigantic crowds—an estimated 250,000 enthusiastic spectators at Reims in 1909, another 200,000 at the races at Issy-les-Moulineaux along the Seine outside Paris in 1911—whose infatuation with and faith in aviation electrified French aircraft constructors. This national passion for aviation was the essential context for the French army's adoption of the airplane, with the Reims air meeting providing the catalyst for French military aviation and the French army's purchase of airplanes.[5]

In Germany between 1909 and 1911, the press and popular scientific literature portrayed the Zeppelin as a symbol of German inventive spirit and greatness, a peerless wonder weapon. The Air Fleet League and the German Aviators Association were instrumental in persuading the army to attempt its own airplane construction in 1909 and to subsidize the operation of an airfield at Johannisthal near Berlin.[6]

In 1909 and 1910, as aviation publicists observed the rapidity with which the military responded to aviation, the airplane's potential for peace or war came under increasing discussion, evoking ambivalent responses as Felix Ingold's work on aviation literature amply demonstrates. German engineer N. Stern found the airplane's significance not in its military but in its cultural effects and proclaimed that it would help avoid war, bind nations together, and unify diverse peoples. But German author Paul Scheerbart calculated that aerial militarism would lead to the dissolution of armies and navies through fears of aerial war, while Frenchman Lucien Jeny believed that air war would be so gruesome that war would die "of its own excesses." German Wilhelm Kress thought that "the flying machine will become a frightful weapon of war and will thus help to make wars more seldom."[7] In these prognostications, the authors acknowledged the tendency toward the military application of the airplane, but counted on fearful expectations of air war, or air war itself, to end war or at least to lessen its occurrence.

England lagged behind France and Germany in the development of aviation. After Zeppelin's flight in 1908, press magnate Lord Northcliffe's *Daily Mail* carried speculations about Germany's use of airships to invade England. H.G. Wells's *The War in the Air*, published in 1907, had already dramatically portrayed the destruction of cities and ultimately of civilization by gigantic airships and planes in the first major aerial conflict. Northcliffe launched a campaign for aviation in the 15 February 1909 *Times* that discussed how air raids could assist a foreign invasion force.

The Aerial League of the British Empire, founded in January 1909, held a large meeting in London on 5 April with extensive press coverage that emphasized British aerial unpreparedness compared to German readiness. In a speech on 21 April, published prominently in the *Times*, Lord Montagu of Beaulieu proclaimed London, the nerve center of the government, defenseless and open to strategic air attack. A May editorial of the aviation journal *Flight*, the official organ of the Aero Club, echoed this fear. R.P. Hearne's book *Aerial Warfare*, published in 1909, proclaimed that everything was at the mercy of the Zeppelin, whose raids would destroy morale and disable military forces. Spurred by this "airship scare," a few members of Parliament formed the Parliamentary Aerial Defense Committee to press for military aviation, though the British government continued by and large merely to observe aviation progress in 1910.[8]

In 1911 the press and the Parliamentary Aerial Defense Committee increased the pressure on the government to involve itself with aviation. The aviation journal *Flight* praised the airplane's value for reconnaissance and its role in French and German maneuvers, and decried the "hopelessness" of the British government's complacent attitude toward air defense, its neglect of aviation compared to the continental powers, and particularly its failure to support a domestic aviation industry. A flying meeting at Hendon airdrome in May demonstrated the use of planes for reconnaissance and bombing to members of parliament, and new First Lord of the Admiralty Winston Churchill, who was already keenly interested in aviation. In the fall the politicians challenged the War Office to buy more airplanes, and under mounting pressure Prime Minister Herbert H. Asquith asked the Committee of Imperial Defense to propose measures necessary for establishing an efficient air service.[9]

After the Moroccan crisis of 1911, Europe expected war. In this increasingly bellicose atmosphere, all aspects of aviation, including the exploits of civilian pilots, became indissolubly tied to the military. France's great civilian aviators such as Roland Garros and Adolphe Pégoud were national heroes, defenders of French honor. The Circuit of Anjou in 1912, which the French army also used as a test, occurred in such dreadful weather that only Garros completed the course. Journalist René Bazin commended the participants for risking themselves for France and likened them to knights protecting a nation in peril.[10]

In Germany the army effectively controlled civilian aviation ventures through its pervasive influence in German society, playing upon chauvinistic notions of cultural supremacy to bolster military aviation. Government and industry organized a National Aviation Fund for Germany in its "hour of national danger" to protect its preeminence in applied science and make the German nation the "powerful engine that would drive her planes to victory in peace and war." The "pioneers in this great new cultural task" who "risk their lives in the patriotic endeavor to secure for Germany in this area an equal place in the universal struggle of nations" deserved the active support of the entire nation.

The fund raised over 7.2 million marks, which bought 62 airplanes for the army and financed the training of 162 field pilots by August 1914. It built airfields that the military would control in wartime, provided partial funding for the civilian German Research Institute for Aviation, and sponsored civilian competitions that became virtually long-range reconnaissance flights for military two-seaters and their crews. When some manufacturers attempted to use these contests to promote sport aviation and a market for small, fast planes, the civilian aviation sport associations effectively thwarted their efforts and zealously defended the army's priorities.[11]

The English government officially formed military and naval air services in 1912, and amid agitation from the press and parliament for larger forces they nonetheless grew slowly in the two years before the war. In *Daily Mail* articles H.G. Wells speculated whether Britain, behind in submarines, airships, and airplanes, was not "backward, unorganized, unimaginative, [and] unenterprising" compared to the continent.[12]

In *The Culture of Time and Space, 1880–1918*, historian Stephen Kern observed that at the turn of the twentieth century, aviation engendered ambivalent visions—aerial warfare's terrifying potential as well as a great technological revolution transcending old boundaries and uplifting human consciousness.[13] While premature expectations of the apocalyptic or the transcendent had surrounded aviation from its infancy, what actually occurred in prewar Europe was the militarization of flight. Sport aviation languished, the era of great races and tournaments ended, and accidents had cooled public enthusiasm for air transport. In an atmosphere of heightening nationalistic bellicosity, and in the absence of substantial sport or commercial markets, military aviation's supporters molded popular attitudes to benefit their cause. Aircraft manufacturers, indissolubly tied to the military—their essential if not exclusive source of contracts by 1912—sponsored civilian aviators, whom the press lionized as defenders of national honor.

In Europe the competition for national superiority in aviation had engendered national stereotypes. French accounts often depicted German aviators as fat, florid types in large slow planes, while proclaiming that the energy and initiative necessary to use airplanes accorded marvelously with traditional Gallic audacity. The Germans lorded the Zeppelin over other powers as a symbol of their presumed cultural supremacy. Articles in the German aviation magazine *Deutscher Luftfahrer Zeitschrift* anticipated pinpoint and unstoppable Zeppelin attacks on enemy targets in the dark of night.[14] The British, who had little to gloat about until the victories of Sopwith seaplanes in international racing competitions in 1914, then quickly claimed that the mantle of leadership in aviation had passed to them.[15]

If the English had been relatively slow to support military aviation, some of them had early understood the implications of the airplane for colonial domination and white supremacy. In 1910 the Committee of Imperial Defense directed the War Office to consider the use of the airplane against "uncivilized countries such as the Sudan, Somaliland, and the north-west frontier of India." A possible joint project of the Colonial Office and the navy in 1914 entailed plans to have the white population employ aircraft to control and threaten the empire's native populations in the event of black uprisings. Rudyard Kipling had early viewed aviation, like the navy, as a tool to unify and protect the Empire, and in debates on airships in the House of Commons in 1909, one MP had commented on the value of airships for imperial security. Charles Grey, editor of *Aeroplane*, wanted to use the airplane to impress European superiority on large native populations, while military theorists advocated the use of aircraft in "savage war" against native populations.[16] While the British merely contemplated the use of aircraft to police the empire, the French and Italians used airplanes in campaigns in North Africa in 1911 and 1912. Flight thus assumed a nationalist, imperialist, and military appearance by 1914.

Throughout the prewar era, individual authors, the press, and aviation organizations pressured government to develop military aviation. From the beginning, the development of military aviation was inextricably intertwined with public perceptions and expectations of its future importance for aggression or defense. In lockstep with naval and army leagues and other organized pressure groups outside of government, proponents of aviation sought to promote their particular object of interest to the government.

The Zeppelin had generated unrealistic expectations in Germany that a minuscule fleet could deliver a telling first strike against enemies. The airplane generally had inspired much popular excitement but not such apocalyptic visions, since mass destruction was clearly beyond the capabilities of the fragile craft of the day. Yet the literature of the prewar era had foretold nearly every role that aircraft would play in the First World War, including the bombing of civilians with the assumption that civilian morale would disintegrate into panic and chaos.[17] Such attitudes anticipated the postwar concentration of aerial theorist Giulio Douhet on the bombing of civilian populations to force nations to accept defeat. The intimate connections between the civilian and military arenas in aviation provided an appropriate context for a weapon that would both galvanize and directly threaten civilian populations in the coming total war. Finally, the public of the prewar era already considered aviators heroes, conquerors of speed, altitude, and distance in the heavens, and masters of the use of technology in the conquest of nature. In France the practice of national *Deuil*, or mourning, was already evident in the case of the death of well-known aviators. In the air services in all countries a different type of warrior, a new hero, arose, exemplified by the dashing and audacious "Lieutenant Daedalus Icarus Brown," RFC pilot of "fame and renown" as proclaimed in British doggerel.[18]

Although most armies had emphasized slow, stable aircraft for the air arm's major anticipated task of reconnaissance, ironically the war would catapult the flying machine again into the forefront of public imagination as a vehicle of the war's greatest individual heroes, the aces, who were reminiscent of those prewar aviators who had mastered the skies. Wartime aerial combat, the realm of aviation in which there had been the least prewar experimentation and speculation, would reintroduce some aspects of sport aviation that the prewar French and German military had sought to escape—the emphasis on the exploits of the individual, and the high-performance airplane, faster, more maneuverable, riskier to fly, occasionally even dangerous to its own pilots. The aura of prewar sport would return, though in a context so deadly that it altered the nature of the game.

During the First World War aviation evolved from an instrument of reconnaissance used singly in 1914 to a weapon for fighting, bombing, and strafing in 1918. Its effectiveness as a weapon required its deployment en masse against the enemy. Aviation emerged as the most advanced and innovative technological arm of battle, epitomizing the new total warfare in its requirement of meshing the military, political, technological, and industrial aspects of war—the front and the rear, military and civilian. By 1918 air services that had begun the war with some 200 front line airplanes had 2,000 to 3,000 airplanes at the front; national aviation industries that employed a few thousand workers at most in 1914 to deliver a hundred planes a month employed hundreds of thousands of workers to deliver thousands of planes and engines monthly in 1918.

In what had become an aerial war of attrition above the one fought in the trenches, those responsible for aviation recognized the importance of mass. Winston Churchill, who became Minister of Munitions on 20 July 1917, wanted to replace the attrition of men with a war of machines using "masses of guns, mountains of shells, clouds of aeroplanes."[19] The French aviation journal *La Guerre Aérienne*, in an editorial in August 1918, recognized that fundamental to aviation's "new phase of its evolution"—collective effort as opposed to individual action—was the French industrial effort, which enabled the new doctrines using aviation en masse over the battlefield.[20] Understanding the importance of the collective effort was fundamental to the aviation mobilization during the war, yet this is not the essence of the popular impression of the air war, which seems to have been divided into two strands. The first concerns conceptions of aerial combat and the aerial hero; the second, strategic bombing.

Lee Kennett, in his history of military aviation in the First World War, notes that by 1916 the public in the combatant countries knew the names and exploits of the great pilots, and that Germany probably led the way in placing the aviator before the public.[21] The experiences of two of Germany's greatest aces, Oswald Boelcke and Manfred von Richthofen, are instructive regarding their recognition and roles.

Early in 1916 Oswald Boelcke, one of Germany's first and most famous aces, received Germany's highest award for valor, the "Pour le Mérite." The German public already knew his name because of his aerial victories, as military and civilians followed the close competition between Boelcke and Germany's other master flier of the day, Max Immelmann. Jaunty verses appeared in the paper *Der Tag* about their neck and neck race to shoot down enemy planes. Boelcke received constant requests from the press for his photograph, and he acknowledged that as a Knight of the "Pour le Mérite," he could not keep himself out of the press.

Visiting Frankfurt in the spring, Boelcke commented that wearing the medal at home guaranteed public notice. Crowds stared at him in streets and even at the opera, where during intermission they crowded around him. The opera singer reappeared to sing an encore, but instead sang a verse in Boelcke's honor. The audience went mad, clapping, shouting and stamping its feet. Boelcke was so startled that he fled.

Life in his home town, Dessau, was somewhat calmer. Daily deputations of youth and others visited his house. Once when he left home for the war, local youth escorted him to the station to cheer as his train departed. He was even invited to lunch and tea with the duke and duchess of the region.

Oswald Boelcke crashed to his death on 28 October 1916, the victim of a collision in combat after having gained 40 victories. The army first staged a magnificent funeral service for him in the large cathedral at Cambrai on 31 October. One of the generals in attendance read the text, which praised Boelcke's eternal greatness, his love of country and iron sense of duty, and declared that every German child knew his name and loved him as a national hero. Six black chargers drew the gun carriage bearing Boelcke's coffin. While aviators flew overhead, rising ace Manfred von Richthofen led the cortege, flanked by lancers and footguards, to the train station, where another general eulogized Boelcke in the name of the Emperor. The train then took him home to Dessau, where he lay in state with an honor guard of noncommissioned officer pilots.

The German nation in mourning sent condolences to the Boelcke family. Once again, during the lengthy funeral in Dessau, eulogies emphasized Boelcke's role as an inspiration to Germany's youth to protect the Fatherland. Story and verse proclaimed that every German boy vowed to be "a Boelcke."[22]

Manfred von Richthofen was the heir apparent to wear Boelcke's mantle, and his experience in 1917 and 1918 paralleled that of his mentor, even unto death. As historian Peter Kilduff recounts, Richthofen always received a hero's welcome in his home of Schweidnitz, with delegations of youth groups to greet him and crowds of people to stand in awe in front of his house. After the press had reported his fifty-second victory, crowds greeted him in Cologne as well. Richthofen recognized that part of the hero's role was to inspire the people, and so he, like any media personality of today, signed autographs for the admiring throng. His presence also inspired soldiers, such as an infantry column that cheered him while he was returning to the front in July, an experience that obviously pleased the cavalryman.[23] The pictures and biographies of aces like Boelcke and Richthofen flooded the press, and even wartime memoirs appeared before the end of the war. Lee Kennett notes that the first two editions of Richthofen's memoirs, *Der rote Kampfflieger*, which appeared in 1918, ran to a half-million copies.[24]

Richthofen played the role to which many famous fliers became accustomed in the Second World War, that of touring the home front and visiting factories to encourage the workers to do their part for the war effort. In a Germany increasingly stalked by the danger of revolution, where workers struck to protest food shortages, the ace visited factories to convince them to return to work, although he feared that they would not do it for much longer.[25]

The young hero himself did not have much longer to live, as he fell to groundfire in the British lines on 21 April 1918, after claiming 80 victories in the skies over the Western Front. The service in Berlin on 2 May was a striking blend of the military, the patriotic, and the religious. Held at the Garrison Church with the streets approaching it thronged by Berliners, the funeral featured an altar draped in black, and a black funeral wreath replete with splintered propeller and four machine gun barrels. The royal family joined the Richthofens in the pew, as air officers and a noncommissioned officers' honor guard stood at attention.[26]

The authorities had feared the effect of the deaths of aces like Boelcke and Richthofen on morale, and that a corollary of their celebrity would be that the public who cheered their victories would lose heart at their deaths. Despite these official concerns, it was nearly impossible to keep the young aces from combat when millions of young men in the army had no choice but to return to the front until they were killed or wounded. The great fliers, drawn like moths to a flame by the thrill of the hunt and their sense of duty to their country, in particular often to their less fortunate brothers in the trenches, returned again and again to the front.

The fighter pilots were also the darlings of France. If bad weather halted frontline operations, they flew to Le Bourget and were driven to Paris, where the populace idolized and feted them. Worshipful women wrote them constantly, and once, as aces Georges Guynemer and Alfred Heurteaux left a restaurant, they found the jewels and addresses of adoring female patrons stuffed in their coat pockets.[27]

French fighter pilot Jean Villars labeled the air arm a privileged group, with "clean hands, interesting work, individual combat," a knightly group in which personal valor still counted. The fighter pilots were the youngest, the most ardent and capable. Ace René Dorme once observed that his sportive combats provided a "gala spectacle" for the "brave infantry in the trenches." These pilots, worshipped by the public, became the focus, even the prisoners, of a cult of heroism, fostered by journals like *La Guerre Aérienne*.[28]

The legendary Georges Guynemer was France's greatest hero, and the frail youth fully expected to die in the service of his country. Upon his death (following 53 victories) on 11 September 1917 during the Battle of Flanders, French teachers instructed schoolchildren that he had flown so high that he could not descend. On 19 October the National Assembly and Senate enshrined "Capt. Guynemer, symbol of the aspirations and enthusiasm of the army of the nation," in the Pantheon, "whose cupola alone has sufficient span to shelter such wings." The slender youth embodied the victory of the spirit over the flesh, of France's will to endure despite its grave wounds.[29]

In England the Royal Flying Corps characterized air combat as a sport, a notion that stemmed from its composition—a corps of commissioned officers who were recruited as much as possible from the ranks of public school sportsmen and were attracted to war flying for the adventure. R.M. Neill wrote to his school newspaper urging Westminster boys to join the RFC, advising them that "any sportsman will realize that, apart from fighting, there is absolutely nothing to touch flying as a sport." Six weeks later Neill perished in action.[30]

Consonant with the attitude equating war with sport, RFC training remained rudimentary and instilled no sense of professionalism compared to its French and German counterparts. Historian Michael Paris suggests that this attitude stemmed in part from the prewar fallacy equating flying with riding, a skill which all gentlemen allegedly mastered. Paris notes that R. Wherry Anderson's popular account of the air war published in 1917 said that air fighting had replaced lion hunting as the finest sport.[31]

Published wartime dispatches compared the air war to a medieval tournament or a dangerous rugby game. From RFC Headquarters Philip Gibbs's column, "Daily Chronicle," which appeared in *Flight* in

February and August, depicted the RFC as "Knights-Errant of the Air," recalling the Black Prince in Flanders during the Hundred Years War. In a war with precious little romance, he found it in the "daily tourneys" in the air, as fearless British fliers attacked unequal odds with the ardor of schoolboys flinging themselves into a football scrimmage.[32]

As both the air war and the composition of the RFC expanded, by 1917 recruits from the upper classes were scarce, and the War Office prevented the RFC from taking a disproportionate share of public school boys. In the fall the pilot candidates had included very few graduates from the great English public schools. Yet British aviation magazines continued to romanticize both the corps and the sporting, chivalric, heroic, and sacrificial images of the air war. As casualties mounted, *Flight*'s obituaries of officer aviators became less elaborate but adhered to a certain form, containing comments such as "a keen sportsman, a good shot, and a good rider to hounds," or "a keen big-game shot." Reports about fliers maintained a jaunty, sportsmanlike air, such as that of the famous polo player whose chief regret about aviation was that polo would hardly thrill him again.

The Times correspondent on 15 April 1917, chronicled the lone airman who returned, riddled from a long-distance mission, to make his report, and after apologizing for a rough landing caused by his smashed foot, "then, duty done, he died." *The Aeroplane* of 30 May carried "The Lament of the Broken Pilot," who bid farewell to France, "the land of adventure and knightly deeds,/where the pilot faces the foe/in single combat as was of yore—/giving him blow for blow." No longer among the "throng of chivalry, youth, and pride," where his comrades entered "the airy lists in the name of Freedom and Right," our broken pilot would now keep their "armour bright." Exclusive London stores like Abercrombie and Fitch advertised aviation clothing intended to dress the wealthy young sportsman knight stylishly and appropriately for the airy lists.[33]

Memoirs and accounts of the war make it amply clear that what little chivalry may have existed in aviation died in the mass combats of 1917 and 1918. Yet that "winged aristocracy" of aviators,[34] their exploits romanticized by the press, provided a source of heroes to rally the masses during the slaughter of 1917. The RFC command, unlike its German and French counterparts, sought to secure its niche as part of a mass army in which most soldiers would never receive individual recognition by initially paying no attention to individual fliers. When the War Cabinet desired to publish the names of outstanding pilots in October, RFC commander Hugh "Boom" Trenchard opposed such special treatment on the grounds that it would be unwise and invidious. Yet the very impersonal nature of mass warfare required publicized heroes and ensured the lionization of these men as the war continued. [35]

Ultimately, the war of the masses bequeathed to them a new individual hero, the aviator. Prime Minister David Lloyd George praised his airmen as constituting a heroic "cavalry of the clouds," referring to them as the noble spirited "knighthood" of the war who recalled to mind the legends of chivalry."[36]

Laurence Goldstein's book, *The Flying Machine and Modern Literature*, considered the postwar memoirs of air aces the closest approximation to knightly tales of old, catalogs of warriors' repeated trials by combat with an avowed moral purpose.[37] Felix Philipp Ingold, in *Literatur und Aviatik*, pointed out that wartime provided the means and theater for a contemporary re-creation of the duel: visible actions had certain moral norms; for instance, the pilots received certain privileges, such as being invited to dine with a victorious opponent or a burial with full military honors. The number of kills, the measure of the new hero, quantified the successes of the pilots. The masses celebrated pilots as popular heroes and honored them as demigods, objects of an unparalleled secular holy cult. These air heroes, convinced that they were personally responsible for saving or increasing the honor of their nation, believed that God watched over them and occasionally even likened themselves to gods, elevated above everything earthly.[38]

The exhilaration of flight, the conquest of space and speed, the sense of mastery over others and the environment that was absent in land warfare, composed the attraction of military aviation. In many respects the airplane established itself as the ideal weapon for Western man, who regards his technical mastery as proof of his superiority over others. Air warfare was the apotheosis of warfare in modern, technological, and industrial society. It literally and figuratively enabled its combatants to rise above the anonymity of mass society and modern warfare to wage a clean and individual struggle. The melding of man and machine was striking. That aerial fighting was furthermore a small man's preserve reinforced the idea of the airplane as extending, or enhancing, the ability of some to participate in warfare. It allowed the preservation of notions of sport and individual combat in a war in which land and naval conflict amply demonstrated that modern warfare had rendered such ideals obsolete and ludicrous.

Yet ideals of sport, chivalry, and individual combat in no way comport with strategies of bombing enemy cities and civilians with relative impunity and in such impersonal fashion that the prospect of future aerial depredations on civilian populations became attractive to air planners after the war.

Early in the war sentiment in German military, political, diplomatic, and business circles gained strength for using air warfare to crush British resistance. In late August 1914 the German minister in Stockholm, Franz von Reichenau, fervently hoped that Germany would dispatch airships and aircraft regularly to bomb England until "the vulgar huckster souls" of those "cowardly assassins" would forget how to add. Industrialist Walther Rathenau also advocated a large air force to work "on the nerves" of the English towns.[39]

The German government sought to do exactly that, but lacked the large air force that Rathenau desired. It began with Zeppelins in 1915. Domestic wartime propaganda in Germany proclaimed the Zeppelins vital war weapons that wreaked much havoc in England and crippled civilian morale. Although this was not the case, propaganda insisted that because of this popular confidence in the Zeppelin, its ruthless deployment against England spurred patriotic enthusiasm and sacrifice. Although the drone of a Zeppelin overhead on a mission to bomb England encouraged German seamen below, the Zeppelin campaign ultimately failed and large bombers superseded the Zeppelins. A focus on the heroism of the airship crews replaced the prewar litany about invincible Zeppelins.[40] Ultimately, the German bombing campaign waged by giant multi-engine airplanes from September 1917 to May 1918 failed to wreck British resolve and drive them from the war.

In France, on 5 July 1915 parliamentary deputy Pierre Etienne Flandin demanded the bombardment of German industrial centers. Politicians were not the only ones with such ideas. In August Professor A. le Chatelier of the Collège de France, in a memorandum on aviation to the government, reasoned that if it was impossible to break the German front on land, then it could be crossed by an aviation arm of a thousand bombers whose attacks in the Rhine zone by day and night would result in victory.[41] Yet this reasoning was going on as the French high command was renouncing its hopes for strategic aviation because of the losses in its bombing of German industrial cities and deficiencies in its bombers, as well as its awareness that Paris would be Germany's prime target for reprisal raids in any strategic air war.

In England in 1915 politicians and civilian publicists were increasingly dissatisfied with and occasionally hysterical about the aerial war effort. At a War Council meeting on 24 February participants contemplated aerial attacks on Germany aimed even at distributing a "blight" on or burning Germany's next grain crop. In June members of parliament advocated destroying Essen and other vital German centers with daily massed raids. In a patriotic manifesto in the *Daily Express*, H.G. Wells argued that two thousand planes could demolish Essen, and even if one thousand were lost, it would be cheaper than the Battle of Neuve-Chapelle or the loss of a battleship. Wells demanded ten thousand planes with reserves and personnel. Undersecretary of War Tennant, when queried in the House of Commons about the possibility of producing three thousand planes in six months, replied that private industry could not deliver them and the proportion of the air service to the army was adequate.[42]

By 1918 civilian officials held the most sanguinary expectations of the British Independent Force of bombers. On 10 September 1918 Secretary of State for Air Lord Weir urged Trenchard to start "a really big fire" in one of the German towns. A week later he advised Trenchard that reports of bombing railroads were harming their cause, as the public, impatient for results, wanted to hear of raids on munitions works and other industrial targets. All the authorities acknowledged that the Independent Force was incapable of causing significant material damage but assumed that it could injure morale. By late 1918 Trenchard believed that striking at armaments production centers would undermine the morale of the most vulnerable segment of the German population, the working class, and quickly end the war. In fact, postwar surveys of those regions of Germany under Allied occupation indicated that the raids had only a minor impact upon civilian morale and productivity. The raids, however, affected the morale in England, raising it through Trenchard's reports to the Air Ministry and the press.[43] The war ended with the value of strategic bombing unproven, but with the notion uppermost in the minds of some practitioners and theorists of aviation that the bombing of civilians could undermine their morale and potentially end wars.

With the end of the war came the legacy of aviation. The English multi-volume work, *The War in the Air*, constitutes the only official history of the air war published in any country. Michael Paris points out that the initial volume focused on the individual and the heroic, thus giving the "official seal of approval" to the prewar and wartime emphasis on the individual exploits of the great pilots. Postwar biographies, combat reminiscences, and popular works reinforced the emphasis on the heroic and the individual in the examination of the air war.[44]

The French and Germans also continued to eulogize their aerial heroes and to examine the air war primarily from the perspective of aerial combat. It is particularly instructive to examine for a moment the German experience in the postwar era, as the losers struggled through the chaos of the early Weimar Republic desperately in need of heroes.

George Mosse's work, *Fallen Soldiers*, points out that the emphasis on the chivalric and individual in German accounts harked back to the ideals of preindustrial warfare that made the war and its modern technology easier to accept, an idea that is certainly applicable to all three of the major powers. This new warrior elite enabled myths about the nation and national elites to be extended in the romanticization of their aerial exploits. These new knights could conquer the sky using technology yet simultaneously give the comfort of recalling the mythical fighters and gods of yore.[45]

Peter Fritzsche's discussion of Ernst Jünger's work, *Storm of Steel*, continues with this line of reasoning. Jünger believed that industrial war reduced most men to victims, but empowered a minority, in particular aviators, who could employ technology to extend their power. These individuals were a new aristocracy that blended the knight and the machine age and who had risen from the middle class, often from urban environments. Such an interpretation reflected the fact that the great majority of aces in Germany and elsewhere were from the middle class. Ruthless, technologically capable, these men would shape the postwar industrial society.[46]

Boelcke and Richthofen were the symbols of this elite. On the fifth anniversary of Boelcke's death, Dessau built an imposing memorial to him, and he remained the symbol of the ideal German hero, manly, heroic, and self-sacrificing, resurrected by nationalists and later by the Nazis when the occasion demanded.[47] Immediately after the war the German government moved Richthofen's body to the German military cemetery near Albert. In 1925 it had the body exhumed and returned to Germany on a special train for an elaborate state funeral in Berlin presided over by Weimar president and First World War Commander-in-Chief Paul von Hindenburg. Manfred von Richthofen's burial in the *Invalidenfriedhof*, where some of Germany's other great heroes lay, returned the hero to German soil and provided the occasion for an outpouring of nationalist sentiment.[48]

The concentration on the "knights of the air" that was evident in all countries stems from a natural tendency to emphasize the heroic. The very circumstances of the First World War encouraged a mythologizing of the air war into a single image of individual combat, deadly but chivalrous. Mass slaughter on an unprecedented scale rendered individuals insignificant. Aerial heroes provided a much-needed, though misleading, affirmation of the importance of the individual and of youth in a slaughter of both. The fighter pilots consequently became not only the symbols of aviation but also the ultimate heroes of the First World War. They were the darlings of the press and civilians, the perfect symbols of an upstart arm that displayed many of the wayward tendencies of youth, in particular a lack of discipline. Ironically, the concentration on the individual exploits of a few fighter pilots has given an archaic, anachronistic image to the most innovative arm of the war, one requiring mass deployment to be effective in the conflict.

Conversely, the darker side of the legacy, the myths of strategic bombing of civilian populations, reminded those that chose to pay attention that the air weapon was truly the child of the era of total war, which conflated civilian and military targets and deemed the bombing of women and children an acceptable means of winning a war. The experience of the First World War provided little evidence of civilian collapse under aerial bombardment beyond some panic in London during early German air attacks. Yet the presumption of civilian vulnerability to aerial bombardment persisted. It was simply assumed that they had to be more vulnerable than a disciplined soldiery to the depredations of aerial raids. Both of these illusionary images—the romantic idealization of individual aerial combat rooted in the past and the brutal vision of massive civilian destruction foreshadowing the future—constituted the dual legacy for airpower in the twentieth century.

Notes to Chapter 13

1. Peter Fritzsche, *A Nation of Fliers: German Aviation and the Popular Imagination* (Cambridge, MA: Harvard University Press, 1992): 3.
2. Kriegswissenschaftliche Abteilung der Luftwaffe, *Die Militärluftfahrt bis zum Beginn des Weltkrieges 1914* (3 vols., 2d rev. ed., edited by Militärgeschichtliches Forschungsamt. Frankfurt: Mittler und Sohn, 1965–66), 1:1–73, passim.
3. Fritzsche, 6–43.
4. Edmond Petit, *La Vie quotidienne dans l'aviation en France au début du XXe siècle*

(1900–1935) (Paris: Hachette, 1977), 79. Louis Morgat, "L'Aviation en Berry avant la Grande Guerre," *Revue Historiques des Armées,* 1980, no. 1: 159–60.
5. Petit, 80. Félix Marie, *Les Origines de l'Aéronautique militaire (novembre 1909-novembre 1910)* (Paris: Lavauzelle, 1924), passim.
6. John H. Morrow, Jr., *Building German Air Power, 1909–1914*(Knoxville: University of Tennessee Press, 1976), 14–47. Jürgen Eichler, "Die Militärluftschiffahrt in Deutschland 1911-1914 und ihre Rolle in den Kriegsplänen des deutschen Imperialismus," *Zeitschrift für Militärgeschichte* 24, no 4 (1985): 350–60.
7. Felix P. Ingold, *Literatur und Aviatik: Europäische Flugdichtung, 1909–1927* (Basel: Birkhäuser Verlag, 1978), 104–5, 116–7.
8. On Wells, see Stephen H. Kern, *The Culture of Time and Space, 1880–1918*(Cambridge, MA: Harvard University Press, 1983), 252–53. On England in general, see Alfred Gollin, *No Longer an Island. Britain and the Wright Brothers, 1902–1909* (Stanford: Stanford University Press, 1984), 433–68; Alfred Gollin, *The Impact of Air Power on the British People and Their Government, 1909–1914* (Stanford: Stanford University Press, 1989), 1–190 passim.
9. *Flight* 3 passim, but particularly no. 46 (18 November 1911: 994 and no. 51 (23 December 1911): 1100.
10. Petit, 83–84, 95.
11. On German aviation from 1912 to 1914, see Morrow, *German Air Power in World War I,* 7–11; Morrow, *Building German Air Power,*48–103.
12. *Flight* 5, no. 5 (1 February 1913): 107–8; ibid., no. 9 (1 March 1913):243–44; ibid., no. 15 (11 April 1913): 415.
13. Kern, 72, 194, 242–47, 287, 310–11, 317.
14. Eichler, "Militärluftschiffahrt," 407–10.
15. Harald Penrose, *British Aviation: The Pioneer Years, 1903-1914*(London: Putnam, 1967), 513–15.
16. Thomas A. Keaney, "Aircraft and Air Doctrinal Development in Great Britain, 1912–1914" (Diss., University of Michigan, 1975), 221, 247–48. Michael Paris, *Winged Warfare: The Literature and Theory of Aerial Warfare in Britain, 1859–1917* (Manchester: Manchester University Press, 1992), 39, 91, 139. *Aeroplane* 3, no. 7 (15 August 1912: 159–60; ibid., no. 15 (10 October 1912): 359–60.
17. Paris, 29, 59.
18. *Aeroplane* 3, no. 14 (2 October 1913: 374.
19. Randolph S. Churchill and Martin Gilbert, *Winston S. Churchill* (vols. 2–4 (Boston: Houghton Mifflin, 1967, 1971, 1975), 4:61.
20. *La Guerre Aérienne,* no. 82 (6 June 1918):474; ibid., no. 90 (1 August 1918):612.
21. Lee Kennett, *The First Air War, 1914–1918* (New York: Free Press, 1991), 154.
22. Johannes Werner, *Knight of Germany. Oswald Boelcke. German Ace* (New York: Arno Press, 1972 [1932]), 145, 164, 172, 233–36.
23. Peter Kilduff, *Richthofen* (manuscript to be published by Smithsonian Institution Press in the United States, an imprint from Arms and Armour Press, 1993), 165, 183, 184, 219–20.
24. Kennett, 160.
25. Kilduff, 269–70.
26. Kilduff, 333–4.
27. "L'Aéronautique militaire pendant la Guerre de 1914–1918," (2 vols. in *Icare, revue de l'aviation française*. Special numbers in 1978 and 1979) 2:29.
28. Lieutenant Marc [Jean Béraud Villars], *Notes d'un pilote disparu (1916–1917)* (Paris: Hachette, 1918), 165–74, 212–13. Jean-Pierre Dournel, "L'image

de l'aviateur français en 1914–1918," *Revue Historique des Armées*, 1975, no. 4: 78.
29. "Guynemer et les Cicognes," *Icare, revue de l'aviation française*, no. 122 (1987): 27, 74, 87.
30. Peter Parker, *The Old Lie: The Great War and the Public School Ethos* (London: Constable, 1987), 266.
31. Paris, 217–18, 225.
32. *Flight* 8, no. 5 (3 February 1916): 97; ibid., no. 33 (17 August 1916): 705–6.
33. *Flight*, 9, no. 16 (19 April 1917). *Aeroplane* 12, no. 22(30 May 1917).
34. Arthur Gould Lee, *Open Cockpit: A Pilot of the Royal Flying Corps* (London: Jarrolds, 1969), 43, 52–53.
35. Trenchard CRFC 2160 (G), 5 October 1917, AIR 1/522/16/12/5, Public Record Office (PRO).
36. David Lloyd George, *The Great Crusade: Extracts from Speeches Delivered during the War*, (New York: Doran and Co,), 212.
37. Laurence Goldstein, *The Flying Machine and Modern Literature* (London: Macmillan, 1986), 89.
38. Ingold, 224–26.
39. Fritz Fischer, *Germany's Aims in the First World War* (New York: W.W. Norton, 1967), 280–82.
40. Fritzsche, 46–58.
41. Philippe Bernard, "A propos de la stratégie aérienne pendant la Première Guerre Mondiale: Myths et Réalités, *Revue d'histoire moderne et contemporaine*, 16 (1969): 360–61.
42. AIR1/2319/223/29/1–18, Public Record Office. *Flight*, 7, no. 26 (25 June 1915: 446–48, 455; ibid., no. 30 (23 July 1915): 525–26, 539–42; ibid., no. 43 (22 December 1915); 798, 802.
43. Weir to Trenchard, 10 September 1918; Weir to Trenchard, 17 September 1918; MFC 76/1/94, Trenchard Papers, Royal Air Force Museum. H Montgomery Hyde, *British Air Policy between the Wars, 1918–1939* (London: Heinemann, 1976), 42. Paris, 242.
44. Walter A. Raleigh and H.A. Jones, *The War in the Air*, vols. 1–6 (Oxford: Clarendon, 1922–37). Paris, 6–7.
45. George L. Mosse, *Fallen Soldiers. Reshaping the Memory of the World Wars* (New York: Oxford University Press, 1990), 117–23.
46. Fritzsche, 62–64, 82, 96, 98, 100.
47. Werner, 237–40.
48. Kilduff, 352–53.

Select Bibliography

The two most recent general histories of the air war in the First World War are Lee Kennett's *The First Air War, 1914–1918* (New York: Free Press, 1991) and John Morrow's *The Great War in the Air: Military Aviation from 1909 to 1921* (Washington: Smithsonian Institution Press, 1993). Of the most recent works discussing aviation and culture, two of the most interesting are frequently cited in this essay: Peter Fritzsche, *A Nation of Fliers: German Aviation and the Popular Imagination* (Cambridge, MA: Harvard University Press, 1992) and Michael Paris, *Winged Warfare: The Literature of Aerial Warfare in Britain, 1859–1917* (Manchester: Manchester

University Press, 1992). Laurence Goldstein's work, *The Flying Machine and Modern Literature*, (London: Macmillan, 1986), is also very informative on the subject, as is Felix P. Ingold's book, *Literature und Aviatik: Europaeischer Flugdichtung 1907–1929* (Basel: Birkhaeuser Verlag, 1978). Stephen H. Kern's study, *The Culture of Time and Space, 1880–1918* (Cambridge, MA: Harvard University Press, 1983), places attitudes about aviation in the larger context of changing attitudes about time and space at the turn of the twentieth century.

CHAPTER 14

COMMUNITIES IN MOURNING

J.M. Winter

Grief is a state of mind; bereavement a condition. Both are mediated by mourning, a set of acts and gestures through which survivors express grief and pass through stages of bereavement.[1] Many of these moments are lived within families supported by social networks. This facet of the social history of bereavement in the Great War has never been treated in a comparative framework.

In all combatant countries, families were torn apart by war. Nothing could have reversed completely this tide of separation and loss. But after 1914 there was also a gathering together, as people related by blood or by experience tried to draw strength from each other during and after the war. The bonds thus formed were powerful and in many cases durable. The process of their formation and expression is at the heart of this essay.

In all countries touched by the war, there was a progression of mutual help, a pathway along which many groups and individuals sought to provide knowledge, then consolation, then commemoration. These elements were always there, though the language in which they were expressed varied considerably.

We can identify the initial stages of bereavement in terms of discovery, of how relatives and friends heard the awful news about casualties, and what some of them were able to do about it. Some were near the front lines. Most were too far away to find out for themselves

---

Notes for this chapter begin on page 350.

what had happened. Moreover, the sheer scale of the conflict made it difficult, if not impossible, to discover the whereabouts of individual soldiers, whether alive or dead, missing or at base camps, on leave or in transit. Mistakes proliferated.

Even when people were informed accurately that a man had been wounded, there was almost always a void of silence about what he had suffered and what were his chances of recovery. Into these silent spaces, fears and rumors flooded. The same silences attended the terse official messages about men who died in uniform.

As we shall see, some people were able to penetrate the maze and go to the bedside of a wounded man. Most were unable to do so. Instead, many different groups were formed to try to act on behalf of those who could not reach their loved ones, and to replace bureaucratic formulae by further information or by simple statements of fact. Some groups were officially sanctioned; most were private bodies of people committed to offering to those in mourning or unsure about the fate of their loved ones the only solace that they believed could help: the truth, or that part of it which could be confirmed.

Out of this effort to burn away the wartime fog of confusion, misinformation, and stylized official language, a set of organizations worked to find out what had happened to individual soldiers and thereby to link families at home with the men at the front and in captivity. The search for the fate of soldiers, and the effort to comfort the bereaved, created a kind of kinship bond among families in wartime and those who set about helping them. Everyone in mourning for a soldier was a victim of war, and to see the ways they were helped (and the ways they helped each other) enables us to appreciate the importance of kinship—familial or socially defined—in the process of coming to terms with bereavement in wartime.

From 1914 on, kinship bonds widened, through a process of informal or figurative "adoption." For a time, Red Cross volunteers, searchers, and officials *joined* the families of men at war. They stood as proxies for parents, wives, brothers and sisters, and expressed in a hundred ways what Meyer Fortes has described as the essence of kinship, a kind of "amity" or "artificial brotherhood" based on a "set of normative premises" of "prescriptive altruism," a "bond of moral obligation to help and support one another," "an ethic of generosity" parallel to early notions of "Christian charity."[2]

Consolation was a second objective of this broadened experience of kinship during and after the war. Helping people through the early days of their loss prepared the way for other forms of material assistance. The Protestant voluntary tradition came into its own in this effort, but Jewish and Catholic groups also worked to ease the plight of widows, orphans, and aged parents who had lost their sons in the war. Men who suffered mutilation or illness during the war needed long-term help, and joined in the wider population of victims of war who created and were served by such organizations. As in their search for information about individual soldiers in wartime, these groups tried to compensate for the shortcomings of central authorities, too mean or preoccupied to provide adequately for those whose circumstances were reduced by the war.

From consolation and support, it was a short step to commemoration. The bonds shared by those in mourning, by widows, ex-servicemen, the disabled, the young and the old alike, were expressed openly in ceremonies of collective memory. On Armistice Day and on other important dates on the calendar, groups and associations drew attention to the victims, both living and dead. Such efforts marked indelibly much of interwar communal life. In this essay we attend to some of these phenomena.

Discoveries

For families with someone in the army, waiting was an onerous and unavoidable reality. "Every day, every hour, ... they probe the unknown," wrote one Frenchman of parents during the war. The mother with her vacant stare, the father pacing, trying to convince himself that their son will be all right, were there in all combatant countries.[3] "Such distress, to know nothing, to be alone ... like a beast," were the despairing words of one woman who learned later that her husband would not return.[4]

When their wait was over, and the bad news came, it took many forms. In France the mayor received from the military authorities notification of the deaths in uniform of local residents. It was his duty to pass on the message to the family. On his way from the *mairie*, he or his deputy was watched from classrooms and alleyways by people young and old, glad to be passed by, apprehensive for those whom he sought.[5] In Britain, the message came by letter to the families of men in the ranks, by telegram to officers' families. Some messages arrived by telephone. Further afield, cables, sometimes supplemented by phone calls, were the rule. In Australia, clergymen delivered the news.

Delays in passing on the news of death on active service were inevitable. Some were lengthy. The family of the poet Wilfred Owen learned of his death one week after he was killed, as it happened, on Armistice Day. Their other son, Harold, was in the Royal Navy, on a ship off Africa. At sea, there was no way for him to learn what had happened until his mail caught up with him around Christmas, six weeks later. And yet Harold Owen says he knew before the family letter arrived, following a "vision" of Wilfred in his cabin one evening at sea, in December 1918.[6]

Those less telepathic had to await official notification. The problem was, though, that up to half of the men killed had no known grave; many people could go on doubting that their loved ones were indeed dead. When we consider as well how far flung were the families of those serving in the Great War, we begin to appreciate how scarce a commodity was verified evidence of life and death for millions of civilians all over the world.

Near the Front Lines

People who lived near the theaters of military operations had an option closed to those further afield. If notified in time, they could try to find their wounded and attend to them in hospital. The history of one British family able to be with their son before he died is a story of their good fortune. Worse off were those so far away that they had no chance to say good-bye or to engage in any material rite of passage on the spot. Where people lived is critical to understanding the different ways families and those around them confronted the loss of their loved ones.

When he joined the army in 1917, Malcolm Wakeman was an 18 year-old Mancunian, the son of a modestly prosperous building materials merchant. He had been an apprentice clerk at two Manchester banks and one insurance company, training to join his father's business. His course in wireless telegraphy in the Manchester Technical School came to an abrupt end when he was conscripted.[7] He joined the Royal Air Force and was commissioned as a flight observer in a two-man plane.

Wakeman was posted to France on 14 July 1918. He was an ordinary young man, without much imagination and full of schoolboy notions. He wrote to his family about the adventures of flying, and entertained them with a story of a crash landing, after which he and his pilot were picked up, brought to an officers' mess "where we had a jolly good dinner and a top pole lunch." He commented on how his plane caught some anti-aircraft fire, and how his co-pilot had to stand on the wing with his foot in a hole to stop petrol leaking. He was keen that his mother send him caramels and boiled sugar sweets.[8] His last letter, written on 1 October 1918, announced that "things are going absolutely OK."[9]

The next day Wednesday, 2 October, his plane was shot down on patrol near the German lines in the Ypres sector. The family in Manchester received this cable from the War Ministry four days later, at 1:30 p.m. on Sunday 6 October: "Regret to inform you that 2/Lt M.W. Wakeman Royal Air Force reported missing on October the Second Letter follows. Secretary Air Ministry." Around 8:30 the same day a second cable arrived: "Your son wounded head Doing well evacuated base OC 53rd Squadron."[10]

The Wakemans decided to travel to France immediately. They took the night train to London, then traveled by boat train to France. They reached the base hospital near Calais on Monday evening, and saw their son for an hour.[11] The doctors thought his head wounds were not life-threatening, and he had no other injuries. Remarkably, his plane had not exploded on crash-landing, though it was still carrying a full bomb load. Wakeman's co-pilot, Lt. Basil Pierce, had been killed, and the injured man asked his parents to inform Pierce's mother. This they agreed to do, because like the Wakemans, Mrs. Pierce had received initial notification only that her son was missing in action.[12] Reassured as to the prospects of Malcolm's recovery, Mr. Wakeman decided to return to England on Wednesday 9 October. Mrs. Wakeman remained with her son.[13]

On Thursday 10 October an x-ray revealed that a bullet was lodged in Malcolm Wakeman's skull. The wound was inoperable, but they still hoped for a slow recovery.[14] One week later, at 2 a.m. on 18 October, Mrs. Wakeman was telephoned to come to the hospital, about two miles from her hostel. Since no car was available, she had to walk through the rain with a Royal Army Medical Corps orderly to reach her son. She got to his bedside around 4 a.m. He had died about one hour before.[15] Later that day she cabled the news to her husband.[16] The military doctor asked her for permission to perform a post-mortem to provide some clues to help similarly wounded men in the future. She agreed, and saw the site of her son's grave. She then returned to England on Saturday 19 October.[17]

The funeral was held two days later, on Monday 21 October. Malcolm Wakeman was buried alongside an American officer. About 100 American servicemen saluted the two men. The chaplain who conducted the service, and who had attended Malcolm, added a personal note to the Wakemans. "Everything was done with all reverence. ... I was so touched by the calm devout spirit of your son—& I felt his loss more than that of any other whom I laid to rest out here, in sure and certain hope of the resurrection."[18]

After the funeral, Mrs. Wakeman was bedridden for a time. Her husband presented a more stoical front, and proceeded to try to tie up his son's affairs. This entailed an entirely unanticipated set of bureaucratic wrangles with the military. First came the matter of retrieving his son's effects. This took two months and three letters to achieve. Then came the correction of the date of death: the army had it as 20 October; the Wakemans knew better. This too was done after a delay.[19]

These minor irritations were bad enough for a bereaved couple. But what annoyed Wakeman most was that his request was denied for reimbursement of the fare of £8/12/8 he had paid to be with his son before he died. The Air Ministry were prepared to reimburse those too poor to pay provided they went in advance to their local police station. They thought Wakeman was not in this category. The bereaved father exploded. He was not a "convict" required to report to the police station; he had no time to comply with such rules before catching the night train to London. Furthermore, he was

> surprised at the Air Ministry trying to treat anyone in such a shabby & what I may say rather brutal manner. ... The sum I paid out was a big item for a man of modest resources & I should like to state that I am not one of those fortunate individuals who are highly paid for doing a little work in many of the Government Offices, and I have not gone about for the last few years with my eyes closed. I am engaged in business & unfortunately my trade has suffered very much during the war through lack of labor and my sales have amounted to only about half of the pre-war figure.

How can these people "lay down one law for the poor and another law for those people who are careful and try to pay their way & who are not 'Rich' nor are spongers on the public service for office." Threats to write to prominent figures followed. Two months later, he won the argument.[20]

Such callousness on the part of public servants did not deflect Wakeman from his belief that his son's death had been in a good cause. In the weeks and months following his son's death, he conducted a long correspondence with the mother of the co-pilot of his son's plane, and with other bereaved parents. "There is such a bond of emotion between us," wrote Mrs. Pierce, a bond felt by many other friends who had lost their sons in the war.[21] The family mourned together, and tried to help others in the same situation. Wakeman sent a two-franc piece to the orderly who had conducted his wife to the hospital on the rainy night his son had died.[22] He also sent serviette rings to the hospital, to mark the dedication of the sisters who attended his son. They too were part of the community of kindness helping those in mourning during and after the war. One nurse replied: "Tradition says that 'Time is a great healer'. If so Time will have her hands full for the next few years. This awful war has broken more than one heart and crippled more than one man."[23]

For Wakeman, the symbol of that extended family in mourning was the Royal Family. He treasured the royal cable expressing the grief of the King and Queen, and in language more direct than that he used to any of his neighbors and relatives, he opened his heart to his monarch. He told of the action in which his son was killed, quoted from his son's last letter, and enclosed his son's photograph. "You will see how serious and keen he looks." Speaking perhaps as one father to another, he continued:

> To myself & wife it is a real pleasure to have our Sovereign's telegram—*our loss is great, he was our only Son*—I have now no Son to succeed to my important chemical business, nor even to carry on the name of Wakeman.

This one story, repeated millions of times, tells us something of the initial stages of grief experienced by those in mourning for fallen soldiers during and after the war. The Wakemans were fortunate. They could act; they could try to help. And once their son had died, they tried to help others. Some bureaucratic problems were inevitable in wartime, but most people realized that if they were to find solace, the state or the army was not where they would find it. It was from their friends, their neighbors, sometimes their churches, their families that hope came. Together they formed a wide circle of those who knew the sorrow of war, and worked both then and in later years to lessen its bitterness.

The language that some used in speaking to the bereaved was euphemistic and elevated. But others, especially comrades in arms, took a different path. When they wrote to parents or widows, at times they told the truth, unvarnished and direct. A.S. Lloyd was a

British soldier killed on 8 August 1916. From the front, his friend Julian Yeatman described Lloyd's fatal injuries to Lloyd's mother:

> If I have wearied you with so many words at a time of stress, I am very sorry, but it is only fair that the parents of soldiers, the real sufferers from the war, should have some of these things which go to compensate.[24]

In Distant Lands: Supplementing the Story

What of the millions who lived too far from the front to have undertaken the Wakemans' journey? How did they react to the same bad news? There is abundant evidence of alternative ways in which families tried to help, or to confirm or supplement the official story.

One distant case reveals the basic elements of this search for details, a multi-national effort to find some shred of evidence about the men who had fallen. Here we can see the emergence of support groups dedicated to helping families grieve by telling them what had happened. Among the furthest removed from the main theaters of military operations were Australian families. Over 330,000 Australians served in the Australian Imperial Force. Of these, approximately 60,000 were killed or died on active service, a casualty rate at or above that suffered by the British, French, or German armies.[25] The fate of these men 12,000 miles from home at Gallipoli and in France was communicated to their families by clergymen,[26] who were notified by official cable, at an interval of about 10 to 14 days after the event. At times the delay was longer still. But as was the case elsewhere, the terse language of the army's formal regret was just the beginning of the quest for the "truth" about the men at the front. The truth they wanted was more detailed and in most cases less anodyne or strictly formal than the standard messages expressing official regret and noble thoughts.

The bereaved received two kinds of additional information. The first was a letter from an officer in the dead man's unit. This was slightly less stylized than the official communiqué. It was handwritten, but it usually contained three stock messages: the man in question was loved by his comrades; he was a good soldier; and he died painlessly.[27]

Whatever balm these words provided, most people knew that they were not wholly true and always incomplete. Bereaved parents, wives, siblings, children wanted to know more. Many yearned to share the last moments of their man; to know what he knew; and at least for a moment, to attempt to feel what he felt. This kind of identification with the fallen required a more human and to a degree more brutal disclosure of information than the state or the army provided.

Fellow soldiers and voluntary organizations often spoke a different language, and communicated a surprisingly vivid and disturbing set of images of combat and death to people in mourning during the First World War. For this reason, we must discount or qualify the argument that civilians did not know how awful trench warfare was.[28] They were *told* about it by those who were there, often in the immediate aftermath of learning that their father, husband, brother, son, friend, colleague had died at war.

Perhaps half of the men who died in action were unidentified or unidentifiable. Thousands simply disappeared. Even when remains were gathered together, the chaos and danger of the battlefield precluded the orderly recovery of bodies and identification tags. On Gallipoli, the site of a nine-month Allied landing in 1915, burial parties worked at night, in the dark. And for much of the period the heat was so intense that bodies quickly putrefied and stank. Burial details simply dumped the bodies into collective graves without retrieving identification tags. So tens of thousands of families were notified by cables indicating that their men were missing and presumed dead.[29]

That presumption left a huge gap for conjecture. What if the man was a prisoner of war? What if he was lost and wandering around the battlefield? What if he was wounded and in need of care? The families of missing men were put in an excruciatingly difficult position: aware that something dreadful had happened, but not able to identify how bad it was.

To help discover the truth, voluntary organizations were set up in many countries. Their natural model was the Red Cross, the accepted intermediary between combatants with special responsibility for prisoners of war.[30] We can follow these expressions of the "amity" of wartime "adoptive kinship" in a number of cases. One particularly active institution was the Australian Red Cross Information Bureaux, set up in 1915 in Melbourne, Sydney, and Adelaide, with offices in Cairo, Paris, and London. Their agents were the eyes and ears of the families at home, scouring the hospitals, base depots, war fronts, and prisoner of war camps for news of casualties and evidence of their survival or death.

We are very fortunate in that the voluminous records of one part of this organization have been preserved. This is the primary reason why it is useful at this point to concentrate on the Australian case. But it was not unique; the Red Cross had offices serving every combatant nation. What we see here is the outline of a story which could be (and should be) told from the point of view of civilians on both sides of the conflict.

Those who worked for the Red Cross came from many parts of Australian society. James (later Sir James) A. Murdoch was a prosperous retail trader in men's wear in Melbourne. In October 1915 he volunteered to serve with the Australian branch of the British Red Cross. He administered depots in Boulogne and Rouen before becoming Chief Commissioner of the Australian Red Cross in 1917.[31] He was surrounded by an array of soldiers and civilians whose job it was to cater to the needs of Australian soldiers and their families at home. The most energetic of them all was Vera Deakin, daughter of the prewar Prime Minister Alfred Deakin. She volunteered for Red Cross work in September 1915, and opened an enquiry office of the Red Cross in Cairo the day after she and her companion, Winifred Johnson, set foot in Egypt. The next year she moved to London and served as secretary of the central enquiry office in Victoria, just behind Buckingham Palace.[32]

Deakin returned to Australia in 1919, after three years of ceaseless work in London, to get at the truth about the fate of Australian soldiers. From 1 to 21 November 1916, for example, her office received 1,402 enquiries, and sent 1,036 cables to Australia, supported by 1,358 reports.[33] In 1917 the work load increased as casualties mounted. In that year, Deakin and her co-workers fielded approximately 4,000 enquiries per month. Her searchers sent in over 32,000 reports on missing soldiers. They traveled throughout Britain and scoured the Western Front. They handled 4,500 reports from officers, matrons, chaplains, and other soldiers.[34] They engaged in a substantial correspondence with the International Red Cross, and through them, with German authorities responsible for Prisoner of War camps. They quarreled with officers worried that censorship regulations were violated by direct communications between the Red Cross and the men in the ranks who could say whether or not a mate had been killed. Deakin testily replied that "the greater part of our work deals with unofficial information received direct from the men and naturally not within the scope of a battalion orderly room."[35] They wrangled with overworked medical officers, exasperated that tired nurses were troubled by Red Cross enquiries.[36] Deakin was steadfast. Her office would continue to ask for details concerning the last hours, deaths and burials of Australians, as we have had so many instance of the sisters or chaplains letters to the next of kin having gone astray, either owing to submarines or incorrect or old addresses.[37]

And they had the delicate task of deflecting problematic cases. One mother suspected foul play when her son died in a Turkish prisoner of war hospital 48 hours after contracting the "Spanish flu"; none was involved.[38] Another mother wrote about the whereabouts of her son, who had sent her a mysterious card in September 1917. The card read:

> I am a prisoner in Germany; wounded; first night I ran away to France, got hit, taken to Bruges. Do not know the name of place. Will meet you some day. Feeling weak. Trying to escape with a mate of mine. He is going to send this letter if possible. Fancy Christmas Day.

In fact he had been absent without leave since August.[39]

Most of their work was more serious. The real difficulty was squaring contradictory evidence concerning those missing in action. The wife of Corporal C.T. Owen wrote to Deakin from South Australia in September 1916. She had received a cable telling her that her husband had been wounded. A second cable arrived with the news that he had been wounded and was missing. The Red Cross investigated. Three soldiers reported three different stories: one said Owen had been killed at Pozières on the Somme; a second was sure he had been wounded but was in hospital in England; a third said he was a prisoner of war. To make matters worse, Mrs. Owen tracked down the soldier who testified to her husband's death. Back in Australia, he denied ever having said it. In this case, there was no resolution. Owen was one of thousands whose body was never found. He had vanished without a trace.[40]

Where final answers were established, and verified information was gathered, Deakin cabled the results to Australia, where they were forwarded to state headquarters. Red Cross workers on the spot then wrote to families, including verbatim, uncensored, and at times contradictory reports on the missing.

In the regional offices, the same diligent voluntary system provided the essential link between front and home front. In Adelaide, for example, in October 1915 a prominent solicitor, Sir Josiah Symon, appealed to the legal profession of the city to come forward and put their investigative experience at the disposal of the Red Cross. Their job was to link up with agents in every hospital in Egypt, Malta, or any other place where Australian soldiers were in treatment. They prepared lists of local men in military hospitals, provided families of those dying in hospitals with this fact, and searched for information on the missing and on others "for whom further enquiry is necessary." He told his colleagues that

> The object aimed is to assist in relieving the anxiety and suspense of the relatives and friends of our men at the front by collecting and communicating to those interested information as to their whereabouts and welfare, supplementing as much as possible the information which the Defence Department obtains, and receiving and dealing with specific enquiries whenever and as far as possible.[41]

The local enquiry office opened in January 1916, and provided a meeting point for anxious relatives and friends for the rest of the war.

Missing, Presumed Dead

They investigated three classes of cases: men who had vanished, presumed dead; wounded men; and prisoners of war. In the case of the missing, enquiries carried on throughout the war and occasionally well after the Armistice. Two ordinary cases illustrate this point. Pte J.A. Briggs disappeared at Pozières near Mouquet Farm on or around 10 August 1916. He was listed as missing on 28 September 1916. The Red Cross searchers found a soldier in Briggs' platoon who said he had been killed. His name was therefore added to the list of missing, presumed killed, and the change was communicated to Briggs' father in Western Australia on 3 January 1917. But the presumption still left room for doubt. Inquiries continued. The Red Cross wrote to one member of Briggs' unit for information to "enable us to satisfy his relations that no error had been made." The man confirmed that he had seen Briggs "cut in two by a shell" near Mouquet farm, while helping a wounded man out of the line. Then the Red Cross found Sergeant C.J. Drake, who had also served with Briggs. Drake was in a German prisoner of war camp in Soltau. He wrote to the Red Cross in November 1917 about Briggs:

> He was my best pal and I have tried everywhere to find out all I can about him. ... I do not think there is any chance of the poor boy turning up but if I happen to hear anything of him in this country I will let you know at once.[42]

Briggs' body was never found, but his fate was determined beyond a reasonable doubt.

Similar efforts were made by the Red Cross on behalf of the family of two brothers killed on the same day, also in the Pozières sector of the Somme. Four days after Pte Briggs had vanished, on 14 August 1916, both Pte Stephen Charles Allen and Pte Robert Beattie Allen, serving in the 13th Battalion of the AIF disappeared. A few weeks earlier, Stephen Allen had sent his mother a poppy growing in his sap. In the files of the Australian War Memorial, the poppy is still there, pressed into the letter.[43] By mid-August, there was no trace of either man. In March 1917, the commanding officer in the Allens' unit, Captain J. Wills, wrote to Mrs. Allen that there was a faint possibility that her boys were alive and in a prisoner of war camp.[44] The Red Cross investigated. They found Will Hale, a man wounded in the same operation that cost the Allen brothers their lives. Hale had also served there with his own brother, who had been wounded as well. This is what he told the Red Cross, and repeated in a letter of June 1917 to the Allens' sister:

> I seen a good lot of your Brothers from the time I met them, and was not more than five yards off when the shell caught us. Your two poor Brothers were between my Brother and I. When the shell exploded I knew by the screams that someone had caught it. I could not get through for some time, as I was half silly through the shock. However when I could get through, my brother was seriously wounded, and your to Brothers were laying there, they had been shifted, because when I was returning to the front line again I could not see them. My brother is having a rough time he is still in Hospital, he cannot walk but gets about on crutches as best he can. I expect he will be home in a few months time. I am pretty well again my hand is not much good to me at the present but I have hopes that in time it will come alright.[45]

In August 1917, another soldier in the 13th Battalion wrote to Mrs. Allen that "Bob was blown up by a shell."[46] Formal certificates of death were issued on 25 September 1917, more than a year after the men had vanished, but still enquiries continued.[47]

We can see here most of the elements of adoptive or informal kinship ties: the extension of the family searching for evidence about the disappeared brother; the essential liaison role of the Red Cross in that effort; and the painstaking work of finding reliable evidence of the fate of the men long after official death certificates were issued. This band of men and women kept hope alive as long as they could. But when they found evidence that pointed towards the unavoidable conclusion that the men had been killed, that evidence was transmitted verbatim to the families affected.

This openness can be confirmed by examining the case records of the South Australia branch of the Red Cross. Cpl K.C. Moore of the 52nd Battalion of the AIF was lost near Bullecourt on 11 April 1917. In October, Moore's brother was told by the Red Cross that there was no trace of the man. It was possible he was a prisoner of war. But, the Red Cross went on, three of Moore's fellow soldiers reported that he was killed on 11 April. One said Moore "by mistake had walked into the German trenches." The family was given the full text of the reports; the testimony slips correspond exactly to the text of the letter sent to the family. The Red Cross added

> We regret that the foregoing reports are contradictory and that no definite tidings have been obtained. However we thought you would be anxious to have every particular which comes to hand. Our Commissioners will continue this enquiry and immediately we obtain any further tidings whatever, we will again communicate with you as we understand a little of your great anxiety.

Still the confusion went on. On 21 November, another soldier told the Red Cross that Moore had been taken prisoner, but the weight of evidence was solidly against the family's hope that he had survived. The formal death notice was delivered in early 1918, but searches continued among prisoner-of-war files in Germany after the Armistice. Nothing ever turned up. This too was communicated to the family.[48]

This straightforwardness was not exceptional. F.L. Donnelly was killed on 8 August 1918. The family received the report of the man who had carried him from the field "after he had been hit in the back by an explosive bullet. He died on the way out on the stretcher."[49] The family of Cpl L. Marks was told that three distinct witnesses confirmed that his head was blown off by a shell, and that he had been killed "instantaneously."[50]

However harsh the imagery, it conveyed reality and finality. Less fortunate were the parents of the missing, whose fate was uncertain. Here too the truth was not obscured by lofty language or delicate euphemisms. Pte J.R. Skinner was lost at Lone Pine on Gallipoli on 6 August 1915. His Sergeant, T. Pestell, gave this account to the Red Cross, which it passed on to Skinner's family. Pestell himself had been shot through the neck and was unconscious. He woke to find Skinner next to him, shot in the right breast; "a gaping wound showed there. ... His case was a very bad one, his eyes were protruding almost as if in death."[51] Two days later Pte D. James also disappeared on Gallipoli. One comrade told the Red Cross that he fell away from the Turkish lines. "It was terrible, the men were falling like rabbits. Many were calling out for Mothers and Sisters.' James' body was never found.[52]

Occasionally, the Red Cross went out of its way to help the bereaved to learn of the final days of fallen soldiers whose graves were known. This was most likely in the case of prominent soldiers in well-documented encounters. Lt Col Ernest Brown was killed on Gallipoli in the August 1915 charge at Lone Pine. The progression from official language to fuller information is evident in the correspondence Brown's widow received. First came the cable to the local clergyman, the Rev. Newmark, instructing him, a week after Brown's death, to "convey deep regrets and sympathy of the Commonwealth government."[53] Then, the following week came the condolences of one of the officers in Brown's unit, the 3rd Battalion. "After all", Major Gallagher wrote, "it is a glorious thing to die for one's country and loved ones: that is really what we are fighting for."[54] Four weeks later came a factual report from another man serving on Gallipoli. He told the widow

> It appears that he was first injured in the head by a shot which affected his mind, and shortly after he was killed outright in leading a charge of his men: I give you these details from a reliable source, which you can depend on.[55]

Other accounts, with additional details, followed.[56]

This case was unusual, in that it involved a high-ranking officer in a highly publicized encounter, out of which legends quickly grew.[57] The fact that the dead man was a professional soldier also separated his story from that of the volunteers who fell around him. This lay behind Major Gallagher's noble rhetoric. But even here, in this special case, we observe the two important parts of the work of the Red Cross. It served as a conduit for information on all victims of war, and helped the local community support those in mourning.

Other Casualties: The Wounded and Prisoners of War

Locating the sick and the wounded was a second facet of the work of the Red Cross. Families receiving notification of casualties were rarely told initially the nature and seriousness of the injury or where the soldier was being treated. Once he was located they had a chance of finding out how bad the situation was.

Again, those in close proximity to the front had a hard time in locating their men, but people further afield were in an impossible situation. The Red Cross tried to act on their behalf.

A "poor washerwoman" in South Australia was "heartbroken" to learn that her son, Pte P.W. Kyloh, was wounded in action in 1915. Friends (presumably her employers) wrote to the Red Cross on her behalf, and paid the costs of the enquiry. She was lucky. Red Cross searchers found her son in a British hospital. He had a serious back wound.[58] Other parents sought similar information time and again during the war. As soon as possible, the Red Cross passed on the news that soldiers were recovering in hospital.[59] At times, this information happily superseded erroneous notifications of death in action.[60]

After the dead and the wounded, the third group under the scrutiny of the Red Cross were prisoners of war. Here the institution fulfilled its traditional intermediary role. First, it informed the families of prisoners of their safety, health, and whereabouts. One of Vera Deakin's co-workers, Miss M.E. Chomley, ran the prisoners' desk of the Australian Red Cross office in London. In May 1917 she found an Australian soldier, Pte E.H. Dowd, in the list of prisoners of war in Minden camp. She wrote to Dowd that she had informed his wife, and hoped thereby "to relieve her anxiety." A year later he was still in captivity. His wife wrote to Chomley that Dowd "is suffering very much from nervous breakdown and I fear is in a very bad state of health." The best the Red Cross could do was to ensure that regular parcels arrived, with an assortment of tea, sugar, milk, raisins, jam, cigarettes, soap, cornflour, beef, sausages, cheese, and lentils. Shoes were provided too, but getting the right size was a hit or miss operation.[61] The Red Cross pressed the Germans to exchange this wounded prisoner, but he was released only after the Armistice.[62]

The Red Cross also pressed Turkish authorities to release wounded prisoners of war. Pte T.H. Dowell was a wounded Australian held in a Constantinople hospital. His leg and knee were mangled at Lone Pine in 1915. Two years later he was still in captivity. He wrote to Miss Chomley in March 1917.

> Is it possible for you to do anything to help the exchange along? There are some of us here who greatly need good doctors to attend to us. My own wound has broken out again after six months at the camp. And there are two other Australians here who are just as bad.[63]

Chomley passed on the request, but nothing happened. They despaired. Dowell wrote his sister that "another year in this country would just about see me off."[64] The only thing that Miss Chomley could do was to try to keep his spirits up by ensuring that parcels would arrive and that friends would write to him. She chided one former prisoner friend of Dowell: "I dare say you remember what it feels like to be cut off from the world and your friends."[65] She tried to celebrate Anzac day—commemorating the Australian landing at Gallipoli on 25 August 1915—with Dowell by letter in 1918.[66] And she kept Dowell's family informed about his condition.

Dowell made it. He was released after the Armistice and sailed to Australia on 15 November 1918, profoundly grateful to those who remembered him and pressed his case for freedom.[67] All prisoners of war were painfully aware that thousands of others had been less fortunate. They died in camps and were buried in Germany or the Middle East. Here too the Red Cross served as their surrogate family, ensuring (in so far as they could) that they be buried with dignity and that their families be notified as soon as possible.[68] Given the numbers involved and the chaos of the last months of the war and the first months of peace, it was inevitable that some families waited for years in hope, and in vain, with their hopes dashed long after the Armistice. Pte C.P. Down died in Germany in a prisoner of war camp on 23 March 1917. The Red Cross received documentation of his date and place of burial only in October 1919. Then and only then did his family in Australia receive notification of their son's death.[69]

In each of these cases, we can see how voluntary workers assisted families to cope with the anxieties of war. I have chosen one particular case, that of the Australian Red Cross, but it can stand for support networks which sprang up in every combatant country. Nothing was easy in this work, but the most straightforward tasks entailed helping the wounded or imprisoned either materially or in keeping in touch with their families. Second, the Red Cross opened channels through which the families of men thousands of miles from home sought information and received it, even when it was painful. Not to know was worse than finding the truth. This was also at the heart of the hardest job of all: to shrink the massive lists of men missing, presumed dead, by finding those who had seen what had happened. Only with such confirmation could families escape from the shadows of uncertainty. To help them do so was one face of humanity in war.

Consolation and Support

The meaning of "adoptive kinship" as "Christian charity" in the original sense of the term, [70] is evident in the work of groups and individuals who helped those whose lives were damaged by the war: the disabled, widows, and orphans. What could be done for these people was limited. For some the state of medical science and the character of injury made recovery either very long-term or impossible. But even those who could return to a full productive life faced massive material problems of reintegration and retraining. While state support was given to these victims of war, it was almost always inadequate to cover the hidden (and not so hidden) costs of rehabilitation. The army of the disabled was too large; the limits on state expenditure were too restrictive. Some groups organized to defend their interests and extract from the state a level of adequate or decent treatment initially denied to them. Most had to look to their own resources, to their families, and to their "adoptive kin" for a hand on the road to recovery. What those who helped could do was strictly limited, but that fact should not obscure the humanity of what they did.

Mutilés de Guerre

In every year between the wars, men died of wounds or disease contracted on active service. Mourning began for many, after years of caring for ex-servicemen. Most of this repetitive and entirely unglamorous service happened within families; virtually all of it went unrecorded. Sometimes the disabled were cared for by friends. Charles Berg was an Australian soldier who enlisted at the age of 19. He saw service at Gallipoli and in France, and was wounded in the spine by shrapnel. His mother died shortly after he returned home. For 17 years he was cared for by a neighboring couple, Mr. and Mrs. J. Semple, who did what they could "with unremitting kindness" to help a man who, throughout his life, "hardly knew what it was to be free from pain."[71] This was not an isolated case. In 1940, a Lambeth woman, Elizabeth Grace, answered an enquiry about an Australian man who had died in England as a result of war injuries.

> Robert Rae came to us during the war with a friend of ours from Australia. He spent all his sick leave with us and after the war was over made his home with us. My husband and I treated him as one of the family as he had a wounded arm and weak lungs and was advised not to go back to Australia till he was stronger. He passed away in Colindale Hospital with lung troubles through the effects of gas on Jan. 17, 1924.[72]

Care of this kind cannot be valorized. It went on unrewarded and in many cases unnoticed in millions of households after the war. All of these families needed material assistance; rarely did they receive what they needed. The history of the struggle for adequate war pensions has been told elsewhere.[73] For our purposes, what emerges from this story is the strength of the bonds forged among the wounded and disabled themselves.

These ties emerged during the war itself. In 1916 a French association of the disabled started to publish a newspaper with the following title: the *Journal des mutilés, réformés et victimes de guerre*. It broadcast the existence of a host of local groups, under the sponsorship of mayors or prefects. Out of this activity came a large national organization. The first congress of war wounded met at the Grand Palais in Paris on 11 November 1917. Delegates named by 125 societies representing 125,000 disabled men were there.[74] In the years that followed, a myriad of societies sprang up in towns, villages, and cities to voice the demands and aspirations of these men and the millions of others who joined them. One of the most poignant of such groups was the association of disfigured men, those with face wounds so terrible that they bought their own property for collective holidays and rest.[75]

Most of these groups were entirely local in character, and many represented small town, *petit bourgeois* aspirations for an escape from political or class conflict through the perpetuation of the camaraderie of the trenches, the spirit of social solidarity they had known in the army.[76] These groups were inclusive: they spoke for all victims of war, not just old soldiers. This is reflected in the baroque name of one of the largest French organizations: the *Union Fédérale des associations françaises des mutilés, réformés, anciens combattants de la grande guerre, de leur veuves, orphelins, ascendents*. The president of this organization, Gaston Vidal, a teacher, journalist, and officer, wounded several times, winner of the Croix de guerre with nine citations, was a man who loved his country and hated war. No jingoism here, just the vision of a man who believed, as he told a Marseilles audience in May 1919, that "the voice of the dead speaks for all the widows, the parents, the orphans they left behind."[77] "What affects widows, affects us all," he wrote in June 1919.[78]

Many activists in this movement had no illusions as to the evanescence of adequate public support for their cause. One wounded man spoke out at a meeting of war wounded in Nancy as early as April 1916. He said, "Today we are welcome, but after the war no one will speak of us and work will be hard to find."[79]

This unknown soldier's words were prophetic. It is true that the victory parade on Bastille Day 1919 was led by the *mutilés de guerre*.[80] But over time, the honor due to the wounded and the infirm became more rhetorical than real. The nations remembered; but words could not feed the victims or their families. For their survival, they could look only to themselves and the groups of "fictive kin" which rallied around them. This was as true of German or Austrian veterans as it was of the British, the French, or any of the vast army of officially recognized *mutilés de guerre*, estimated by the International Labour Organization as numbering ten million men in 1923. This is probably an underestimate.[81]

Widows and Orphans

Perhaps three million of the nine million men killed in the war left widows behind. If British figures are an indication of the approximate size of these young families, each widow had two small children to look after. Six million children were deprived of their fathers by the First World War.[82] How did they mourn and what became of them?

In most cases we shall never know. What was mourning like for Flora Kennedy-Smith, an Australian woman twice widowed by the war: first in 1916, through the death of her first husband in France; then in 1933, when her second husband passed away, a victim of his war wounds?[83] And what could have lifted the spirits of Elsie Bennett, whose father enlisted after a furious row with his wife, who shamed him into joining up? Bennett was killed in 1917 at the age of 37. His wife was never forgiven by the family for his death. In Elsie Bennett's school, a Thanksgiving service was organized on Armistice Day. When the National Anthem was played, Elsie refused to stand up. The headmaster asked why. "All the other little boys' and girls' Daddies would be coming home now; but her Daddy would never come home again." She was caned for disobedience.[84]

We must not overestimate the appeal of fictive kinship for victims of war. Callousness and compassion were both in evidence in the postwar years. But even when kindness replaced such brutality, most people could do nothing to shield widows and orphans from the harshness of their fate.

Before the war, widowhood meant poverty for the mass of the population.[85] War widows were in an even more unfavorable situation. After 1914, millions of women faced a bleak financial future as a result of the death of their husbands in military service, despite the provision of state widows' pensions in all combatant countries. These entitlements followed the provision of wartime separation allowances, money payments to wives made by the state as the surrogate wage-earning husband.[86]

It is true that war pensions extended significantly the notion of welfare as a right rather than a privilege. This was of particular importance in the long-term history of pensions, especially in France and Britain.[87] In the short-term, though, money payments in the form of widows' pensions rarely reached average wage levels. In addition, such transfer payments were reduced drastically in real terms by rampant price inflation.[88] In 1916, the widow of a private soldier killed in the German army received 33.30 marks per month. The *average* monthly wage for a skilled worker on the eve of the war was between 120 and 150 marks.[89] Though inflation, especially after 1916, was more savage in Germany than on the Allied side, war widowhood almost always meant deprivation or poverty.

The scale of the problem was so vast that no one dreamt it could be remedied through state action alone. In Germany, for example, there were approximately 525,000 war widows and over one million war orphans in 1920.[90] According to one survey of war widows in Darmstadt at the end of the 1920s, whatever level of public assistance they received, the income of most of these women was lower than it would have been if their husbands had lived *and* remained employed. The unemployment crisis in Berlin in the early 1920s[91] and in all of Germany later in the decade made such comparisons highly academic, but the inference to be drawn was clear. The state was in no position to prevent widows and children from suffering distress after the war.

In many ways the "victors" were no better off. Pension levels never approximated wage levels. Furthermore, distress came in many forms, all of them bleak. Private Albert Claydon was a British soldier killed in 1918. His widow Kate, with two young daughters to raise alone, suffered a nervous breakdown shortly after the war. She died in an Epsom mental hospital in 1974.[92] In such cases, it is impossible to separate the impact of war from longer-term instabilities. But even emotionally robust widows faced daunting problems in trying to rebuild their lives.

The gap between what the state could or would provide and what war widows and their families needed to survive was covered irregularly and partially by a host of voluntary institutions during and after the war. In Britain, the Soldiers and Sailors' Families Association carried on very much in the spirit of Victorian philanthropy.[93] In Germany, the bewilderingly complex system of welfare provision was administered largely by municipal authorities and charitable organizations at the local level.[94] In France, a host of charities, many Catholic, did what they could.

On 15 March 1917, an assembly of 14 French organizations in aid of war orphans convened in Paris. In this period, "orphan" usually meant a child whose father had died. Speakers drew attention to these children's plight, treated with greater urgency, according to Françoise Thébaud, than that of their mothers.[95] In fact, because the vast majority of children whose fathers died on active service were very young,[96] there was no way to separate the problems of widows and orphans during and after the war.

To try to compensate in part for official parsimony and perpetuate the wartime community of shared sacrifice, many other groups emerged to help widows and children in the spirit of "fictive kinship." This may be described succinctly with reference to one of the most enduring of such groups. *Legacy* was (and is) an association of Australian veterans, dedicated to perpetuating the spirit of mutual assistance fostered by the men who had volunteered for the first AIF. General Sir John Gellibrand was instrumental in setting up a "Remembrance Club" in Hobart, Tasmania, in March 1923. The club was dedicated to "reviving the old comradeship and esprit de corps of the A.I.F." and to render "mutual assistance" to members in business and other matters.[97] A few months later in Melbourne a "Legacy Club" was founded by discharged former soldiers. A former sapper, Frank Doolan, was acting secretary, and devoted himself to promoting the cause of helping war orphans.[98] By 1925 a consensus had emerged that these groups, and others like them, should dedicate themselves to looking after the children of dead comrades, something many had already been doing. As the official historian of the AIF, C.E.W. Bean put it, they knew that

> a field of great importance was the care, guidance and encouragement of the families of those comrades who, through death, were themselves no longer there to give those benefits. ... In a great many cases someone was needed to act virtually as guardian and sponsor, with the thought, help and advice that our dead comrade would have given.[99]

By 1926 a national association had emerged. The Melbourne branch formed a Boys' Club, with "a membership of 175 boys, all sons of deceased soldiers." It helped sponsor a cafeteria for daughters of dead soldiers attending the East Sydney Technical College, and organized "motor picnics" for 150 wives and children of fallen comrades.[100] Orphans were placed in apprenticeships. A "big brother movement" took charge of English war orphans coming to Australia.[101] By the 1930s, *Legacy* helped young people find jobs in a very inclement economic climate.[102]

By assisting these children, ex-soldiers both eased the burden war widows faced and helped rebuild family life. These former soldiers self-consciously tried to repay the debt they owed to their fallen comrades. But the damage inflicted by the war was so deep that such manifestations of "fictive kinship," while admirable, could not eliminate the problems faced by millions of families.

Consider the case of two war widows. Their husbands succumbed years after the Armistice to war-related infirmities. They thus became widows after many years of caring for disabled men. For two decades, Mrs. Rebecca Hinds, a Tasmanian woman, looked after her disabled husband Joseph, who finally died of his wounds in Sydney in April 1941. With no savings, and with a bare £2.2.0 a week as war pension, she was unable to keep up payments on her home. When asked by the Australian War Memorial to verify her husband's particulars, so that his name could be accurately inscribed on his country's roll of honor, she mused:

> I have filled in the enclosed form as you requested. But at the same time I am not in favour of all this kind of thing, as we wives and mothers do not need them to remind us of those we have lost. I think it would be more fitting to put the money to better use for those that are living and finding it hard to live these days. ... Why worry over the dead, I'm sure they would not wish it, if they only knew just how we who are left are treated.
> They gave their lives 'tis true and I often wonder what for?[103]

Mrs. Hinds' case may have been extreme; there is no record of *Legacy* or similar groups coming to the rescue. In any event, she was not alone in facing adversity after the death of a war invalid she had spent much of her life nursing. Violet Selma Aiken's husband Harry served in the Australian army. He died in England in 1928. His wife wrote that he was

> a long sufferer from his war injuries ... and was nursed the last 18 months night & day in our little home here by myself after he had been in many hospitals & sanitoriums in France and United Kingdom. I am proud to be his widow but regret that because I live in the mother country I have since 1932 had my 9/- a week stopped from my war widow's pension. I am told it is the exchange rate that is the cause of this. It is a struggle to live in these times. ... I appreciate my husband's name being erected on the "Hall of Memory" immensely but what about those left behind?[104]

What indeed? These letters hint at the grim world of uncertainty and precariousness faced by most war widows without independent means. They also highlight the link, and occasional clash, between the lofty phrases enjoining everyone to remember the dead and the harsher official treatment of their survivors. Local charity and benevolence healed some of these wounds; others remained unattended.

Commemoration

So far I have presented aspects of the work of men and women in several countries to help soldiers and their families through the chaotic days of the war and the difficult period of adjustment to postwar life. I have used the notion of "fictive kinship" to describe such efforts at truth-telling and solidarity. A third area in which such bonds are evident is in wartime and postwar commemoration. Here I offer some preliminary remarks on the ways commemoration and mourning were inextricably entwined.

War memorials are collective symbols. They speak to and for communities of men and women. Commemoration also happened on a much more intimate level, through the preservation in households of possessions, photographs, personal signatures of the dead. That is why it mattered so much to parents to retrieve the kit of their sons after notification of their deaths.[105]

Comrades in arms often wrote to widows and parents, often offering condolences and memories in equal part. One British soldier engaged in a long correspondence with the widow of his officer, Alan Lloyd. A year after Lloyd's death, Gunner Manning sent Mrs. Lloyd the following poem about her husband:

In Memoriam

A year has passed since that sad day
When God called my dear friend away
God took him home
It was his will
Forget him. No I never will.

O how I miss you dear friend
I often wish that you were here
When trials come and friends are few
Dear friend O how I long for you.

Mrs. Lloyd sent parcels to her dead husband's unit, and followed the fortunes of these men after the war. Manning told her of his troubles. One of his brothers had been killed; another was a prisoner of war in Germany; a third, bedridden, "with no hope of recovery." He would "never go down mine again"; and seemed resigned to an arranged marriage. He hoped to open a pub in Manchester.[106] There is the whiff of class difference about this correspondence, but it reveals also the notion that mourning for the same man created a strong bond between the two.

Those who went on pilgrimages to war cemeteries and sacred sites—Verdun, Ypres, Langemark—also developed affinities with parents, widows, sons and daughters like themselves, who were there to remember the dead. Mr. and Mrs. Wakeman returned to their son's grave in France in 1923. They took advantage of the services of the "St Barnabas Hostels," simple hostleries not very different from the ones they had stayed in five years before. This organization was founded in 1919, after it was apparent that help was needed for the "many Pilgrims miles from their hotels, vaguely wandering about in search of cemeteries and with no sign-posts to guide them thereto."[107] Instead of charging as much as £35, as one London travel bureau did for a visit to Loos, St Barnabas did so, first for £14, and by 1923, for £4.0.0. The Wakemans, like other pilgrims, were met at Calais by a St Barnabas "lady worker." The organization noted that "the tact and sympathy of these unselfish women has soothed many a Sorrowing Pilgrim, and brought a glimmer of peaceful sunshine into many a desolate and lonely heart." They were then conducted by car to the cemetery, and returned to a small hotel in time for their return the following day to England. Similar journeys could be made to the cemeteries of the Somme and Ypres, beginning in 1924, facilities were available to conduct pilgrims to Gallipoli, Palestine, and Italy. A fund for those who could not pay even this modest fee enabled 2,000 "poor relations" to visit their sons in 1923 alone.[108]

The history of the pilgrimage movement is a subject worthy of a book in itself.[109] For our purposes, what matters most is the way it drew upon and added to the kinship bonds already forged by war victims and their families. Those who made the journey (for many both physically and emotionally difficult), did so in the company of others like them, who knew what it meant to mourn fallen soldiers. Kipling's short story "The Gardener" speaks of this community of people in mourning. So does Abel Gance's film *J'Accuse*, set in 1937 among the countless graves at Douaumont. And so too does Käthe Kollwitz's timeless war memorial, for her son in Vladslo, Belgium.. In this community, men were not privileged over women. Indeed, the imagery of mothers on pilgrimage tending the graves of their sons is at least as present and certainly as powerful as that of General Plumer, in 1927, telling each set of parents, visiting the Menin Gate in Ypres, 'He is not missing. He is here'.[110]

One final example may point to the union of such people in an even wider community of suffering and solace. As Annette Becker has shown, after the war one Parisian parish priest, Abbé Alfred Keller, dedicated himself to creating a manifestation of Catholic compassion for "humanity in distress." He sponsored a housing project for poor families, each of which "adopted" a dead soldier of the Great War. They were unrelated formally, but the dead man's name was placed over the door of each apartment. In the courtyard is a chapel decorated by murals painted by Desvallières. The murals portray the soldier's war as the way of the Cross.[111] This "Cité de souvenir," dedicated in 1934, still stands in a quiet street in the 14th *arrondissement* of Paris. Over the gate is the following inscription: "To honour the dead by an act of life and so that large families can adopt them" ["une descendance adoptive"].[112] Here dwell the living and the dead, children born after the war, and young men who never had the chance to know the fullness of family life. This instance of fictive kinship in a Catholic form illustrates my central theme: the powerful, perhaps essential, tendency of ordinary people, of many faiths and of none, to face the emptiness, the nothingness of loss in war together.

Notes to Chapter 14

1. I am grateful to Ken Inglis for discussions on this point. The literature on this subject is vast. For a start, see the classics: Sigmund Freud, "Mourning and Melancholia," in *Collected Papers*, trans. by Joan Riviere (London, Hogarth Press, 1950), iv, pp. 152–70; M. Klein, "Mourning and its relationship to manic-depressive states," *International Journal of Psychoanalysis*, xxi (1940); J. Bowlby, 'Processes of mourning', *International Journal of Psychoanalysis*, xliv (1961); J. Bowlby, 'Pathological mourning and childhood mourning', *Journal of the American Psychoanalytic Association*, xi (1963). For syntheses see C.M. Parkes, *Bereavement. Studies of Grief in Adult Life* (London, Tavistock Publications, 1972); C.M. Parkes and R.S. Weiss, *Recovery from Bereavement* (New York, Basic Books, 1983); G. Gorer, *Death, grief and mourning in contemporary Britain* (London, Cresset, 1965); B. Schoenberg *et al.* (eds), *Bereavement: its psychosocial aspects*

(New York, Columbia University Press, 1975); Horowitz, Mardi J., 'A model of mourning: change in schemas of self and other', *Journal of the American Psychoanalytical Association*, xxxviii, 2 (1990), pp. 297–324.
2. Meyer Fortes, *Kinship and the social order. the legacy of Lewis Henry Morgan* (Chicago, Aldine, 1969), pp. 241, 251, 110, 123, 239. For the distinction between blood kinship, fictive kinship and figurative kinship, see Julian Pitt-Rivers, 'The kith and the kin', in J. Goody (ed.), *The Character of Kinship* (Cambridge, Cambridge University Press, 1973). For other approaches to the subject, see Ernest Gellner, 'Ideal language and kinship structure', *Philosophy of Science*, xxiv (1957), pp. 235–41; Rodney Needham, 'Descent systems and ideal language', *Philosophy of Science*, xxvii (1960), pp. 96–101; Gellner, 'The concept of kinship', *Philosophy of Science*, xxvii (1960), pp. 187–204; Maurice Bloch, 'The moral and tactical meaning of kinship terms', *Man*, vi (1971), pp. 79–87. I am grateful to Dr Barbara Bodenhorn for drawing my attention to these references.
3. Jacques Garmier, *Homage à mon ombre* (Macon, Protat Frères, 1916), pp. 11, 21.
4. Jane Catulle-Mendes, *La prière sur l'enfant mort*, as cited in Françoise Thébaud, 'La guerre et le deuil chez les femmes françaises', Colloque sur l'histoire culturelle comparée de la première guerre mondiale, Historial de la grande guerre, Péronne, Somme, July 1992, p. 8.
5. Pierre-Jakez Helias, *Le cheval d'orgueil. Memoires d'un Breton du pays bigoudin* (Paris, Plon, 1975), pp. 8–9. See also the reference to the sad announcement in J. Giono, *Le grand troupeau* (Paris, Gallimard, 1931).
6. Harold Owen, *Journey from Obscurity* (Oxford, Oxford University Press, 1968), pp. 232–4.
7. Imperial War Museum, Wakeman Papers 67/305/1 (hereafter WP), Malcolm Wakeman to Capt E.F. Falkner, recruiting officer, Town Hall, Manchester, 2.3.17.
8. WP, Malcolm Wakeman to parents, 24.7.18; 10.8.18; 17.8.18.
9. WP, Malcolm Wakeman to parents, 1.10.18
10. WP, Cables dated 6.10.18 and 7.10.18; the time of receipt identified from Miss Waken to Mrs Pierce, 8.10.18.
11. WP, Wakeman to G. Hickling, 22.10.18.
12. WP, Wakeman to Mrs Pierce, 10.10.18.
13. WP, Cable, Wakeman to family 'Malcolm cheerful. Home tomorrow. Wakeman'.
14. WP, Mrs Wakeman to Wakeman, 17.10.18 and 18.10.18.
15. WP, Wakeman to F.W. Anthony, 22.10.18; Wakeman to Marion Kate Winser, 23.10.18.
16. WP, Cable 1.10.18.
17. WP, Wakeman to Couther, 22.10.18.
18. WP, Chaplain Beadle to Wakeman, 21.10.18.
19. WP, Letter of Wakeman to Air Ministry 29.20.18, 5.11.18, 4.12.18, 29.12.18.
20. WP, Wakeman to Air Ministry, 16.12.18, 31.12.18; Air Ministry to Wakeman, 30.12.18, 27.1.19.
21. WP, Mrs Pierce to Wakeman, 7.11.18; Mrs Helen Eright to Wakeman, 19.10.18; Hilda Trotter to Wakeman, 23.10.18.
22. WP, Wakeman to Private W.R. Osborn, 29.10.18.
23. WP, Sister Alice Collinge to Wakeman, 21.11.18.
24. Imperial War Museum, A.S. Lloyd papers, R. Julian Yeatman to Mrs Lloyd, 10.8.16.
25. For full information, see the data-base prepared by Peter Dennis and Jeff Grey of the Australian Defence Forces Academy, Canberra.

26. This was not the case in Britain, where the cable came unadorned. I am grateful to Michael McKernan of the Australian War Memorial for help on this point.
27. The examples are legion in both the Imperial War Museum and Australian War Memorial collections.
28. For further support in the French case for the argument that front and home front were closely linked, see Stéphane Audoin-Rouzeau, *Men at war. Trench journalism and national sentiment in France 1914–1918* (Oxford, Berg, 1992).
29. Mortlock Library of South Australia, Adelaide. Red Cross papers, (hereafter RCPA), SRG 76/32, Papers on establishment of Australian Red Cross Society Information Bureau, suggestion of Mr Hackett, n.d.
30. On the earlier history of the Red Cross, see R. Durand and J. Meurant (eds), *Préludes et pionniers. Le précurseurs de la Croix-Rouge 1840–1860* (Geneva, Société Henry Dunant, 1991). I am grateful to F.B. Smith for drawing my attention to this collection. See also P. Boissier, *Histoire du Comité international de la Croix-Rouge. t.1. De Solférino à Tsoushima* (Paris, Plon, 1963); André Durand, *Histoire du Comité international de la Croix-Rouge. t.2. De Sarajevo à Hiroshima* (Geneva, Institut Henry-Dunant, 1978); Geoffrey Best, *Humanity in Warfare* (London, Hutchinson, 1980).
31. Australian War Memorial, Canberra. Red Cross Papers (hereafter RCPC) 1 DRL/428, Report of the work of the Australian Red Cross, Jan. 1917, p. 19.
32. RCPC, 1 DRL/428, Miss L.A. Whybrow to the editor, *British Australasian*, 23.4.19.
33. RCPC, 1 DRL/428, Wounded and missing Inquiry Bureau, Report, 1–21 November 1916.
34. RCPC, 1 DRL/428, Report for 1916–17.
35. RCPC, 1 DRL/428 Deakin to Lt Col. Scott, 56th Bn AIF, 9.8.17.
36. RCPC, 1 DRL/428, Major Brambury to Deakin, 15.9.16.
37. RCDC, 1 DRL/428, Deakin to Miss Schofield, sister in charge, 20th Casualty Clearing Station, BEF, 25.7.18.
38. RCPC, 1 DRL/427, Mrs G. Marriott to Miss Whybrow, 29.4.19.
39. RCPC, 1 DRL/428, L. Owen to Vera Deakin, 23.11.17.
40. RCPC, 1 DRL/428, file on Corporal C.T. Owen, 1916.
41. RCPA, Call to the legal profession 26.10.15.
42. RCPC, 53/6, Files of Missing Men, J.A. Briggs.
43. RCPC, 53/6, Files of Missing Soldiers, S.C. Allen and R.B. Allen, letter of Stephen Allen to mother, 8.7.16.
44. RCPC, 53/6, File on Allen brothers, Capt Wills to Mrs Allen, 1.3.17.
45. RCPC, 53/6, File on Allen brothers, Will Hale, Wogga Wogga to Miss Allen, 16.6.17.
46. RCPC, 53/6 File on Allen brothers, Sgt Assenheim to Mrs Allen, 28.6.17.
47. RCPC, 53/6, File on Allen brothers, Charles Fry to Miss Allen, 5.2.18.
48. RCPA, SRG 76/1/2432, File on Cpl K.C. Moore.
49. RCPA, SRG 76/1/6776, File on F.L. Donnelly.
50. RCPA, SRG 76/1/36–39, File on L. Marks.
51. RCPA, SRG 76/1/36–39, File on J.R. Skinner.
52. RCPA, SRG 76/1/36–39 File on D. James.
53. RCPC, 53/6, File on E.S. Brown, cable of 17.8.15 to Rev. Newmark.
54. RCPC, 53/6, File on E.S. Brown, Major Gallagher to Mrs Brown, 21.8.15.
55. RCPC, 53/6, File on E.S. Brown, Gerald Campbell to Mrs Brown, 24.9.15.
56. RCPC, 53/6, File on Lt Col. E.S. Brown. Clippings and letters collected by E.N. Watter.

57. A pine tree exists next to the Australian War Memorial in Canberra, grown from the seeds of a cone sent home to his mother by a soldier at Gallipoli.
58. RCPA, SRG 76/32, Papers of South Australian Red Cross, Letter of Agnes Rigney to Sir Josiah Symon, 28.9.15.
59. RCPA, SRG 76/32, letters of Mrs Snell to Symon 4.12.15; 19.4.16; Agnes Rigney to Symon, 28.9.15; Mrs Donaldson to Symon, 27.11.17.
60. RCPA, 76/1/4797, file on Frederick William Dumont.
61. RCPC, 55/4, Prisoner of War files, Files on E.H. Dowd. This file is typical of thousands of others in this invaluable collection.
62. RCPC, 55/4, Prisoner of War files, File on E.H. Dowd.
63. RCPC, 55/4, Prisoner of War files, File on T.H. Dowell, Dowell to Chomley, 2.3.17.
64. RCPC, 55/4, Prisoner of War files, File on T.H. Dowell, Amy McFarlane to Australian Red Cross, 20.6.18.
65. RCPC, 55/4, Prisoner of War Files, File on T.H. Dowell, Chomley to Pte P. O'Connor.
66. RCPC, 55/4, Prisoner of War files, File on T.H. Dowell, Chomley to Dowell, 25.4.18.
67. RCPC, 55/4, Prisoner of War files, File on T.H. Dowell, Chomley to (brother) F.E. Dowell, 16.12.18.
68. RCPC, 55/4, Prisoner of War files, Files on A.C. Down, died of wounds 9.10.18.
69. RCPC, 55/4, Prisoner of War files, File on C.P. Down.
70. See footnote 2.
71. AWM 164, Roll of Honour forms, obituary of Charles Berg.
72. AWM 164, Form on Robert Rae, letter of Elizabeth Grace to Hayes, 28.9.40, addressed: 54a Kennington Rd, Lambeth.
73. First and foremost, in a magisterial manner, by Antoine Prost, *Anciens combattants et la société française 1914–1939* (3 vols, Fondation nationale des sciences politiques, 1977); R. Whalen, *Bitter Wounds. German victims of the Great War 1914–1939* (Ithaca, New York, Cornell University Press, 1984); Graham Wootton, *The Politics of influence. British ex-servicemen, Cabinet decisions and cultural change (1917–57)* (London, Routledge, 1963); Wootton, *The Official History of the British Legion* (London, Macdonald & Evans, 1956); Charles Kimbell, 'The Ex-service movement in England and Wales, 1916–1930', PhD Stanford, 1990.
74. Archives nationales (AN), Paris, F7/13243, files on Associations des mutilés et victimes de guerre.
75. Sophie Delaporte, 'Les blessés de la face de la grande guerre', Maitrise, Jules Verne Université de Picardie, 1992.
76. See the rhetoric presented and analysed by Prost in *In the Wake of War. Anciens combattants and French society 1914–1940*, trans. H. MacPhail (Oxford, Berg, 1992).
77. See the file on Vidal in AN, F7/13243, and report of lecture at Marseilles, 18 May 1919.
78. AN, F7/13243, Vidal, 'Pour les veuves de guerre', *Le Pays*, 1.6.19.
79. AN, F7, 13243, report of meeting in Nancy 21.4.16.
80. See the discussion in chapter 1.
81. AN, F7, 13243, Figures from *Liberté*, 31.7.23.
82. Calculations based on J.M. Winter, *The Great War and the British People* (London, Macmillan, 1986), ch. 8.
83. AWM 164, form for K.S. Williams.
84. IWM, Papers of J. Bennett, 83/14/1, Note of Mrs Estelle Perrett, 1.2.88.
85. D. Thompson, 'The poor law and the elderly in England, 1850–1900', Cambridge PhD, 1980.

86. Susan Pedersen, 'Family allowances and state policy in France and Britain 1870–1940', PhD Harvard, 1985.
87. See Harriet Jackson, 'Widows and pensions in France 1870–1940', PhD, New York University 1995. See also Theda Skocpol, *Pensions and the State* (Cambridge, Mass., Harvard University Press, 1993) for comments on the earlier impact of the U.S. civil war on subsequent welfare measures.
88. Jeffrey Lerner, 'The public and private management of death in Britain, 1890–1930', PhD Columbia University, 1981, Tables 2–3, pp. 233, 235.
89. R.W. Whalen, *Bitter wounds. German victims of the Great War, 1914–1939* (Ithaca, New York, Cornell University Press, 1984), p. 76.
90. Whalen, *Bitter Wounds*, p. 131.
91. J. Cole, 'Demobilization', in J.M. Winter and J.L. Robert, *Paris, London, Berlin*, ch. 7.
92. IWM, Claydon papers, Note of Len Wade on Father-in-law Pte Albert Claydon.
93. See the forthcoming Cambridge MLitt thesis of Ingrid James, 'Widows and widows pensions in Britain during and after the First World War'.
94. T. Bonzon, 'Transfer payments', in J.M. Winter and J.L. Robert, *Paris, London, Berlin*, ch. 10.
95. Thébaud, 'La guerre et le deuil', p. 10.
96. Whalen, *Bitter Wounds*, p. 77.
97. E. Hilmer Smith, *History of the Legacy Club of Sydney* (Sydney, Waite and Bull, 1944), p. xi.
98. Mark Lyons, *Legacy. The First Fifty Years* (Clayton, Victoria, Lothian, 1978), pp. 14–15.
99. Bean, in Smith, *Legacy Club of Sydney*, p. xiii.
100. Smith, *Legacy Club of Sydney*, 'Year 1926–7', pp. 6–15.
101. Smith, *Legacy Club of Sydney*, pp. 25, 35.
102. Lyons, *Legacy*, p. xiv; see also M.H. Ellis. *The Torch. A Picture of Legacy* (Sydney, Angus and Robertson, 1957).
103. AWM 164, Mrs Rebecca Hinds to Hayes 22.10.41.
104. AWM 164, form of Harry Richard Aiken, letter of Mrs Aiken to Hayes, 6.3.40.
105. See the Wakeman papers in the IWM for details on this point.
106. IWM, A.S. Lloyd papers, Manning poem, July/August 1917; Manning to Mrs Lloyd 23.11.18.
107. IWM, Wakeman papers 67/305/1, The St Barnabas Hostels, *How to reach 'the Hallowed areas' in France and Belgium*, 1923.
108. Wakeman papers, *How to reach the 'Hallowed Areas'*, pp. 4–11.
109. We await the Cambridge PhD thesis on the subject by David Lloyd.
110. Australian War Memorial archives, Longstaff clippings, 'Great War Picture', *Hobart Mercury*, 20 Nov. 1929, and Will Longstaff, *The Menin Gate at Midnight* (n.d.), text in Australian War Memorial, Canberra. I am grateful to Mrs Marie Wood for her help in tracing these references.
111. On Desvalliers, see Jean-Philippe Rey, 'Desvallières et la guerre de 1914–1918', *Bulletin de la société historique de l'art français* (1988), pp. 197–211. Found, through the kindness of Annette Becker, in the library of the Centre Georges Pompidou in Paris.
112. I am grateful to Dr Becker for drawing this work to my attention. It is discussed in her *La guerre et la foi* (Paris, Armand Colin, 1994), pp. 128ff.

Select Bibliography

Audoin-Rouzeau, Stéphane. Men at War. Trench Journalism and National Sentiment in France 1914-1918. Oxford: Berg, 1992.
Becker, Annette. La guerre et la foi. Paris: Armand Colin, 1993.
Best, Geoffrey. Humanity in Warfare. London: Hutchinson, 1980.
Boissier, P. Histoire du Comité international de la Croix-Rouge. t. 1. De Solférino àTsoushima. Paris: Plon, 1963.
Catulle-Mendes, Jane. La Prière sur l'enfant mort. As cited in Francoise Thébaud, "La guerre at le deuil chez les femmes francaises," Péronne: Somme, 1992.
Durand, André. Histoire du Comité international de la Croix-Rouge. t.2. De Sarajevo àHiroshima. Geneva: Institut Henry-Dunant, 1978.
Durand, R. and Meurant, J. (eds.), Préludes et pionniers. Le précurseurs de la Croix-Rouge 1840-1860. Geneva: Société Henry Dunant, 1991.
Ellis, M.H. The Torch. A Picture of Legacy. Sydney: Angus and Robertson, 1957.
Fortes, Meyer. Kinship and the Social Order. The Legacy of Lewis Henry Morgan. Chicago: Aldine, 1969.
Freud, Sigmund. Standard Edition of the Works of Sigmund Freud.
Garmier, Jacques. Homage à mon ombre. Macon: Protat Frères, 1955.
Goody, J. (ed.) The Character of Kinship. Cambridge: Cambridge University Press, 1973.
Gorer, G. Death, Grief and Mourning in Contemporary Britain. London: Cresset, 1965.
Helias, Pierre-Jakez. Le cheval d'orgueil. Memoires d'un Breton du pays bigoudin. Paris: Plon, 1975.
Lyons, Mark. Legacy. The First Fifty Years. Clayton, Victoria: Lothian, 1978.
Owen, Howard. Journey from Obscurity. Oxford: Oxford University Press, 1968.
Parkes, C.M. Bereavement. Studies of Grief in Adult Life. London: Tavistock Publications, 1972.
Parkes, C.M. and Weiss, R.S. Recovery From Bereavement. New York: Basic Books, 1983.
Prost, Antione. Anciens combattants et la société francaise 1914-1939. 3 vols., Fondation nationale des sciences politiques, 1970.
Prost, Antione. In the Wake of War. Anciens combattants and French Society 1914-1940. Translated by H. MacPhail. Oxford: Berg, 1992.
Schoenberg, B. et al. (eds.) Bereavement: Its Psychosocial Aspects. New York: Columbia University Press, 1975.
Skocpol, Theda. Pensions and the State. Cambridge: Mass., Harvard University Press, 1993.
Smith, Hilmer E. History of the Legacy Club of Sydney. Sydney: Waite and Bull, 1944.
Whalen, R. Bitter Wounds. German Victims of the Great War 1914-1939. Ithaca, New York: Cornell University Press, 1984.
Wooten, Graham. The Official History of the British Legion. London: Macdonald & Evans, 1956.
Wooton, Graham. The Politics of Influence. British Ex-servicemen, Cabinet decisions and Cultural Change (1917-1957). London: Routedge, 1963.
Winter, J.M. The Great War and the British People. London: Macmillan, 1986.
Winter, J.M. and Robert, J.L. Paris, London, Berlin. Cambridge: Cambridge University Press, 1995.
Winter, J.M. Sites of Memory. The Persistence of Tradition. Cambridge: Cambridge University Press, 1995.

NOTES ON CONTRIBUTORS

Frans Coetzee teaches in the history department at George Washington University. A recipient of fellowships from the ACLS, Fulbright Foundation, and the NEH, he is the author of *For Party or Country: Nationalism and the Dilemmas of Popular Conservatism in Edwardian England* (1990) and co-editor of *World War I and European Society* (1995).

L.L. Farrar, Jr. has taught at Stanford, the University of Washington, Trinity College (Hartford, Connecticut), and most recently at Boston University. He is the author of *The Short-War Illusion* (ABC-Clio, 1973), *Divide and Conquer* (East European Quarterly Press, distributed by Columbia University Press, 1978), and *Arrogance and Anxiety* (University of Iowa Press, 1981), and is presently at work on a re-evaluation of the role of nationalism as a cause of World War I.

John Horne is a senior lecturer in Modern French and European History at Trinity College, Dublin, where he was also the first Director of European Studies. He has published in French labor and social history and the comparative history of the First World War, including *Labour at War. France and Britain, 1914–1918* (Clarendon Press, 1991). He spent 1994–95 as a Member of the Institute of Advanced Study, Princeton, and as a Visiting Fellow of the Rutgers University Center for Historical Analysis.

Susan Kingsley Kent teaches British History at the University of Colorado, Boulder. She is the author of *Sex and Suffrage in Britain, 1860–1914* (Princeton University Press, 1987) and *Making Peace: The Reconstruction of Gender in Interwar Britain* (Princeton University Press, 1993). She is currently writing a textbook, *Gender and Power in Britain, 1660 to the Present*.

Francesca Lagorio is scholarship holder at the IRSIFAR (Institute for Italian Study from Fascism to Resistance of Rome). She is working on Italian war widows and on this subject she has published *La solitudine imposta. Alcune note sulle vedove di guerra*, (The imposed loneliness. Some notes about war widows of the second world war, in, a c. di Bruna Michelletti e Pier Paola Poggio, *l'italia in guerra 1940–43*, Annali della Fondazione "Luigi Micheletti", Brescia 1990–91, Brescia, 1992; *e Appunti per uno studio delle vedove di guerra nell'Italia del '900*, (Remarks for a study on war widows in twentieth century Italy) in "Rivista di storia contemporanea", Loescher Editore, Torino, 1995. She is also working on Private Violence in Rome during 1943–45.

James F. McMillan is Professor of European History at the University of Strathclyde. He is the author of *Housewife or Harlot: The Place of Women in French Society 1870–1940* (Harvester Press, Brighton and St. Martin's Press, 1981), *Napoleon III* (Longman, 1991), and *Twentieth Century France: Politics and Society 1989–1991* (Edward Arnold, 1992), as well as many articles on aspects of modern French history.

John H. Morrow, Jr. is Franklin Professor of History and Associate Dean of the College of Arts and Sciences at the University of Georgia. His most recent book is *The Great War in the Air: Military Aviation from 1909 to 1921*. (Smithsonian Institution Press, 1993).

Giovanna Procacci is Professor of Social History at the University of Modena. She has worked extensively on the First World War in Italy and is the author of *Soldati e prigionieri italiani nella grande guerra* (Editori Riuniti, 1993), and editor of *Stato e classe operaia in Italia durante la prima guerra mondiale* (Angeli, 1983).

Marsha L. Rozenblit is an Associate Professor of Modern Jewish History at the University of Maryland, College Park, where she has been teaching since 1978. The author of *The Jews of Vienna, 1867–1914: Assimilation and Identity* (State University of New York Press, 1993), she has also written many articles about Austrian Jewry, exploring such issues as religious reform and national identity. She is currently at work on a book about the impact of World War I on the German-speaking Jews of Austria-Hungary.

Dr. Eve Rosenhaft is Senior Lecturer in the Department of German at the University of Liverpool, teaching modern German history and women's history. Her publications include *Beating the Fascists? The German Communists and Political Violence 1929–1933* (Cambridge University Press, 1983), *The State and Social Change in Germany 1880–1980* (Berg, 1990), and numerous articles on German social, labor and women's history since the nineteenth century. She is currently working on a social history of Germany, 1890–1990.

Marilyn Shevin-Coetzee teaches in the history department at George Washington University. A recipient of fellowships from the ACLS, NEH, and the Alexander von Humboldt Foundation, she is the author of *The German*

Army League: Popular Nationalism in Wilhelmine Germany (1990) and co-editor of *World War I and European Society* (1995).

Leonard V. Smith is Associate Professor of European Social History at Oberlin College. His first book, *Between Mutiny and Obedience: The Case of the French Fifth Infantry Division during World War I* (Princeton University Press, 1994), was awarded the Paul Birdsall Prize from the American Historical Association for the best book on the subject of European military and strategic history since 1870.

Gary D. Stark is Professor of History and Dean of Arts and Letters at the University of Central Arkansas, and has published on the institutional and legal context of cultural life in modern Germany. He is currently engaged in a larger study of state censorship of art, literature, drama, and film in Germany between 1871 and 1918.

John Steinberg teaches Russian History at Georgia Southern University. He is in the process of completing a study on the Imperial Russian General Staff in the Belle Epoque.

Jay Winter is University Lecturer in History and Fellow of Pembroke College, Cambridge. He is the author of *Socialism and the Challenge of War* (1974), *The Great War and the British People* (1986), and the forthcoming book *Sites of Memory*, among others.

Fredric Zuckerman is a Senior Lecturer in History at the University of Adelaide, Adelaide South Australia, and has completed a book entitled *The Tsarist Secret Police in Russian Society, 1880–1917*, to be published by Macmillan and New York University Press later this year. At present, he is completing a manuscript on the activities of the Imperial Russian Secret Police in western Europe in the pre-First World War period, and is working on a book dealing with Russian-American economic relations between 1914 and 1922. He has published articles in several journals including the *Journal of Contemporary History* and the *History of European Ideas*.

INDEX

Action Française, 116, 120, 128
Aerial League, 307
Anti-clericalism, 114–115, 119–129
Asquith, Herbert, 308
Association of Mothers and Widows of the Fallen, 185–189
Aviation, 305–321

Barbusse, Henri, 243, 252–258, 261–264, 267–268
Barres, Maurice, 124, 235
Bauer, Lt. Col. Max, 89
Belmont, Ferdinand, 230, 234
Benedict XV (Pope), 117–121, 128
Benedikt, Clothilde, 200, 203
v. Bethmann Hollweg, Theobald, 118, 140
Boelcke, Oswald, 312–313, 320
Brittain, Vera, 165–167, 170
Bryce Report, 158–159
Borden, Mary, 166–168, 170
Burgfrieden, 68

Caporetto, 8–9, 11–13, 22
Catholic Center Party, 65, 98
Catholic Church, 113–115, 120–123, 125
Cavour, Count, 7
censorship
  in France, 139
  in Italy, 12
  of film, 60, 62–64, 67–70, 73–75
  of press, 59–61, 65–66, 68, 72–73
  of theater, 59, 61–62, 67, 70–71, 74–75
Churchill, Winston, 308, 312
Clemenceau, Georges, 120, 122, 126, 141
Cochin, Augustin, 231–232
commemoration, 189–190, 325, 348–350
compulsory savings schemes, 81–102

Dallolio, Gen. Alfredo, 14–15
Defence of the Realm Act, 139
Dorgeles, Roland, 252–254, 258–259, 261–268
Dragomirov, M.I., 286, 288–289
Dubarle, Robert, 230, 232–233
Duhamel, Georges, 243

Eteve, Marcel, 231, 233

Fawcett, Milicent, 156
Feminism, 154–155, 159, 165, 170–172
Fictive kinship, 326–327, 346–347

Garros, Roland, 308
German Air Fleet League, 306
Giolitti, Giovanni, 3–5, 7
Globachev, Gen. K.I., 35, 37, 39, 42–44, 47–48, 50–52
Grey, Sir Edward, 141
Grunwald, Margarethe, 203, 208
Grunwald, Rabbi Max, 204
Güdemann, Rabbi Moritz, 203–204

Index

Guillaumin, Emile, 229
Guynemer, Georges, 315

Heroism, 226–232, 242

Industrial Mobilization (MI), 14–15, 23
Italian Socialist Party (PSI), 6, 15

Jews [see also women, Jewish]
  and nationalism, 200–213
  and Zionism, 202, 204, 206, 208–209, 211–212
  in Austria, 199–213
  in Galicia, 200, 204–207

Khvostov, A. N., 38
Klimovich, E. K., 38
Kurlov, P. G., 39, 49
Kuropatkin, A. N., 286–287, 289

Labriola, Arturo, 12
Lavisse, Ernest, 231
Liebknecht, Karl, 257
Liszt, Franz von, 86–87
Living standards, 16–18, 82–87, 95–97
Lloyd George, David, 141; 317
Ludendorff, Gen. Erich, 66, 71, 138

Martynov, Col. A. P., 37, 42, 44–48, 50, 52
Masculinity, 164, 251–269
Massoulier, Paul, 126
Mattutat, Hermann, 96
Miliutin, D. A., 276–278, 280, 281, 286
Mutiles de guerre, 342–345
Mutinies, 235–241
Müller, Anitta, 209–212

Nationalism, 133–134, 137–138, 140, 142, 144–146, 306, 309–310
National Aviation League, 306
Neutrality, 5, 6, 10–11, 117–119
Nicholas II, 39, 50, 287, 288, 295

Orlando, Vittorio Emanuele, 22

Pankhurst, Christabel, 171
Pankhurst, Emmeline, 163
Pankhurst, Sylvia, 157
Pegoud, Adolphe, 308
Peguy, Charles, 226, 229
Petrov, Lt. Gen., 291–294
Plehve, V. K., 33
Poincare, Raymond, 113
Popular protest
  in Italy, 18–23
  in Germany, 82, 93–94
  in Russia, 45–52
Propaganda, 10, 11, 136–138, 158–159, 318
Protopopov, A. D., 38–39, 50–51

Rathenau, Walther, 318
Republican Association of Veterans, 263
Revolution of 1905, 34–35, 41–44, 46, 285
Richthofen, Manfred, 313–314, 320
Russian Army
  maneuvers of, 285–294
  military education in, 277–284
  promotion in, 281–283
  reform of, 276–281

Sacrifice, 233–235, 240, 243
Salandra, Antonio, 5–7, 11
Samsonov, A.V., 294, 296
Schundliteratur, 63, 65–66
Shell shock, 252
Shturmer, B. V., 38
Sternheim, Carl, 70
Strikes [see Popular protest]
Social Democratic Party, 94–95
Surveillance, 30–33

Total War, concept of, 57, viii

Union sacree, 113, 116, 121–122, 226

Vasil'ev, A. T., 39, 50–51
Voluntarism (see Women)

War aims, 139–141
War culture, 229, 234, 238, 242
Wells, H.G., 309, 319
Widows, 176–190, 344–345, 347–348
Wilhelm II, 60, 63
Women
  and protest, 20, 82, 93
  and voluntarism, 96–98, 123, 201–203, 206–210
  and Zionism, 202, 204, 206, 208–212
  attitudes towards, 90–92, 97, 100
  Jewish, 199–213
working class
  character of family, 97–101

Youth
  and crime, 86–89
  and popular entertainment, 60, 64–66, 76
  and protest, 82, 93–94
  and work, 82–85, 90, 101

Zemgor, 40–44
Zeppelin, 306–307, 310–311, 318
Zweig, Stefan, 200

www.ingramcontent.com/pod-product-compliance
Lightning Source LLC
Chambersburg PA
CBHW052009070526
44584CB00016B/1675